► MASTERING PAGEMAKER ON THE IBM PC

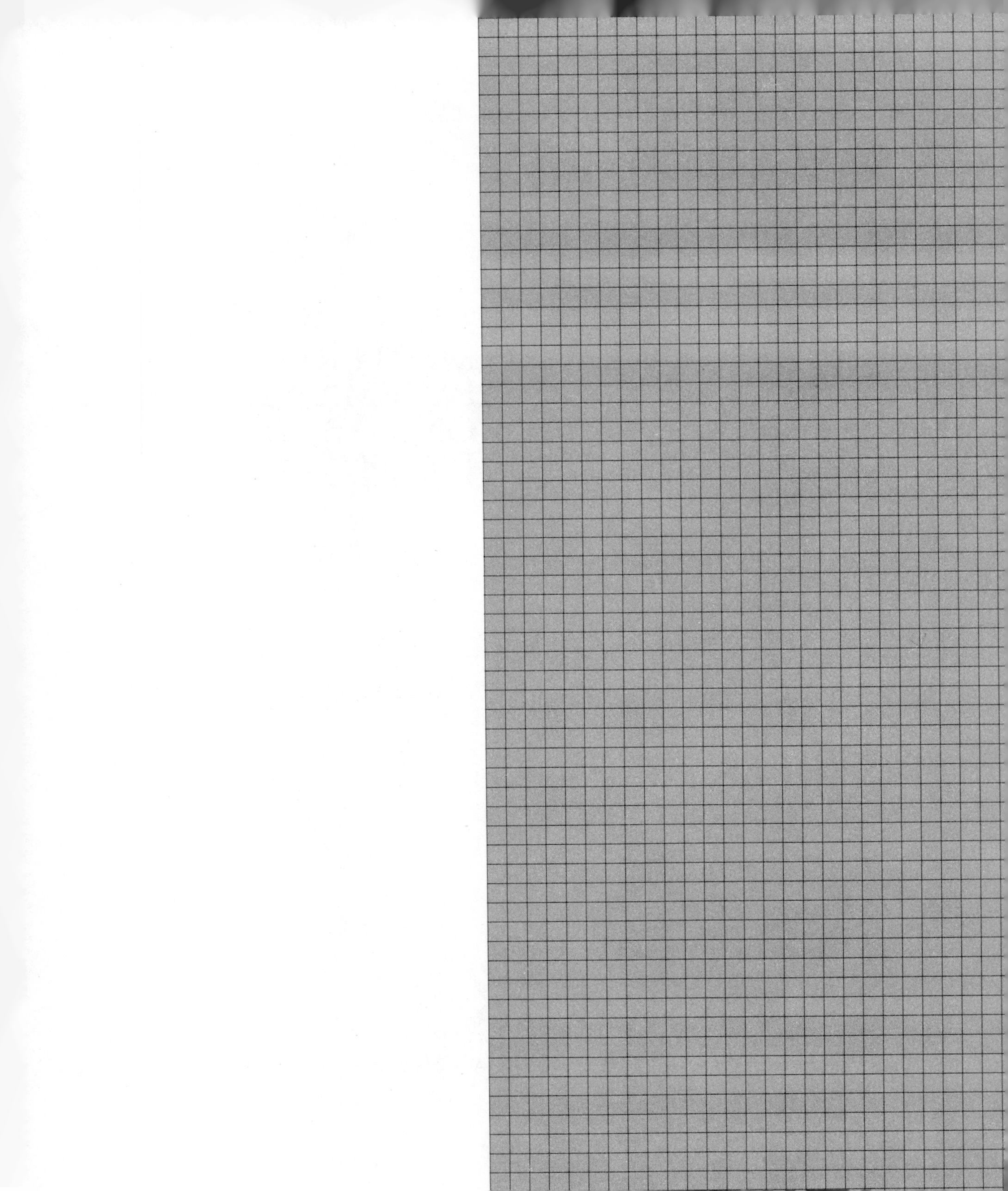

►MASTERING PAGEMAKER® ON THE IBM® PC

Second Edition

Antonia Stacy Jolles

► SAN FRANCISCO ► PARIS ► DÜSSELDORF ► SOEST

Cover Design by Thomas Ingalls + Associates
Cover Photography by Casey Cartwright
Book Design by Ingrid Owen

Library of Congress Card Number: 88-62343
ISBN 0-89588-521-2
Manufactured in the United States of America
10 9 8 7 6

► To my parents, Sifu's of a sort.

► . . . what is the use of a book . . . without pictures and conversations?

Lewis Carroll
Alice's Adventures in Wonderland

ACKNOWLEDGMENTS

I want to thank my family for supporting me in my work: my parents for their constant faith in my abilities, and my grandmother for her absolute belief in me. Always deep thanks to my heart-mate Coleen and our favorite human in a dog's body, Bodhi.

Special thanks to the staff at SYBEX who worked on this second edition. To my developmental editor, Cheryl Holzaepfel, for her guidance and for putting up with my travel schedule. To Peter Weverka, my copy editor, for his constant helpful phone calls. And to all the SYBEX staff who helped put this second edition together: Dan Tauber, technical reviewer; Bob Myren and Scott Campbell, word processing; Olivia Shinomoto, typesetting; Sonja Schenk, screen reproduction; Julie Kawabata, indexing; and Eleanor Ramos, graphic artist. Without them, this book never would have happened.

And thanks again to the staff at SYBEX who worked on the first edition of this book. To my editor, Bonnie Gruen, for her constant patience. To the acquisitions editor Chuck Ackerman, for having faith in me. And to all the SYBEX staff that made that book possible: Olivia Shinomoto and John Kadyk, word processing; Michelle Hoffman, graphic production; Dawn Amsberry, typesetting; Jeff Green and Suzy Anger, proofreading; and Ingrid Owen, design.

CONTENTS AT A GLANCE

TABLE OF CONTENTS

INTRODUCTION

If you produce a neighborhood newsletter, a company publication, sophisticated manuals or documentation, or you are publishing your own poetry or greeting cards, you are a prime candidate for desktop publishing. With PageMaker, you can be in control of the entire publication from start to finish.

▶ WHO SHOULD READ THIS BOOK

Mastering PageMaker on the IBM PC is for the computer user with word processing and perhaps graphics experience. You will learn how to design a publication, so you do not need any previous design experience, but the book does assume you are able to develop your own text and graphics with other software packages. You then go step-by-step through the process of using PageMaker to integrate the two into professional-looking publications.

▶ HOW TO USE THIS BOOK

You'll find that *Mastering PageMaker for the IBM PC* offers several features that you won't find in the manual that comes with the program. Two lists of PageMaker commands—one arranged alphabetically, the other according to menus—are inside the front and back covers of the book. Throughout the book you'll see margin notes that provide additional information about the subject being discussed. The notes may give you practical hints, refer you to other chapters or sections in the book, or warn you of a possible problem.

The Fast Track section at the beginning of each chapter summarizes the chapter's contents, lists the steps or keystrokes needed to complete specific tasks, and points you to the page where you can find a more detailed explanation. In some cases, the Fast Track entry will be all you need to get going. In other cases, you can use the Fast Track to pick out the points you are interested in and then go directly to the information you need. Also note that Fast Tracks cover the chapters' primary topics; they do not cover every option, exception, or caveat discussed in the text.

Mastering PageMaker on the IBM PC is divided into five parts. Part 1 gets you started using PageMaker, but if you haven't yet installed PageMaker, you probably will want to go first to Appendix A, Installing Pagemaker. Chapter 1 will show you how to use Microsoft Windows and a mouse, which you must have in order to work with PageMaker on the PC. Chapter 2 teaches you how to start the PageMaker program and introduces you to page setup. Chapter 3 explains the PageMaker publication window in detail. You learn about PageMaker's pull-down menus and pasteup tools that will help you create professional-looking publications.

Part 2 covers publication design. Chapter 4 introduces you to publication design principles, and in Chapter 5 you will learn about master page design. In Chapter 6 you will complete your template design for creating a typical newsletter.

In Part 3 you learn how to work with text in PageMaker. Chapter 7 teaches you how to work with text blocks and how to integrate the text you create with your word processor into your layout. Chapter 8 teaches you how to work with text once it is placed in your layout. You learn to use PageMaker's own text capabilities to make changes to the text in your publication. In Chapter 9 you will learn some typography techniques used by typesetters, such as text kerning and justification, to give your publication a polished, professional look.

In Part 4 you learn how to work with graphics in PageMaker. Chapter 10 teaches you how to integrate the graphics you create with your graphics software into your PageMaker publication. In Chapter 11 you learn how to use PageMaker's graphics capabilities to enhance your publication design.

Part 5 brings the text and graphics together. In Chapter 12 you learn about graphics techniques such as drop shadows and shading that add to the professional quality of your publication. In Chapter 13 you learn how to print your publication, and in Chapter 14, you use all the skills you've learned to customize the templates provided by PageMaker.

The appendices provide useful supplemental information. Appendix A explains how to install PageMaker and Microsoft Windows on your hard disk. Appendix B provides a list of the keyboard equivalents to the mouse commands you frequently use in PageMaker. Appendix C lists the default settings for the menu options and dialog boxes found in PageMaker. Appendix D is a glossary of the terms you will encounter while using this book. Appendix E is a list of further reading about publication design. Appendix F is a list of the hardware and software that is compatible with PageMaker.

The figures in this book were created with PageMaker on an AST 286 computer. Since you probably are using a different computer and printer, your screens may vary slightly from the figures in this book. The fonts available to you may also slightly alter the way your screen looks, because in most cases, PageMaker displays your font on the screen. Otherwise, the figures should appear exactly as they do on your screen.

How you use this book of course depends on your own experience. If you are already familiar with Microsoft Windows and are using a mouse on the PC, you can skip Chapter 1. If you are already familiar with layout design, you can probably skip the discussion of design principles in Chapter 4. However, if all this is new to you, you should probably begin with Chapter 1 and read the book all the way through. By the time you reach the end, you will be a proficient PageMaker user.

WHAT'S NEW IN PAGEMAKER?

This book covers PageMaker versions 1.0, 1.0a, and 3.0. Version 3.0, the most recent version, brings you many new features that will help you produce professional-looking publications. This book gives you complete information for upgrading from version 1.0 and 1.0a to version 3.0. Features that are new to 3.0 include

- Style sheets—repeatable formats that you design
- Autoflow—successive flow of text from your long word processed files
- Text wrap—automatic wrapping of text around graphics of any shape and size
- Spot color—colors you apply to text and graphics for output on your color printer
- Templates—over 20 predesigned templates that you can modify to meet your needs
- Image control—you control the contrast and lightness or darkness of illustrations and scanned images
- Export filter—lets you move text changes made in PageMaker back out to your word processed file

HARDWARE AND SOFTWARE REQUIREMENTS

In order to run PageMaker and follow the examples in this book, you must have an IBM PC AT with MS-DOS, or any highly compatible 286 computer. PageMaker 1.0 and 1.0a run within the Microsoft Windows environment using version 1.03. PageMaker 3.0 runs within the Microsoft Windows environment using version 2.0. The Windows environment requires a display that can accommodate a Windows screen driver such as an EGA, CGA, Hercules, or compatible display card. Your computer must have a hard disk with a minimum of 10 megabytes of storage. The PageMaker software requires a minimum of 512 KB of memory. However, because Windows and PageMaker take up a lot of memory space, 640 KB is recommended. A mouse is required to run the program as well.

► PART I:

GETTING STARTED

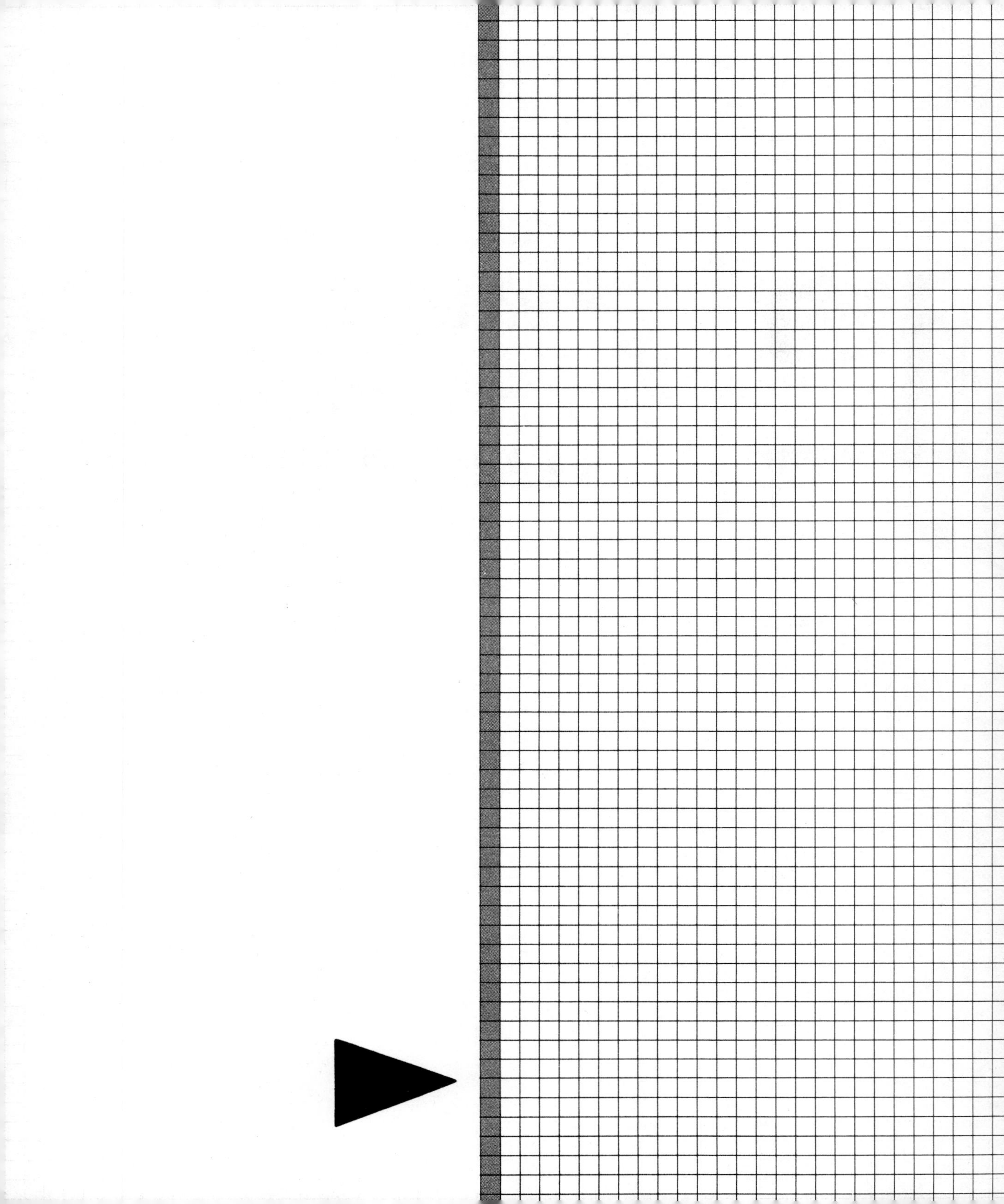

1 GETTING ORIENTED

When converting Macintosh files to PC files, 14

convert 1.2, 2.0, or 2.0a Macintosh files to PC PageMaker 1.0 files. Convert Macintosh PageMaker 3.0 files to PC PageMaker 3.0 files only.

To convert your old PageMaker 1.0 or 1.0a files to 3.0, 14

load the old files into PageMaker 3.0 and save the file again, indicating the name.

To use the keyboard to perform commands,

refer to the list of PageMaker's keyboard equivalents for mouse commands in Appendix B.

PageMaker is a page composition program that integrates text from your word processing program, and graphics from your paint and draw programs, into one publication. First you develop the text using your word processing program. Next you create graphics using draw and paint programs. At this point you are ready to combine the two in a PageMaker document.

PageMaker lets you edit a layout again and again until it is just the way you want it. You may choose multiple column formats, different typefaces, type sizes, and fonts. You may reproportion, rotate, enlarge, or shrink a graphics image. You can enhance the look of your document with borders, line art, and shading. Many of the tools used by graphic artists are available to you in PageMaker.

► USING WINDOWS

PageMaker 1.0 and 1.0a require the Windows 1.03 environment. Using an earlier version of Windows with PageMaker 1.0 or 1.0a will cause problems in text formatting. If you run PageMaker 1.0 or 1.0a in an updated Windows environment, such as 2.0, the Toolbox icons will not be displayed.

In order to make PageMaker work, you must be running the Microsoft program called Windows. PageMaker will only run within the Windows environment. There are many versions of Windows on the market today, and PageMaker 3.0 can run under several of them.

Windows 2.0 is included with PageMaker 3.0. The runtime version allows you to run only PageMaker; you cannot run some Windows applications using this version. But other versions of Windows 2.0 and Windows 386 allow you to run PageMaker 3.0 and Windows-compatible applications at the same time.

► WORKING WITH WINDOWS

PageMaker works within the Windows environment allowing you to use the features Windows has to offer. These features include pull-down menus, icons, and dialog boxes. (You'll learn about these features shortly.) Under the full version of Windows, PageMaker's screen can be split into several windows where different applications may be run at the same time. You can also split the screen between PageMaker and another application, or you can lay one window over another. These features allow you to keep one application open while working in another, and to move quickly between applications without exiting.

This multiple-window capability of Windows even lets you run a Windows-compatible word processor or graphics program simultaneously with PageMaker. For example, with your graphics program, you can develop a bar chart in one window, and then paste it directly into PageMaker's publication window.

Windows also gives PageMaker its *pull-down menus* capability. With this feature, when you select a menu title, PageMaker displays the menu commands as if you had "pulled" them down from the top of the screen, scrolling the menu commands below the menu title you selected. Each pull-down menu contains a list of commands for performing certain operations.

► THE CONTROL MENU COMMANDS

The Windows runtime version has a menu of commands called the Control menu (Figure 1.1). The Control menu, available to you within PageMaker, supplies commands for defining your window environment.

The "Size" command is for changing the size of a window on your screen. Select this command and the pointer changes to a four-directional arrow. Now you may use the directional arrow keys on your keyboard to resize the window. Window size can also be altered by positioning the mouse pointer on the edge of a window, and changing the window to the size you want.

The "Restore" command returns a window to its former size. If you have used the "Size" command to enlarge a window, and you wish to bring it back to its original size, use the "Restore" command.

The "Move" command moves a window to a new location on your screen. Like the "Size" command, selecting the "Move" command changes the pointer to a four-directional arrow. You may pick up the window and move it to a new location on your screen. A window may also be moved by dragging the title bar to a new location.

The "Minimize" command in the Control menu allows you to shrink a window into an icon that represents the application. This way, although the window is not displayed, it is available for quick access. The window remains open, the applications remain running, and clicking on the icon redisplays it.

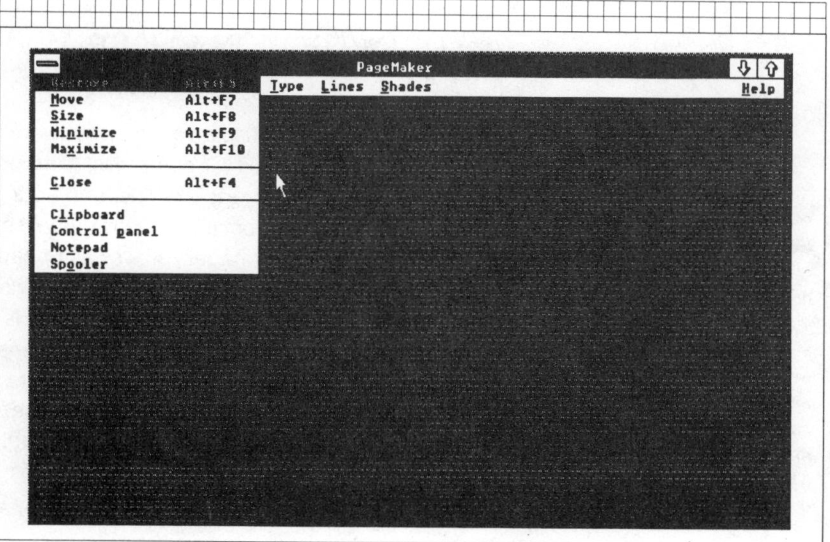

Figure 1.1: The Windows Control menu

The "Maximize" command makes a window expand to full screen size. This command is used when you want to focus attention on one window.

The "Close" command shuts a window. Once a window has been shut, opening it again requires restarting the application.

The Clipboard is an application that opens a window and displays the contents of the Clipboard. You'll hear more about the Clipboard later.

The Control Panel helps you define your operating environment. Select the Control Panel and three menu titles are displayed—the Installation menu for installing printers or fonts for your printer, the Setup menu for defining your printer settings, and the Preferences menu for defining settings such as screen color and mouse speed. The Control Panel is also used to change the date and time, the blinking of the cursor, and the double-click rate on your mouse button.

The "Notepad" command runs Windows' simple word processing program. With it you can type in text, open a file, or move text to the Clipboard.

The last command in the Control menu is the "Spooler" command. Spooler is a separate application, like Notepad. Spooler displays the print queue. Files listed in the queue have been sent to the printer. Spooler displays them in the order in which they will print. Commands are provided to help you control your printing.

The Windows Control menu commands are available to you when you are running PageMaker. For more information about installing and using Windows, refer to the Windows *User's Guide*.

► USING PAGEMAKER WITH YOUR WORD PROCESSING PROGRAM

You will probably use a variety of software programs for your desktop publications. Most of your text will come from word processors. Most of your graphics will come from graphics applications, and your photos from scanning. PageMaker can use the output from many word processors, paint programs, draw programs, scanned and video images, as well as Encapsulated PostScript files.

PageMaker 3.0 has a built-in export filter that can be used with Microsoft Word 4.0. Thanks to the export filter, text you edited in PageMaker can be exported to where it originated (Word 4.0) with all revisions included. Text can also be exported in Document Content Architecture (DCA) format and as a text-only, or ASCII file.

PageMaker recognizes a word processed file by its file name extension, but sometimes the extension PageMaker recognizes is different from the word processor's default extension. In these cases, you must rename your word processed file with the extension recognized by PageMaker for your word processor.

PageMaker recognizes a word processed file by its file name extension, but sometimes the extension PageMaker recognizes is different from the word processor's default extension. In these cases, you must rename your word processed file with the extension recognized by PageMaker for your word processor.

PageMaker recognizes the following extensions:

Word Processor	**Extension**
HP AdvanceWrite	.AW
HP Executive MemoMaker	.WS
Lotus Manuscript	.DCA
Microsoft Word	.DOC
MultiMate	.DOC
Olivetti Olitext Plus	.OTX
Samna Word	.SAM
Windows Write	.WRI
WordPerfect	.WP
WordStar 3.3	.WS
XyWrite III	.XYW

PageMaker can also recognize IBM Document Content Architecture (DCA) files from AdvanceWrite, Lotus Manuscript, Office Writer, IBM DisplayWrite 3 and 4, Samna Word, Volkswriter 3, and WordStar 2000. DCA format makes files interchangeable among applications. PageMaker can recognize all DCA-formatted files as long as they have .DCA or .RFT file extensions.

An ASCII file contains just text, no format or type specifications. ASCII files are also called *text-only files.* If your word processor is not directly supported by PageMaker, or if you want to use PageMaker's format specifications only, save your word processed file as a text-only file. Be careful though, because when some word processors save a text-only file, that file still may contain some formatting commands, like tabs, spaces, and end-of-line returns. Use Notepad from the Windows Control menu to delete all formatting commands. Delete all carriage returns (they act as end-of-line breaks) as well. When a text-only file is placed in PageMaker, default values for type specifications are assigned. Remember to name text-only files with the .TXT file extension.

You can also import database and spreadsheet files into PageMaker by making them text-only files, but the result varies between applications. This is because each database and spreadsheet application converts files to text-only format differently. Although you should be able to place any spreadsheet or database file into PageMaker, you may have to make adjustments to the file once it is placed.

To use a database or spreadsheet file, save it as a text-only file. Open the text-only file and clean up the format with your word processor. You may have to add tabs or end-of-line returns. Now your spreadsheet or database file is ready to be placed in your PageMaker publication.

► USING PAGEMAKER WITH YOUR GRAPHICS PROGRAM

PageMaker imports graphics from paint and draw programs, clip art programs, scanned or video images, as well as graphics programs. For a list of graphics programs and files that can be used by PageMaker, see Appendix F.

It is up to you to select a file format that PageMaker can use. Some graphics applications let you select the file format. The selection you make depends upon your system setup and the complexity of the graphic. If you have trouble placing a graphic, try changing the saved format to another PageMaker-compatible format.

After you've placed a graphic into PageMaker, it stays the same size as it was created, and you can't erase any part of it except by cropping. (PageMaker does provide some handy graphics tools for resizing or cropping a graphic.) Text included with the graphic cannot be changed either. There are tools for drawing boxes, circles, lines, and line and shade patterns around your graphics. Use your own graphics software to make your original file as near perfect as possible before you place it in PageMaker, since these tools are designed only to supplement this software.

► COLOR GRAPHICS

PageMaker has many applications for creating color graphics. With PageMaker 3.0, you can use the Colors palette to select a variety of colors for your graphic. First, use your graphics software to separate your graphic into distinct parts. Then, by bringing each part of the graphic into PageMaker separately and giving each part a new color from the Colors palette, you can build a multicolored graphic.

► SCANNING GRAPHICS

Scanners convert the hard copy of an image into a graphics file. Scanners work best on line art and photographs, although more complicated graphics can also be scanned. Scanners, when you specify it, use the Tag Image File Format, or TIFF, to save a graphic in a bit-mapped file, a halftone image, or a gray-scale image. TIFF is used by most scanners for placing files in PageMaker. If your scanner does not save files in TIFF, a paint-type format can also be placed in PageMaker. Saving files in a paint-type format allows you to edit them using your paint software before placing them into your PageMaker file.

Before selecting a resolution for your scanner, consider the characteristics of your graphic or photograph and the type of output device you are using. A large TIFF file means having to wait a long time for your image to print. Likewise, the higher the resolution you select for your scanner, the longer it will take to print your image.

When scanning basic line art graphics or halftones, the scanner resolution should match the resolution of your output device. For example, if you are using a laser printer with a 300 dpi (dots-per-inch) resolution, set the scanner for 300 dpi. Line art and halftones should be saved in TIFF black-and-white format, or in a paint-type format.

Gray-scale images use 16 to 256 tones of gray. They produce excellent results using resolutions less than 300 dpi. Using a 300-dpi laser printer, scan a graphic using the gray-scale TIFF format at 75 dpi. (When printing to a linotronic device with 1200 dpi, scan the graphic at 150 dpi or higher.) When using PageMaker to enlarge a graphic, select a high resolution to preserve the detail in the enlarged image. Scanning a gray-scale image creates a smaller file that prints quickly. Gray-scale images are easily manipulated by PageMaker. They produce excellent images from a low scanning resolution.

Very large files are sometimes created when scanning an image, and PageMaker has an interesting way of quickly placing these files. PageMaker places scanned files larger than 64K by linking a low-resolution screen version of the image to the original scanned version. On your screen, PageMaker displays the low-resolution version, but this screen version is internally linked to an original high-resolution version, the one you want to see at print time. When it comes time to print your PageMaker publication, PageMaker searches its directory for the high-resolution original and prints it. You also have the option of printing the low-resolution screen version of your image.

Many scanners can be used with PageMaker. The graphics application used with the scanner helps create the scanned images. See Appendix F for a list of scanners and the compatible software that can be used with PageMaker.

► USING VIDEO IMAGES

The arena of desktop publishing has really expanded, offering everything from image capturing of line art and halftones, to video image capturing. Video images may be captured using a video camera, a videodisc, a VCR, or a camcorder. The TIFF format for capturing scanned images can be used by PageMaker. So can Encapsulated PostScript, if you have a PostScript laser printer.

► PREPARING GRAPHICS FILES FOR PAGEMAKER

In most cases, it is a good practice to prepare your files as thoroughly as possible before placing them in PageMaker. Remember, PageMaker provides some graphics and text features for making changes to a file after it has been placed into your layout, but these features have limitations. The text and graphics features of PageMaker are not as extensive as the specialized features provided by other programs.

► USING FILES FROM DRAW-TYPE PROGRAMS

PageMaker recognizes many different drawing programs according to their file name extension. You can place these files easily into your layout.

Many drawing programs allow you to select the format for saving your graphic. The format you select depends largely upon the complexity of your graphic. And complex graphics with many lines and details create large files once they are saved. The largest file PageMaker can place is 64K. If your graphic file is larger than that, PageMaker will warn you that your file can't be placed. However, there is a way to get around this predicament. Split your graphic into several small files, and reassemble these files one at a time in your PageMaker layout.

There is one more consideration to make when placing a graphics file in a PageMaker layout. The text included with a graphic, a caption for example, cannot be edited with PageMaker's text tool. Also, the typeface and text enhancements of your graphics software may not be recognized by PageMaker. In such cases, PageMaker substitutes its own type specifications automatically, but this could affect the positioning of the text in your graphic.

► CGM FORMAT

The Computer Graphics Metafile (CGM) format is a standard drawing file format used by many draw-type programs. The Graphic Software Systems (GSS) subset of CGM files can be placed directly into your PageMaker layout, or you can use a program to convert other draw-type files to the GSS subset of the CGM format. When placing a CGM formatted file into PageMaker, the file must have the .CGM extension.

► EPS FORMAT

An Encapsulated PostScript (EPS) file can be used to create complex graphics, but you will need a PostScript printer to print them. For structuring purposes, a file saved using the EPS format is given a PostScript code. By reading this code, PageMaker is able to structure, or construct the graphic in your layout. This reading may take a few seconds. When PageMaker is ready to place the graphic, a symbol on the screen will indicate a PostScript graphic. A screen version of the graphic can be displayed at this point if your EPS file also includes a TIFF or metafile version of the graphic.

If a screen version of your graphic cannot be displayed, PageMaker can still place your graphic in the layout for printing. Instead of a screen version, you will see a box surrounding the graphic area. The box will include special comments to identify your graphic.

► HP-GL FORMAT

Many draw-type programs are able to use the Hewlett-Packard Graphics Language (HP-GL) format. This format is partly supported by PageMaker—PageMaker does not recognize all the commands used by this format. You may find pieces missing from your graphic once it is placed in PageMaker. Only experimentation using HP-GL–created graphics will show you what works in PageMaker.

To use a file in HP-GL format, plot the graphic to disk with the application set up for an HP plotter such as the HP 7470A or the HP 7475A. Once the file is plotted to disk, you must change the extension to .PLT before placing it into your PageMaker layout.

► NAPLPS FORMAT

The North American Presentation Level Protocol Standard (NAPLPS) format is a video file format used by General Parametric's Videoshow. Several applications allow you to save your file using the NAPLPS format. However, all files using this format must use the .PIC extension. You may have to change the extension on a NAPLPS file before placing the file in PageMaker.

► WINDOWS GDI FORMAT

Some draw-type programs use the GDI file format within Windows graphics. All files using this format must have the .WMF file extension in order to be used in PageMaker. After saving your graphics file using the GDI format, you may have to change the file extension to .WMF.

► CONVERTING AND TRANSFERRING PUBLICATIONS

If you are using PageMaker 3.0 on your PC, you may be wondering how to transfer your old files from earlier versions of PageMaker on the PC. Or if you have been using a Macintosh, you may need to convert your Macintosh files to the PC. Aldus has made it fairly easy to transfer and convert these files. Most of the programming code used to create the original Macintosh version of PageMaker was used to create the PC-based version too.

► CONVERTING MACINTOSH FILES TO PC FILES

To convert a file from your Macintosh machine to your PC, use one of the many communications programs for moving files from one machine to the other.

You also can get a PC-compatible drive for the Macintosh SE or II. And, some networks allow PCs and Macintoshes to use each other's hard disks.

If you are transferring Macintosh PageMaker 1.2, 2.0, or 2.0a files to the PC, they may be used by PageMaker 1.0. However, if you are using PageMaker 3.0 on the PC, your Macintosh files must be using PageMaker 3.0, or be converted to PageMaker 3.0 on the Macintosh, before they can be used by PageMaker 3.0 on the PC.

Since draw-type files cannot be transferred from the Macintosh to the PC, PageMaker will indicate the location of these graphics in your layout by displaying a box marked with an X. Also, graphics that are linked to a publication because they are larger than 64K must be transferred separately from the publication. In all other respects, your Macintosh PageMaker files are fully transferrable to your PC.

► CONVERTING PAGEMAKER 1.0 FILES TO PAGEMAKER 3.0 ON THE PC

Once you have updated your PageMaker 1.0 with 3.0, you can convert most of the publications you have already created simply by opening the old file. Your 1.0 publication is loaded into 3.0, creating a file that is sometimes 20% larger. The new 3.0 version of the publication will be untitled, so you must save it under a new name. Meanwhile, your old 1.0 version of the publication is unchanged. In addition, publications in PageMaker 3.0 use a different file extension than PageMaker 1.0 publications. PageMaker 3.0 uses the file extension .PM3. This lets you know which of your publications has been converted to the new version.

► USING YOUR INPUT DEVICES

PageMaker has several input devices for developing a publication. If you have been using a PC or compatible, you are already familiar with the keyboard. PageMaker uses a second input device, a mouse. If you haven't used a mouse on your PC or compatible, don't worry. Using a mouse is very easy.

► USING THE MOUSE

To learn how to select menu commands with the keyboard instead of the mouse, see Appendix B.

The mouse is used to perform a variety of functions, chiefly to select menu commands, to place text, and to place graphics. Because you have been using an IBM PC AT or compatible, you might never have used a mouse. But to use PageMaker, you must learn to use one. And you'll find that using a mouse is quite easy. Basic mouse techniques take only a little practice to master.

The first function of the mouse is to control the arrow-shaped pointer on the screen. The pointer is your main tool in PageMaker; you will be using it often to choose commands and to perform various other functions. Move the mouse around on your desktop and the arrow on the screen moves too. To move the pointer to the right, simply slide the mouse across your desktop to the right. The pointer directly follows this movement on the screen. To move the pointer up the screen, slide the mouse away from you across your desktop, and so on. Play around with the mouse and you will soon get a feel for how it works.

Keep in mind that the movement of the pointer on the screen is electronically connected to the rolling ball on the bottom of the mouse. The location of the mouse on your desktop is not the guiding factor. You can pick the mouse up and move it to a different location on your desktop without moving the pointer on the screen.

Once you have figured out how to point to the screen item you want, you are ready to learn another function of the mouse—using the mouse buttons. Your mouse has one, two, or three buttons located on top. For most actions, just one button is needed. If your mouse has two or three buttons, the main mouse button is the one on the left side within easy reach of your index finger. The other buttons are used occasionally and will be explained later. If you are left-handed, the Microsoft Windows Control Panel allows you to switch the main mouse button to the right-most button, which is closest to your left index finger. Refer to your Windows *User's Guide* for help.

Mouse buttons are used two ways. *Clicking* a mouse button means to quickly press and release the button. *Pressing* means to press a mouse button and hold it down while you move, or *drag* the pointer to a new location. Once you have positioned the pointer on a new spot, you release the mouse button. In some cases, you may be asked to use the mouse button a third way called *double-clicking*. Double-clicking means to give the button two clicks, one after another without moving the pointer. PageMaker 3.0 has some functions that require you to triple-click your mouse button. To do so, click the button three times in quick succession.

When you point at something on the PageMaker screen and click the mouse, you are *selecting* that item. As you learn PageMaker, you will be asked to make many selections.

► USING THE KEYBOARD

You will find yourself using the mouse quite often. However, you can also use the keyboard to perform many of the same functions you would use the mouse for. Some operations actually run more quickly from the keyboard than from the mouse.

Of course, you have to use the keyboard for every PageMaker job that requires text to be keyed in. But you can also select many menu options with the keyboard instead of the mouse. A list of PageMaker's keyboard equivalents for mouse commands can be found in Appendix B. Feel free to use any combination of keyboard and mouse-activated commands. PageMaker has provided you with both options for your convenience.

► PRINTING WITH PAGEMAKER

When you're ready to print a PageMaker publication, you can choose from many different models of laser printers, all of which allow low-cost, high-quality graphics and text printing. You can use your laser-printed publication directly or use it as a camera-ready copy. (*Camera-ready* copy refers to high-quality pages that can be photographed to produce printing plates.)

Many laser printers use the Hewlett-Packard Printer Command Language, or PCL. See Appendix F for a list of PCL laser printers supported by PageMaker. Soft downloadable fonts may be installed for PCL printers. These fonts come on a diskette and can be transferred from your computer to your printer.

PageMaker also supports many laser printers that use the PostScript page description language. See Appendix F for a list of laser printers supported by PageMaker's PostScript driver.

PostScript printers offer a variety of resident fonts. In addition, you may use downloadable fonts transferred from your computer for use by your printer.

Typesetters can also be used in conjunction with PageMaker. Appendix F has a list of Pagemaker-compatible typesetters.

Dot-matrix printers are also supported for draft copies. But keep in mind that the purpose of desktop publishing is to create typeset quality or near typeset quality publications with a desktop computer. Appendix F lists the dot-matrix printers that are supported by PageMaker.

All the printer drivers you use with PageMaker are supported in the Windows environment. Other printer drivers that work within Windows may also be used by PageMaker.

► SUMMARY

Desktop publishing is a unique application that ties together other applications. You must use your word processor to create most of your text, and graphics programs, spreadsheets, and scanners to create your images. PageMaker brings it all together in a professional-looking layout that works for you.

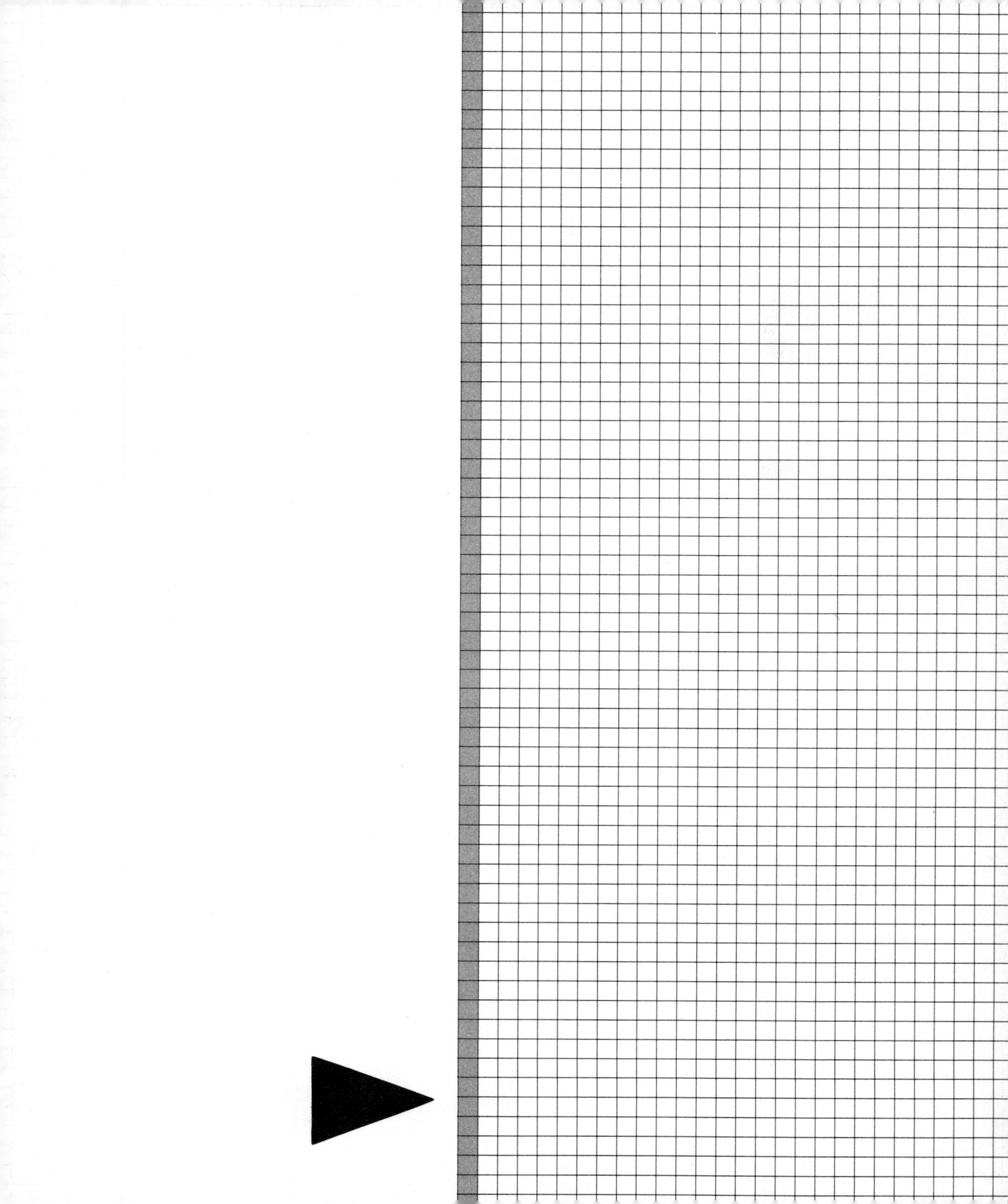

▶ 2 STARTING PAGEMAKER

To log on to PageMaker, 24

change to the subdirectory containing PageMaker, by typing CD\PM for PageMaker 1.0 or CD\PM3 for PageMaker 3.0, then pressing ↵.

To start PageMaker, 24

type WIN PM if you installed a full version of Windows, or PM if you installed the runtime version, then press ↵.

To select a menu from the menu bar, 25

point to the menu title and click the mouse button.

To designate your target printer, 27

select the "Printer setup" option from the File menu and click on that option. Click on the printer you want to select, then point to OK and click the mouse button.

To open a new publication, 31

select the "New" option from the File menu and click the mouse button. Enter the page specifications in the Page Setup dialog box, then click OK.

To save your work, 35

click on the "Save" command in the File menu.

To exit from PageMaker, 38

click on the Windows System box and select the "Close" command, or double-click on the Windows System box.

The best way to learn to use PageMaker is to develop a publication. Once you've created one publication, the same steps can be used to create a variety of publications, from newsletters to flyers and brochures. In this chapter, you'll learn to start PageMaker, to make selections from the menus, to choose a target printer, and to open a publication. You will continue to develop this publication in the following chapters.

► DEVELOPING A PUBLICATION

As you follow along with this book learning how to use PageMaker's many features, you will create a typical business communications newsletter. This will give you the opportunity to use PageMaker's features as they are being explained. With computers, the best teacher is hands-on training.

The purpose of our newsletter is to discuss the desktop publishing issues that are important to our target audience of desktop publishers. Our newsletter will be two pages long and will have a feature article, a smaller article, and a graphic from a paint or draw program. We will use several graphics features of PageMaker to enhance the overall look of the newsletter.

But first, in order to follow along as we create our newsletter, you need to have a few files ready to place into our PageMaker layout. Remember, PageMaker works best with text created using your word processor, and with graphics created using your paint or draw programs.

You need to create two stories with your word processor, a very short one (about three or four paragraphs), and a longer one, which should be a little over a page long. If you like, you may use your word processor to type the following stories, which we will use as examples in our newsletter. You can use documents from your own files, though, if you want to.

The first article in our newsletter is the following:

> **Personal computers are becoming faster and more powerful, and page makeup programs are approaching the capabilities of systems with five- and six-digit price tags. Telling the best page makeup programs through all the hype is getting harder and harder.**
>
> **The page makeup program you select will depend upon the type of publications you plan on developing. Some programs work best on small publications with limited amounts of text and high-quality graphics, such as brochures, flyers, and newsletters. Other programs work best for larger publications with dense text, such as technical manuals or books.**
>
> **The PageMaker version 3.0 from Aldus incorporates features from both ends of the spectrum and is ahead on the road toward the dedicated desktop publishing workstation. With all its advantages, PageMaker represents the top of the line in desktop publishing.**

The second article is the feature article of our newsletter. This article is as follows:

> **If you've never thought of yourself as an artist or graphic designer, desktop publishing may overwhelm you with its task of designing a page on a computer. It's easy to be intimidated by the vast array of choices you have to make. Which typeface should I use? What about type sizes, graphics, and formatting? Too many choices can seem to ruin all the advantages gained from desktop publishing.**
>
> **You can avoid the pitfalls by sticking to a few simple rules that graphic artists have followed for years. First, the design you create must be based on the content of your publication. You must determine the critical elements of your publication and use your design to highlight the levels of importance.**
>
> **In a newsletter, the most important element is the masthead of the newsletter. This should be the largest element of the first page. Next in importance are the titles of the articles and any special features or announcements that you want to catch your reader's eye quickly. The masthead itself should be first in importance, with the titles following in an order of importance that is defined simply. Avoid using too many type sizes and enhancements such as bolding and italicizing to make your point. The simplest approach is usually best.**
>
> **Selecting a typeface for your publication is another important step in determining its character. With all the fonts available on laser printers today, it's hard to determine which one to select in each case.**
>
> **Some typefaces have a flowery feel to them with serifs and bold lines. These typefaces work well for the invitations to an art opening, but not for technical publications. A plain typeface might be best for your company's annual report. The best approach is to use only one or two typefaces in each publication. Too many typeface changes can be distracting to a reader's eye.**
>
> **In the end, the best desktop published documents will be those that take a simple and direct approach. Leave enough white space to allow your reader's eye to relax on the page. Use your graphics to guide your reader's eye along the page, pointing out the topics of importance. It is better to use a simple layout design than to clutter the page with a complex design.**

Now that you have your text, you need to create a graphic with your paint or draw software. The graphic may be a simple company logo, or even a standard file that came with your software. The graphic we've created here for developing our newsletter is a PageMaker screen captured using Hotshot Graphics version 1.0 (Figure 2.1).

Once these files are ready to use, go to the next section to start PageMaker and begin learning about its many features for laying out a newsletter or other type of publication.

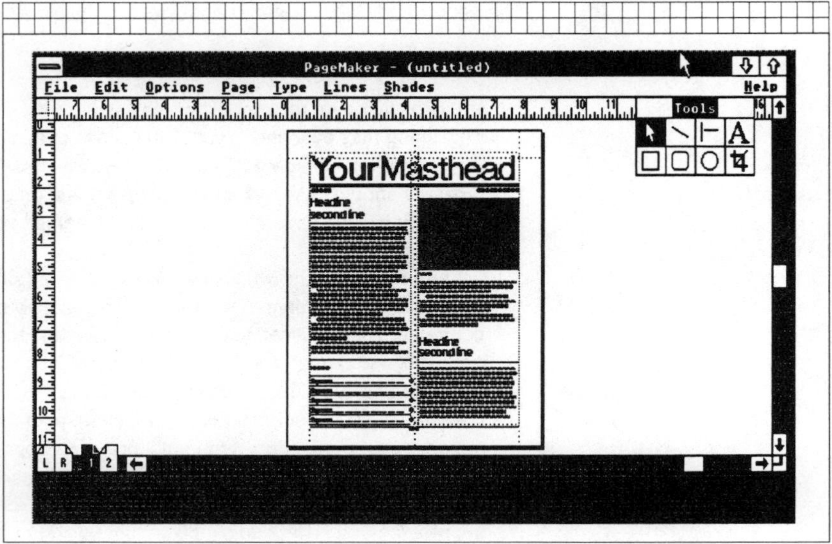

Figure 2.1: PageMaker screen with masthead and article titles

► STARTING PAGEMAKER

Before you start PageMaker, be sure you have correctly installed the program on your computer. Appendix A gives detailed instructions on installation.

When you turn on your computer, the disk operating system (DOS) loads up automatically. If necessary, enter the time and date when you are prompted. You should now be logged onto the main, or *root* directory on the C drive. The C prompt should appear on your screen.

To begin working with PageMaker, you must change to the subdirectory containing Windows and PageMaker. If you set up PageMaker according to the directions in Appendix A, the name of the subdirectory for PageMaker 1.0 should be PM, and the name of the subdirectory for PageMaker 3.0 should be PM3.

To change to the PM subdirectory, type

CD\PM

and press ↵ (Enter). To change to the PM3 subdirectory, type

CD\PM3

and press ↵. A new C prompt is displayed.

You are now ready to start PageMaker. If you installed a full version of Windows, type

WIN PM

and press ↵. If you installed the runtime version of Windows, type

PM

and press ↵.

The PageMaker copyright screen in Figure 2.2 is displayed on your screen.

From here you can start a new publication or open one you've already created. The copyright box in the middle of the screen will remain there until you click the mouse button to initiate a command.

The copyright screen displayed here is from PageMaker version 3.0. If you are using PageMaker version 1.0, your screen may look slightly different.

► SELECTING A MENU FROM THE MENU BAR

Notice the row of menu titles at the top of the copyright screen. This is called the *menu bar.* The menu bar title selections are File, Edit, Options, Page, Type, Lines, and Shades. Hidden under each of these menu titles is a listing of menu command options, each of which performs a specific function. You will learn about all these options as you read through this book. For now, let's view the File menu. Position the pointer on the word File on the menu bar. Click and hold the main mouse button. The copyright box in the middle of the screen will disappear and you will see the gray desktop and a list of command options in the File menu shown in Figure 2.3.

Figure 2.2: The PageMaker copyright screen

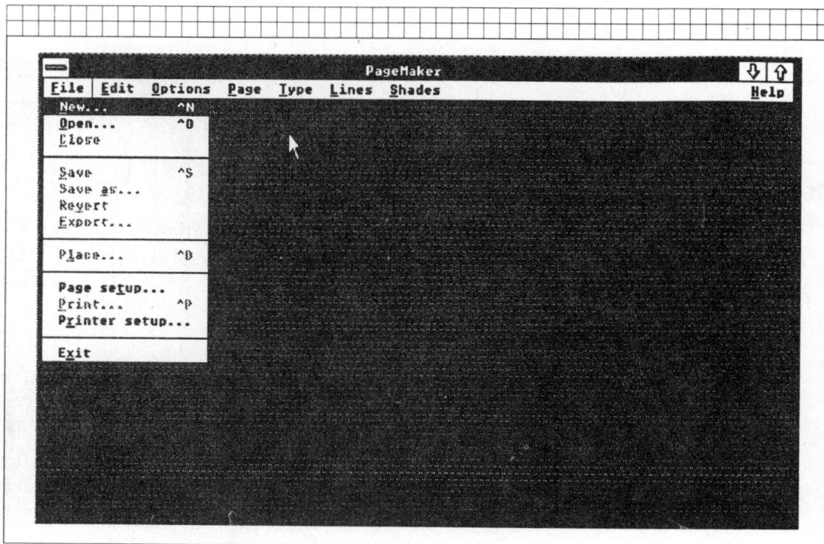

Figure 2.3: The File menu

Hold down the mouse button and drag the pointer down the list of commands. Notice that some of the menu command options are in black and some are in gray lettering. The active menu options appear in black. The gray menu options are not available for use right now. When a command option is appropriate to the task you are performing, it becomes an active command displayed in black. To choose a menu option, you must stop the pointer on the one you want and release the mouse button. To avoid choosing an option, move the pointer away from the menu options and release the mouse button. Also notice that each option has one letter underlined. You can display menus by holding down the underlined letter while you press the Alt key.

► SELECTING THE CONTROL MENU

Now look just above the menu bar in the upper-left corner of the screen. The small box containing two horizontal lines is called the *Control menu box*. This is the box where the Windows commands you may want to use while in PageMaker (which were discussed in Chapter 1) can be accessed. Choosing an option from the Control menu works just the same way as choosing a command option from one of the menus listed in the menu bar.

Position the pointer in the Control menu box. Click and hold the mouse button. The Control menu command options, shown in Figure 2.4, scroll down the screen just like those on the menu bar do. These commands are discussed as they are

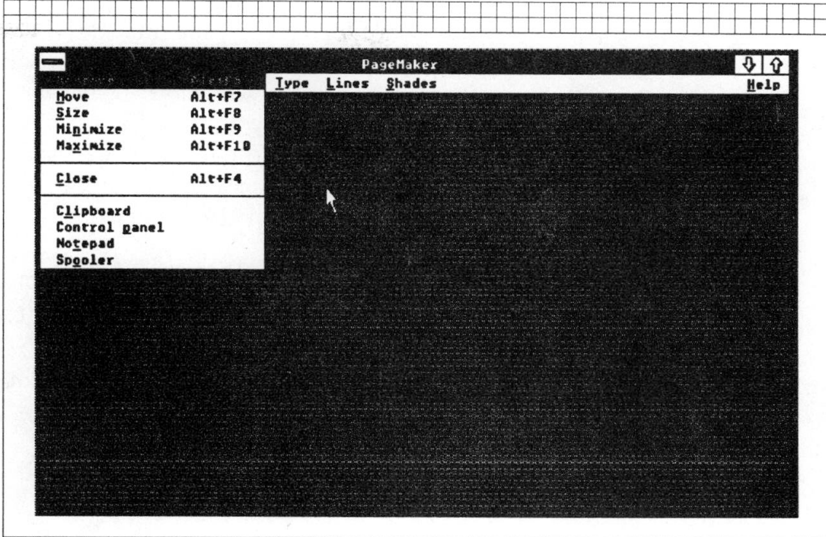

Figure 2.4: The System menu

used throughout the book. For more information on the Windows Control menu, refer to the Windows documentation. Return to the gray desktop by clicking away from the drop-down menu.

► CHOOSING A TARGET PRINTER

Before you begin a new publication in PageMaker, you must indicate which printer you will use to print your final publication. This printer is called the *target printer*. Each printer works with a specific set of type specifications and paper sizes. Once you have indicated a target printer, PageMaker displays only the options available to you based on that specific printer.

However, this does not mean that the target printer has to be hooked up to your computer. For instance, you may know a professional print shop able to print your publication from a disk using their high-quality printers. (More and more print and copy shops are providing these services as desktop publishing becomes popular.) In this case, you must indicate to PageMaker which target printer you plan to use at the print or copy shop.

If, after you've finished your publication, you choose another target printer, you may have to go back over the publication to touch up any changes that occurred as a result of the change. A printer change usually affects the line length and page breaks of a publication because PageMaker has to make the text specifications match the fonts, styles, and sizes available on the new target printer.

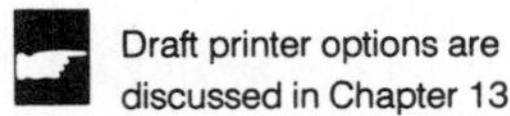

Your choice of target printer refers only to the printer you will use to produce your final pages. PageMaker provides a draft printer option for running draft copies on a printer other than the target printer. When you use this option, type specifications for the draft printer are automatically substituted. The specifications for the final pages of your publication are not affected.

Let's now designate the target printer for our newsletter. The target printer you choose may be different than the one shown here. Go ahead and make the selection that is appropriate to your system.

1. Position the pointer on the File menu in the menu bar.
2. Click the mouse button to display the menu options. (You will see the menu shown in Figure 2.3.)
3. Slide the pointer down the list of command options. Point to the ''Printer setup'' option.
4. Click on the ''Printer setup'' option.

A box like the one in Figure 2.5 appears in the middle of the screen. This is called a *dialog box.* A dialog box is PageMaker's way of asking you to supply more information so that your command can be carried out. The Printer Setup dialog box lists the printers and plotters you have already installed. The printer does

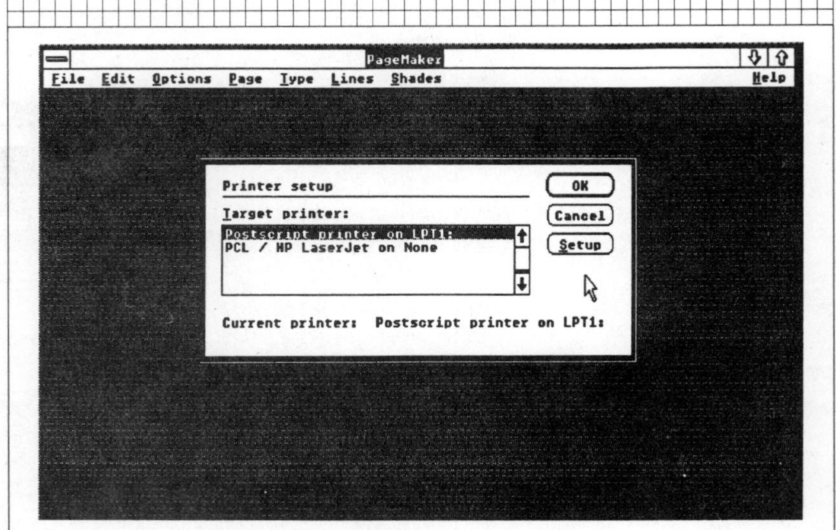

Figure 2.5: The Printer Setup dialog box

not have to be attached to your computer. However, the PM print driver must be installed when you run the PM Install program (see Appendix A).

Now you're ready to designate your printer.

1. Move the pointer to the printer you want to select. If your list of installed printers is too long to fit in the box, point to the arrow in the vertical scroll bar on the right side of the box (see Figure 2.5), then click the mouse to scroll through the list of printers. This scroll bar lets you display hidden names on the printers list.
2. When your choice is displayed, click the mouse button. The printer you selected is highlighted.
3. Point to OK and click the mouse button, or double-click the mouse on your printer choice directly, which selects your printer and OK at the same time.

The dialog box for the printer you selected should now be displayed on your screen. The sample in Figure 2.6 shows the dialog box for a PostScript laser printer. If the printer you selected has additional options, another dialog box appears on the screen, overlaying the first one, such as the one shown in Figure 2.7 for the PostScript printer. (The dialog box you see varies with the printer you selected.) With the mouse, select the options you want and click OK when you are ready, or double-click on the final selected option. The opening screen is redisplayed without the dialog boxes.

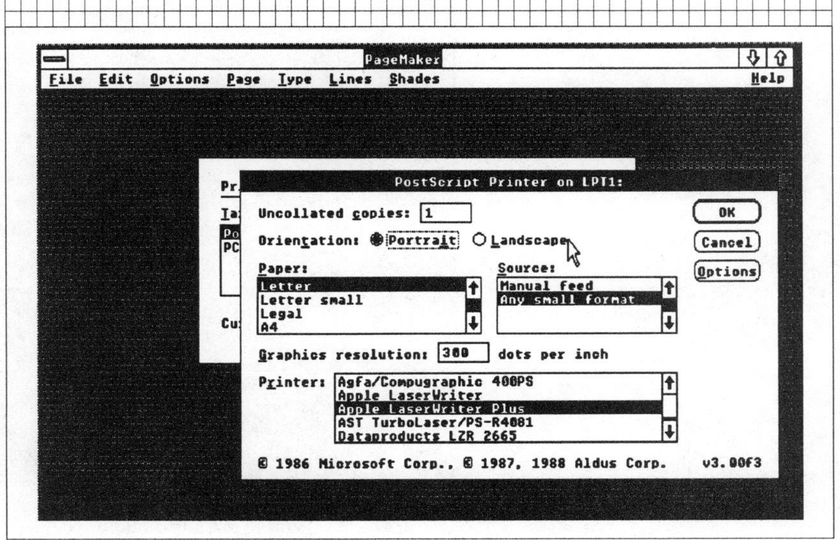

Figure 2.6: A PostScript printer dialog box

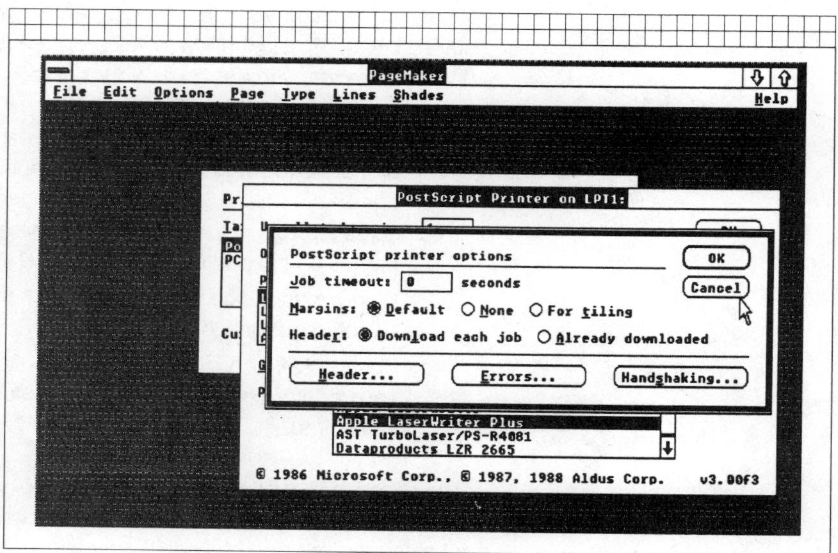

Figure 2.7: A second dialog box overlaying the first

Figures 2.8 and 2.9 illustrate the dialog boxes for PCL laser printers.

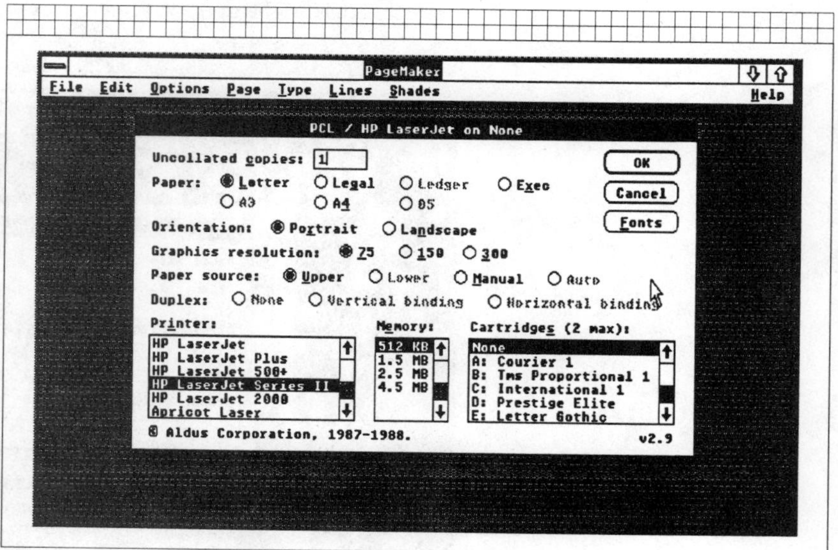

Figure 2.8: A PCL laser printer dialog box

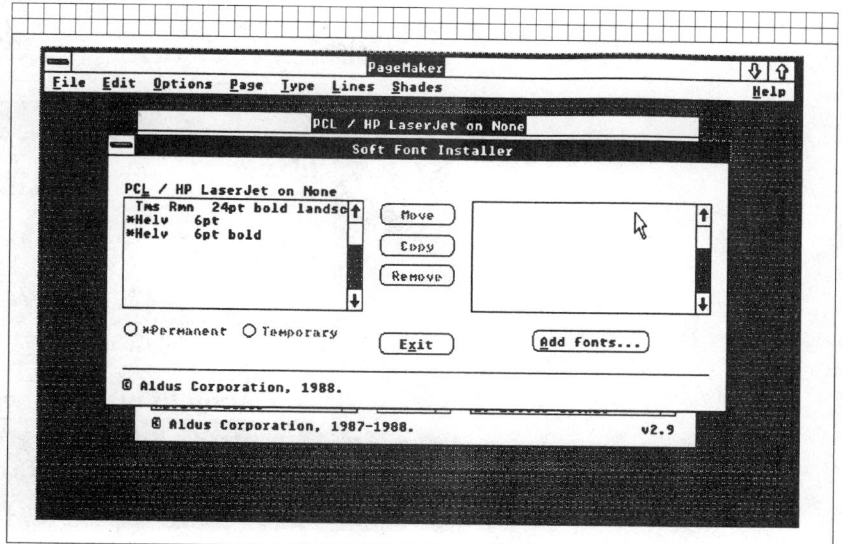

Figure 2.9: A PCL font installer dialog box

► OPENING A NEW PUBLICATION WITH THE PAGE SETUP DIALOG BOX

After you have chosen your target printer, you will again see the gray desktop. You are now ready to start a new publication, your newsletter.

To start a new publication:

1. Point to the File menu in the menu bar.
2. Click the mouse button to display the menu.
3. Point to the "New" option and click the mouse button.

You will now see the Page Setup dialog box (shown in Figure 2.10) on your screen.

This dialog box requires you to enter information about how you want your pages to be set up. To do this, you will enter information in the text boxes, which are the rectangular boxes for text entry. We will be using the keyboard to enter this information. To begin, you must select a text box by positioning the pointer in the box. The pointer icon then changes to the text icon, the I-beam. Click the main mouse button and the cursor is displayed. Now type in the information.

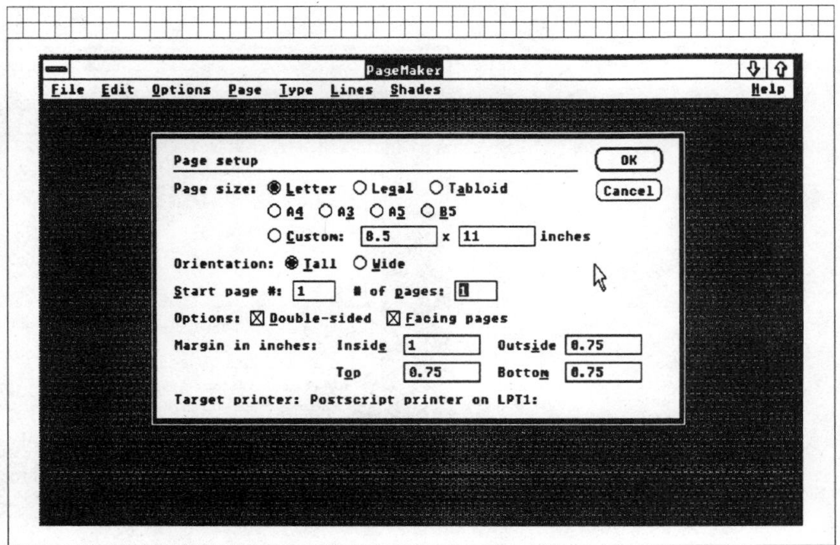

Figure 2.10: The Page Setup dialog box

You will set up the page using other items on the Page Setup menu, too. You will make these selections with the mouse. The square boxes with X-marks turn functions on or off. If an X-mark appears in the box, the function is turned on. Clicking the mouse in the box turns the function off and causes the X-mark to disappear. The option can be turned on again with a click of the mouse.

You use the circular option buttons to indicate your choice from a group of options. The button containing the dark circle is the selected, or current choice. To change the selected button, point to the option you want and click the mouse. You can choose only one circular option button at a time. Clicking on an option button in a group automatically turns the previous choice in that group off.

The command buttons, labeled OK and Cancel, tell PageMaker when you have finished with a dialog box. Clicking OK lets PageMaker know you have made your selections and are ready to proceed. Clicking Cancel lets PageMaker know you want to stop working with a dialog box. Clicking Cancel returns you to the gray desktop.

The options already selected in the Page Setup dialog box are called *default values.* PageMaker chooses these options for you automatically, but you can change them. Changing default values and choosing new options are explained below.

► PAGE SIZE

The circular option buttons determine the page size of your document. The letter selection designates 8.5-by-11-inch paper. US legal indicates 8.5-by-14-inch paper. The tabloid option is a standard newspaper size of 11-by-17 inches. A4 is a European standard of 210-by-297 millimeters, or 8.268-by-11.693 inches. A3 selects a European standard of 11.693-by-16.535 inches. A5 selects a paper size of 5.827-by-8.268 inches. B5 is another European standard paper size of 182-by-257 millimeters, or 6.929-by-9.842 inches. While your printer may not use most of these page sizes, you may be using an outside printer that does. You can also specify any custom page size you want by typing in the exact measurements of the page.

The maximum paper size that PageMaker allows is 17-by-22 inches. The size you select does not have to correspond to the paper in your printer, but it is a good idea to select a size equal to or smaller than the paper your printer uses. However, if you select a size larger than the paper in your printer, PageMaker provides a command called Tiling to accommodate this. Refer to Chapter 13 for a detailed explanation of tiling.

For our newsletter, we will select Letter, PageMaker's default value, a standard 8.5-by-11-inch paper size, so you do not need to make any changes.

▶ ORIENTATION

The next circular button option asks you to choose the orientation for your publication. All the pages of a document must share the same orientation, but you can get around this limitation by creating two separate files. Create one for pages you want to orient horizontally and one for pages you want to orient vertically.

The default Tall publication orients the contents of a page vertically. This is the way we are most used to seeing our documents. Tall orientation is also called *portrait* orientation. A Wide publication orients the contents of a page horizontally. This is also referred to as *landscape* orientation.

For our newsletter we will select Tall, PageMaker's default orientation. So leave the value as it is already selected.

▶ STARTING PAGE NUMBER

The Start Page # box contains the default entry of 1. If the first page number of your document is not 1, type the page number you want to use, up to 999. For instance, suppose you are combining two files, and the first file begins on page 1, but the second file begins on page 20. In this case, you would enter 20 in the Start Page # box of the second file. You may also create a unique page numbering system using master pages. Master pages will be explained later.

Our newsletter will start with page 1, so leave the PageMaker default as it is.

Next, you must indicate the number of pages for your publication. Our newsletter will be two pages long (but we can always add more pages later). To designate the number of pages:

1. Click the I-beam in the # of Pages box to display the text cursor.
2. Type in 2, since we will be creating a two-page newsletter.

When you know how many pages are in your publication, type in the number right away, up to 128, in the # of Pages box. This way, with several pages formatted from the start, you can move easily from formatted page to formatted page. Later you can always insert or remove pages.

► SINGLE, DOUBLE-SIDED, OR FACING PAGES

In the PageMaker default value, the Page Setup dialog box has an X-mark in the option titled "Double-sided." This means your publication is to have both left-hand (even-numbered) and right-hand (odd-numbered) pages. If you want a single-sided publication, remove the X-mark from the "Double-sided" option by pointing to the box and clicking the mouse.

If you are working on a double-sided publication and you want to display both the left-hand and the right-hand pages on the screen, make sure there is an X-mark in the Facing Pages box. You also have the option of displaying only one page at a time of a double-sided publication. To do this, click the Facing Pages box to make the X-mark disappear.

For our newsletter, we want a single-sided format. To select this format, click on the Double-sided box so that the X-mark disappears, which unselects that option. Notice that the X-mark in the Facing Pages box also disappeared.

► MARGINS

Margins define the area of a page that contains the text and the graphics. PageMaker's default value has the inside margin set at 1 inch, and the outside, top, and bottom margins set at .75 inches. (You'll learn about inside and outside margins in a moment.) But like other page setup default values, you can change them to meet your needs. When you set your margins, remember that your printer has certain margin requirements. For example, setting the margins at 0 eliminates them altogether, but your printer may not be able to handle text or graphics near the paper's edge. PageMaker measures the margin units in inches. You can change this using the "Preferences" option in the Edit menu.

For the purpose of double-sided and facing pages, the right and left margins are referred to as the inside or outside margin. On left-hand pages, the inside margin is on the right side, and the outside margin is on the left. On right-hand pages, the inside margin is on the left side, and the outside margin is on the right. This method of referencing margins may take some getting used to at first, but if you have your publication professionally bound, the distinction between inside and outside margins becomes important. For instance, you may need to allow a larger inside margin to accommodate the space taken by the binding.

Our newsletter is a single-sided publication, so PageMaker automatically refers to the margins as right, left, top, and bottom. To set the margins for our newsletter:

1. Click the I-beam in the Left Margin text box.
2. Type in .5 to set the left margin at half an inch.
3. Repeat this process for each margin text box, setting the right and top margins at .5 inches. Set the bottom margin at 1 inch.

► TARGET PRINTER

The last selection in the dialog box displays the name of the target printer. If you have been following the instructions in this chapter, you should have already indicated your target printer and it should show up here. If your target printer is different than the one indicated in the dialog box, go to the section "Choosing a Target Printer" and define your target printer. The target printer indicated here determines which type specification options will be available to you as you design your publication, so choose your target printer correctly before going any further.

Your page setup screen should now look like the one in Figure 2.11. Click on the OK button at the top right-hand corner of the Page Setup dialog box and begin your publication.

You should now have the PageMaker publication window displayed. You will learn all about the publication window in the next chapter, but before we go on, let's learn how to save our work and exit from PageMaker. Be sure to save your work whenever you want to leave your newsletter.

► SAVING YOUR WORK

The Save commands are located in the File menu (see Figure 2.3). There are two Save commands, "Save" and "Save as." "Save" is used to save a publication that has already been saved and given a title. Selecting this command saves your most recent changes under the title that is displayed in the title bar at the top of the publication window. Use the "Save as" command for a file that hasn't yet

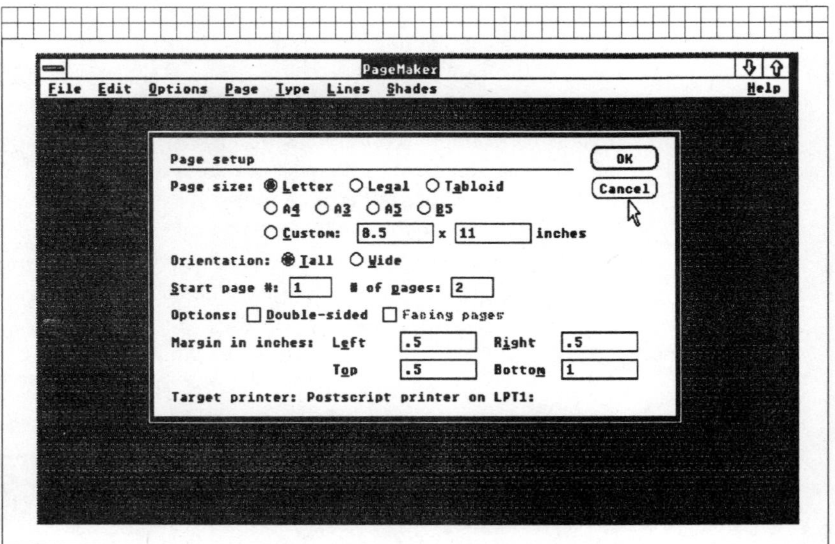

Figure 2.11: Completed Page Setup dialog box for our newsletter

been saved. Since we just opened our publication, and it has never been saved before, we must use the "Save as" command.

It's a good habit to save your work frequently to ensure that your work isn't lost if you encounter an unexpected disaster, such as a power failure or equipment problems.

To save your work:

1. Click on the "Save as" command, and the Save As dialog box, shown in Figure 2.12, is displayed.
2. To name our publication, position the pointer in the Name box. When the icon changes to the I-beam, click the mouse button to display the cursor.
3. Now type in the name of our newsletter. Let's call it NEWSTEMP.

These options are not available in PageMaker versions earlier than 3.0.

If you are using version 3.0, notice the Publication and Template option buttons. These options give you a choice of how to save your file. A *template* is a file containing only layout specifications. By saving the layout specifications separately in a template file, you save yourself the trouble of using the Page Setup dialog box each time you create a new publication.

Let's save our work as a template to produce our monthly newsletter. Later we will add the articles and graphics.

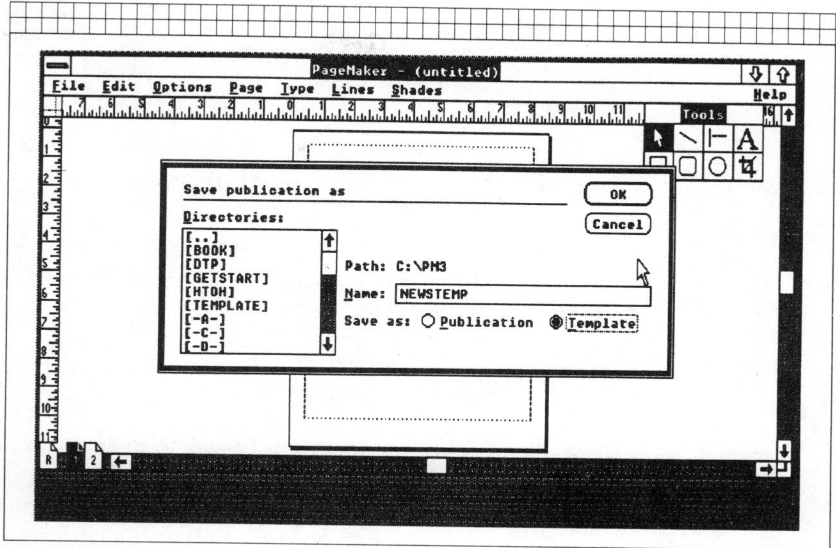

Figure 2.12: The Save As dialog box

4. Click on the Template option button to indicate you want this saved as a template. PageMaker 3.0 saves templates with a .PT3 extension, and publications with a .PM3 extension.
5. Click on the OK button and the publication is saved as a template.

► CLOSING THE PAGEMAKER WINDOW

Once the template or publication is saved, you will see your publication displayed in the PageMaker window. Now, let's close the PageMaker window as if we were finished with our template. In the next chapter, we will open the template again and add more elements to the layout. To close a template or publication:

1. Display the File menu.
2. Click on the "Close" option.

Once the template has been saved, you are immediately returned to the gray desktop. If you had forgotten to save your work, PageMaker would have displayed a dialog box, like the one in Figure 2.12, asking you to save your work before closing. This precaution ensures that you won't accidentally close a publication or template without saving it and lose your work.

► EXITING FROM PAGEMAKER

Now let's exit from PageMaker and return to the DOS prompt. To exit from PageMaker:

1. Click on the Windows System box to display the command options.
2. Click on the Close command.

You should now be out of PageMaker. The DOS prompt is displayed on your screen. You can now turn off your computer, or read on as we develop a PageMaker publication.

► SUMMARY

You're now on your way to developing a PageMaker publication. You've learned some PageMaker basics and have opened up the publication you'll be using in the next chapter. There you will learn how to open a publication that has already been started, and continue developing your newsletter template.

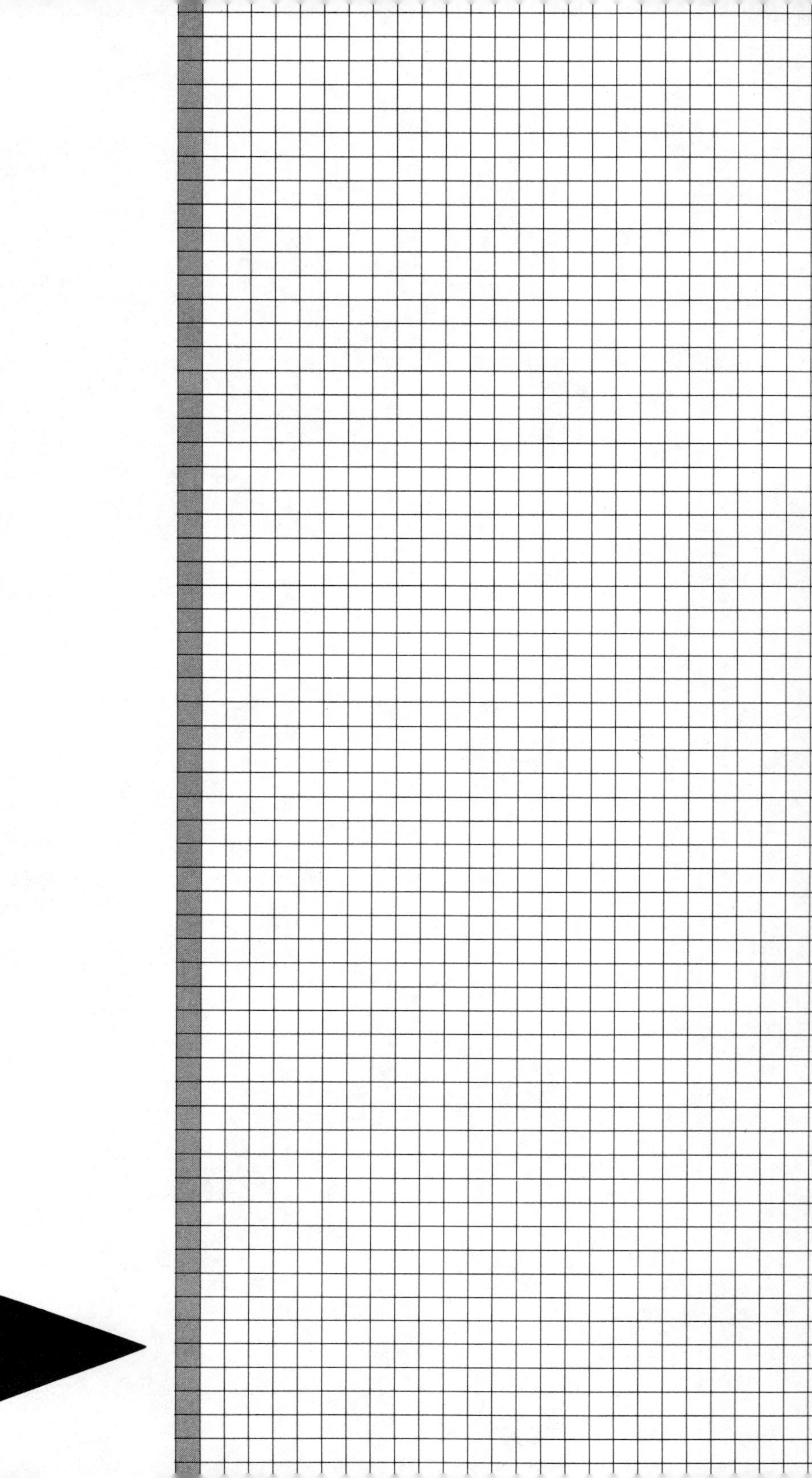

3 PAGEMAKER'S MAIN WORK AREA: THE PUBLICATION WINDOW

To see a list of the directories 44

on your hard disk and floppies, and the names of the files they contain, click on the File menu, then select "Open." You will see the Open Publication dialog box. The directories are listed on the left side of the box.

To open an existing file, 44

select the "Open" command from the File menu, then double-click on the directory name to see a list of file names in that directory. Click on the file name, then click on OK to open the file.

Use the arrow-shaped pointer 46

to select menu options, move around in the publication window, select tools, and perform many other functions.

The pasteboard 46

is the blank area surrounding the page in the publication window; use it to store text and graphics before you're ready to place them in your publication, or as a scratch pad to develop text or graphics.

Use Microsoft Windows commands 47

through the Control menu box. This is the small box with horizontal lines in the upper-left corner of the publication window. Click on the box to display the Control menu.

To move your publication in the window, 47

use the gray scroll bars to the right and at the bottom of the screen.

To move to a new page, 48

use the page icons shown at the bottom left of the publication window.

Enhance your page with PageMaker's graphics tools. 49

Use the text tool to add text, the drawing tools to draw shapes and lines, and the cropping tool to trim a graphic.

To change the size of your view of the page, 50

use the Page menu commands. Select "Page" from the menu bar, then select one of the five view options.

In the last chapter, we began developing the template for our newsletter. A template, you remember, is a file containing layout specifications, graphics, and text that you want to have in every edition of your newsletter. We designated a target printer for our publication. We selected page setup options from the Page Setup dialog box. In this chapter, we will learn about the publication window, PageMaker's main work area. We will also learn to use the Toolbox feature, which provides electronic tools for adding text and graphic enhancements.

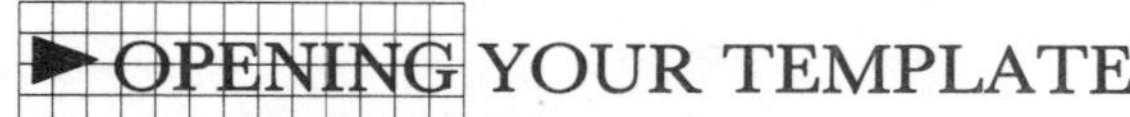

► OPENING YOUR TEMPLATE

To open a template:

1. Click on the File menu to display the commands.
2. Click on the "Open" option to open an existing template or publication. This displays the Open Publication dialog box, shown in Figure 3.1.

The scroll box, on the left side of the Open Publication dialog box, lists files and directories to select from. Directories are bracketed, while file names are not. To find a file name within a specific directory, double-click on the directory name. The file names within the directory will be displayed. If you want to return to a list of directories from a list of file names, double-click on the two bracketed dots. In the

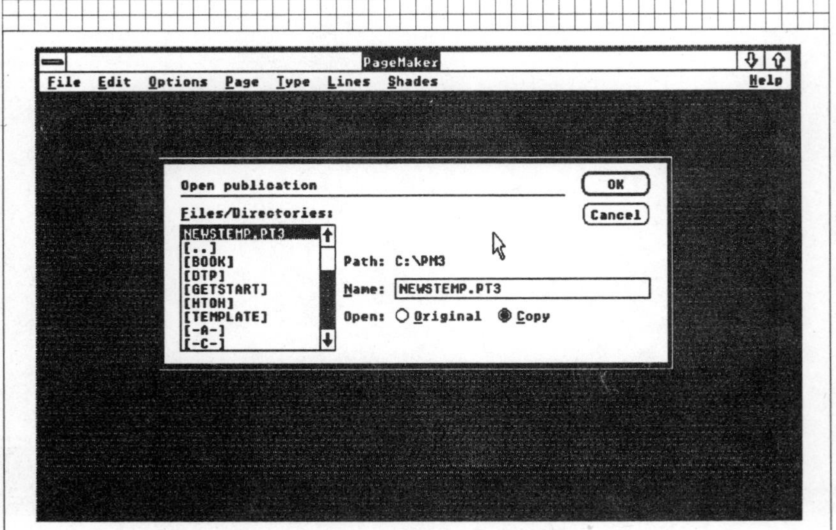

Figure 3.1: The Open Publication dialog box

same way, from the list of directories, double-clicking on the two dots within the brackets displays the list of files in the currently selected directory. Notice the ↑ and ↓ symbols to the right side of the scroll box. Clicking on these arrows scrolls the list of directory and file names up or down. In this way, you can read the names that are hidden from view.

3. Find the NEWSTEMP.PT3 file and click on it to highlight it.
4. You are opening an original template. If you were going to modify a template and intended to save your modified copy under a new name, you would select the "Copy" option button. This would give us a copy of the file, leaving the original template unchanged.
5. Click on OK to open the template.

The publication window is now displayed, as shown in Figure 3.2. You will do most of your PageMaker work in the publication window. It is displayed whenever you create a new publication or edit an existing one.

▶ PAGEMAKER'S PUBLICATION WINDOW

Many items on this screen are probably mysterious to you. Let's go over each part of the screen before we begin working with it. Understanding what

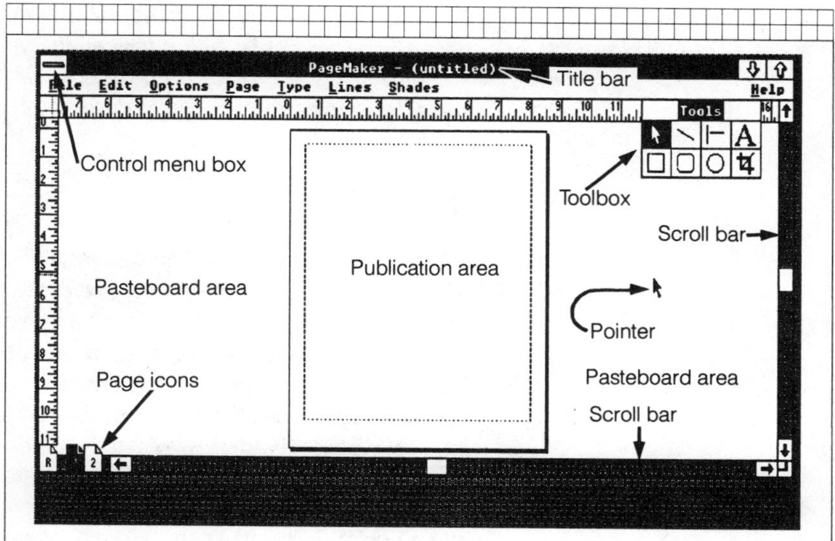

Figure 3.2: The publication window

each element of the publication window does is essential to working with PageMaker in an efficient and comfortable manner.

► THE POINTER

We have already used the pointer to select menu option commands, but let's review it quickly since it is such an important element. The pointer is the small arrow on the screen. It is controlled by the mouse. In PageMaker, you will work with many different tools to perform operations as diverse as selecting text and manipulating graphics, and the pointer is used to select the tools you need. For example, when you entered text into the dialog box, you saw the text icon change into an I-beam. The pointer also changes into other icons, depending on which operations you want to perform.

► THE PUBLICATION AREA

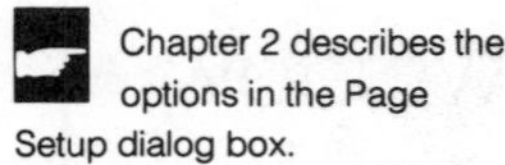
Chapter 2 describes the options in the Page Setup dialog box.

The rectangular box bordered by dashed and dotted lines is the place where your publication appears. PageMaker displays either one page or two facing pages at one time. If you created a double-sided publication and you checked "Facing pages" in the Page Setup dialog box, then two pages are displayed. If you created a single-sided publication, or if you created a double-sided publication but you didn't check "Facing pages" in the Page Setup dialog box, then only one page appears on the screen at a time, as in Figure 3.2. The dotted and dashed lines indicate the specifications you gave for the margins. The size and orientation of the displayed page are also dependent upon the information you entered into the Page Setup dialog box.

► THE PASTEBOARD

The space surrounding the rectangular box is called the *pasteboard*. The pasteboard is like a graphic artist's work table. Here you may set aside text and graphics until you are ready to place them. You can also move text or graphics off the page and place them on the pasteboard. In fact, a good way to work with PageMaker is to line up all the graphics for your publication on the pasteboard. This way you can see the elements you want to include in your publication, rather than having them hidden away in a file. When you are ready to place a graphic in your publication, it is there on the pasteboard ready for you to use.

The pasteboard can also be used like a scratch pad. You can develop your text and graphics on it, and when the text or graphic is complete, you can then place it anywhere you want in the publication. The entire pasteboard area is too large to be displayed on your screen at one time. Soon you will learn to use the scroll bars to get to the hidden areas of the pasteboard.

► THE TITLE BAR AND THE CONTROL MENU BOX

The *title bar* is the highlighted horizontal line at the top of the publication window. The title bar contains the PageMaker program name and the title of your publication. A new publication is untitled until you save it and give it a name. But once a publication has been saved, titled, and brought up again, it becomes an existing publication, and its title and the disk drive and directory where it is stored will be displayed in the title bar.

At the left side of the title bar is a box containing two horizontal lines. This is the *Control menu box* that you previously saw on the copyright screen. The Control menu lists the commands for Microsoft Windows, which are discussed in Chapter 1. The command options in the Control menu are selected in the same way as the command options in the menu bar.

► THE SCROLL BARS

The *scroll bars* are the gray bars located vertically on the right side and horizontally at the bottom of the screen. The scroll bars are used to move the publication vertically and horizontally in the publication window in three ways. Click in a scroll bar's gray area to move large distances. The white rectangles indicate where your publication is located relative to the scroll bar. Try using both the scroll bars to move around in the publication window. Notice how the pasteboard area extends beyond what was originally displayed on your screen. This entire pasteboard area is available to you.

To scroll the page only a short distance, position the pointer at either end of the gray scroll bar area in one of the boxes containing the ←, →, ↑, or ↓ symbols. Click the mouse and the publication scrolls slightly. Continue clicking the mouse to scroll the publication a small step at a time.

The scroll bars can be used a third way. Position the pointer in the white rectangular box in a scroll bar. Click and hold the mouse button down. Now move the mouse, sliding the rectangular box along the length of the scroll bar. Notice how your publication moves around in the publication window.

► THE GRABBER HAND

The scroll bars move the page around on the screen to display more pasteboard area, but suppose you want to "pick up" a page and quickly move it around. For this purpose, PageMaker includes a *grabber hand.* The grabber hand moves in any direction, unlike the scroll bars.

To grab the page, move the pointer anywhere inside the page in the publication window. First, press and hold down the Alt key, then click and hold the mouse button down. The pointer changes into an icon that looks like a small hand. This is the grabber hand. Move the mouse and the grabber hand moves on the screen, picking up the page with it. When you have the page positioned, release the buttons.

► THE PAGE ICONS

Master pages are used when you want every page of your publication to conform to a particular format. The first step in creating a master page is to position the pointer on the L or R page icon and click the mouse button. Developing a master page is explained in Chapter 7.

Several page icons are located at the bottom left-hand corner of the screen. The two icons labeled L and R are the master page icons. They stand for the left-hand (L) and right-hand (R) sides of a double-sided publication. If your publication is single-sided, as ours is, you only see the R icon, as in Figure 3.2.

The 1 and 2 page icons refer to the pages of the publication that have been developed. The highlighted icon indicates which page is being displayed. Your publication can have up to 128 pages. An icon for each page number appears along the bottom of the screen as each page is developed, but if you have more than 20 pages, PageMaker may not display all the page icons at one time. In this case, arrows appear on either side of the page icons. Click on the arrows to display the hidden page icons, in the same way you click on the scroll bar arrows to position the publication.

► THE MICROSOFT WINDOWS ICON

If you are using a runtime version of Windows you won't see the Microsoft Windows icon. See Chapter 1 for more information on runtime and full versions of Windows.

If you started PageMaker from the Windows MS-DOS Executive Window using a full version of Windows, a floppy disk icon will be displayed in the gray area at the bottom left of the screen. This is the Microsoft Windows icon and you can use it to bring up the Windows screen you use to start up PageMaker.

► MORE PUBLICATION WINDOW FEATURES

The horizontal ruler, at the top of the screen, and the vertical ruler, on the left side of the screen, are to help you align text and graphics in your layout.

The ↑ and ↓ arrows in the upper right-hand corner of the screen let you zoom in and out of the publication window.

Use the pointer to click on the "Help" option, located just below the ↑ and ↓ arrows, when you need help with PageMaker.

► THE TOOLBOX

A graphic artist uses a variety of tools to paste up a layout. A similar set of tools is available to you to perform the same functions using PageMaker. PageMaker's Toolbox overlays the publication window in the upper right-hand corner of the screen. There you will find eight electronic tools for creating a page.

To select a tool, move the pointer to the box containing the tool of your choice. Click the mouse button. The pointer icon then changes into a new icon, one corresponding to the tool you want to use.

You can use any tool as a pointer to make selections from the menu bar, to scroll through the publication window, to move from one page to another (using the page icons), or to choose a tool from the Toolbox. Let's look at the tools PageMaker provides.

► THE POINTER

You are already familiar with the arrow-shaped pointer. It is the tool you used to select text and graphics and to choose menu options. When you choose a new tool with the pointer, the pointer changes to the icon of the tool you chose. To return to the pointer again, just move the tool icon you're using to the pointer box and click the mouse.

► DRAWING TOOLS

The \ and |– symbols are used to draw lines and rules. The pointer changes to a crossbar when you select these tools. The line begins at the intersection of the crossbar.

The □, ▢, and ○ symbols are used to draw squares, rectangles, ovals, and circles. You would use them, for example, to draw shapes for framing graphics or text. Once you've selected one of these tools from the Toolbox, the tool symbol becomes a crossbar. One corner of the shape begins at the intersection of the crossbar.

► THE TEXT TOOL

The box containing **A** is the *text tool.* The text tool is used to insert text and to select text on the screen for correcting or replacing. We have already used the text tool icon in the shape of an I-beam in Chapter 2 when we saved our newsletter, NEWSTEMP, in the Save As dialog box.

▶ THE CROPPING TOOL

The ⌗ symbol indicates the *cropping or trimming tool*. This tool is used like a pair of scissors to crop, or trim, a graphic.

▶ VIEWING THE PUBLICATION WINDOW

The publication window first displays your publication so that an entire page fits within the screen area. If you are creating a double-sided publication with facing pages, both the left and right pages are displayed. The actual size of your document when it is printed probably is bigger than the screen of your computer. For this reason, PageMaker can adjust the size of your publication on the screen so that the entire page (or pages) fits within the publication window. PageMaker refers to this view of the publication as the *Fit-in-window view.*

PageMaker offers five views. The Fit-in-window view is one of these. Commands in the Page menu (Figure 3.3) allow you to select many views of a publication. In a moment, we will experiment with the different views. But first, let's look at them one at a time.

The Fit-in-window view allows you to see the entire page. However, the clarity of the text and graphics is lost when the publication is shrunk to fit in your screen. Therefore, PageMaker provides an *Actual Size* view that displays your publication with all elements in the actual size in which they will be printed. The hitch is, since

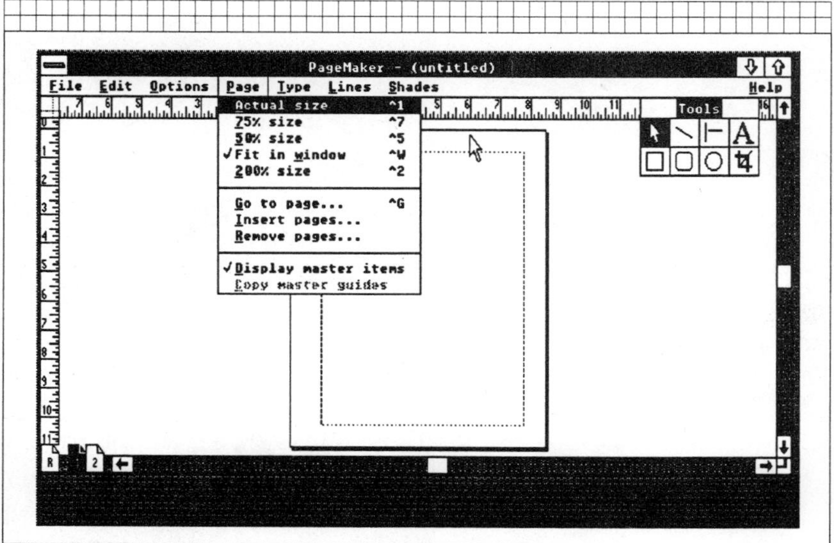

Figure 3.3: The Page menu showing the view options

your screen is probably smaller than the size of your publication, you can only view a portion of a page of your publication at a time. You must use the scroll bars in the publication window to move around on the page and view it all.

Two other views allow you to reduce the Actual Size view. The "50% size" and "75% size" options show you the Actual Size view reduced by 50% or 75%. A fifth option, "200% size," doubles the size of the elements seen in the Actual Size view.

► CHOOSING THE CORRECT VIEW

Ruler guides are explained in Chapter 5.

You may choose any size view when working on your publication, since all PageMaker commands work with all view sizes. But the view you should choose depends upon the actions you are performing. Certain sizes provide an easier view for carrying out certain commands. The ruler guides that help you lay out a page change size according to the view, and larger views display finer increments between the markings on the ruler guides. All views, however, display the ruler markings accurately.

When you choose a view, you should also consider the precision needed for the task you are performing. The Fit-in-window view gives you an idea of how the whole page fits together. This view works best to determine the overall balance of the page. The 75% and 50% views work well when you are adding enhancements to the page. Boxing in graphics, or placing lines or borders on the page can be performed well using these view sizes.

The Actual Size view provides clarity in the text. Smaller views make the text unreadable, but at actual size, the text can be read, entered, and edited easily. The Actual Size view of a page also works well to place graphics and text.

The "200% size" option gives you the most precision. At this size, the increments of the ruler markings are large. You can place text and graphics on the page precisely. This is a good view to use when you create your layout grid. Placing the grid guidelines can be done quickly and accurately from this view.

► SELECTING A VIEW

Remember that there are keyboard equivalents to these mouse commands. See Appendix B.

The view commands are located in the Page menu (Figure 3.3). To select a view, point in the menu bar to "Page" and click and hold the mouse button. The Page menu scrolls down the screen. Move the menu pointer down the list of commands. A check-mark next to a command option indicates the current view. To select another view, highlight the command option you want (each option is automatically highlighted as you move down the list). Release the mouse button. The new view is check-marked and is displayed in the publication window.

PageMaker provides some shortcuts to changing the view of a page. To select the Fit-in-window view, hold down the Alt and Shift keys simultaneously. Click the main mouse button. PageMaker displays the Fit-in-window view of the page.

To display the page at its actual size, point to the portion of the page you want centered on the screen. Hold down the Alt and Ctrl keys, and click the mouse button. To return to the Fit-in-window view from here, hold down the Alt and Ctrl keys and click the mouse button.

The 50% and 75% size views can only be selected from the Page menu. However, there is a shortcut to displaying the page at 200%. Hold down the Alt, Shift, and Ctrl keys simultaneously. Click the main mouse button. Repeat the process to move to an Actual Size view from the 200% size view.

When you change views, PageMaker retains a memory of the portion of the page you were just viewing. So when you return to that view, you are returned to the exact location on the page you were last viewing.

► SUMMARY

In this chapter, you have learned about the elements of the publication window. This is the main work area of PageMaker. Here you use PageMaker's many tools that enable you to produce an attractive document, such as the pasteboard, the grabber hand, and the Toolbox. You also have learned about the many ways you can view a publication. In the next chapter, you will learn basic design principles to help you use PageMaker's publication window to create a desktop publication.

► PART II: DESIGN BASICS

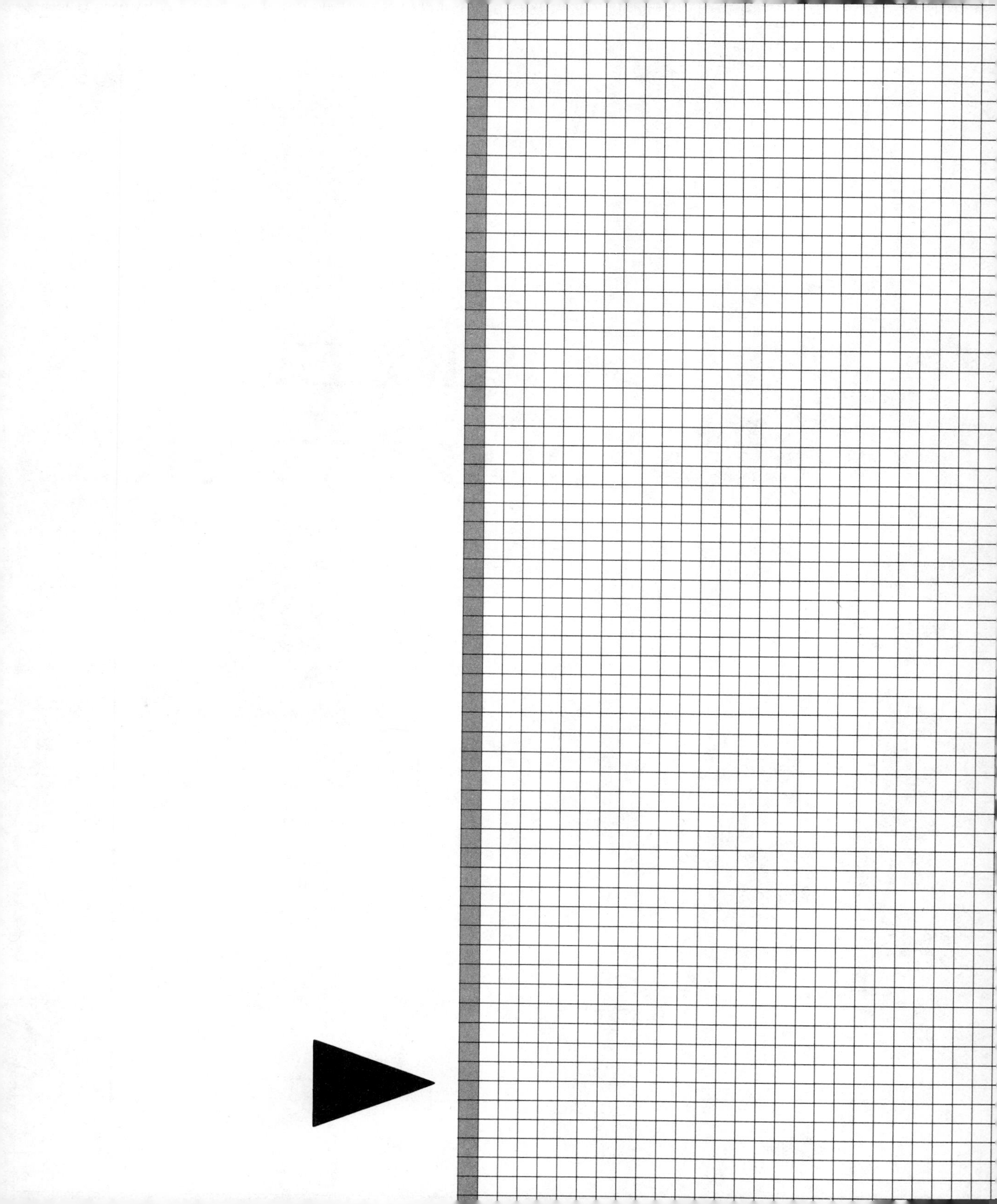

4 DESIGNING YOUR PUBLICATION

Fast Track

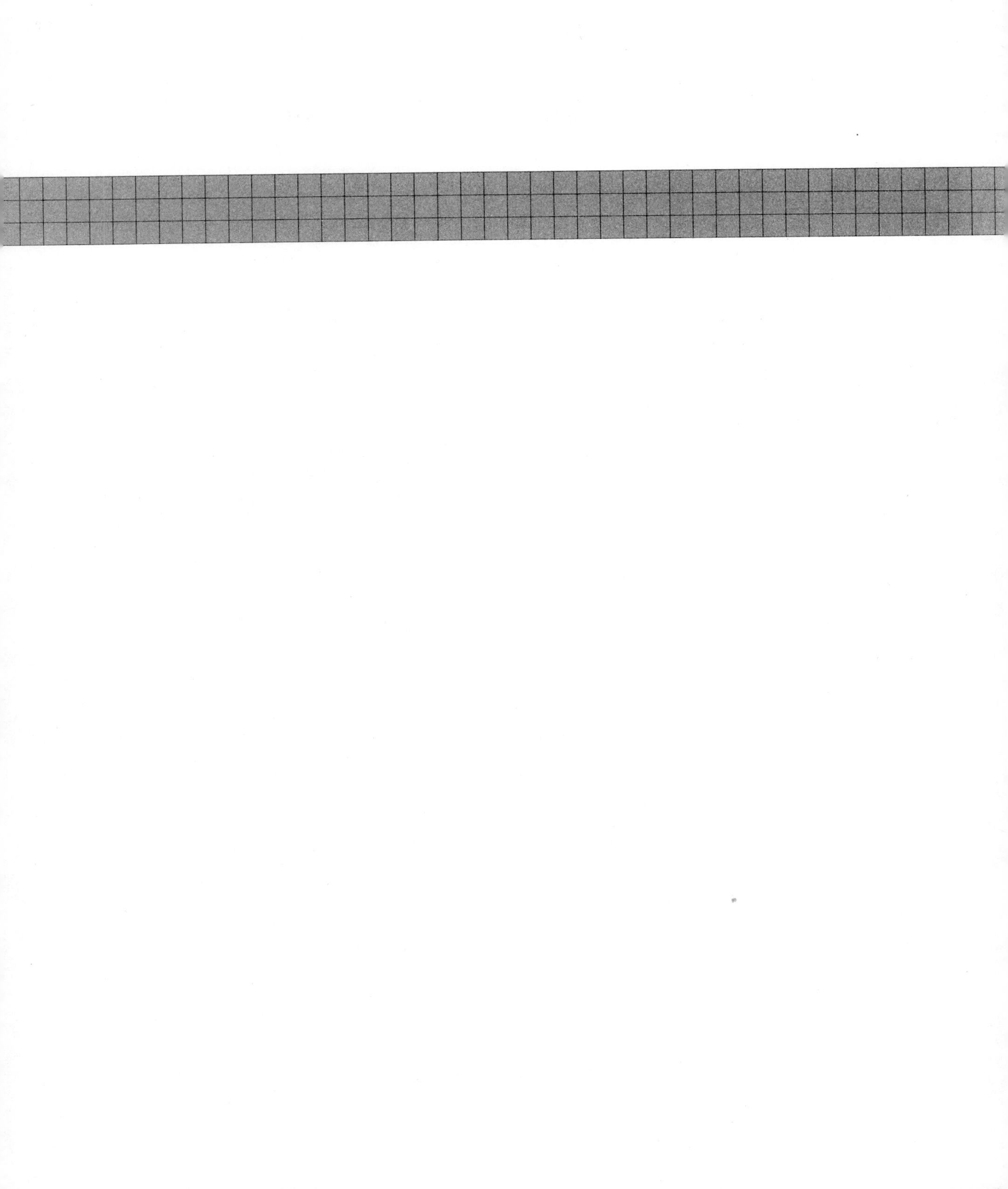

If you are new to desktop publishing, the skills of publication design may be unfamiliar to you. This chapter will give you some basic design principles to work with in creating visually appealing publications.

We will first discuss the initial design considerations you must address before beginning any publication. We then will design our own newsletter, as well as outline the steps to take in designing other publications.

▶ FOLLOWING GOOD DESIGN PRACTICES

For a list of books about publication design, refer to Appendix E.

Learning the principles of page design is the key to making an effective desktop publication. Good page design relies on basic standards that graphic artists have been following for years, such as balance, simplicity, consistency, and contrast. It is best to begin with a simple page format; you can embellish the layout as your design experience develops. When you are planning your design, remember that the purpose of a layout is to make your publication attractive and easy to read. The text itself is only one part of the design. Once a page is laid out, look at the whole page as one shape. The text and graphics should divide the white space in a balanced manner.

Remember, your publication should be a union of form and function. The format you choose should reflect the content and help facilitate the communication of the material.

Before you begin, let's get familiar with the basic steps in developing a publication. The typical stages of publication are writing, editing, design, illustration, pasteup, and printing. In conventional publishing, each of these steps is carried out by individuals trained in each task. PageMaker is designed to handle each of these steps. In fact, as you work with PageMaker, you will change hats frequently. You will be writer, editor, designer, illustrator, pasteup artist, and printer. This chapter will help you develop skills for the design part of the process. Later we will begin using the PageMaker design tools.

▶ MAKING YOUR INITIAL DESIGN CONSIDERATIONS

Begin developing your publication design with a planning session. Your initial session should address three main issues:

1. What size will my publication be?
2. What is my target audience?
3. What writing style is most appropriate for this audience?

Always keep these three considerations in mind as you design your publication.

Start by defining the kind of publication you wish to create. Is it a small newsletter, a tabloid, a manual, or a book? The size of the document influences the kind of page layout best suited for communicating your information. Our newsletter about desktop publishing will have a few short articles. A three-column format on 8.5-by-11-inch paper works well for a small newsletter like ours.

If we were creating a large newsletter with long articles, we might consider using a wider column format. A two-column format, for example, would enable our readers to take in more of an article with one span across the page. Or, we could use a tabloid size, or perhaps an 8.5-by-14-inch size for even larger newsletters with a three- or four-column format. These are the decisions you must make early in the planning session.

Next, you must determine your audience. You should gear the format of your document and your writing style to the target audience. Is it made up of readers, scanners, or nonreaders? Avid readers may expect to see a document with lots of text, whereas nonreaders and scanners may look for the main topics to jump from the page and catch their eye. Is the audience well acquainted with the topic material, or are they novices? Is the audience naturally interested in the material, or is some persuasion necessary? Always keep your audience in mind. Your design layout should encourage your audience to read your publication.

Our audience is desktop publishers. This is a group of scanners who want to grab significant information off the page quickly. They are not interested in reading through dense text. They want to know the latest trends in software, or helpful design hints that they can quickly incorporate in their own document designs. Boxes or windows of information would work well for our target audience. Scanners like the information to leap off the page.

The third important factor to consider is the kind of writing style you will use to communicate your information. Will page after page of dense text hold your reader's attention, or should you provide lots of visual breaks? For example, lawyers are accustomed to reading dense pages written in complex language, so a legal newsletter can have a dense format and a complex writing style. But our audience of desktop publishers is looking for a highly formatted newsletter with a light and direct writing style. They want boxes and lines that guide their eyes to the significant information on the page.

Now it's time to consider the actual layout of our publication. You must decide on format details such as page size, margin size, the number of columns, and type specifications. To help you lay out the page, you'll set up a layout grid. Later, you'll use this design to decide where to place your illustrations. Make your decisions based on the information you have considered so far: the target audience and the type of publication you are designing. It's important to keep a running file of the design decisions you've made during your initial planning session so that you can refer to them as you develop your publication.

Let's review the design decisions we've made so far:

1. We decided on a short, two-page newsletter. We can add pages later as the newsletter develops.
2. We defined our audience as desktop publishers. They are "scanners" interested in quickly learning new desktop publishing skills.
3. We decided to use a light and direct writing style to quickly inform our audience about trends and shortcuts in desktop publishing and design.
4. We decided to use 8.5-by-11-inch paper, since our newsletter has only two short articles.

► CHOOSING A TYPEFACE

In this section you will learn about selecting the typeface for your publication. A *typeface* is a set of characters, including letters, numbers, and special characters, that share a cohesive design. A *font* is more than a typeface. It is the complete set of the characters in a typeface, plus all the enhancements such as boldface and italic. Commercial printers have hundreds of typefaces to choose from, but desktop publishers are limited to the typefaces available on their printers.

Before you choose a typeface, you must decide on the type sizes and enhancements (such as boldface, italics, and underscoring) you want to use, and where you want to use them. Be sure you document each decision you make so that you can refer to it.

Choosing a typeface for your document is a very important step and should be one of the first decisions you make. It is important to choose the typeface before designing the format because some typeface styles and sizes work better with certain page formats. Therefore, the decision you make now about the typeface will affect your future decisions about formatting.

► SERIF AND SANS SERIF TYPEFACES

There are two categories of typefaces, *serif* and *sans serif.* Serif typefaces have a cross line extending from the end stroke of each letter. Sans serif typefaces do not have this line. Serif typefaces make large blocks of dense text easier to read and often are a good choice for the main body of your text. Sans serif typefaces catch a reader's eye and work well for headlines, short copy, or ad layouts. Below are examples of serif and sans serif typefaces.

This is Palatino, a serif typeface.

This is Helvetica, a sans serif typeface.

The typeface you choose should enhance the communication and overall appearance of your document and portray its personality. Is this a scholarly, technical, or lighthearted document? Choose a typeface that invites people to read the text. Typefaces designed to catch the reader's eye are usually difficult to read in large doses, but they are good for titles or headlines. Other typefaces designed to make reading easier are ideal for the main body of text in dense documents.

As you can see in Figure 4.1, in our newsletter for desktop publishers, we will use a sans serif typeface for the title in the masthead. (The masthead contains information about the publication, including the title.) Also the masthead and headlines will be boldface to make them stand out on the page. The typeface I have selected for the masthead is Helvetica. Helvetica is an easy-to-read sans serif typeface that makes titles and headlines stand out well. If you have a PostScript printer, Helvetica is available to you. If not, substitute a typeface from your printer that you feel meets these criteria.

For the article headlines and the main body of text, I have selected Palatino type, a serif typeface. Most newspapers use serif typefaces in the main body of text. By choosing a serif typeface, we give our readers something familiar—they should immediately feel comfortable reading the newsletter.

► MIXING TYPEFACES

Avoid using more than one or two typefaces in your document. The temptation to mix many different typefaces within one document can lead to clutter and confusion in your design. As a general rule, if you decide to change the typeface within a document, be sure your decision is based on good design principles. For example, in our newsletter, we choose Helvetica for the masthead, but changed the typeface to Palatino for the main body of text to bring some familiarity to our publication. Until you become more familiar with publication design, it's a good idea to keep the main elements of text—the article headlines, figure captions, and article text—in the same typeface.

PageMaker 3.0 has provided style sheets to help you maintain consistent specifications throughout your publication. See Chapter 6 for a discussion of style sheets.

You can add interest to your document by using different text enhancements from the same typeface (boldface and italics, for example), but don't overdo it. A word put in italics will make it stand out from the surrounding paragraph, but an entire paragraph in italics is difficult to read. The same is true of boldfaced text. Boldfacing is an effective highlighting tool for a headline or a title, but it must be used sparingly and consistently. Decide how you want to use these text enhancements early on so that you use them consistently.

► POINT SIZE

Another typeface decision you must make concerns point size. A *point* is the standard measuring unit for type. One point equals 1/72 of a linear inch. Most

Month Day, 1989
Volume #

DeskTop News

PageMaker 3.0

Personal computers are becoming faster and more powerful, and page makeup programs are approaching the capabilities of systems with five- and six-digit price tags. Telling the best page makeup programs through all the hype is getting harder and harder.

The page makeup program you select will depend upon the type of publications you plan on developing. Some programs work best on small publications with limited amounts of text and high-quality graphics such as brochures, flyers, and newsletters. Other programs work best for larger publications with dense text such as technical manuals or books.

The PageMaker® version 3.0 from Aldus incorporates features from both ends of the spectrum and is ahead on the road toward the dedicated desktop publishing workstation. Figure 1 illustrates one of the new features of PageMaker 3.0, templates. With all its advantages, PageMaker represents the top of the line in desktop publishing.

Learning To Make Type Specifications

If you've never thought of yourself as an artist or graphic designer, desktop publishing may overwhelm you with its task of designing a page on a computer. Which typeface should I use? What about type sizes, graphics, and formatting? It's easy to get intimidated by the vast array of choices you have to make.

Let's discuss a few simple rules that graphic artists have followed for years. First, the design you create must be based on the content of your publication. You must determine the critical elements of your publication and use your design to highlight the levels of importance.

In a newsletter, the most important element is the masthead of the newsletter. This should be the largest element of the first page. Next in importance are the titles of the articles and any special features or announcements that you want to catch your reader's eye quickly. The masthead itself should be first in importance, with the titles following in an order of importance that is defined simply. Avoid using too many type sizes and enhancements to make your point. The simplest approach is usually best.

Selecting a typeface for your publication is another important step in determing its character. With all the fonts available on laser printers today, it's hard to determine which one to select in each case.

cont. on pg. 3

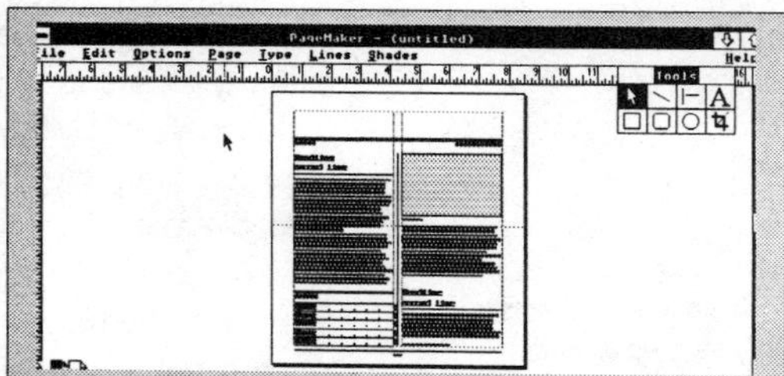

Figure 1: PageMaker 3.0 Newsletter Template

DeskTop News 1

Figure 4.1: Page 1 of the printed newsletter.

typefaces come in a variety of point sizes, from 6-point to 72-point. The main body of text is usually printed in the 9-point to 12-point range, depending on the typeface you choose. Ten-point type is considered the best for readability. Figure 4.2 shows a variety of point sizes.

6-point type
8-point type
10-point type
12-point type
14-point type
18-point type
24-point type
36-point type
48-point type
60-point ty
72-point

Figure 4.2: Type in the Palatino typeface from 6 to 72 points

Changes in point size catch the reader's eye and can enhance the appearance of your document. Changing point sizes is also an effective way of establishing a hierarchy of headings. A hierarchy of headings means that the titles, subtitles, and text are sized according to how important they are. Be consistent with your sizing. For example, the masthead, at the top rung of the hierarchy, should be larger than the figure titles, the lowest rung.

Our newsletter needs a large title to let our readers know immediately what they are reading. Our title, "Desktop News," will use 36-point type. The article headlines will be in the Palatino typeface, at half the point size (18 points) to distinguish them as less important than the title. Figure titles will use the same typeface at an even smaller point size of 10, to communicate their lesser importance in our layout. The main body of text will also use the Palatino typeface, but at a very readable 12-point size.

► LEADING

The vertical space between lines of type is called *leading.* This is the amount of spacing between the tops of capital letters in two successive lines of text. You can use the leading that PageMaker provides automatically (called *auto leading*), or you can specify your own leading to within one-half point. Leading, like type size, is measured in points, with one point equaling 1/72 of an inch. PageMaker's auto leading specification calculates leading at 120 percent of the type size. This means that for a type size of 10 points, PageMaker uses 12 points of leading. (PageMaker rounds off its auto leading calculations to the half point.) Figure 4.3 shows some leading examples.

If you haven't worked with leading, use PageMaker's automatic option until you become more familiar with it. When you begin to feel comfortable with leading, you can experiment with selecting your own. For our newsletter, we will use PageMaker's auto leading specification.

This is 10-point Palatino type with a 10-point leading. It is called 10/10.

This is 10-point Palatino type with a 14-point leading. It is called 10/14.

This is 12-point Palatino type with a 12-point leading. It is called 12/12.

This is 12-point Palatino type with a 14-point leading. It is called 12/14.

Figure 4.3: Palatino type in 10- and 12-point sizes with various leading

▸ LAYING OUT THE PAGE

Now that we have made all our typeface decisions, let's consider page structure. Page structure decisions are those involving the number of columns on each page, the placement of your illustrations, and the setting of a layout grid.

The first step is to determine your information breakdown. Is the content organized in a logical manner? Do you need one, two, or three columns per page? PageMaker allows you to create up to 20 columns per page, but for readability, a publication with two to three columns is usually best. You can set the column width and the space between columns yourself, or you can have PageMaker calculate them automatically.

Graphic layout artists usually use pasteup boards with nonreproducible blue lines that act as a grid. The blue lines are visible to the eye, but are not printed. In the same manner, PageMaker provides several types of nonprinting grid lines to help you plug in text or graphics quickly and precisely.

▸ DEFINING THE COLUMNS

Remember, PageMaker's default standards for column width and spacing are based on the principles used by graphic layout artists, so you should have a good reason for deviating from these standards.

If you are calculating your own column width and spacing, it helps to first draw a diagram. First, determine the margin widths and subtract the margin space from the total width of the page. You must base the column width and spacing on the amount of printable area available on the page. Next, decide on the number and width of each column. Then determine how much space is left over for the spacing between columns and distribute it evenly between the columns. The number of columns minus one determines the number of spaces between columns.

Keep in mind that a column should not be narrower than 20 to 25 characters, and not be wider than 60 characters. Narrow columns are easy to read, but the number of characters that can fit in a column is sometimes determined by type size and the typeface style.

In our desktop publishing newsletter, we will use a three-column format. We'll be sticking with PageMaker's automatic selection for column size and column spacing. In the next chapter, you'll get hands-on experience in establishing the column sizes.

▸ CREATING THE LAYOUT GRID

In our newsletter, we will be laying down several column, margin, and ruler guides to help us place text, titles, and figures on the page. These guidelines will be explained in Chapter 5.

You are now ready to create your layout grid, the main building block for designing your page format. The grid divides the page into proportional areas to give you a structure on which to organize your design elements such as headings, text, and graphics. A layout grid is made up of margin, column, and *ruler guides* that appear as dotted lines on your screen, but do not print. They can help you position text, graphics, headings, and page numbers on the page. You can use as many ruler guides as you want.

You should now be well acquainted with the basic design decisions you need to make each time you design a publication. Let's review the design decisions we've made so far.

1. We decided on a short, two-page newsletter. We can add pages later as the newsletter develops.
2. We defined our audience as desktop publishers. We decided they are "scanners" interested in quickly learning new desktop publishing skills.
3. We will use a light and direct writing style to quickly inform our audience about trends and shortcuts in desktop publishing and design.
4. We decided to use 8.5-by-11-inch paper, since our newsletter has only two short articles.
5. We'll use one typeface for the masthead title, and another for the headlines, figure captions, and the main body of text.
6. We established a hierarchy of point sizes: Helvetica 36-point for the masthead title; Palatino 18-point for headlines; and Palatino 10-point for other page specifications such as page number and figure captions.
7. We decided to use Palatino 12-point type for the main body of text so that it will be familiar and readable.
8. We will have a three-column format using PageMaker's standard defaults for column width spacing.
9. We decided to use column, margin, and ruler guides to help align text and graphics on the page.

Now you're ready to consider how to use design elements to enhance the appearance of your newsletter.

► USING DESIGN ENHANCEMENTS

PageMaker provides many design enhancements for dressing up a page. Learn the purpose of each type of enhancement and you can make design selections wisely. Remember, selecting too many design enhancements can clutter a page, and that would violate one of the basic principles of good design—simplicity.

► USING BORDERS FOR VISUAL IDENTITY

PageMaker's graphics tools can be used to draw borders around a page. Adding a border gives a page visual identity and a dignified appearance. For example, certificates and diplomas often have a surrounding border, and it gives them an official appearance. A formal border or frame helps to strengthen the impact of the information on the page. Figure 4.4 shows an example of such a border.

Borders can also provide a design standard that can make your publication more recognizable. For example, suppose your company publishes two newsletters for investment bankers, each with a different topic focus. One newsletter focuses on markets and marketing, and the second on banking technology. Using the same surrounding border for both newsletters will help trigger recognition of your company from your audience. Each time they see the border, they will know the newsletter is one of yours.

Using a border has a second, more practical function. Most laser printers can't print to the edge of the page. A border can help define this nonprintable area so you won't try to place text and graphics off the printable area.

► GUIDING THE READER'S EYE WITH RULER LINES

Ruler lines (sometimes called just *rules*) are horizontal and vertical design enhancements. For example, a thin line, called a hairline, between columns is a type of ruler line (see Figure 4.5). This ruler line helps distinguish columns from one another. In this case, the hairline is a vertical line. You could place a horizontal line below a heading, for example.

A ruler line should be used when you want to guide your reader's eye to information (such as a heading) or across a column of text. However, too many ruler lines can create a grid effect that breaks the page into too many compartments. Decide on a judicious use of ruler lines in your layout, and then stick to it.

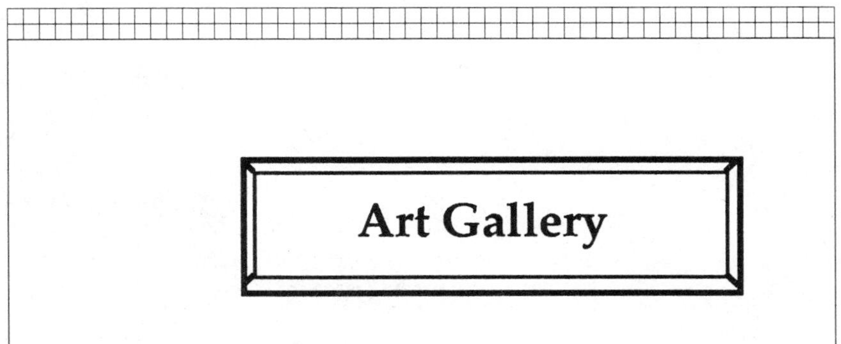

Figure 4.4: Borders can give text a dignified appearance.

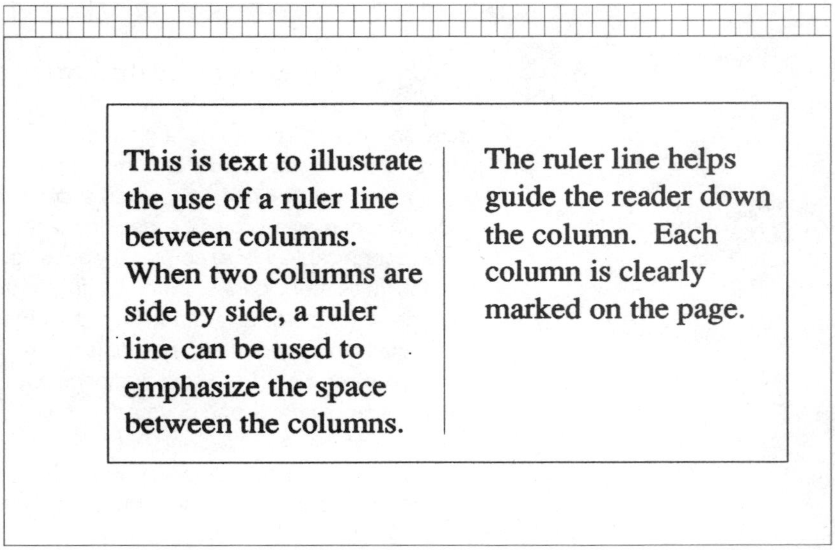

Figure 4.5: A hairline ruler line between text columns

► BALANCING THE PAGE

We already learned how to use type sizes to establish a hierarchy of headings. The amount of space taken by a graphic or photo also indicates its importance to your reader. An accounting chart in an annual report, for example, should occupy a more important spot than the company logo that appears on every page. Proportion the elements on the page to emphasize those that you think are most important.

► KEEPING A CLEAN PAGE WITH WHITE SPACE

White space is the blank area that surrounds text or graphics on a page. White space is used to make the elements on the page stand out, just as a mat is used to set off a picture in a frame. White space helps to focus the reader's attention on the main point. Using white space also aids the readability of your page because it keeps the page from looking dense and cluttered. A common design error is to use white space too sparingly, so don't be afraid to add it to your page layout.

▶ USING REVERSES

Reverse or *inverse* graphics and type on a page quickly catch your reader's attention. In reverse type, the text is white against a dark background (see Figure 4.6). However, because of the darkness that this enhancement adds, it is a good practice to limit reverses to one or two per page.

When you use reverse type, limit it to short pieces of text, since long passages in reverse type are hard to read. Sans serif type is easier to read in inverse than serif type. In addition, be sure you use adequate space around the type to increase its visual identity.

▶ ACCENTUATING BOXES AND SCREENS

Boxes and screens in your layout accentuate the surrounded text or graphic. A *screen* is a shaded area used to highlight text or a graphic. PageMaker has tools to create a box around text or graphics, and the Shades menu can be used to create a screen on the page.

A *sidebar* is a narrow column of text that contains information that highlights or elaborates the main text.

A screen is best used to distinguish a unique column of text, such as a sidebar. Figure 4.7 shows a sidebar shaded with a screen. Screens are often enclosed in a box, but can be used without borders, or with a partial border (at the top and bottom, for example).

A screen can also be used to set off a table of information or a graphic. Screens, however, can sometimes make complex text or a detailed graphic hard to read. For instance if the graphic has minute details, a screen may actually obscure them. A screen is most effectively used with a simple graphic or text, and should be used with a legible typeface that uses a heavy line. Figure 4.8 shows examples of typefaces with heavy and lighter lines. Also, be sure to use a legible point size.

Figure 4.6: An example of reverse type

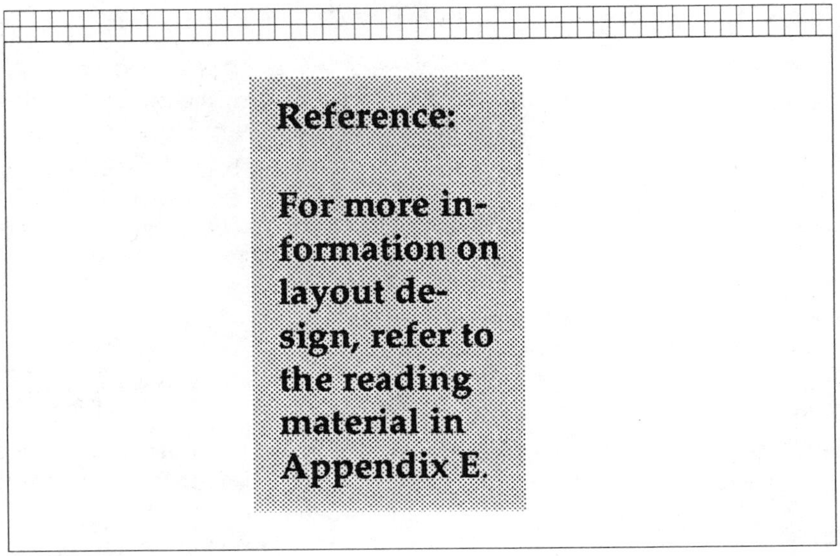

Reference:

For more information on layout design, refer to the reading material in Appendix E.

Figure 4.7: A shaded sidebar

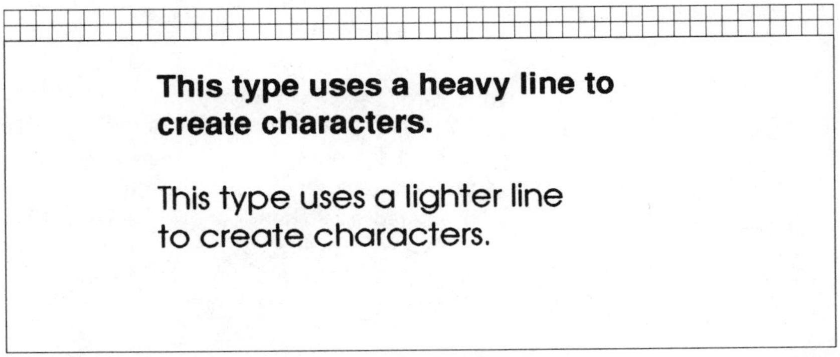

This type uses a heavy line to create characters.

This type uses a lighter line to create characters.

Figure 4.8: Examples of typefaces with heavy and lighter lines

► ADDING INTEREST WITH PULL-QUOTES

Pulling a quote from an article and framing it on the page helps to increase the reader's interest. This graphic enhancement is called a *pull-quote.* The pull-quote should appear in a larger point size than the main text, be surrounded by white space, or be enclosed in a box to help it stand out on the page.

The pull-quote should be a key sentence or phrase—something that gives your reader a quick impression of the content of the page. An enhanced pull-quote will draw in the reader and increase his or her desire to read on.

As you design your publications, you will discover other design enhancements. Keep in mind that each enhancement should serve a particular function. Though adding enhancements can be fun, be sure they also have a practical purpose. Used wisely, design enhancements can greatly increase the communications ability of your publications.

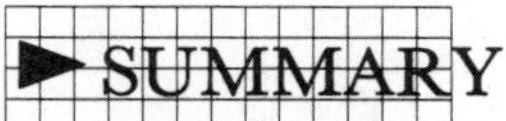

► SUMMARY

In the next chapter, you will learn how to use PageMaker to apply the new skills you just learned. Keep in mind that you will not need to go through each of these these design steps each time you produce a publication. Once you develop a publication design you feel comfortable with, you can use it again and again whenever it is applicable. You'll probably find that you only need to develop a few designs, which will become standards for most of your documents. Next, you will design a template for your newsletter that will contain all the elements that you will use in every edition of the newsletter. This way, you will not have to reinvent your newsletter each time you publish it.

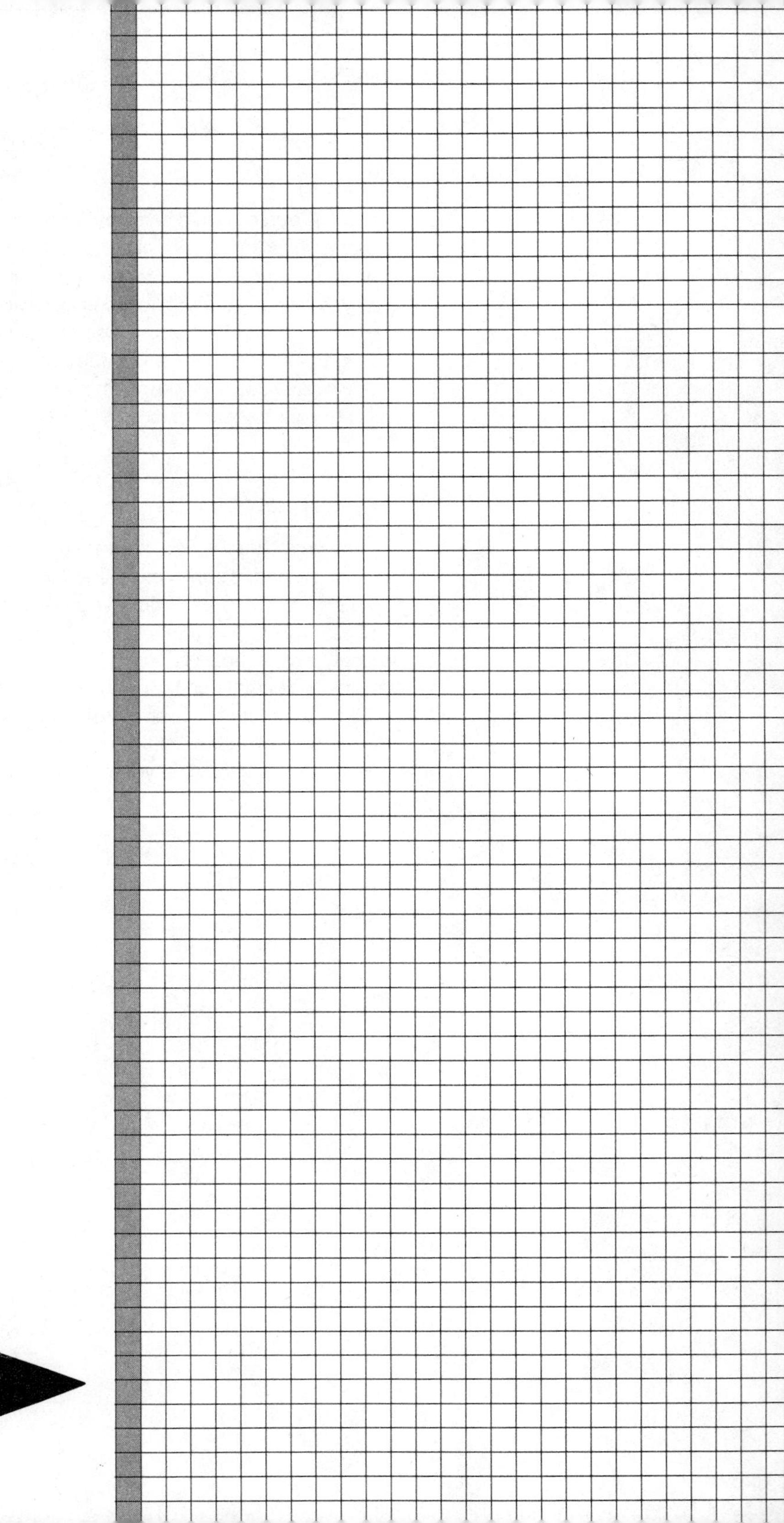

5 SAVING WORK WITH MASTER PAGES

To begin creating master pages, 78

click on the master page icon at the bottom left-hand corner of the publication window.

To set up a layout grid, 79

select your measuring system, indicate your zero point, display the rulers, place any nonprinting ruler guide, and choose the number of columns.

To number pages automatically, 90

indicate the position of the page number with the text tool, then press the Shift-Ctrl-3 key combination.

To add a ruler line to the master page design, 92

first select the perpendicular line tool from the PageMaker Toolbox. Click on the Lines menu, choose the type of line you want, then position the crossbar where you want the line to begin. Now click and hold down the mouse button and move the crossbar to where you want the line to end. Release the mouse button and the line appears.

To customize a master page, 94

click on the page number you want to modify and make changes to the master page elements.

ation	Waiting To Be Shelved Item 0
cription	Used book in acceptable condition. Binding shows heavy wear, shifted spine, cover, and/or pages. More markings/writing may be present. May have some stickers and/or sticker residue present. Pages have water stains and/or some wavy pages. If applicable, book's access code, disc, and/or accessories are not included unless otherwise specified. All items shipped Monday - Friday. Fast shipping - Books ship in envelope. All items pictured use stock photos. Due to volume, we are unable to provide extra pictures.
N	0895885212
ployee	cinnie

If anything is incorrect, please contact us immediately at gwbooks@goodwilltucson.org and we will make it right. Thank you again for your purchase and please leave

With a onetime-only publication, you can skip the step of creating a template. However, if you have any inkling that you may create a similar publication in the future, you may want to store it as a template so it can be used again.

Now that you have been introduced to the basics of publication design, you are ready to use PageMaker to make the job easy. In this chapter, you will learn how to use PageMaker to create master pages, which you will use later to create a template for publications.

The *master pages* include a layout grid and any text or graphics you want to have on every page of a publication. A layout grid is made up of column guides and ruler guides. By placing guides on the master pages, you save the time of having to place a layout grid on each page of your publication. Other master page elements include page numbers and graphics elements such as ruler lines. Remember, consistency is very important in producing a good publication, and master pages enable you to repeat elements such as nonprinting guides, and text and graphics features such as headers and footers, on every page to give your publication a consistent look.

A *template,* sometimes called a dummy publication, contains only the master pages and the layout grid. It also can include customized pages, such as a title page, or text or graphics (such as a logo) that you want to see consistently in every edition of the publication. It does not contain the text and graphics that are unique to each edition.

► CREATING MASTER PAGES

Set up your master pages before you paste up any text or graphics. This way, not only will your layout grid be consistent throughout the document, but you will also avoid having to make adjustments after you have placed text and graphics in the publication. Remember, PageMaker lets you make changes to the master page elements on any page.

You can either create a master page that repeats its design on every page of your publication, or if you have a double-sided publication, you can create unique designs for each set of facing pages. The facing pages can either have different formats, or they can have similar formats that mirror each other, so that the left-hand page is the reverse of the right.

Once you select the master elements of your publication, you can still customize pages as you go along by choosing the specific elements you want to use on each page. For example, in our newsletter, you will create a three-column layout. However, on one page of the newsletter, you will include a graphic that extends across two columns. In this case, you will abandon the master page layout for that page or that graphic, and return to it when you are ready to continue with the three-column layout.

Let's practice by setting up the master page elements for our newsletter. Chapter 2 introduced you to the Page Setup dialog box. There you selected the page size, the number of pages in your publication, the orientation of your pages, a single- or double-sided publication, and more.

If you are not logged onto PageMaker, with the publication window displayed, follow these steps to open a copy of the NEWSTEMP.PT3 template:

1. Select the "Open" command from the File menu. You will see the Open Publication dialog box, as shown in Figure 5.1.
2. Click on the NEWSTEMP.PT3 file. (If you are using Pagemaker version 1.0 or 1.0a, the publication title is NEWSTEMP.PUB.)
3. Click the OK command button.

You should see the publication window. You're ready to create a master page.

1. Point to the R (for "Right") master page icon at the bottom left-hand corner of the publication window.
2. Click the mouse button. The master page icon is selected.

You now see the master page displayed on your screen as shown in Figure 5.2. In the next section, you will introduce elements to this page that will appear consistently on all pages of the publication.

► SELECTING THE ELEMENTS OF A LAYOUT GRID

A layout grid is made up of nonprinting horizontal and vertical lines that form a grid across the page on your screen. Once you have designed your grid and figured out where you want the lines to go, you can use the grid to line up text and graphics. You can plan a grid on paper, or create it on the screen using PageMaker's commands.

A PageMaker grid consists of dotted lines indicating the top, bottom, inside, and outside (also called right and left) margins. You can add your own column guides to help line up text and graphics into columns. You can also add ruler guides to help line up titles and page numbers.

But before you set up grid guidelines, you must decide on a measuring system. Once you select a measuring system, you can use the rulers provided by PageMaker to help you line up your guides.

► SELECTING YOUR MEASURING SYSTEM

A cicero, a common unit of measure in Europe, is equal to 4.55 millimeters.

PageMaker gives you a choice of five units of measure—inches, inches decimal, millimeters, picas, or ciceros. PageMaker's default measuring system is

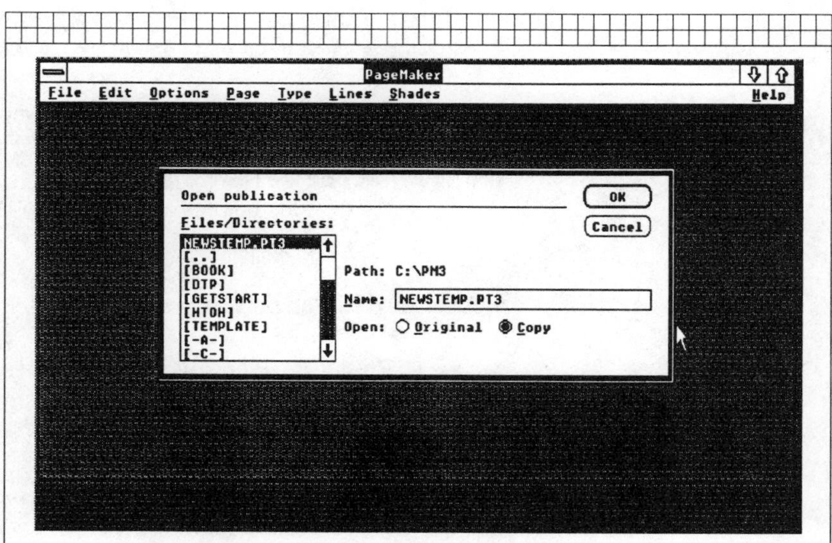

Figure 5.1: The Open Publication dialog box

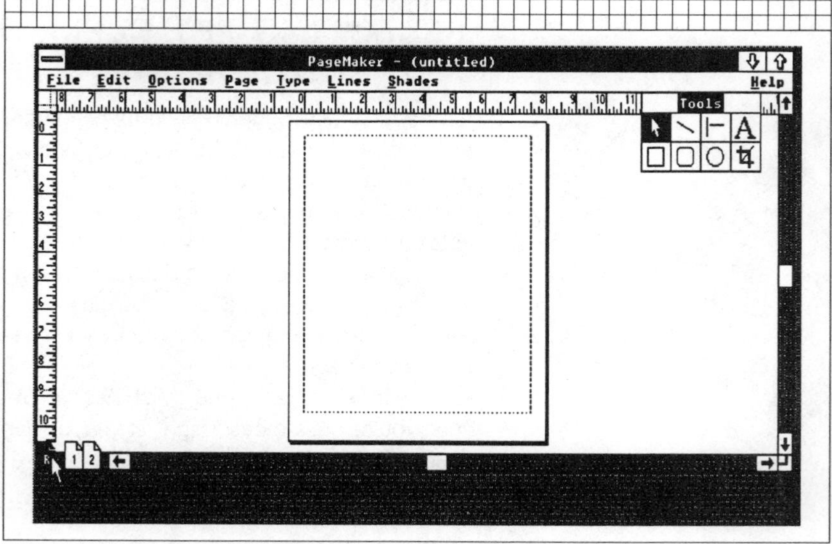

Figure 5.2: Blank master page

inches. However, picas are used by most graphic artists because picas are a very exact measuring standard. A pica is one-sixth of an inch, or 12 points. A point is 1/72 of an inch or 1/12 of a pica.

You must have selected a measuring system in order to answer the measurement questions that will appear in dialog boxes (including the margin designations you already made in the Page Setup dialog box). In addition, PageMaker allows you to display horizontal and vertical rulers in the publication window to help you line up text and graphics on the page, but you must select a measuring system to use the rulers.

Let's select the inches measuring system for our newsletter.

1. Click on the Edit option.
2. Choose "Preferences" at the bottom of the list of menu options. The Preferences dialog box shown in Figure 5.3 is displayed on your screen.
3. In the options under Measurement System, point to the option button next to "Inches" and click the mouse button. The highlight circle appears in the button, indicating that you have selected the inches measuring system.
4. Click on OK in the upper-right corner of the screen.

Note that PageMaker 3.0 also offers three measurement options for using the vertical ruler. The options are "Inches," "Picas," or "Custom." The "Custom" option allows you to measure text according to the leading option you select. Leading, the space between each line of text, was discussed in Chapter 4. Selecting a custom vertical ruler measuring system helps when aligning columns of text. Specifying a

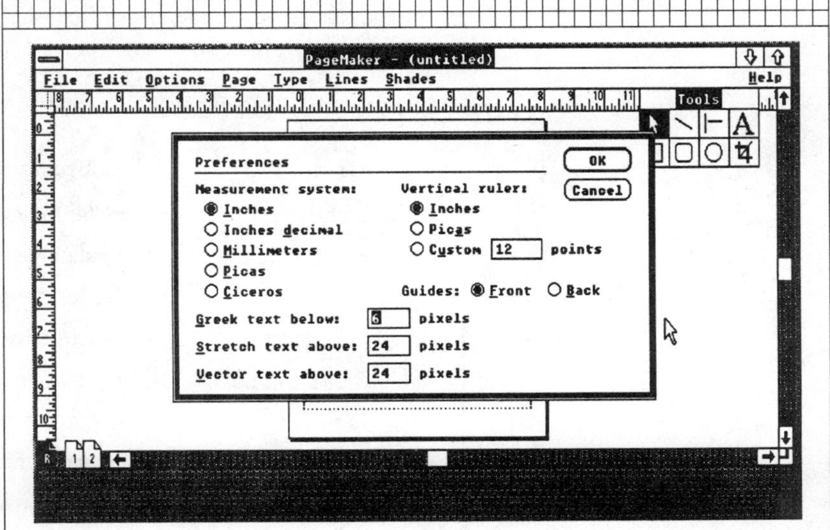

Figure 5.3: Preferences dialog box

measurement in the "Custom" text box controls the distance between tick marks on the vertical ruler. The tick marks are measured in points, the same as leading is.

Changing the Measurement System

Once you select a measuring system, you will probably stay with it throughout the publication. However, if you change the measuring system, keep in mind that the text and graphics already placed on the page may not conform to the new system. You may have to make adjustments.

Use the "Preferences" command from the Edit menu to select a new measuring system. You also can override the measuring system displayed in any dialog box that uses measurements. Each measuring system has a one-character abbreviation that can be used for overriding the selected measuring system. Table 5.1 shows these abbreviations.

▸ USING THE RULERS

You'll find the PageMaker rulers essential. The rulers help you position your guides on the page. The markings on the rulers correspond to the unit of measure you selected. Because you selected inches in the Preferences dialog box, the rulers you display will be marked in inches.

You can also use the rulers to adjust the size of graphics. You can draw lines and shapes with precision and lay them out on the page exactly where you want them. The guides you create using the PageMaker rulers line up text and graphics within a half point of accuracy. That is a mere 1/144 of an inch.

Unit	Abbreviation	Example
Inches	i after the number	5.5i
Millimeters	m after the number	20m
Picas	p after the number	18p
Pica points	p before the number	p6
Picas and points	p between the numbers	18p6
Ciceros	c after the number	8c
Cicero points	c before the number	c6
Ciceros and points	c between the numbers	18c6

Table 5.1: Measuring System Abbreviations

When PageMaker is started, the rulers are displayed automatically. Check to be sure your rulers are selected by clicking on the Options menu. Look at the "Rulers" option. If a check mark appears next to the command, the rulers are visible. You can turn off the rulers by selecting the command again.

Figure 5.4 shows the PageMaker publication window with the rulers displayed. (Note the arrow pointing to the markings on the ruler.) The increments between the ruler markings depend on the size and resolution of the screen you are using. The smaller the view, the larger the increments between markings. The Fit-in-window view of the document has the largest increments; the 200% view has the smallest.

PageMaker also supports Multi-color Graphics Array (MCGA), Video Graphics Array (VGA), AT&T Color DEB, Compaq Portable Plasma, and Tandy 1000 Color.

To use PageMaker, your computer must have a graphics card supported by Microsoft Windows. It can have either an Enhanced Graphics Adapter (EGA), a Color Graphics Adapter (CGA), or a Hercules- or AT&T-compatible Monochrome Adapter. If your computer has an EGA or a CGA display, the rulers are incremented as shown in Table 5.2. If you are using a monochrome display, the rulers are incremented as shown in Table 5.3.

Working with the Zero Point

The *zero point* refers to the point where the zero marks on both rulers intersect. PageMaker automatically places the zero point where the top and left edges of the page intersect, but you can move it wherever you want. You can see the zero

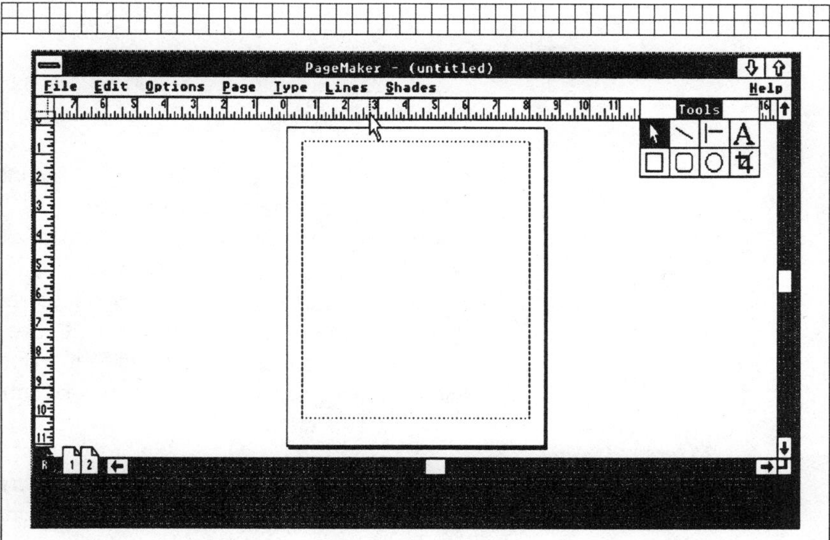

Figure 5.4: The PageMaker rulers

View	Inches	Decimal Inches	Millimeters	Picas and points
Fit-in-window	1/4i	1/2i	1/4 cm	1 pica
50% Size	1/8i	1/10i	1/4 cm	1/2 pica
75% Size	1/16i	1/10i	1/4 cm	1/2 pica
Actual Size	1/16i	1/20i	1/2 cm	1/4 pica
200% Size	1/16i	1/10i	1/10 cm	1/4 pica

Table 5.2: The EGA and CGA Ruler Increments

View	Inches	Decimal Inches	Millimeters	Picas and points
Fit-in-window	1/8i	1/10i	1/2 cm	1 pica
50% Size	1/16i	1/10i	1/2 cm	1/2 pica
75% Size	1/16i	1/20i	1/10 cm	1/4 pica
200% Size	1/32i	1/20i	1/10 cm	1/12 pica

Table 5.3: The Monochrome Graphics Ruler Increments

point marker in Figure 5.5. Look for the two intersecting dotted lines in the upper-left corner, near where the rulers meet.

The zero point is the point of reference for all your pasteup; it provides a starting point from which to measure. After you set the zero point, lock down the location so you don't accidentally move it and lose your point of reference.

When you begin a new publication, the zero point won't be locked down yet, making it easy to move the zero point. In Figure 5.5, the zero point is at the top left edge of the page. For our newsletter, let's move the zero point to the intersection of the top and left margins.

1. Position the pointer on the zero point marker, which is represented by the two dotted lines intersecting where the rulers meet in the box at the upper left-hand corner of the publication window (see Figure 5.5). Notice that the upper-left corner is now highlighted.

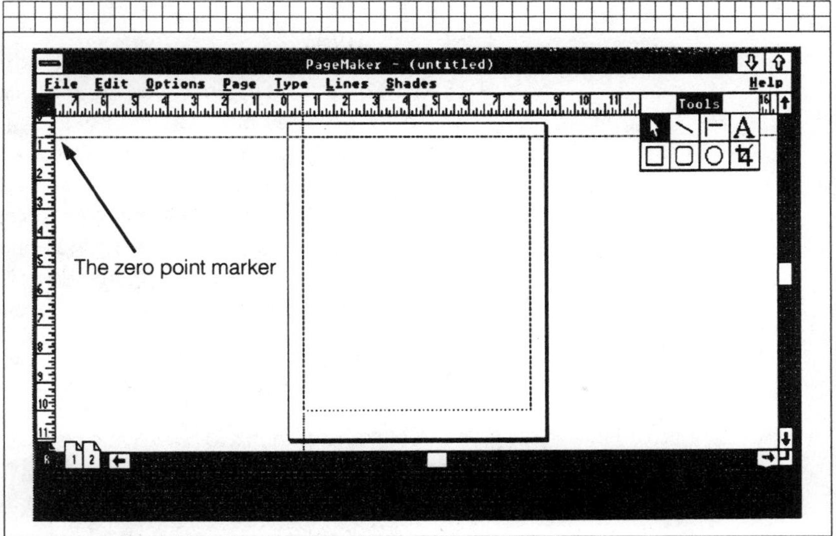

Figure 5.5: The zero point marker

2. With the pointer positioned on the zero point marker, click and hold down the mouse button.
3. Drag the zero point marker to the intersection of the top and left margins. When you move diagonally across the publication window, you will see the mark moving along both rulers.
4. When the zero point marker is positioned at the top and left margins, release the mouse button. The new zero point is set.

Now you must lock the zero point in place so you won't lose your point of reference in the publication.

1. Click on the Options menu.
2. Move down the list of menu command options until "Zero lock" is highlighted, then release the mouse button.

When you release the mouse button, a check mark appears next to the "Zero lock" option. The zero point is now locked in place—you can see the check mark by displaying the menu again. If you click the option again, it erases the check mark, unlocking the zero point.

▸ CREATING A LAYOUT GRID

Now that you have decided on a measuring system, displayed your rulers, and locked the zero point in place, you are ready to set up a layout grid. PageMaker provides three types of nonprinting guides: margin guides, ruler guides, and column guides. You can set guides anywhere on the page. They appear as dotted lines on the screen. The margin guides define the printable area of the page. The ruler guides help to align text and graphics, such as headers or footers and page numbers. Column guides define the boundaries in which text can flow. You learned in Chapter 2 how to set up margin guides in the Page Setup dialog box. Now, establish the rest of your layout grid by setting up ruler and column guides.

▸ LAYING OUT RULER GUIDES

PageMaker provides two ruler guide options, one for laying out horizontal ruler guides, and one for laying out vertical ruler guides. The rulers must be displayed in the publication window in order to select ruler guides.

Let's pull down some horizontal ruler guides from the ruler that runs across the top of the pasteboard area. We will use four horizontal ruler guides to lay out our newsletter. We will set the first at .75 inches on the vertical ruler to align our newsletter masthead. The second guide, set at 1.25 inches, will help us align our title bar. The third ruler guide, set at 9.75 inches, will help us line up a ruler line at the base of the newsletter. The fourth will help us align our page number near the bottom of the page at the 10-inch mark on the vertical ruler.

Let's first place the 10-inch ruler guide:

1. Move your pointer anywhere on the horizontal ruler at the top of the pasteboard area.
2. Hold down the mouse button and move the arrow down into the publication window. The pointer changes to a double-headed arrow, and a dotted line follows the arrow onto the page. This is the ruler guide.
3. Use the ruler markings on the left side of the pasteboard (the vertical ruler) to line up the bottom ruler guide. This ruler guide will help us align page numbers. Position the horizontal ruler guide on the 10-inch mark of the vertical ruler.
4. Release the mouse button. The 10-inch ruler guide is now in place.

Though it appears on the screen, the ruler guide will not print as part of your publication.

5. Now, for our newsletter, place three more ruler guides at the 9.75-, 1.25-, and .75-inch marks on the vertical ruler. Figure 5.6 shows your new ruler guides.

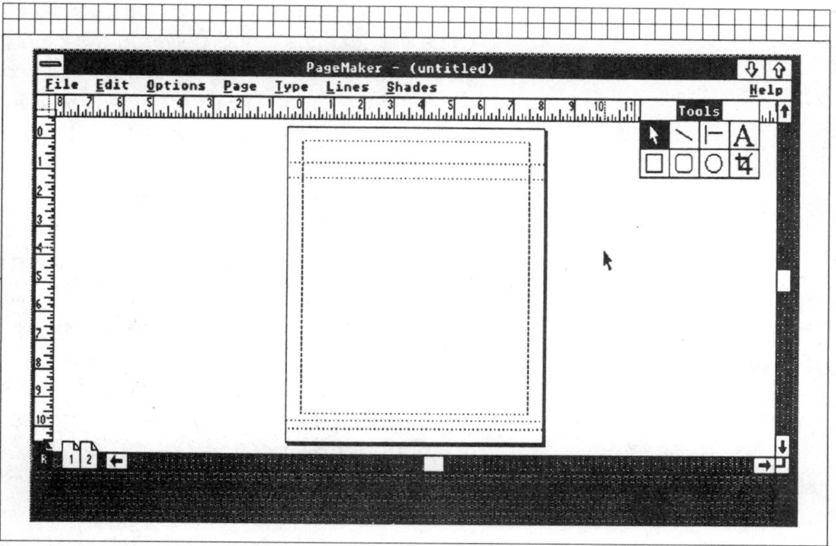

Figure 5.6: The ruler guides

Our newsletter does not require a vertical ruler guide, but if we wanted one, we would establish it in the same way. To create a vertical ruler guide, position the pointer on the ruler at the left of the pasteboard. Click and hold down the mouse button. The pointer changes into a double-headed arrow. Drag the pointer across the publication window. A dotted guide will move with the pointer across the window. Position the vertical ruler guide and release the mouse button.

Moving and Deleting Ruler Guides

If you want to move a ruler guide, position the pointer on the guide. Hold down the mouse button and move the guide to a new location. To delete a ruler guide, point anywhere on the line. Click and hold the mouse button. The pointer again changes to a double-headed arrow. Drag the guideline off the page and to the edge of the publication window, then release the mouse button.

► SETTING UP COLUMN GUIDES

Now you will learn to set up *column guides.* Column guides divide a page into columns. PageMaker lets you set up as many as 20 columns. When you bring text into your newsletter, the text flows into the column, adhering to the column guides. The guides ensure that the text stays within the columns you set.

When you set up column guides, the text flows into the columns line by line. Once the text is aligned between the column guides, you can still move the column guides and adjust the text again if necessary.

PageMaker automatically assumes you want to create columns that all have the same width. Let's set up column guides for our three-column newsletter.

1. Click on the Options menu.
2. Choose the "Column guides" command option and you will see the Column Guides dialog box shown in Figure 5.7.
3. The "Number of columns" box contains a default setting of 1. Type 3 to indicate you want a three-column format.

Now we must decide how much space we want between columns (also called gutter size). We can stay with 0.167 inches, PageMaker's default, or we can establish our own gutters. If you do not specify how much space you want between columns, PageMaker chooses for you. If you choose your own spacing, you must first decide how wide you want your columns to be. Once you've decided that, figure out how much horizontal space all your margins will take up. Add margin space to column space, and see how much space remains for your gutters. If you have three columns, you will have two gutters. Now distribute the remaining space evenly among the gutters to determine the gutter width.

See Table 5.1 for the one-character abbreviations used for overriding a measuring system.

To indicate a gutter size other than the default, point to the "Space between columns" box. Click the mouse button and make a numeric entry in the box. If you

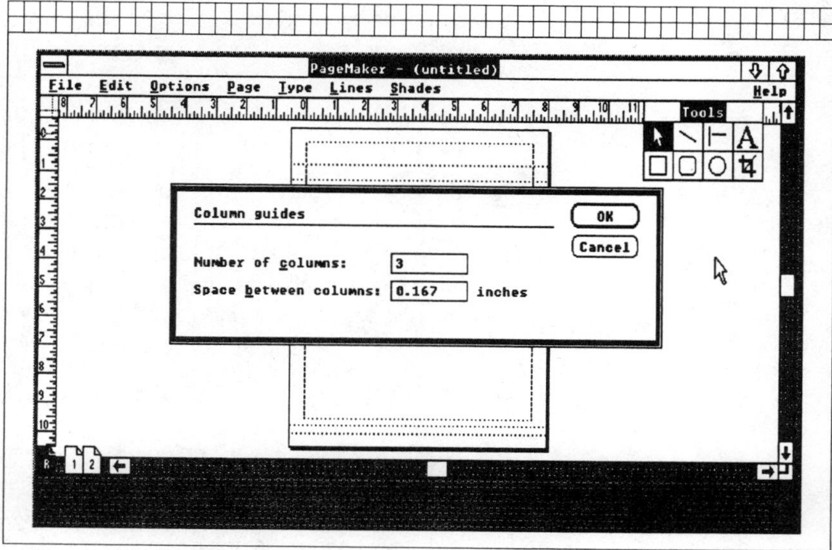

Figure 5.7: The Column Guides dialog box

want, you can override the current measuring system by including an abbreviation with your entry. For our newsletter, however, we will choose PageMaker's default for the gutter size.

4. The "Space between columns" box shows a default setting of 0.167 inches. Click on OK to choose the default.

You should now see the three-column format shown in Figure 5.8. Notice that the leftmost guide is flush with the left margin, and the rightmost guide is flush with the right margin. If you were working on a double-sided publication with facing pages, you could establish different column guides for the left-hand and right-hand pages.

Hiding the Guidelines

Now that you have set up your ruler and column guides, they will continue to be displayed on the page to help you align text and graphics. However, if you want to view the page as it will appear when printed, you can hide the guides temporarily. To do this, select the Options menu. A check mark appears next to the "Guides" command, indicating that the guides are visible. Click on the "Guides" command option and the check mark disappears. Text and graphics are not affected when the guides are hidden. You now can see how your publication looks without the guides in place. It's easy to redisplay the guides. Just select the "Guides" command again.

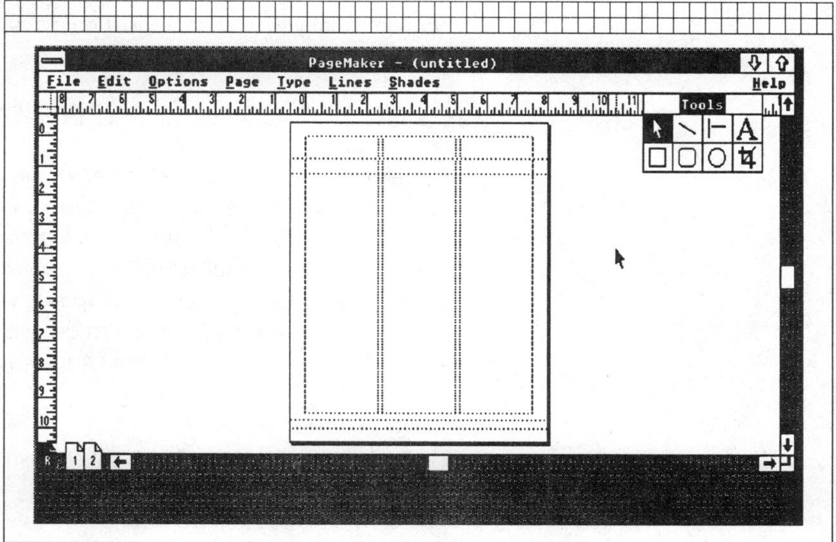

Figure 5.8: The column guides for a three-column format

For now, let's keep our newsletter guides displayed.

► USING THE SNAP TO GUIDES FEATURE

Don't worry about being able to place text and graphics accurately on the layout grid. The Snap to Guides feature makes the guides act like magnets, pulling text and graphics accurately into place on the page. Let's turn the Snap to Guides feature on.

1. Click on the Options menu.
2. Choose the "Snap to guides" command. A check mark appears next to the menu option, indicating that the guides are now acting like magnets.

When you place text and graphics in the layout, PageMaker will automatically align anything you place near a guide, directly on that guide. Occasionally, you may want to place text or graphics near, but not directly on a guide. In this case, you will have to turn Snap to Guides off. To turn the feature off, choose the command again from the list of menu items. The check mark disappears, indicating that the feature is not active.

► COMPLETING YOUR MASTER PAGES

Now that you have finished constructing a layout grid, you are ready to add any other items that you want to appear on every page of your publication.

► NUMBERING PAGES AUTOMATICALLY

PageMaker can automatically number the pages of your publication. You can create a standard page numbering system that prints only the page number, or use a composite page numbering system that includes a number and text, such as A-1. You can also choose where you want to place the page numbers.

For our newsletter, let's use a composite page numbering system. First, however, to read text on the screen, you must use a larger view than the Fit-in-window view of the screen. Let's select the "Actual Size" option.

1. Click on the Pages menu.
2. Select the "Actual Size" option from the list of menu items.

The view changes to the Actual Size view. Now click on the gray scroll bars at the right and bottom of the pasteboard until the bottom left-hand corner of the page is displayed in the window, as shown in Figure 5.9. You are now ready to type in the page number and text and place the page number in your newsletter.

1. Move the pointer to the Toolbox.
2. Point to the box that contains the A text tool and click the mouse button.
3. Move the pointer icon onto the page and it changes to the text tool icon, the I-beam.
4. Indicate the position of the page number by placing the I-beam on the 10-inch vertical ruler guide you established at the left margin.

Notice that we placed the page number outside the text area marked by the margin and column guides of the grid. It is a good idea to choose a page number position outside the text area. This simplifies future page number editing, and insures that the page number will not interfere with the text on the page.

5. Click the mouse button and the flashing cursor is displayed.
6. Now type the text that will appear with the page number:

   DeskTop News Page

7. To indicate the page number, hold down the Shift key, the Ctrl key, and the # key simultaneously. (Instead of the # key you could press 3.)

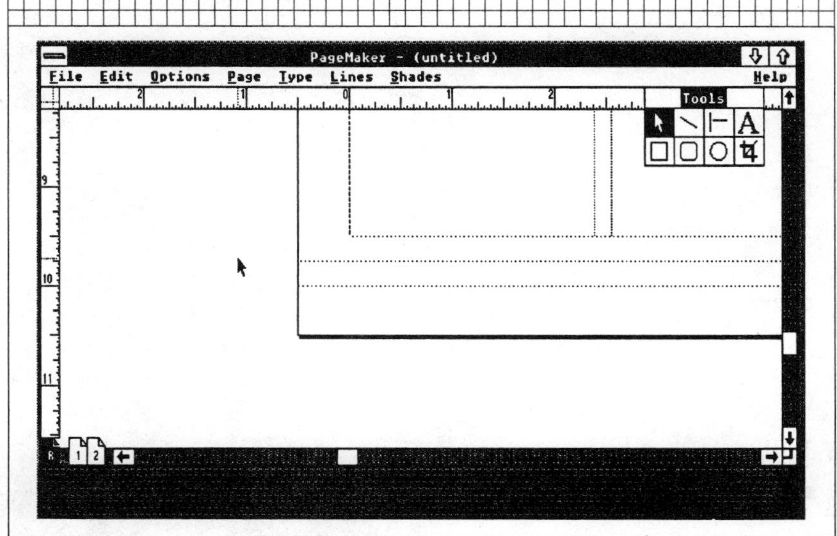

Figure 5.9: The Actual Size view

In the spot where the cursor was, you should now see *DeskTop News Page 0,* as shown in Figure 5.10. Page 0 is indicated because we are still working on the master pages. When we finish our master pages and move to the page of our publication, the 0 will change to indicate the page we are on.

In Chapter 8, you will learn how to designate the font and point size of the page number and its associated text. You will also learn how to move the page number using the text editing features of PageMaker.

► PLACING GRAPHICS ON THE MASTER PAGES

PageMaker provides two line tools in the Toolbox to help you draw a line in any direction. The perpendicular line tool ⊢ draws lines at 45-degree increments. This is the tool we will use to create a line at the top of our newsletter and at the bottom of the page (this line is called a baseline). In Chapter 10 you will learn more about using PageMaker's other graphics tools.

Let's first draw the baseline on the 9.75-inch ruler guide we created.

1. Select the perpendicular line tool from the toolbox. Move the pointer out of the Toolbox and the icon changes to a crossbar, indicating that you are using one of PageMaker's graphics tools.
2. Move the crossbar up into the menu bar and it automatically changes back to the pointer icon.

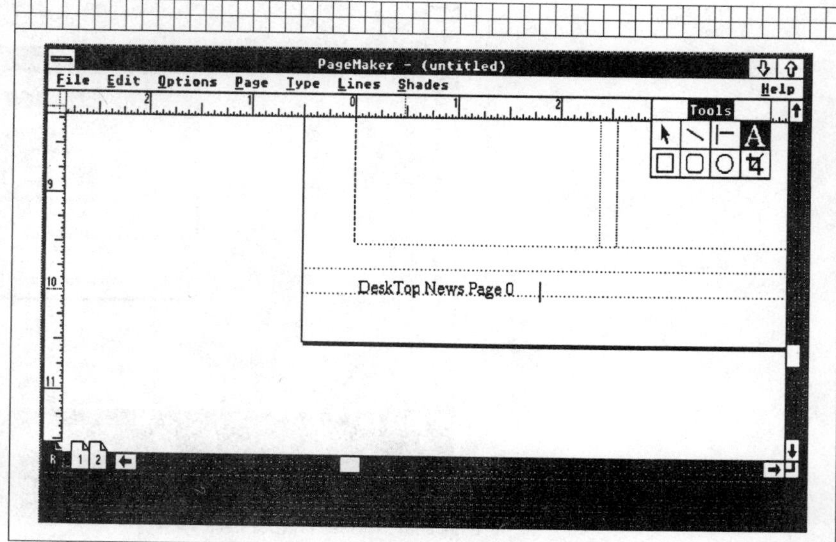

Figure 5.10: DeskTop News page number

3. Click on the Lines menu. You will see a variety of lines and patterns to choose from (see Figure 5.11).
4. Choose the "2pt" option. A check mark next to the option indicates it is selected.
5. Position the crossbar at the intersection of the left margin and the 9.75-inch ruler guide.
6. Click and hold down the mouse button.
7. Slide the crossbar to the right along the ruler guide until it reaches the right margin guide.
8. Release the mouse button, and a 2-point line appears just above the page number, as shown in Figure 5.11.

Notice the small boxes that appear at each end of the line. These boxes are called *handles.* Handles can help you make changes to a graphic. In Chapter 10 you will learn how to use them.

Let's now draw a line just below the masthead of our publication. Click on the gray scroll bars until the top left-hand corner of the page is displayed in the publication window.

1. Use the perpendicular line tool to draw a line positioned on the .75-inch ruler guide. Once the line is drawn, the handles are displayed.
2. Click on the Lines menu.

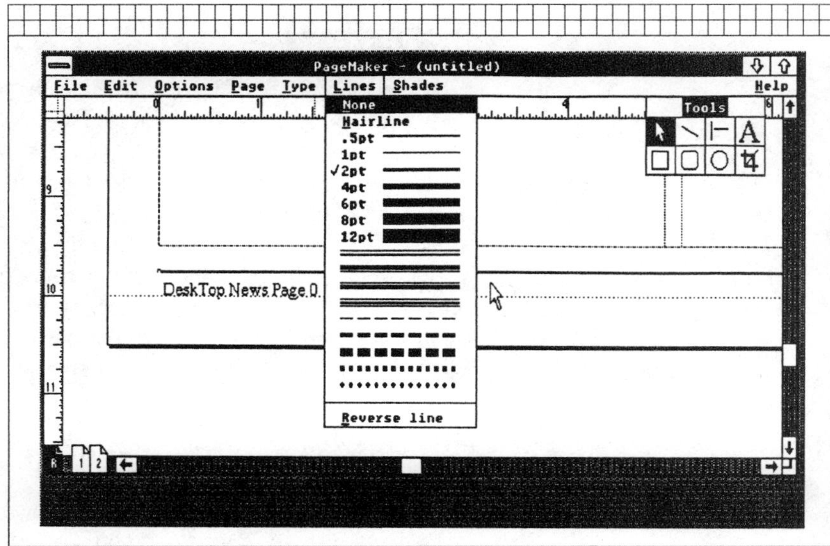

Figure 5.11: The Lines menu and a 2-point baseline

3. Select the "12-pt" option. The line, with its handles, now appears as shown in Figure 5.12. (The handles are the tiny rectangles at the top corner of the line.)

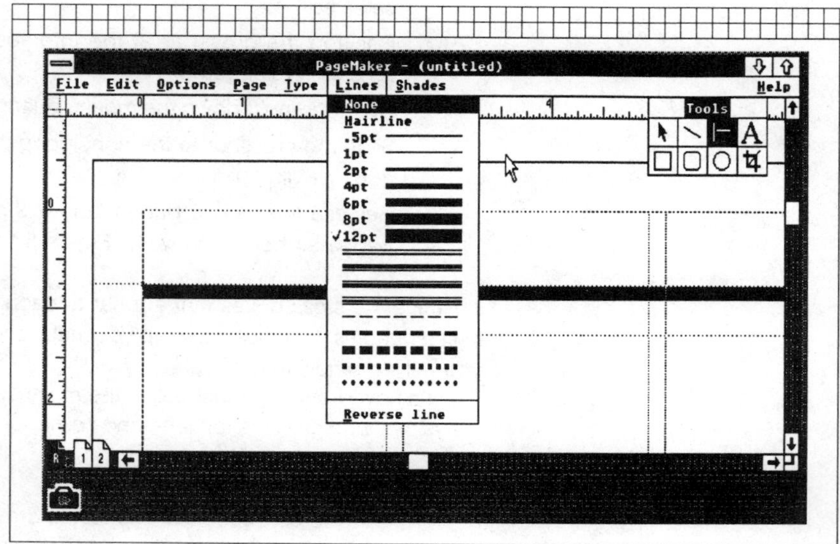

Figure 5.12: The 12-point line

► MODIFYING A MASTER PAGE

You have now laid out the master page elements of your newsletter. If, after you place your text and graphics, you find that you would like to change certain elements of your master page design, you can modify them. To do so, return to the master pages of the newsletter. Click the L master page icon to indicate that you want to make changes to the master pages. Go ahead and make any changes you like. You can change the number of columns or select different nonprinting guides. You can make changes to the text or graphics in the master page layout. Once you've made your changes, click the page icon corresponding to the page number you want to work on next. You can then move from page to page to verify the changes to the master page elements.

► CUSTOMIZING MASTER PAGES

As you move from page to page developing your publication, you may want to make changes to the layout grid you created in the master pages. For example, you may choose not to display the master page items for a particular page. You can remove one or all of the master page elements on a particular page without removing them from the master page. At any time, you can call back the elements you want to use from the master page.

Let's practice customizing a master page by removing a guide from page 2. (Remember that all of the design elements you placed into the master page will be found on all your publication's pages.) The guide positioned at .75 inches was placed there to help us line up the title of our newsletter. Since the title will only appear on page 1, let's remove the guide from page 2. Remember, you can move from page to page by clicking on the page icon displayed at the bottom left-hand side of the publication window. The changes you make to the guides on page 2 do not affect the guides on the other master pages.

1. Move to page 2 by clicking on the page 2 icon. Page 2 is now displayed on your screen with all the master page elements displayed.
2. Point on the .75-inch guide.
3. Click and hold down the mouse button. The two-directional arrow is displayed.
4. Move the guide into the horizontal ruler at the top of the pasteboard.

If, after you have moved the guides around, you decide to restore the original master page guides, be sure you have the right page selected in the publication window. Next, select the Page menu. Choose the "Copy master guides" command. You will see the master guides redisplayed.

Let's now save the master pages. Click on the "Save" command from the File menu. Remember, the file is called NEWSTEMP.PT3.

► SUMMARY

Congratulations! You have completed the first steps toward creating your newsletter. You should now be familiar with creating master pages and selecting elements for a layout grid. All the skills you learned here can be used to create master pages for other kinds of publications. In the next chapter, you will learn how to use master pages to create a template for your newsletter.

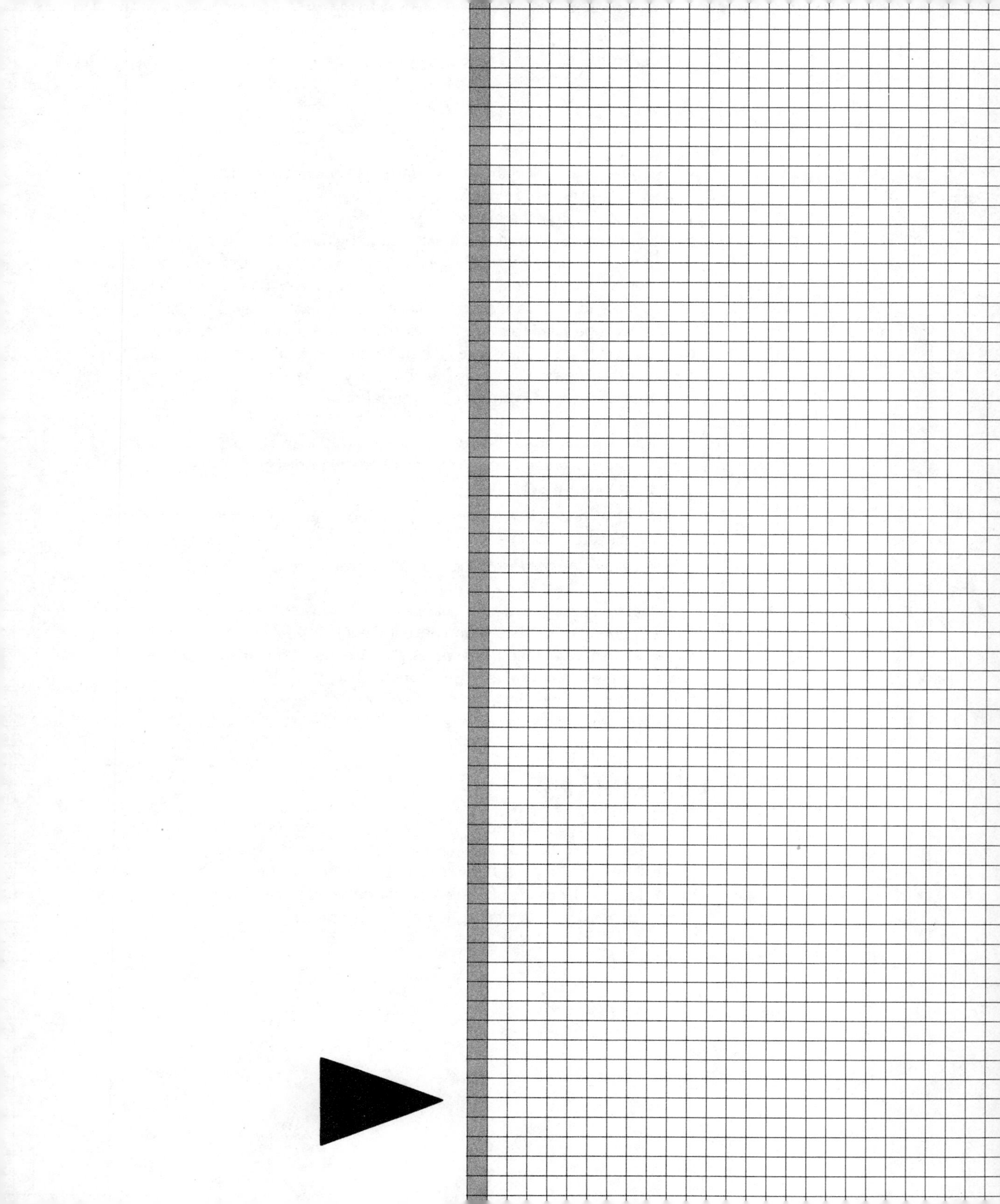

6 ENSURING CONSISTENCY WITH STYLE SHEETS AND TEMPLATES

A template 100

contains a master page design and any page elements that are unique on each page, such as titles and mastheads.

Use PageMaker's style sheet feature 101

to save formatting information, including text typography, paragraph formatting, tabs, and color specifications.

To customize a page, 101

go to your master page design, click on the page icon for the page you want to work on, then add the unique design features to that page.

Apply styles to text with the Styles palette. 103

Click on the "Styles palette" option in the Options menu, then choose from a list of styles in the publication's style sheet.

To create a style sheet, 103

click on the Options menu and choose the "Styles palette" option. Then choose the "Define styles" option in the Type menu. Create your style sheet from this dialog box.

Select the font, point size, type style, and enhancements 103

from the Type Specifications dialog box. From the Type menu, choose the "Type specs" option to display this dialog box.

Select paragraph formatting options, 109

such as alignment, indents, and hyphenation from the Paragraph Specifications dialog box. From the Type menu, choose the "Paragraph" option to display this dialog box.

To move text from the pasteboard onto the page, 112

select the pointer tool from the Toolbox, then position the text where you want it on the page.

In this chapter you will customize the master pages you created in the last chapter to create a template. Not only does a template (also called a dummy or boilerplate) include the master page elements, it can also have elements that are unique for each page. For example, on the first page of your newsletter, you will add a masthead that includes the newsletter title, volume number, and edition date.

Earlier versions of PageMaker do not have the template feature. But you can save the copy under a new name, then open a copy of the saved publication, which allows you to use the original as a template.

The master pages you created in the last chapter include elements that will appear on every page of our newsletter. PageMaker 3.0 allows you to save these master page elements in a template and use them over and over again.

You also will learn to use PageMaker 3.0's style sheets. These allow you to predefine type and paragraph specifications for text that will be included in the newsletter, making it easier for you to maintain consistency throughout the publication. (If you are using an earlier version of PageMaker, you will learn how to establish a consistent style without style sheets.)

▸ USING TEMPLATES

A template is a model that you can use again and again. A newsletter template like the one you will create can be used each month to put out a consistent and recognizable newsletter. For example, your company's quarterly or annual report may be a good candidate for a template. After you have set up the template for our two-page newsletter, you will be able to use the skills you learned to set up templates for other kinds of publications.

Once you've designed a template, you can still change the margins, the starting page number, the type of publication, or the single-sided or double-sided designation. If you make changes after you've placed text and graphics on the page, PageMaker automatically makes the necessary adjustments.

However, it is best to try to finalize your format as soon as possible. Set up the margins before you set up any column guides, and set up column guides before you begin placing text and graphics on the page. Once your column guides and your margins are established, PageMaker anchors your text and graphics in relation to the intersection of the top and left margins. So changing the margins after the text and graphics are in place moves everything, perhaps off the page.

Therefore, find a page format that works for you and stick with it. Different types of publications may require different formats, but keep in mind that the best results come from consistency. When you've settled on a standard page format, make a template as we will do here so you can save the standards to use next time. This saves you the time of setting up a format each time you open a new publication.

▶ PAGEMAKER'S STYLE SHEET FEATURE

With PageMaker 3.0, you can add to the consistency of your publications by using *style sheets*. A style sheet saves formatting information, including text typography, paragraph formatting, tabs, and color specifications, unique to the text and graphics of your template.

For example, you can define unique type and paragraph specifications for the title in the masthead of your newsletter, for the article titles, or for any other text elements in the template. Or, you can specify tab settings for a spreadsheet or database section. You can even apply special colors to text and graphics. All these specifications, once they've been saved in the style sheet, can be applied to the publication each time you create it. This way, when you go back to your monthly newsletter, the same design will be there for you to work with, giving you consistency in publication production.

Earlier versions of PageMaker do not have the style sheet feature, but you do not necessarily need to make text and graphics specifications for your template. If you don't have style sheets, you will have to designate the formatting specifications each time you add new text or graphics, since they cannot be saved in a style sheet. Let's first learn how to customize a template using PageMaker 3.0 with style sheets. Later in this chapter, PageMaker 1.0 and 1.0a users will learn to customize a template without using style sheets.

You may find many cases when you need to add elements to a publication that are unique to that page. PageMaker's style sheets enable you to do such customizing to your template. In this section you'll learn about customizing by adding unique elements to the title page, but you can use these techniques for any part of a publication.

The title page includes many unique elements. The masthead alone has a title, an edition date, a volume number, and more. To place these elements on the title page, you will be using some new PageMaker design tools.

▶ ADDING TEXT TO THE TEMPLATE

Let's begin by placing the newsletter title on page 1. First you'll type the title on the pasteboard, then you'll position the title in the masthead. The first step is to load the template on the screen. Select the "Open" command from the File menu. Click on the NEWSTEMP file. Click OK. The publication window is displayed.

1. Since we are customizing the first page of the template, point to the page 1 icon and click the mouse. Page 1 is displayed on your screen, as shown in

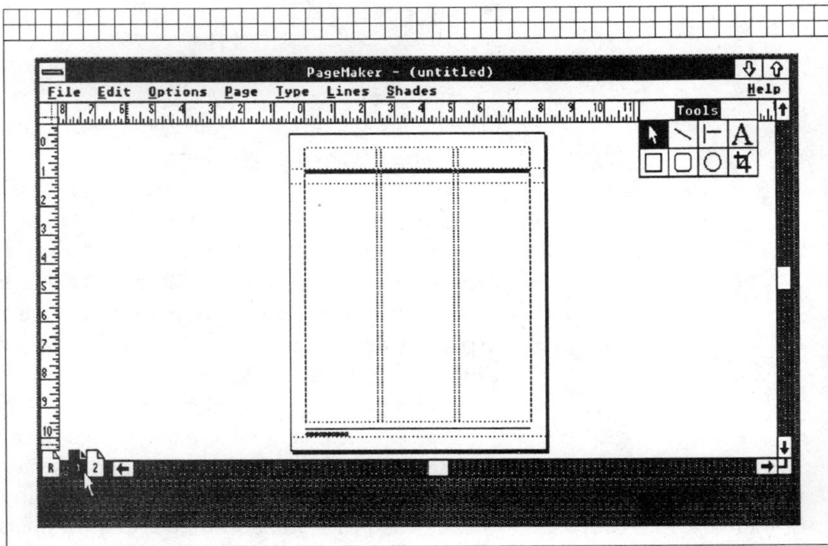

Figure 6.1: Page 1 of the newsletter

Figure 6.1. Notice that it has the top and bottom ruler lines that you placed on the page in the last exercise.

2. Use the gray scroll bars to position a blank space of pasteboard on the screen.
3. Select the text tool from the Toolbox by pointing on the **A** icon and clicking the mouse. The icon changes to an I-beam.
4. Move the I-beam onto the pasteboard and click the mouse. The flashing cursor appears.
5. Type the name of our newsletter:

   DeskTop News

   You can type the title anywhere on the pasteboard.

The title of our newsletter is the most important element on the first page. It needs to attract attention and let the readers know what they are looking at. In Chapter 4 you learned about establishing a hierarchy of importance on the page. This can be done by using different type enhancements (such as bolding or italicizing) to make text stand out, and with variations in type size.

The title of our newsletter, *DeskTop News,* will use a large type size and bolding to catch our reader's eye. But, before we can designate our format, the text must be highlighted so PageMaker can know exactly which piece of text we want to work with. To highlight the text,

1. Select the text tool from the Toolbox if you are not already working with it.
2. Position the I-beam just in front of the first letter of text, in this case, the *D* in *DeskTop News.*
3. Click and hold down the mouse button.
4. Move the I-beam to the right, directly over the text. The text should become highlighted on your screen, as shown in Figure 6.2.
5. When the I-beam is positioned to the right of the last character of text, release the mouse button.

Now that the title is highlighted, you are ready to make your formatting specifications. If you are using PageMaker version 3.0, use the instructions in the following sections to create a style sheet for the title. If you are using an earlier version of PageMaker, go to the section entitled "Formatting Text with PageMaker 1.0 or 1.0a."

► FORMATTING TEXT USING STYLE SHEETS

To use a style sheet, you will need to display the Styles palette in the publication window. The Styles palette uses previously entered format specifications to introduce new page elements quickly.

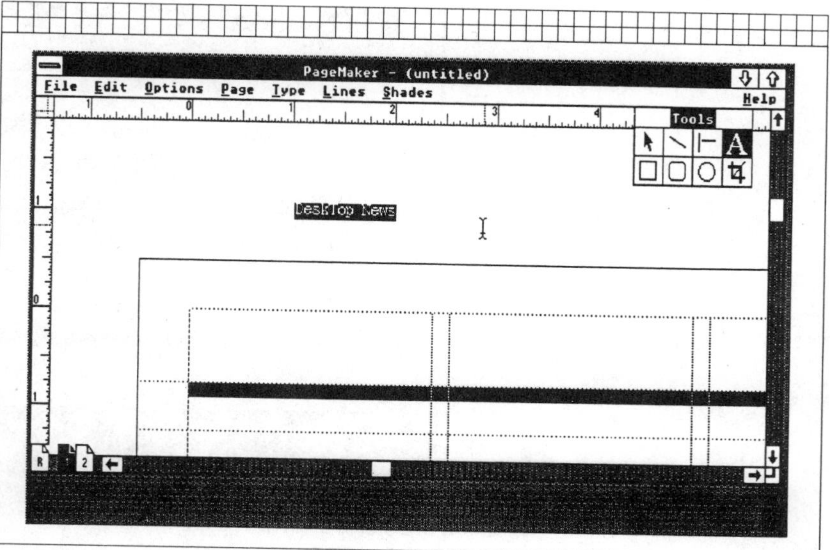

Figure 6.2: Highlighted newsletter title

To display the Styles palette,

1. Click on the Options menu.
2. Click on the "Styles palette" option. A check mark appears next to the option and the Styles palette is displayed in the publication window, as shown in Figure 6.3.

With the Styles palette displayed, you are ready to make some formatting specifications for the title of our newsletter. (The Styles palette will remain on the screen, even when you use other menus.)

1. Click on the Type menu.
2. Click on the "Define styles" command. The Define Styles dialog box is displayed, as shown in Figure 6.4.

The Define Styles dialog box, together with the Styles palette, allow you to create style sheets for each element in your template.

3. Since this is a new style sheet, click on the "New" option button in the dialog box. The Edit Style dialog box is displayed (Figure 6.5).

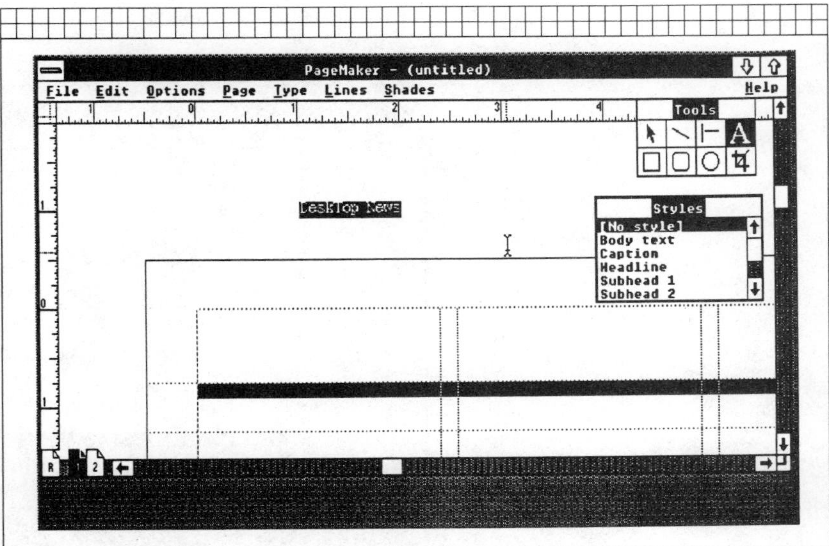

Figure 6.3: The Styles palette

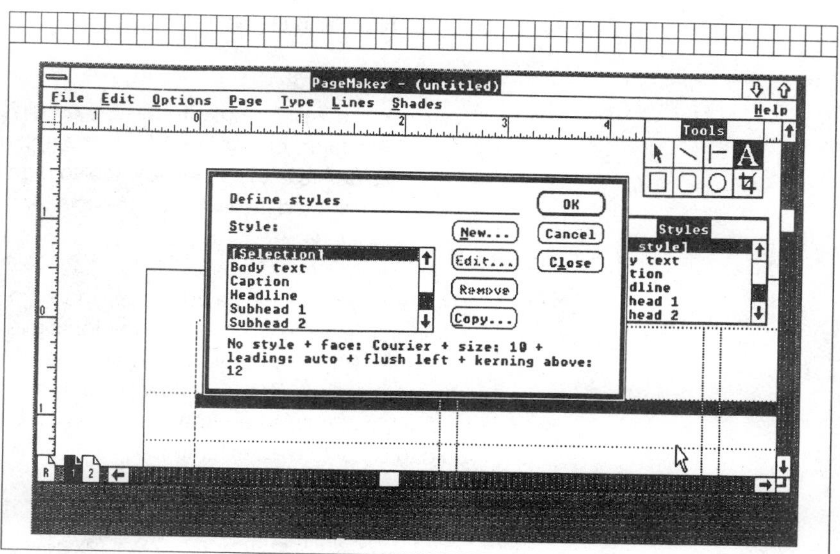

Figure 6.4: The Define Styles dialog box

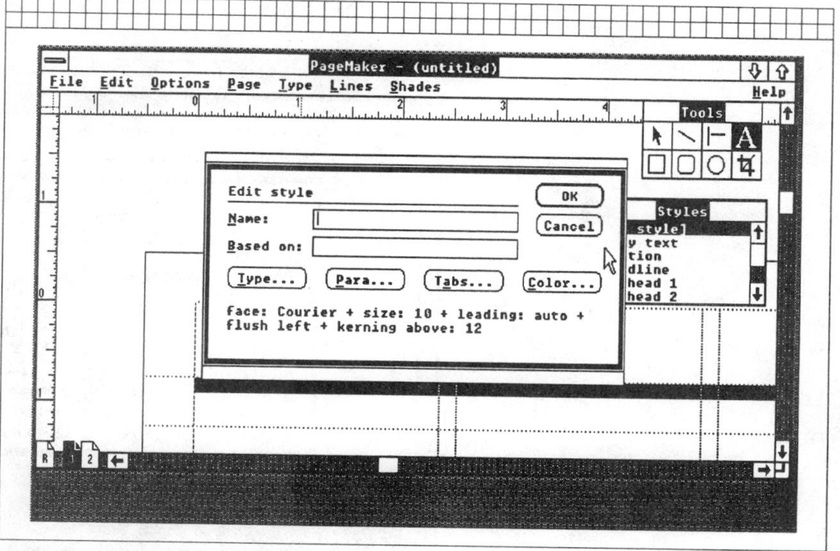

Figure 6.5: The Edit Style dialog box

4. First, fill in the Name field. Type

    Title

5. Press Tab to move to the Based On field. You'll learn more about this field later, but for now, if a name appears in this box, it must be deleted. To delete text, use the text tool to highlight the text in the box, just as you highlighted the title of our newsletter. With the text highlighted, press the Delete key.

Now let's select a font, a point size, and a type style for the newsletter title. PageMaker only lets you choose from the fonts available on your target printer. When you started PageMaker, you designated a target printer, as well as the hard and soft fonts available. You will now select from this list of available fonts. The fonts used in the exercise here may not be available on the printer you are using, but you can substitute a similar font.

6. Click on the "Type" option button. The Type Specifications dialog box, shown in Figure 6.6, is displayed.
7. In Chapter 4, in our design planning session, we chose Helvetica type for the title of our newsletter. Click on the "Helvetica" option in the Font Name and Size field of the dialog box. You may need to use the gray scroll bars to display any hidden options.

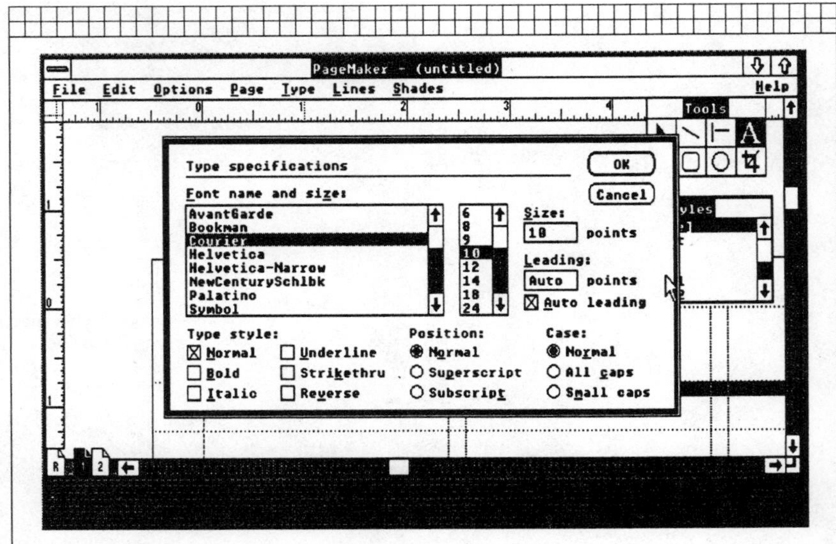

Figure 6.6: Type Specifications dialog box

8. We are using a type size of 36 points, so click on "36" in the Size field of the dialog box. (Again, you may have to use the gray scroll bars to display the larger sizes of type.)
9. Next, select a type style for the title. Click on the "Bold" option. An X-mark appears in the box, indicating that bolding is the current selection.
10. Now that you've made your selections, click on OK. You are returned to the Edit Style dialog box.
11. Click OK again and you are returned to the Define Styles dialog box.
12. Click OK once more and you are returned to the publication window.

The title, *DeskTop News,* is now formatted in 36-point Helvetica bold type. You are now ready to remove the title from the pasteboard and place it on page 1.

▶ MOVING TEXT IN THE PUBLICATION WINDOW

To move text or graphics in the publication window, you must use the pointer tool. This tool acts like a hand, allowing you to pick up text and graphics and place them on the page. Let's place the title on page 1.

1. Select the pointer tool from the Toolbox.
2. Point directly on the title in the pasteboard.
3. Click and hold down the mouse button. A dotted line box appears around the text, letting you know it is ready to be moved.
4. Slide the text on the screen until it is on the page. Place the baseline of the text even with the 1/2-inch mark of the vertical ruler, flush with the right margin, at the 7.5-inch mark on the horizontal ruler. Place it just above the 12-point ruler line, as shown in Figure 6.7.
5. Once the text is accurately placed, release the mouse button.

The title is now positioned in the masthead area on the first page. Skip the next section that shows you how to format your title using PageMaker 1.0 or 1.0a. and go to "Adding and Formatting Text as Placeholders."

▶ FORMATTING TEXT WITH PAGEMAKER 1.0 OR 1.0A

When you format text with earlier versions of PageMaker, you cannot use style sheets. This means that each piece of text must be formatted individually.

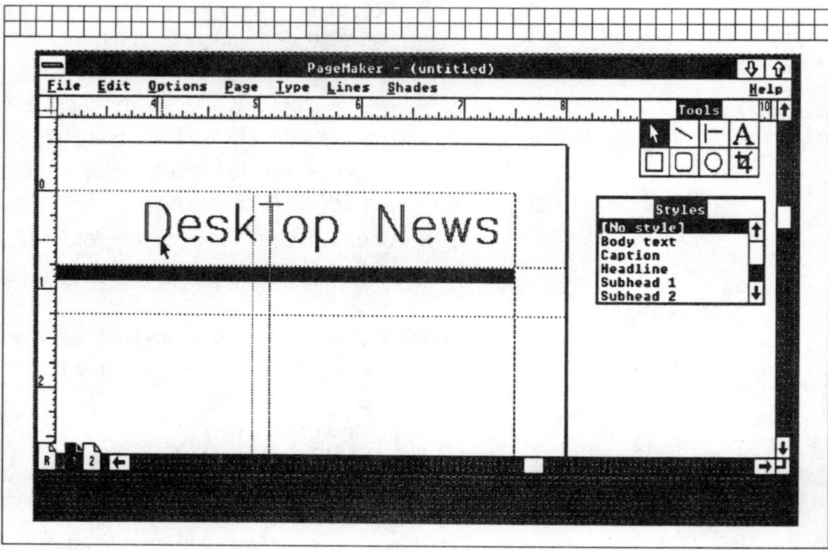

Figure 6.7: Placing the title on page 1

1. Click on the Type menu.
2. Click on the "Type specifications" option. The Type Specifications dialog box, shown earlier in Figure 6.6, is displayed.
3. In Chapter 4, in our design planning session, we chose Helvetica type for the title of our newsletter. Click on the "Helvetica" option in the Font Name and Size field of the dialog box. You may need to use the gray scroll bars to display any hidden options.
4. We are using a type size of 36 points, so click on the "36" in the Size field of the dialog box. (Again, you may have to use the gray scroll bars to display the larger sizes of type.)
5. Next, select a type style for the title. Click on the "Bold" option. An X-mark appears in the box, indicating that bolding is the current selection.
6. Now that you've made your selections, click on OK.

The title, *DeskTop News,* is now formatted with the new type specifications. You are ready to place it on page 1.

1. Select the pointer tool from the Toolbox.
2. Point directly on the title in the pasteboard.
3. Click and hold down the mouse button. A dotted line box appears around the text, letting you know it is ready to be moved.

4. Slide the text on the screen until it is on the page. Place the baseline of the text even with the 1/2-inch mark of the vertical ruler, flush with the right margin at the 7.5-inch mark on the horizontal ruler. Place it just above the 12-point ruler line, as shown earlier in Figure 6.7.
5. Once the text is accurately placed, release the mouse button.

The title should now be accurately positioned in the masthead on the page.

► ADDING AND FORMATTING TEXT AS PLACEHOLDERS

The date and volume number will change with each edition of our newsletter. However, since these items are included in each newsletter, we can format place-holders for them and position the placeholders on the first page of our template. When we produce our newsletter each month, we can insert the formatted date and volume number where the placeholders are.

The first step is to type the placeholders for the date and volume number in the pasteboard.

1. Position a blank area of the pasteboard on your screen using the gray scroll bars.
2. Select the text tool from the Toolbox.
3. Click on the blank area in the pasteboard; the flashing cursor appears.
4. Type

   Month Day, 1989

   Press ↵.
5. Type

   Volume #

The text in the pasteboard is ready to format. We'll begin by highlighting it in the pasteboard to let PageMaker know that this is the text we want to format.

1. Use the text tool to highlight the text.
2. Click on the Type menu.

Use the following instructions if you are using PageMaker version 3.0. If you are using an earlier version of PageMaker, go to the section called "Text and Paragraph Formatting with PageMaker 1.0 and 1.0a."

3. Choose the "Define styles" option from the menu. The Define Styles dialog box, shown earlier in Figure 6.4, is displayed.
4. Click on the "New" button and the Edit Style dialog box, shown earlier in Figure 6.5, is displayed.
5. In the Name box, type

   Level 2

6. In the Based On box, type

   Title

This means that the second level of text in the masthead (the title is the first level in our hierarchy) will use the same font as (or is "based on") the previously formatted title.

You are now ready to select the type and paragraph specifications unique to the second level of text in the masthead.

7. Click on the "Type" option button. The Type Specifications dialog box, shown earlier in Figure 6.6, is displayed.
8. Make the following selections: Helvetica; 12 point; Bold.
9. Once your selections are made, click OK. You will be returned to the Edit Style dialog box.

All second level text, in this case the date and volume number, will now reflect the new type specifications—12-point bold Helvetica.

This second level of text will also include a unique paragraph formatting specification. You will use the Paragraph Specifications dialog box to do this formatting. This menu includes options that determine how a paragraph of text appears, such as hyphenation, indents, and justification.

1. From the Edit Style dialog box, click on the "Para" option. You should see the Paragraph Specifications dialog box, as shown in Figure 6.8.
2. We will right-align the date and volume number in the first column of the masthead. Make sure the text handles lie within the column guides. To specify right alignment, click on the "Right" option button in the Alignment section of the dialog box.
3. Click OK. You are returned to the Edit Style dialog box.
4. Click OK again. You are returned to the Define Styles dialog box.
5. Click OK once more and you are returned to the publication window.

The date and volume number on the pasteboard should have the specifications you indicated. Notice that the Styles palette in the window now contains a "Title"

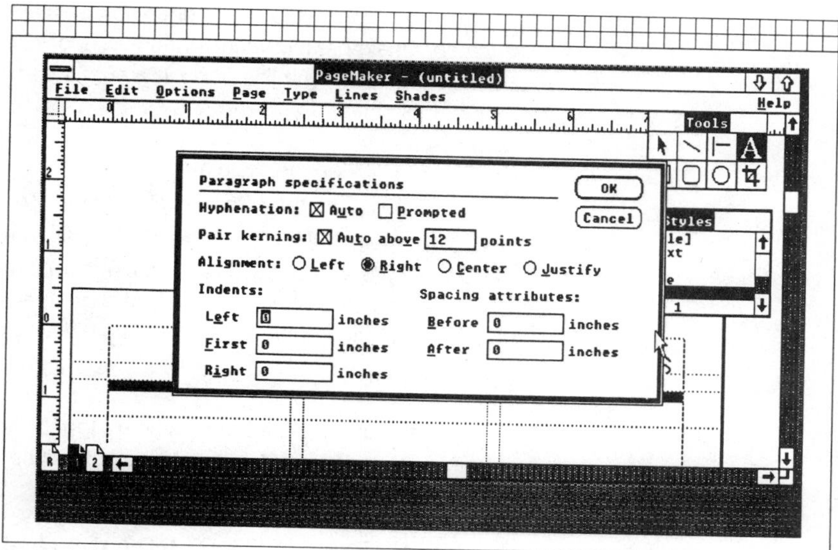

Figure 6.8: Paragraph Specifications dialog box

option and a "Level 2" option. Here you see the advantage of the style sheet. In the future, when you include text that you want formatted with the same specifications as the Title text or the Level 2 text, simply highlight the text, then go to the Styles palette and click on the "Title" or the "Level 2" option. Your text will be formatted, saving you the time of repeating the formatting steps we just completed.

The following section is for PageMaker 1.0 and 1.0a users. If you are using version 3.0, skip ahead to the section called "Moving Text from the Pasteboard to the Page."

► TEXT AND PARAGRAPH FORMATTING WITH PAGEMAKER 1.0 AND 1.0A

PageMaker versions 1.0 and 1.0a do not include style sheets. Therefore, each time you place new text in the publication, you must complete all the formatting steps. Let's format the date and volume number in the masthead.

1. The text in the pasteboard should be highlighted and you should have the Type menu on your screen. Select the "Type specifications" option from the menu. The Type Specifications dialog box, shown in Figure 6.6, is displayed.
2. Make the following selections: Helvetica; 12 point; Bold.
3. Click OK.

The date and volume number now contain the type specifications you indicated. One more formatting change is necessary before the text can be placed in the masthead of the title page. (Be sure the text in the pasteboard remains highlighted so that PageMaker knows which text to act on.)

4. Click on the Type menu.
5. Click on the "Paragraph" option. The Paragraph Specifications dialog box, shown previously in Figure 6.8, is displayed.
6. We will right-align the date and volume number in the first column of the masthead. To specify right alignment, click on the "Right" option button in the Alignment section of the dialog box.
7. Click OK.

The text in the pasteboard is now aligned with the right margin, leaving the left side as ragged text. Continue to the next section and move the text onto the page.

▶ MOVING TEXT FROM THE PASTEBOARD TO THE PAGE

You again will use the pointer tool to move the text from the pasteboard to the page. Remember, the pointer tool acts as a hand to pick up anything in the publication window and move it to a new location.

1. Click on the pointer tool from the Toolbox.
2. Point on the text in the pasteboard.
3. Click and hold down the mouse button.
4. A dotted line box appears around the text and the pointer icon becomes a four-directional arrow, indicating that the text is ready to be moved.
5. Move the text onto the page, aligning the baseline of the volume number with the baseline of the title. Place the text flush with the right column guide in the first column, as shown in Figure 6.9.

PageMaker 3.0 automatically adds a .PT3 extension when you save a file as a template.

The text in the masthead is now complete. Let's save the work we've done so far. (It is a good habit to save your work as frequently as possible.) Save your work just as you did in Chapter 5. However, this time you will save your work as a template if you are using PageMaker 3.0. To do this, just click on the "Template" option button, then click on the "Save as" option from the File menu. We are still calling our newsletter template *NEWSTEMP.*

If you are using PageMaker 1.0 or 1.0a, your newsletter template is complete and you are ready to close the template. Skip the following section for PageMaker 3.0 users and continue to the section, "Closing A Template."

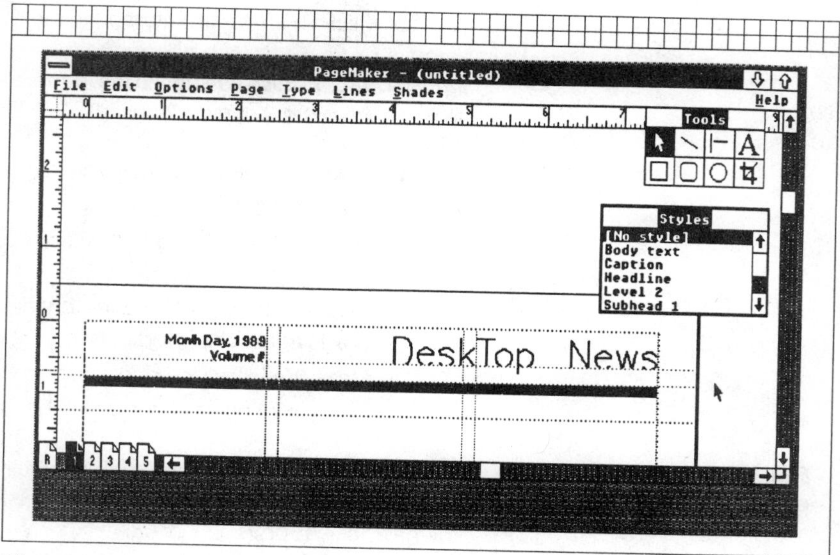

Figure 6.9: Placing the date and volume number in the masthead

If you are using PageMaker 3.0, go to the next section where you will learn to create style sheets for all the text in the newsletter, including the headlines and articles that are unique to each edition.

► CREATING STYLE SHEETS FOR HEADLINES AND ARTICLES

By defining the format specifications for the headlines, articles, and the main body of text, you can save time later on when the articles are placed in the publication. The format specifications are saved under a name in the Styles palette. When the text is placed on the page, clicking a format style in the Styles palette sets up all the formatting specifications you established previously. Let's set up format specifications for our article headlines.

1. Hold down the Ctrl key while clicking on "Headline" in the Styles palette. The Edit Style dialog box, shown in Figure 6.5, is displayed. *Headline* is displayed in the Name text box.
2. Click on the "Type" option. The Type Specifications dialog box, shown in Figure 6.6, is displayed.
3. Make the following selections: Palatino; 18 point; Bold.
4. Click on OK. You are returned to the Edit Style dialog box.

5. Click OK. You are returned to the publication window.

From here, we also can define the formatting specifications for the main body of text, the articles of our newsletter.

1. Hold down the Ctrl key while clicking on the "Body text" option in the Styles palette.
2. The Edit Style dialog box is displayed with the word *body* in the Name box.
3. Click on the "Type" option button and the Type Specifications dialog box is again displayed.
4. Make the following specifications: Palatino; 12 point; Normal.
5. Click OK. You are returned to the Edit Style dialog box.

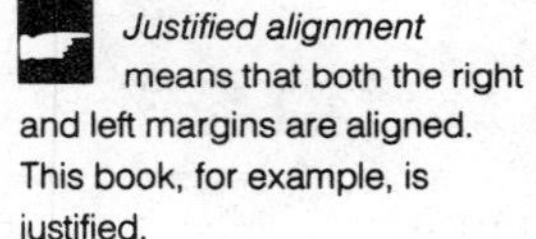

Justified alignment means that both the right and left margins are aligned. This book, for example, is justified.

Now we can make the paragraph formatting specifications for the main body of text in our newsletter, the articles. Let's use justified alignment for the text to give the newsletter a professional look.

6. From the Edit Style dialog box, click on the "Para" option button. The Paragraph Specifications dialog box, shown in Figure 6.8, is displayed.
7. Click on the "Justify" option button in the Alignment section of the dialog box.
8. Click OK. You are returned to the Edit Style dialog box.
9. Click OK. You are returned to the publication window.

The Styles palette now includes all the formatting specifications for the headlines and for the article text that you will need for each edition of the newsletter. The template is finished and you are ready to start using it. First, however, you must save the template again under the same name, NEWSTEMP (just click on the "Save" command from the File menu), then continue to the final section to learn how to close the template.

► CLOSING A TEMPLATE

Before your template is ready to use, it must first be closed. This is because, when you create your first publication, you will open an untitled copy of the template. This way, you'll still have an original, unchanged template that you can use each time you create a new edition of the newsletter.

Before you close the template, be sure you have saved your work. If you have not, a dialog box will appear, asking you if you want to first save your work.

To close your template,

1. Click on the File menu.
2. Click on the "Close" option in the menu.

The template is now closed and you are returned to the gray desktop screen. From here, you can start a new publication or open an existing one. You can also exit PageMaker by selecting the "Exit" option from the File menu.

In the next chapter, you will begin adding articles to your newsletter using the template you just created.

► PART III:

WORKING WITH TEXT

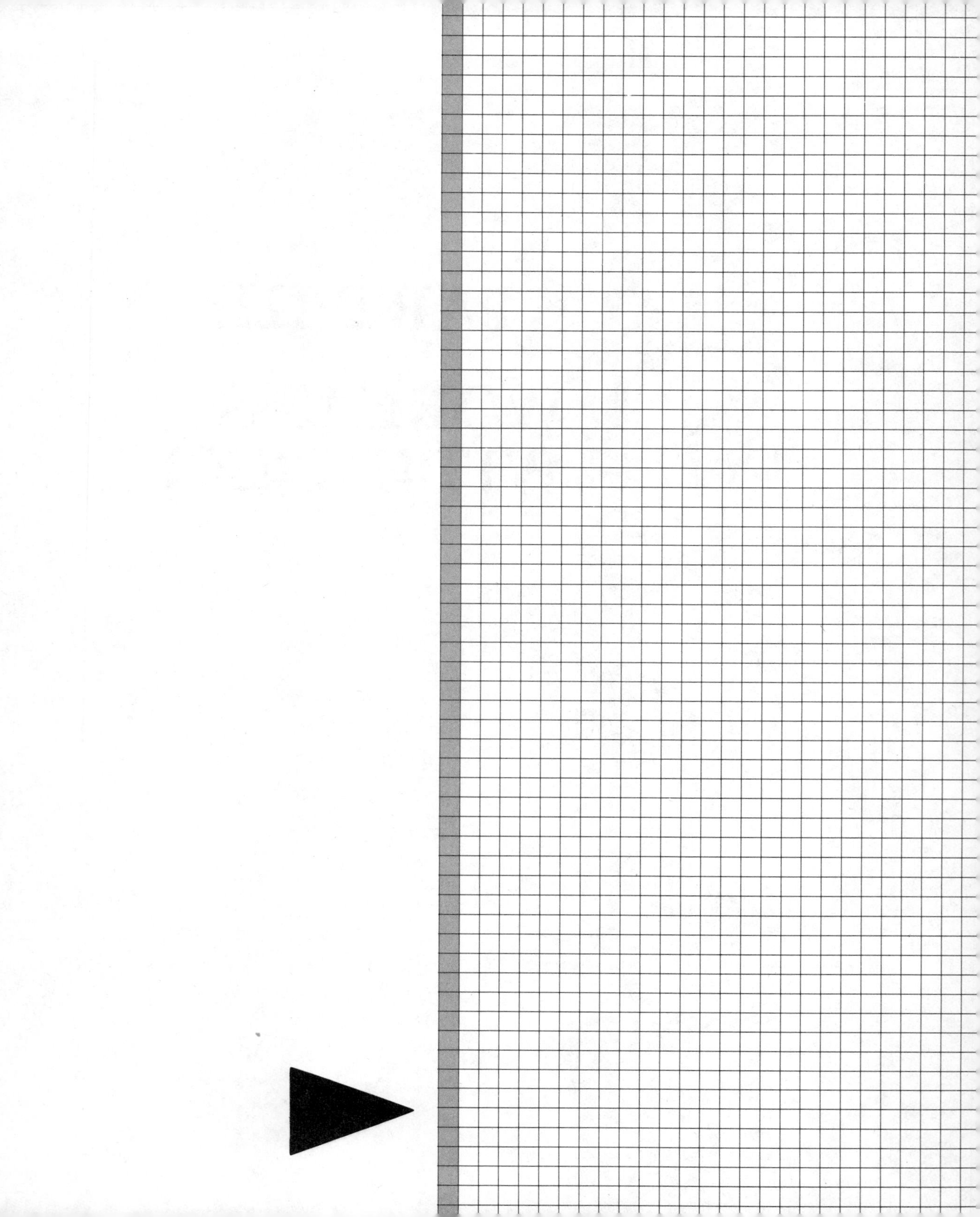

7 WORKING WITH TEXT BLOCKS, PAGEMAKER'S BASIC TEXT UNIT

To place text into PageMaker, 123

select the "Place" command from the File menu. Click on the file name of the text you want to place. This highlights the file name. Click on OK or "Place."

To display the handles on a text block, 123

click anywhere on the text with the pointer tool.

To flow the remaining text in a block, 123

click on the plus sign (+) to load the text page icon.

To autoflow a story into your layout, 128

click on the "Autoflow" command from the Options menu. Select the "Place" command and highlight the story, then click OK.

To resize a text block vertically, 133

click and hold down the mouse button on the middle of the windowshade handle.

To resize a text block horizontally and vertically, 134

click on the corner of the windowshade handle.

To resize a text block vertically only using a corner handle, 134

hold down the Shift key and click on a corner handle.

To break up a text block into several threaded blocks, 135

click on the plus sign (+) and flow the text into the new location. Repeat this step each time the plus sign appears in the windowshade handle.

To select a text block, 135

use the pointer tool to display the handles.

To remove a selected text block, 138

click on the "Cut" command from the Edit menu.

To move a text block, 138

click on the top windowshade handle and the text page icon loads with the text to be placed in a new location.

To delete a selected threaded text block, 140

click on the "Clear" command from the Edit menu.

To consolidate text blocks, 140

merge the handles of one block, then stretch the handles of the other text block to include the block with merged handles.

To align text blocks, 142

use ruler guidelines and the Snap to guides command from the Options menu.

Use the Clipboard, 145

to unthread text blocks, copy, move, and delete text blocks.

To include text from the Clipboard, 145

use the "Paste" command from the Edit menu.

If you are developing large blocks of text, it is best to use your word processor to create the text before placing it in PageMaker.

Now that you have created a template complete with master pages and customized pages, you are ready to begin placing text in your newsletter. PageMaker provides three ways for you to include text in a publication. You can include a complete file you created using your word processor, or you can use the Windows Clipboard to select the parts of a file you want to include. The third way is to use the PageMaker text tool that you worked with in Chapter 6. The text tool works best when it is limited to developing titles, page numbers, headings, etc. The text tool is not a complete word processor. In this chapter you will work with text blocks, PageMaker's way of grouping text, as you place text into your newsletter and alter text.

► USING YOUR WORD PROCESSOR WITH PAGEMAKER

Even though PageMaker can work with files from your word processor, certain specifications are not recognized. For example, PageMaker ignores the right margin specification in a word processed file. This is because text must be broken down to fit into the new columns of your layout, so PageMaker ignores the original right margin specifications. If you indented text from the left margin in your word processed file, PageMaker indents the same distance in the new column. Since it is hard to predict how indentations will affect your PageMaker layout, do not try to calculate them ahead of time. Wait until the text is in PageMaker and then make any necessary adjustments.

PageMaker does recognize the first line indent of a paragraph, but if the indent is wider than the PageMaker column, PageMaker ignores it. When you align tables or columns in your word processor, use the Tab key. Try to plan ahead by not making a table wider than the PageMaker columns you plan on using.

PageMaker recognizes type specifications from your word processor—the font, the type size and style, the line spacing, and position of the text. If your word processor cannot make type specifications, PageMaker will substitute its own by default. (Later you can change PageMaker's default specifications to suit your needs.) PageMaker also makes default substitutions if the type specifications in your word processed file are not recognized by your target printer. However, the original word processor specifications will be saved by PageMaker, so if you find a target printer later on that uses the specifications you want, PageMaker will revert to your original word processor specifications.

PageMaker does not recognize footnotes, page numbers, headers, or footers from a word processor. This is because PageMaker threads all the text from your word processor into a continuous flow, and the headers, footers, etc., you created with your word processor will be flowed into PageMaker's columns along with the rest of the text. The best thing to do is develop your word processed files without any headers, footers, footnotes, or page numbers. Use PageMaker's text tool to make these additions after the text is in place.

PageMaker does not have some of the advanced features that may come with your word processor, such as spell checking. Be sure you use the spell checker from your word processor before you place the text in PageMaker. Use your word processor to make your text as clean as possible before transferring it into PageMaker.

▸ PLACING TEXT INTO YOUR PUBLICATION

In Chapter 2, you created two articles with your word processor. Let's place them into the new PageMaker template you created in Chapter 6.

First, open the newsletter template using the command options from PageMaker's File menu.

1. Choose the "Open" option from the File menu. The Open dialog box is displayed.
2. Click on the NEWSTEMP template you completed in the last chapter.
3. Click OK.

Now your template is displayed in the publication window and you are ready to begin creating this month's newsletter. Let's place the two articles you created in Chapter 2.

1. Click on the File menu.
2. Select the "Place" command option. The Place File dialog box, shown in Figure 7.1, is displayed.

This dialog box displays a list of the files that are stored on PageMaker's disk. The files displayed in the scroll box at the left of the window can come from your graphics or word processor directories. If the file you want to use is in the same directory as PageMaker, use the gray scroll bars to look through the files in the scroll box until you find it. If the file you want to use is in a different directory, you must select this directory by switching to different disks or directories on your system. For example, to display the files in the A drive, click on [-A-]. To list the directories on the current drive, click on [..]. The scroll box will display the names of files on the directory you chose.

Let's select the short article you created in Chapter 2.

3. Move to the directory containing the file and display the file name in the scroll box.
4. Click on the file name to highlight it.

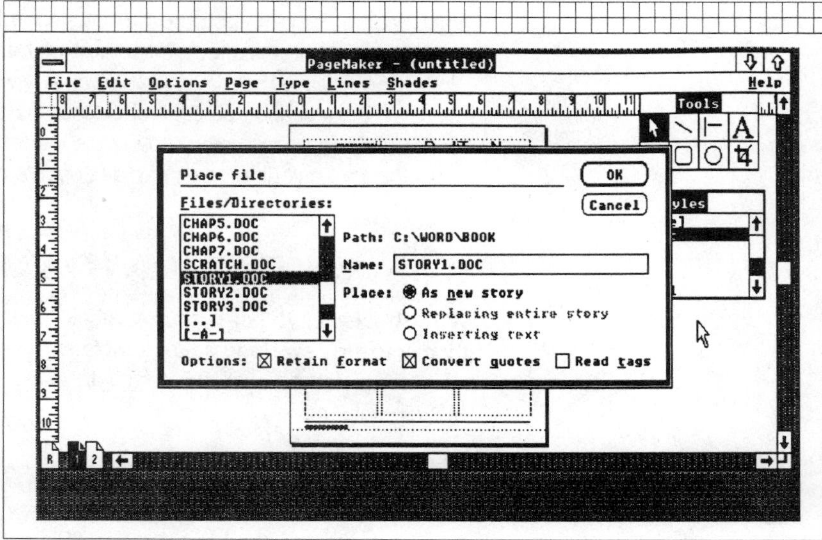

Figure 7.1: The Place File dialog box

> With earlier versions of PageMaker, two option buttons are used. Highlighting the "Retain format" option button retains the formatting commands in PageMaker-compatible word processed files. Highlighting the "Text only" button places the files without formatting commands.

The short story file should now be highlighted in the Files/Directories scroll box. Now look at the options near the bottom of the window. You can retain the format of a PageMaker-compatible word processed file, or you can drop the format commands and place the file as a text-only file. If you want to place the file with the formatting commands intact, leave the X-mark in the "Retain format" option box. Click in the box to delete the X-mark if you want to place the file as a text-only file.

You'll also see some additional options for placing text from a word processor in a publication. The "Convert quotes" option allows you to convert the regular-style quotation marks used by your word processor to the typesetting-style quotation marks used by PageMaker. The "Read tags" option box reads any formatting tags you set in your file, and matches them to the corresponding style formats you created using PageMaker's style sheets. In Chapter 8, you'll look more closely at these options. For now, we'll use the PageMaker default selections.

5. If you used a PageMaker-compatible word processor to create the article, leave the X-mark in the "Retain format" option box (or the highlight in the "Retain format" option button). If you used an incompatible word processor, click on the "Retain format" option box. The X-mark disappears and a text-only place option is selected.
6. Click on OK or the "As new story" button to return to the publication window. (You could also double click on the file name to select the file and return to the publication in one step.) If PageMaker doesn't recognize the

format of the file, the Select File Type dialog box shown in Figure 7.2 will be displayed. Select the correct format for the file and click OK.

Now the publication window is displayed. Notice that the pointer icon has changed to a text icon resembling the corner of a page. This means that the text page icon is now loaded with your short article.

7. Using your mouse, move the text page icon to the top-left corner of the first column on page 1 of the NEWSTEMP template. Align the corner of the text page icon with the intersection of the 1.25-inch ruler guide and the left margin guide.
8. When the text icon is positioned properly, click the mouse button. The text flows into the column. Your publication should now look something like the example shown in Figure 7.3.

See Chapter 8 for an explanation of the export filter.

When text from a word processed file is placed into PageMaker, the original word processed file is not altered. Remember, however, if you alter the file once it is in PageMaker, the original word processed file will not contain your alterations—unless you are using PageMaker 3.0. PageMaker 3.0 has an export filter with which to export files

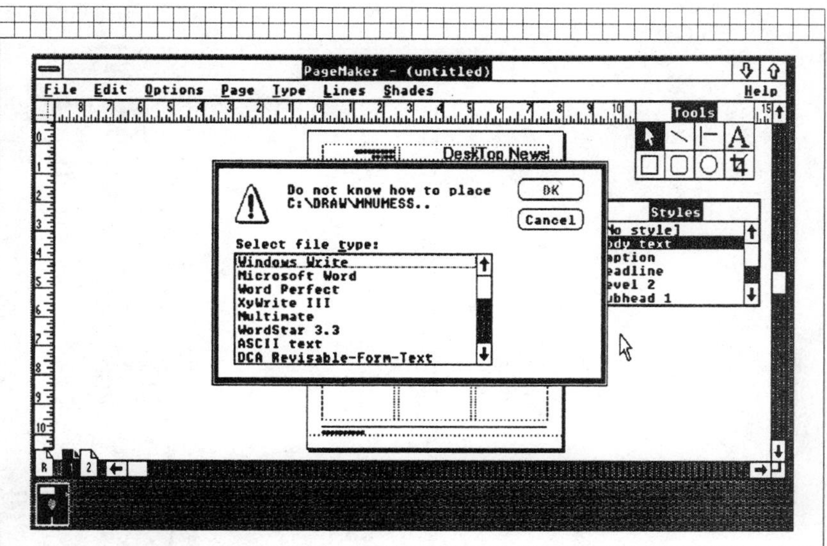

Figure 7.2: The Select File Type dialog box

from PageMaker back to your word processor. You can save any changes you made within PageMaker by using the export filter.

Let's now place the long article.

1. Use the "Place" command to select the second file you created in Chapter 2. Use the same option selections you made in placing the first story.
2. Click OK or "Place." You are returned to the publication window. The text page icon is now loaded with the second article of our newsletter.
3. Position the corner of the text page icon in the second column, at the intersection of the 1.25-inch ruler guide and the left column guide.
4. Once the icon is correctly positioned, click the mouse button and the text will flow into the column.

This chapter also explains two other methods of placing text—Autoflow and Semi-automatic text flow.

Since this is a long article, a handle with a plus symbol appears at the bottom of the text block. This symbol means there is still more text to be placed. Since column two is filled, you'll have to place the text in another location in the newsletter. In this case, you'll place it in column three. Let's continue placing the text.

5. Point directly on the plus symbol in the bottom handle and click the mouse button. The text page icon appears again.
6. Position the icon at the top of the third column on page 1. Align the corner

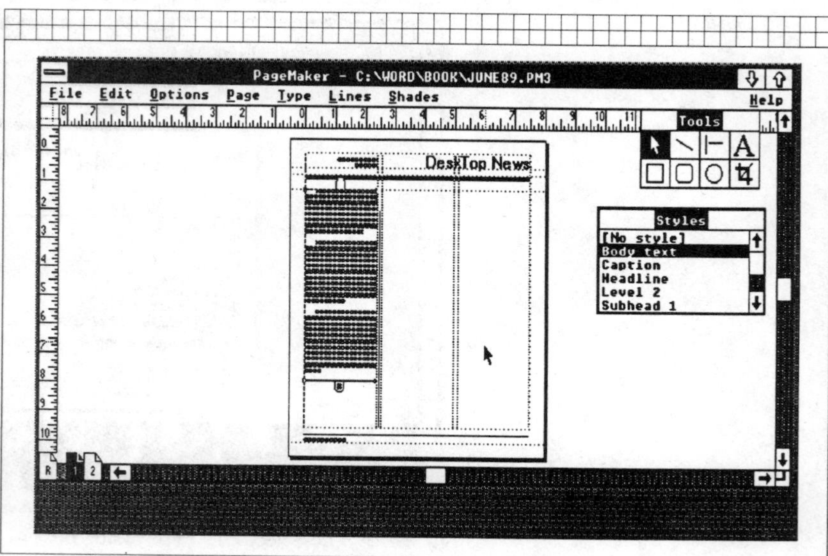

Figure 7.3: First story placed on page 1

of the page with the intersection of the 1.25-inch ruler guide and the left column guide.

7. Click the mouse button.

Snap to guides are discussed in Chapter 5.

The text flows into column three. Your screen should now look like Figure 7.4. If you are having trouble placing the text accurately, remember you can use the Snap to guides feature. This feature gives the column guide a magnetic capability. The Snap to guides feature is located in the Options menu.

However, you still have some text in the second article to place. Let's place the remainder of the article on page 2.

1. Click on the plus sign in the handle at the bottom of the third column. Now the text page icon is loaded with the remainder of the file.
2. Move the text page icon over the page 2 icon at the bottom of the publication window. Notice the text page icon change into the pointer tool.
3. Click on the page 2 icon to display page 2 of the template.
4. With page 2 displayed, position the text page icon at the top of the first column. Align the corner of the icon with the intersection of the 1.25-inch ruler guide and the left margin guide.
5. Click the mouse button and the rest of the text flows into column one.

All of the second article is now placed in our publication. Let's save the work we've done so far. Use the "Save as" command from the File menu. Save the file

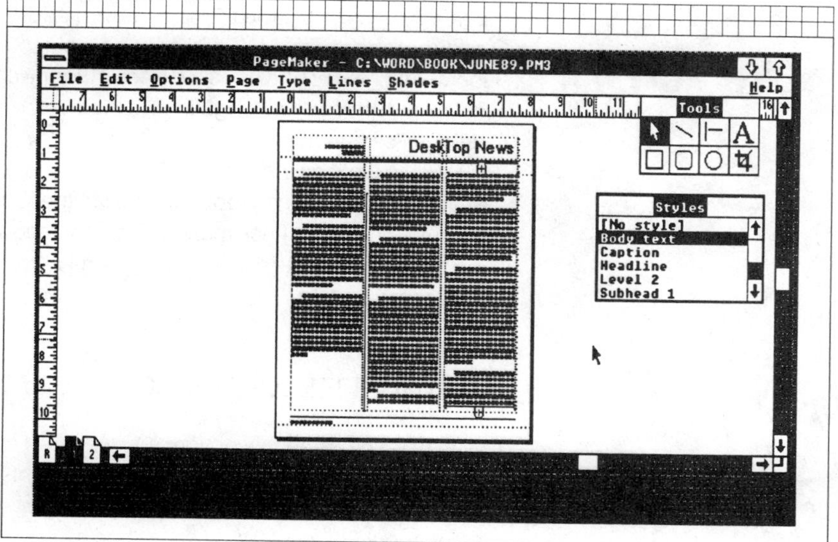

Figure 7.4: Second story placed on page 1

under the name JUNE89, indicating that this is the June, 1989 newsletter. This is the first publication of our newsletter, so be sure the "Publication" option button is highlighted. Once you've saved the file, you will return to the publication window. The name of the publication appears at the top of the publication window.

► OTHER "PLACE" COMMAND OPTIONS

The "Place" command also lets you replace an article with a new one, or insert a passage from a word processed file into your publication. To replace an entire story, you would click on the "Replacing entire story" option button in the Place dialog box (Figure 7.1). To insert text, you would first have to select the insertion point using the text tool. You can select an insertion point within a text block, or between text blocks. With the insertion point in place, you would click on the "Inserting text" option button in the Place dialog box.

► PLACING TEXT WITH THE AUTOFLOW AND SEMIAUTOMATIC OPTIONS

So far you have placed text from your word processed files in your PageMaker layout one column at a time. There is a faster way; in fact, there are two faster ways. PageMaker 3.0 gives you two other options for placing text—the "Autoflow" and "Semi-automatic" options.

The "Autoflow" option flows text into a PageMaker format from column to column, and from page to page. It even adds formatted pages if you don't have enough pages in your publication to place an entire file. The other method included in version 3.0 is called Semi-automatic flow. It flows text to the bottom of a column. A loaded text page icon is then automatically displayed, allowing you to quickly flow the remaining text.

Use the Options menu to set the type of text flow. PageMaker's default setting is manual (no check mark appears next to the "Autoflow" command in the Options menu). Click on a check mark next to "Autoflow" to turn this option on. Interrupting the autoflow of text selects the "Semi-automatic" option. Let's look first at the "Autoflow" option.

► USING THE AUTOFLOW FEATURE

To practice using this option, you will need to create a third story for our newsletter. The content of the story is not important—you could even use text from an existing file—but it should be at least two pages long. I have decided to place a story about Microsoft Word style sheets.

Version 3.0 users should place the third story using the "Autoflow" option; if you are using an earlier version of PageMaker, create the third story and place it in your newsletter publication in the same way you placed the previous two stories.

1. Click on the Options menu.
2. Select the "Autoflow" option. A check mark next to the option indicates that it is selected.
3. Select the "Place" command. (See Figure 7.1.)
4. Highlight the third story file name.
5. Click OK.

Now the icon changes to the Autoflow page icon. Let's position the icon and flow the text into our publication.

6. Click on the page 2 icon to display page 2 in the publication window.
7. Position the Autoflow icon at the top of the second column. Align the corner of the icon with the 1.25-inch ruler guide and the left column guide.
8. Click the mouse button.

Text from your third story automatically flows into the remaining two columns on page 2. In addition, PageMaker added formatted pages automatically so that the remainder of the article could be placed on page 3.

Next, use your resizing skills to align the new text blocks with our format. Align the top of the columns with the 1.25-inch ruler guide. Align the bottom of the columns with the bottom margin guide. When you are finished, page 2 should look like Figure 7.5, and page 3 should look like Figure 7.6.

You have now worked with two methods for placing a word processed file into PageMaker. First you used manual text flow, which places text in a layout one column at a time. This method requires you to click on the plus sign to flow in remaining text. Manual text flow is the only option available in early versions of PageMaker. You just used the "Autoflow" option to flow text in the third article. This method places an entire file in a layout at once. If necessary, extra pages are automatically added to accommodate all the text. The last method offered by PageMaker 3.0 for flowing in text is called Semi-automatic text flow.

► USING SEMI-AUTOMATIC TEXT FLOW

The "Semi-automatic" text flow option does not appear in the Options menu, but it can be accessed at any time while you are using the manual or autoflow methods. To go from "Autoflow" to the "Semi-automatic" flow option, you must

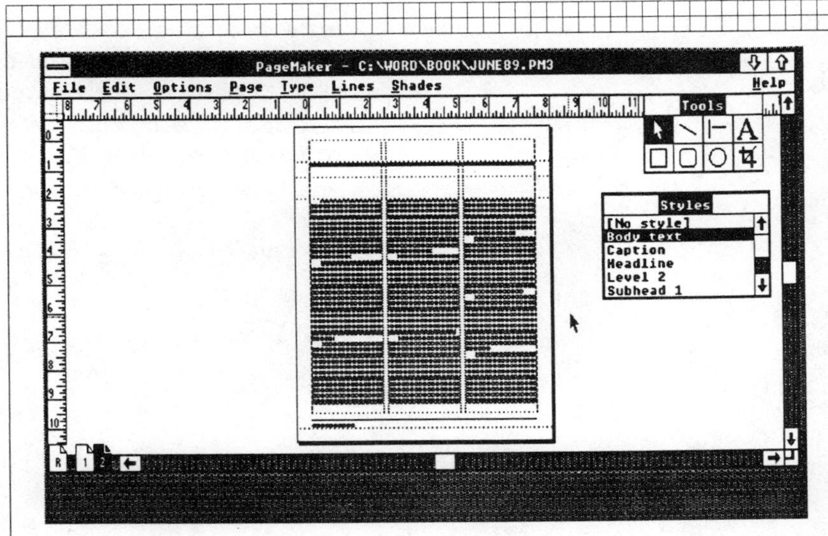

Figure 7.5: Page 2 with the third article resized

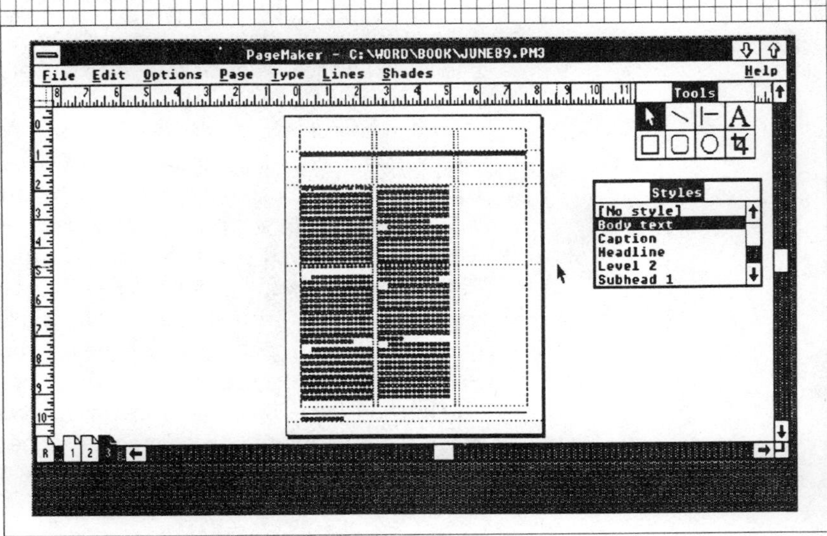

Figure 7.6: Page 3 with the third article resized

have activated the "Autoflow" command. Now, to interrupt the automatic flow of text, click the mouse button. The flow of text will stop and a windowshade handle will appear at the bottom of the text block. At this point you are ready to flow text semiautomatically. Click on the plus sign in the handle. The remaining text is loaded in the Semi-automatic text page icon. Next position the new icon where you want the text to resume flowing and click the mouse button.

To go from the manual to the semiautomatic text flow method, you must switch out of the manual mode by holding down the Shift key and clicking the mouse button. This activates the Semi-automatic text page icon. Now you must position this icon where you want the text to start flowing.

There is another fast way to switch text flow options. To go from manual text flow to Autoflow, hold down the Ctrl key and click the mouse button. Do the same to switch from Autoflow back to manual text flow—hold down the Ctrl key and click the mouse button.

To sum up what we have learned about switching text flow options:

- Hold down the Shift key and click the mouse button to switch from manual to Semi-automatic text flow.
- Hold down the Shift key and click the mouse button to switch from Autoflow to Semi-automatic text flow.
- Hold down the Ctrl key and click the mouse button to switch from Autoflow to manual flow.
- Hold down the Ctrl key and click the mouse button to switch from manual flow to Autoflow.

▸ PAGEMAKER TEXT BLOCKS

The files you just placed into PageMaker have been made into threaded text blocks. A *text block* refers to a grouping of text. PageMaker defines the boundaries of a text block by putting *handles* at the beginning and end, like the ones in Figure 7.4. There are two kinds of text handles. The *window-shade handles,* found at the beginning and end of a block, are used to resize a text block vertically by pulling it down or pushing it up the page. The *square handles,* found at all four corners of the text block, are used to resize a text block horizontally as well as vertically. A text block can be resized both from side to side, and up and down, simultaneously. If the handles are not displayed and you want to display them, point on the text with the pointer tool and click the mouse button. Whereas a word processor treats a file like one big block of text, PageMaker divides a file into many text blocks, each one corresponding to a column in your layout. PageMaker also threads each block of text to the next one in the file. You can always resize a text block, or even consolidate text blocks, because PageMaker keeps track of their order and threads them together.

PageMaker placed your word processed files within the column guides of your layout grid. The text flowed into the columns and stopped when it reached the bottom margin. It would have stopped, likewise, if it had run into something else, such as a graphic, a sidebar, or another article. When an entire text block cannot fit into a column, the windowshade handle on the bottom will show a plus sign (+). This means that more text is waiting to be flowed into PageMaker. But if all the text has been placed, the windowshade handle will show a number sign (#). This sign marks the end of a text block, like the windowshade handle in Figure 7.3.

The text block you last placed is always the selected text block. Another way to tell which is the selected block is to look for the handles—they will be showing.

► ALTERING AND MOVING PLACED TEXT BLOCKS

At times, you may want to unthread text. This is discussed later in this chapter.

PageMaker places your text by threading it together from beginning to end in a string of text blocks. This feature allows you to easily adjust text blocks without having to worry about losing anything.

When you lengthen a text block, PageMaker adds lines by taking them from the next block in the string. This means that lengthening one text block necessarily shortens the next one. In the same way, when you shorten a text block, you push the overflow text into the next block. And that block, in turn, pushes its overflow text into the next one. Only the last text block in a file can lengthen to accommodate all overflow text. Anything you do to one text block affects the others in the string of threaded text blocks.

You have placed two articles in your NEWSTEMP template. The first article, in column one of page 1, is one text block long. The second article has three text blocks, one in column two of page 1, one in column three of page 1, and one in column one of page 2. PageMaker has threaded together the three text blocks of the second article.

Thanks to the threading feature, you can break a text block down into as many text blocks as you like. You can also consolidate, delete, insert, and move text blocks. For example, you would break a text block into smaller blocks to make room for a graphic or a new story. Consolidating lets you thread together text blocks from different word processed files into one story. Or, you can consolidate text blocks when you want to have fewer to work with in a layout grid. Inserting lets you add a text block between already laid-out blocks. You can delete a text block when you don't need it anymore. These options are explained later in this chapter.

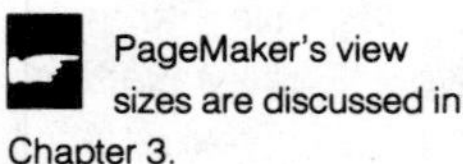

PageMaker's view sizes are discussed in Chapter 3.

You may find it easiest to work with text blocks if you adjust the view to Actual or 75% size. This is done by using the commands from the Page menu. The figures in this chapter appear in the size that best illustrates the functions being performed, which means that the figures are often shown in Fit-in-window view. However, making changes to the text blocks themselves is sometimes easier from the Actual Size view.

► RESIZING A TEXT BLOCK

A text block can be resized both vertically and horizontally. Column guides and margin guides restrict the flow of text into a publication, but sizing a text block is not necessarily limited by these guides.

There are three ways to resize a text block:

- Resize a text block vertically by changing its length.
- Resize a text block vertically by changing its width. (When a column of text is made wider, the length of text in the column decreases.)
- You can change both the length and width of a text block.

Resizing Text Blocks Vertically

Let's resize our text blocks to make room for article headlines at the top of the first page of our newsletter. But first you'll need to align the tops of the articles, which requires a new ruler guide.

1. Select the pointer tool from the Toolbox.
2. Click on the page 1 icon at the bottom of the screen to position page 1 in the publication window.
3. Point on the horizontal ruler at the top of the publication window.
4. Click and hold down the mouse button. The pointer will change into a two-directional arrow.
5. Slide the pointer down into the publication window. This drags down a dotted ruler guide.
6. Position the new ruler guide at the 1.75-inch mark on the vertical ruler.
7. Release the mouse button and the ruler guide is in place.

Now you are ready to resize the text blocks. You will make room at the top of the page for the headlines to our articles, which means that you will change the vertical size of the blocks. Select the text block you want to work with, in this case the text block in column one of page 1, by clicking on it. This makes the handles visible. To resize the text block:

1. Point in the center of the top windowshade handle in the first column on page 1.
2. Click and hold down the mouse button.
3. Slide the handle down and align it with the 1.75-inch ruler guide.

4. Release the mouse button and the text automatically adjusts to accommodate the new space at the top of the page.

Notice that the bottom windowshade handle now contains a plus sign. This is because, when you pulled down the top handle, overflow text was loaded into the bottom one. We must now slide the bottom handle down to accommodate this overflow text.

5. Point on the plus sign in the bottom windowshade handle of the article in the first column.
6. Click and hold down the mouse button.
7. Slide the handle down until it is aligned with the bottom margin guide.
8. Release the mouse button.

Now the remaining text flows automatically into the longer text block. The # sign in the bottom windowshade handle indicates that all the text has fit into the new, longer text block. Repeat these steps to align the article in columns two and three with the 1.75-inch ruler guide. When you are finished, page 1 should look like the one in Figure 7.7.

Resizing Text Blocks Vertically and Horizontally

Point on the center of a windowshade handle, as you did in the above exercise, to resize a text block vertically only. Point on the square corner handle when you

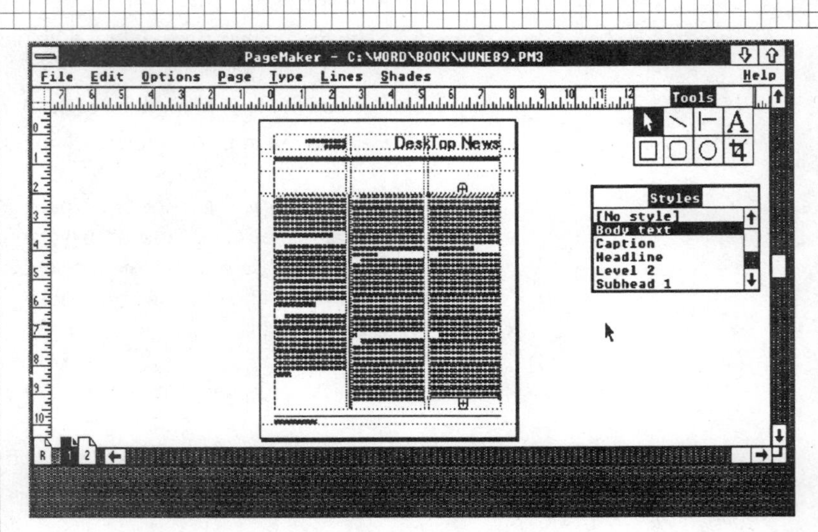

Figure 7.7: Text blocks resized using a windowshade handle

want to resize a text block both vertically and horizontally. When you point on a corner bottom handle, be sure to hold down the Shift key. This prevents the text block from moving horizontally. When you have resized the text block, release the mouse button. PageMaker automatically adjusts if you drag the text block over graphics or other text.

Next, we want to make room for a graphic at the bottom of the first page of our newsletter. The graphic will span across the bottom of columns two and three. First, place another horizontal ruler guide at the 7-inch mark on the vertical ruler. The new guide will mark where the text in columns two and three must end to accommodate our graphic.

This time let's try resizing a text block using a corner handle.

1. Hold down the Shift key.
2. Use the pointer tool to point on the right corner of the bottom window-shade handle in column two.
3. Click and hold down the mouse button.
4. Slide the handle up the column until it is aligned with the 7-inch ruler guide.
5. Release the mouse button.

Now you have shortened the text block in column two to make room for a graphic. Repeat these steps to shorten the text block in column three. Notice that the text automatically flows into the last text block on page 3. Remember, only the last text block in a file of threaded text blocks can automatically lengthen to accommodate all the text from shortened text blocks. Page 1, with resized text blocks, should now look like Figure 7.8.

► BREAKING UP A TEXT BLOCK

If you do not have PageMaker 3.0, each time you place an article longer than one column, you are in effect breaking up the text into threaded text blocks as you place it.

Breaking up a text block into several blocks is useful when you want to make room to insert other stories in between a threaded text block in your layout. On page 3, let's make room to insert a new text block in the second column. We will break up the text block in column two and flow the remaining text into the third column. Use your resizing skills to shorten the text block in column two on page 3. Bring the bottom of the text block up to the 5.5-inch mark on the vertical ruler, as shown in Figure 7.9.

Now we are ready to break up the text block.

1. Select the text block in column two, page 3. Remember, you can tell when a text block is selected because the handles are displayed.
2. Click on the plus sign of the bottom handle of the text block. The text page icon is loaded with the remaining text.

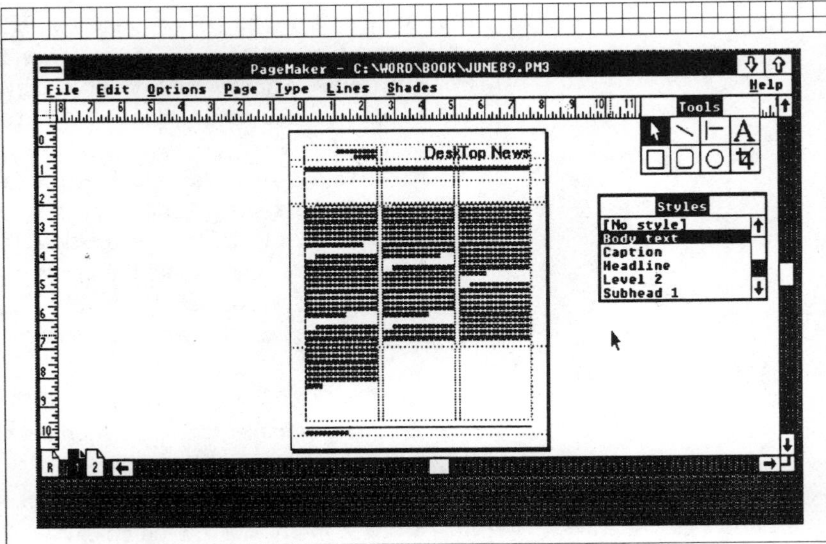

Figure 7.8: Text blocks resized using a corner handle

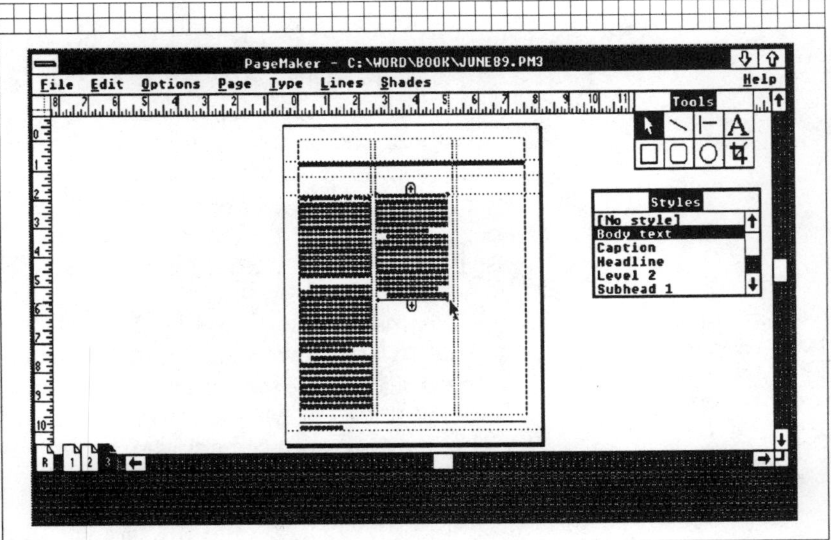

Figure 7.9: Shortened text block

3. Position the text page icon at the top of the third column on page 3. Align the corner of the icon with the intersection of the ruler guide and the left column guide.
4. Click the mouse button and the text will flow into the column.

You have now created another text block in column three. This text block is still threaded to the other text blocks in the same article even though it is positioned in a different column now. PageMaker will readjust for any resizings you make to the first text blocks in the article by resizing the last text block. This feature is very useful when you are working in a newsletter or magazine format and you want to continue a story in a later column or on a later page. You can make changes anywhere in a story without having to readjust the threaded text blocks. You can break up a text block into as many new blocks as you want.

► INSERTING A TEXT BLOCK

You may find you want to insert a text block between already existing text blocks in your layout. For instance, you may decide to continue a story in a different column in order to insert another story, or to make room to place a graphic.

Let's insert a text block between the two blocks of text you just created in columns two and three of page 3. The text block we insert will not be threaded to the third article. It will be a separate text block. Remember, each story is threaded only to its own text blocks. Let's insert a text block created with PageMaker's text tool.

1. Use the scroll bars to position a blank area of the pasteboard on your screen.
2. Point to the text icon in the Toolbox and click the mouse button. This selects the text tool.
3. Position the text tool in the pasteboard and click the mouse button to display the flashing cursor.

Now you will type the text block using the text tool.

4. Since the article I placed was about Microsoft Word style sheets, I'm going to insert a text block that will be a helpful hint to PageMaker users working with Microsoft Word. If you want, you can use my example, or else you can insert a text block pertaining to your own third article. For the purposes of this example, I will type the following text block:

   PageMaker Users:
   Use Microsoft Word style sheets with your PageMaker layout to save time formatting. PageMaker 3.0 imports and exports Word files.

5. Select the pointer tool from the Toolbox.
6. Point on the text block in the pasteboard.
7. Click and hold down the mouse button. A four-directional arrow appears.

8. Position the text block in the blank area at the bottom of column two on page 3, and release the mouse button.

You have now positioned a new text block between threaded text blocks of the third article in our newsletter. Page 3 should now look like Figure 7.10. If you need to resize the text block to make it fit within the column guides, click on the corner handles of the text block and line them up with the column guides.

▸ DELETING AN UNTHREADED TEXT BLOCK

To remove an unthreaded text block, you must first select it. Let's remove the last text block in the second article, the text block in column one on page 2. First, position page 2 in the publication window by clicking on the Page 2 icon. Be sure you have selected the text block in column one.

1. With the text block selected, click on the Edit menu.
2. Click on the "Cut" command. This removes the selected text block.

The "Cut" command moves the text block to the Clipboard, a temporary holding place, where your deleted text is saved in case you want to place it somewhere else. (You will use the Clipboard and the text in it later in this chapter.) Click on the "Clear" command to delete a text block permanently. Either command causes the selected text block to disappear from your publication.

As you can see in Figure 7.11, when you delete or remove a text block, it leaves a blank area where your text block used to be. PageMaker will not automatically fill in the blank area with text blocks in the layout that follow the removed one. You must remove the blank area in the layout that you created when you deleted the text block. This requires you to move text blocks.

▸ MOVING TEXT BLOCKS

We now have a gap in our layout, a blank first column on page 2. Let's move the text blocks in the third article into the first column on page 2.

1. Click on the text in the second column to select it.
2. Click on the blank top windowshade handle. The text page icon will load up with text.
3. Position the text page icon at the top of the first column on page 2. Align the corner of the handle with the intersection of the ruler guide and the left margin guide.
4. Click the mouse button and the text will flow into the column.

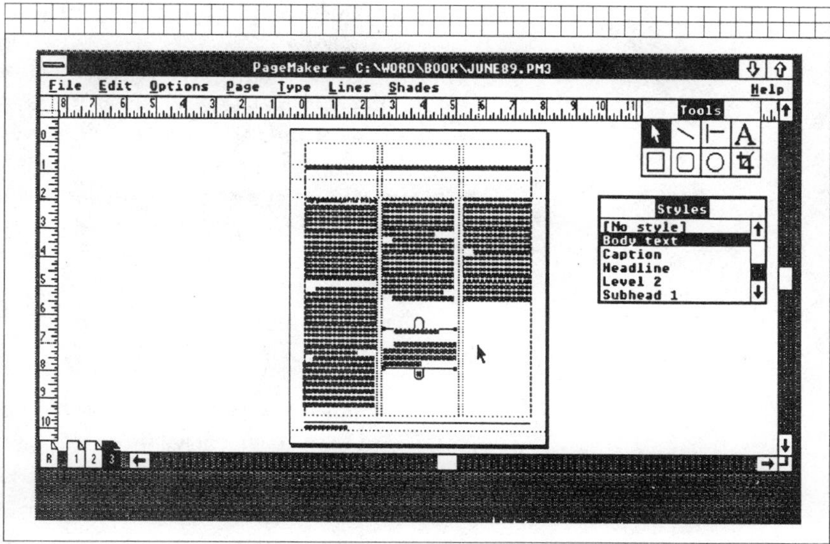

Figure 7.10: The inserted text block on page 3

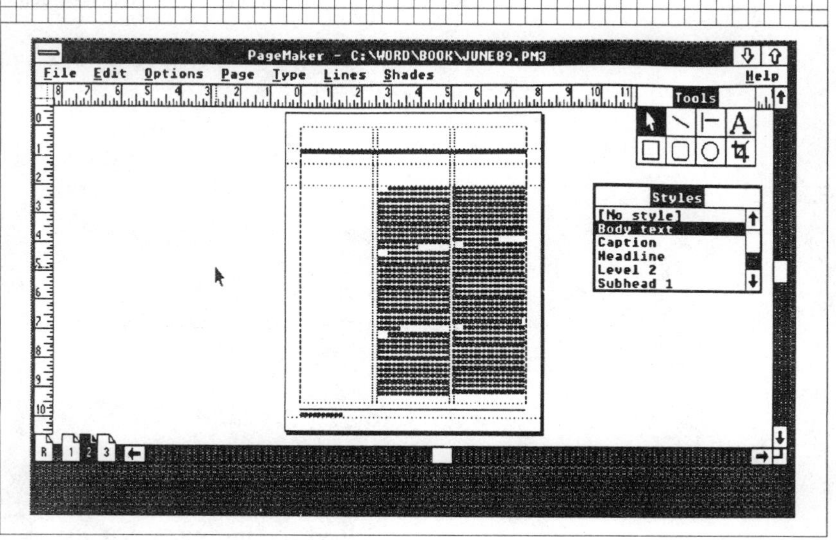

Figure 7.11: Page 2, after a text block was removed

Notice that the article automatically adjusted to flow into the three columns on page 2. The remainder of the article, on page 3, also adjusted automatically to a new position. Remember, this is because the text blocks were threaded together.

► DELETING A THREADED TEXT BLOCK

In this chapter you already practiced deleting a text block. But the text block you deleted was the last text block in the article, so the remaining threaded text blocks were not affected. Deleting a threaded text block in the middle of an article is done differently because you have to consolidate the text blocks that surround the deleted one. Let's delete a threaded text block in the middle of an article.

First, click on the page 3 icon to position page 3 in the publication window. The first column on page 3, a single text block, contains three paragraphs of text. We want to delete the middle paragraph. To do this, we will first need to split the text block into three text blocks. Be sure you have selected the text block in column one of page 3.

1. Shorten the text block up to the bottom of the first paragraph in the column, so that only the first paragraph shows.
2. Click on the plus sign in the shortened text block.
3. Position the text page icon in the blank area just below the shortened text block. Click the mouse button. The remaining text will flow into the column as a second text block.
4. Repeat this procedure to create a third text block for the third paragraph.

Column 1 on page 3 should now contain three text blocks. Let's delete the middle one.

1. Select the middle text block so that the handles are showing.
2. Click on the Edit menu.
3. Click on the "Clear" command.

The middle text block is now removed from the column, as shown in Figure 7.12. The space occupied by the deleted text block remains in the column.

► CONSOLIDATING TEXT BLOCKS

Now that you have deleted a text block, you must get rid of the blank space it left behind. To do so, you must consolidate the text blocks on either side of the blank space. You will find many instances in which you want to consolidate text blocks. You would consolidate in order to have fewer text blocks to work with. Or, suppose you spread a story over several pages of a publication and later decide to put the story onto one page—then you would consolidate. A large text block is easier to work with than many small ones.

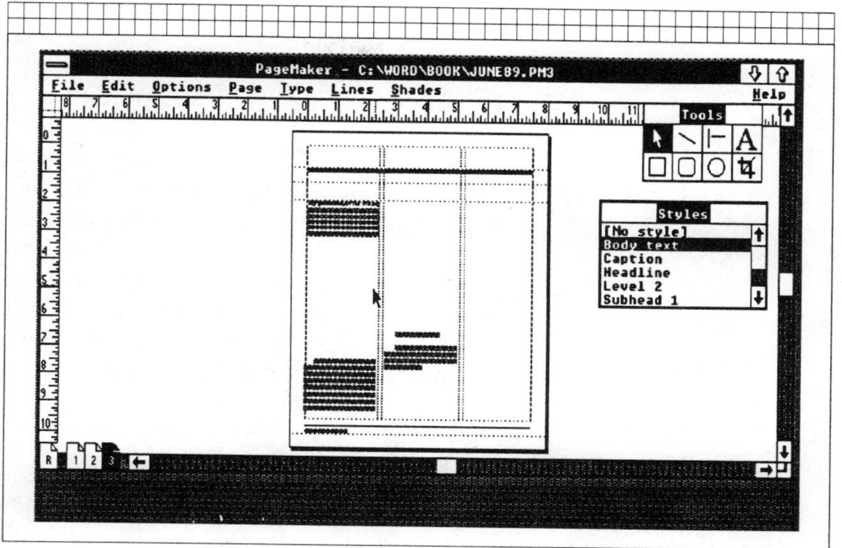

Figure 7.12: Page 3, after deleting a threaded text block

Let's consolidate the two text blocks in column one on page 3. You will have to delete the text blocks without deleting the text. Let's start with the text block at the bottom of the column.

1. Use the pointer to select the bottom text block.
2. Point on either the top or bottom windowshade handle.
3. Click and hold the mouse button.
4. Slide the handle up until it meets the handle of the other text block.

It appears as if the text block is emptied of text, as shown in Figure 7.13. The two plus signs in the handles let you know that text is included in these merged handles, so don't worry about losing the text in the block; it will soon be recovered.

The next step is to make room below the first text block for the text block you are adding to it.

5. Point on the first text block to select it.
6. Point on the bottom windowshade handle.
7. Click and hold down the mouse button.
8. Slide the handle down to lengthen the text block until it includes all the text in the second text block. Release the mouse button.

Figure 7.14 shows the two text blocks consolidated into one.

► ALIGNING TEXT BLOCKS

When you move a text block to a new page, you may need to align it. Aligning makes your publication look professional. Text blocks can be aligned by their left edges or along their baselines. When text blocks are stacked on top of each other, make sure their left edges line up evenly. Text blocks placed side by side should line up on the same baselines. The *baseline* is the line on which the letters sit. So far, you have been moving text blocks using the Fit-in-window view because the handles are visible even from that view. However, when you align text blocks, you may want to change to the Actual Size view for the sake of accuracy.

Aligning Stacked Text Blocks

You probably noticed, when you consolidated the text blocks on page 3, the text block we inserted earlier standing alone in column two. Let's move this text block into the space below the consolidated text blocks in column one. We will then align the two text blocks. Use the pointer tool to pick up the text block in column two and move it into column one.

Notice that the stacked text blocks in Figure 7.15 are not aligned. In this case, since the text blocks are stacked on top of each other, you will align them with the

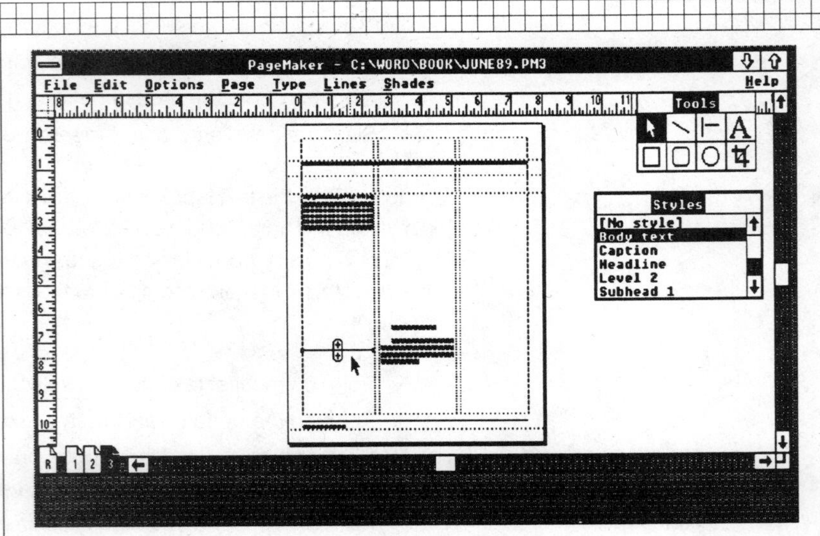

Figure 7.13: Merging the two handles of a text block

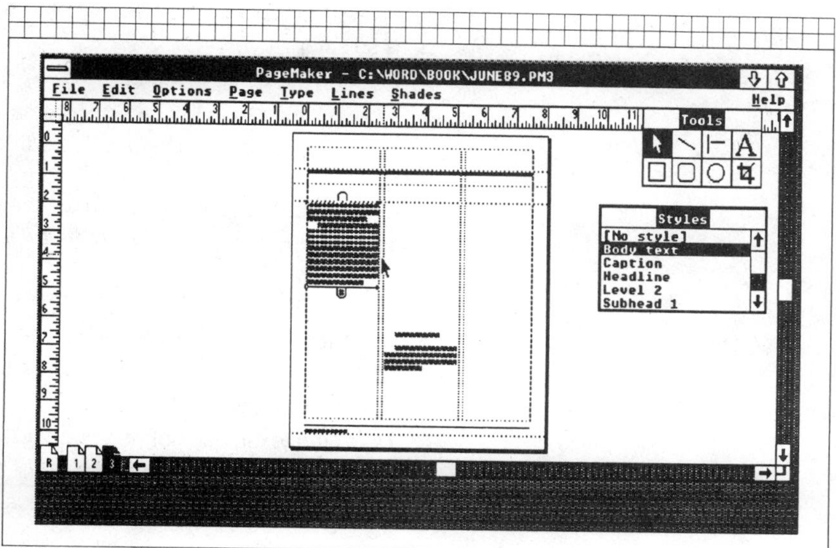

Figure 7.14: Consolidated text blocks

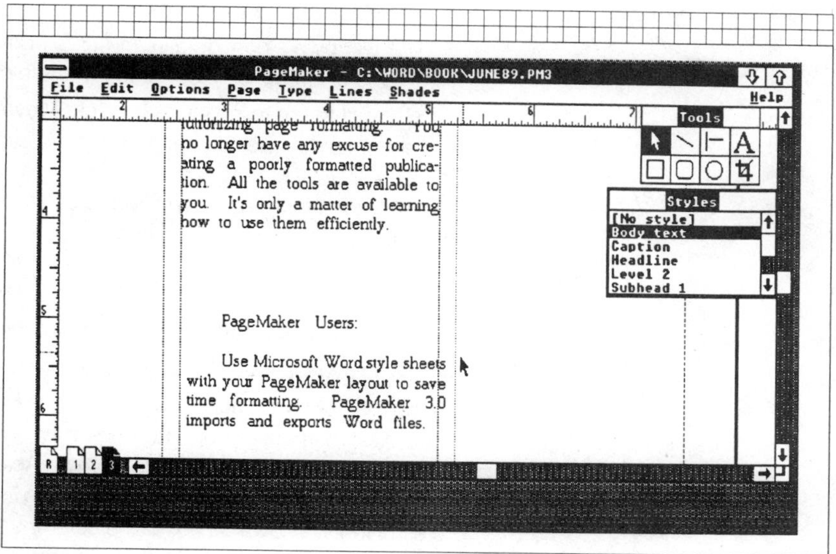

Figure 7.15: Column with two unaligned text blocks

left-hand column guide. If there wasn't a column guide by which to align the text blocks, you would have to drag a ruler guide from the edge of the publication window to give you a guide to follow.

1. To align the left edges of the text blocks, make sure that the top text block is selected.
2. Click on the Options menu.
3. Click on the "Snap to guides" command. A check mark next to the command indicates it has been selected.

The "Snap to guides" command makes the guides act like magnets. The top text block is now lined up perfectly. Let's now align the second text block.

4. Use the pointer tool to select the second text block.
5. Point anywhere in the second text block.
6. Click and hold down the mouse button. The pointer turns into a four-directional arrow.
7. Move the text block until it is lined up with the guide.
8. Release the mouse button. Because the Snap to guides feature is still active, the text block snaps into place.

As explained in Chapter 4, leading is the amount of vertical space between the tops of the capital letters of two successive lines of text.

You may also want to align text blocks so they have the same leading. To do this:

1. Select the top text block.
2. Pull down a horizontal ruler guide from the top of the publication window and line it up with the bottom handle of the text block you just selected.
3. Point to the following text block. Move it until its handle lines up with the horizontal ruler guide, as shown in Figure 7.16.

The two text blocks are now aligned correctly one on top of the other, and the leading in both blocks is the same.

Aligning Text Blocks Side by Side

It's easier to work with the Actual Size view when aligning text blocks side by side than the Fit-in-window view because it makes the text easier to read. Choose the "Actual size" command from the Page menu to select the Actual Size view. To do the following exercises, you should have an Actual Size view of your publication.

You already aligned the stacked text in the first column on page 3. The next step is to align the side-by-side text in the columns. We placed two different articles on page 1, so the columns may not be aligned side by side. Click on the page 1 icon to position page 1 in the publication window. You may find it easier to align text blocks side by side when the Snap to guides feature is turned off.

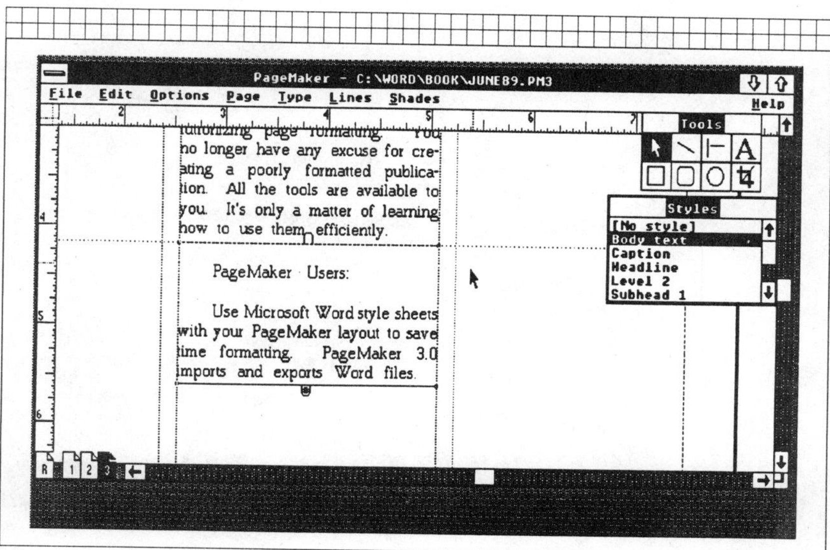

Figure 7.16: Aligned stacked text blocks

1. Pull down a horizontal ruler guide and line it up on the baseline of the text in the first column.
2. Point on the second column of text.
3. Click and hold down the mouse button. The four-directional arrow appears.
4. Line up the baseline of text in the second column with the baseline of text in the first column, as shown in Figure 7.17.
5. Release the mouse button.

You can now remove the horizontal guide. Point on the guide, and click and hold the mouse button. Drag the guide up to the top of the publication window. It will disappear.

► USING THE CLIPBOARD TO UNTHREAD TEXT BLOCKS

Changing the size of a text block or editing text from a text block may require you to make many adjustments to the publication. This is because changes to one text block necessarily affect other text blocks. PageMaker threads text together, which makes text move from one page to the next. The changes you make in the early stages of a publication may affect many pages to come. For example, if you

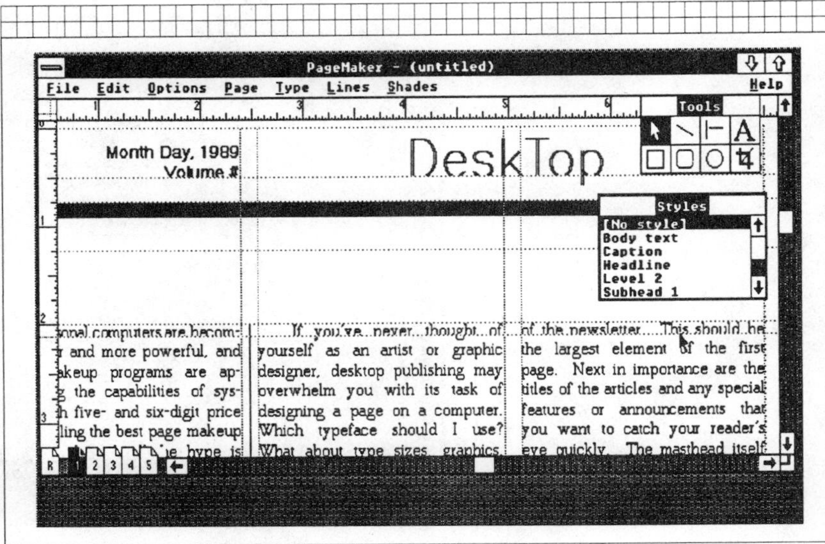

Figure 7.17: Aligning text blocks side by side

delete large portions of text, you may end up with blank spaces at the end of your publication.

PageMaker helps you cope with the problems of threading by allowing you to unthread text. Unthreading is very helpful, for example, when you have completed most of your pasteup, only to find that you need to change the size of a text block significantly. When a text block is unthreaded, you may edit it without affecting the surrounding text blocks.

You can also store text on the pasteboard. This method is preferable because if you later copy or cut another text block to the Clipboard, you may lose your text block. The Clipboard only holds one item at a time.

To unthread text, you must first move it to the Clipboard. The *Clipboard* is a hidden area within Windows for temporarily holding text or a graphic until you are ready to place it in your publication.

A text block, once it has been cut to the Clipboard, is no longer threaded to the other text blocks from which it came. Use the "Paste" command to paste a text block from the Clipboard back into the publication. You can paste the text block on a new page, or even in a new publication. Paste text with either the pointer or the text tool. Use the pointer tool when you want the text block to look exactly as it did when you cut it to the Clipboard. But keep in mind that to paste text with the pointer tool, the text block has to have been cut to the Clipboard using the pointer tool in the first place. By using the pointer tool to cut a text block to the Clipboard, you can retain the original line length of the text block. You must also use the pointer tool to place the text if you want it to be the same line length as before.

Paste with the text tool when you want to flow text into a publication. Start by selecting an intersection point for the text to flow. Text pasted with the text tool flows between the column or margin guide, ignoring the line length of the text block when it was cut to the Clipboard.

In an earlier section, "Deleting an Unthreaded Text Block," you used the "Cut" command to move the remainder of our second article to the Clipboard. Unless you used the "Cut" command since then, that text block will still be on the Clipboard. Let's paste the text block into our publication using the pointer tool.

1. If it is not already selected, select the pointer tool from the Toolbox.
2. Be sure you are positioned on page 3. We are pasting the text block into the second column.
3. Click on the Edit menu.
4. Select the "Paste" command.

The text block is placed in the middle of your screen on top of whatever is there, as shown in Figure 7.18. Now you must position the text block where you want it on the page, using the pointer tool.

5. Point on the pasted text block.
6. Click and hold down the mouse button. The four-directional arrow appears.
7. Move the text block into the second column on page 3.
8. Release the mouse button. The text is now pasted from the Clipboard to page 3. Now save your work.

To paste with the text tool instead of the pointer, select the text tool from the Toolbox. Position the text tool where you want to start pasting. Make sure to paste

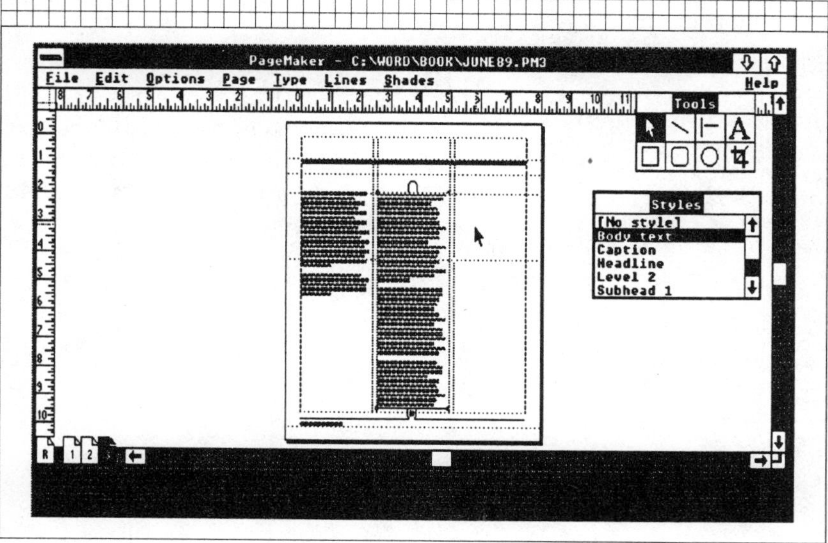

Figure 7.18: Text pasted with the pointer tool

the text outside of any existing text blocks. Click the mouse button to position the flashing cursor. Choose the "Paste" command from the Edit menu. If you paste within column guides, the text block will flow between the column guides until it reaches the end of the text block or the bottom of a page. If you paste the text block in the pasteboard, the line length will carry to the edge of the pasteboard.

► MORE CLIPBOARD USES

You can also use the "Copy" command in the Edit menu to move text to the Clipboard. This command sends a copy of the text to the Clipboard and leaves the text in the publication. You can also use the Clipboard to hold a text file that you created with another Windows application until you are ready to place it into your PageMaker publication. If you installed the full version of Windows, you can also use the Clipboard to cut text or a graphic from one Windows application and place it in your PageMaker publication without exiting PageMaker. Just use the Windows environment to run both programs at once. You can also use the Clipboard to cut and paste between publications, or within one publication. The important thing to remember is that the Clipboard only holds one item at a time.

For more information on using the Clipboard or the Windows environment, refer to the Microsoft Windows documentation.

Any text you move from PageMaker to the Clipboard retains its PageMaker type specifications. However, if you have cut or copied text to the Clipboard and you close PageMaker, the type specifications will be lost next time you reopen PageMaker. This happens because PageMaker assigns its default specifications to text in the Clipboard when you close PageMaker. Text from other Windows applications are also given PageMaker's default specifications.

► SUMMARY

In this chapter you learned how to place word processed files into your PageMaker publication. You also learned how to manipulate text blocks. In the next chapter, you will use PageMaker's own text writing capabilities to add and change text in your PageMaker newsletter.

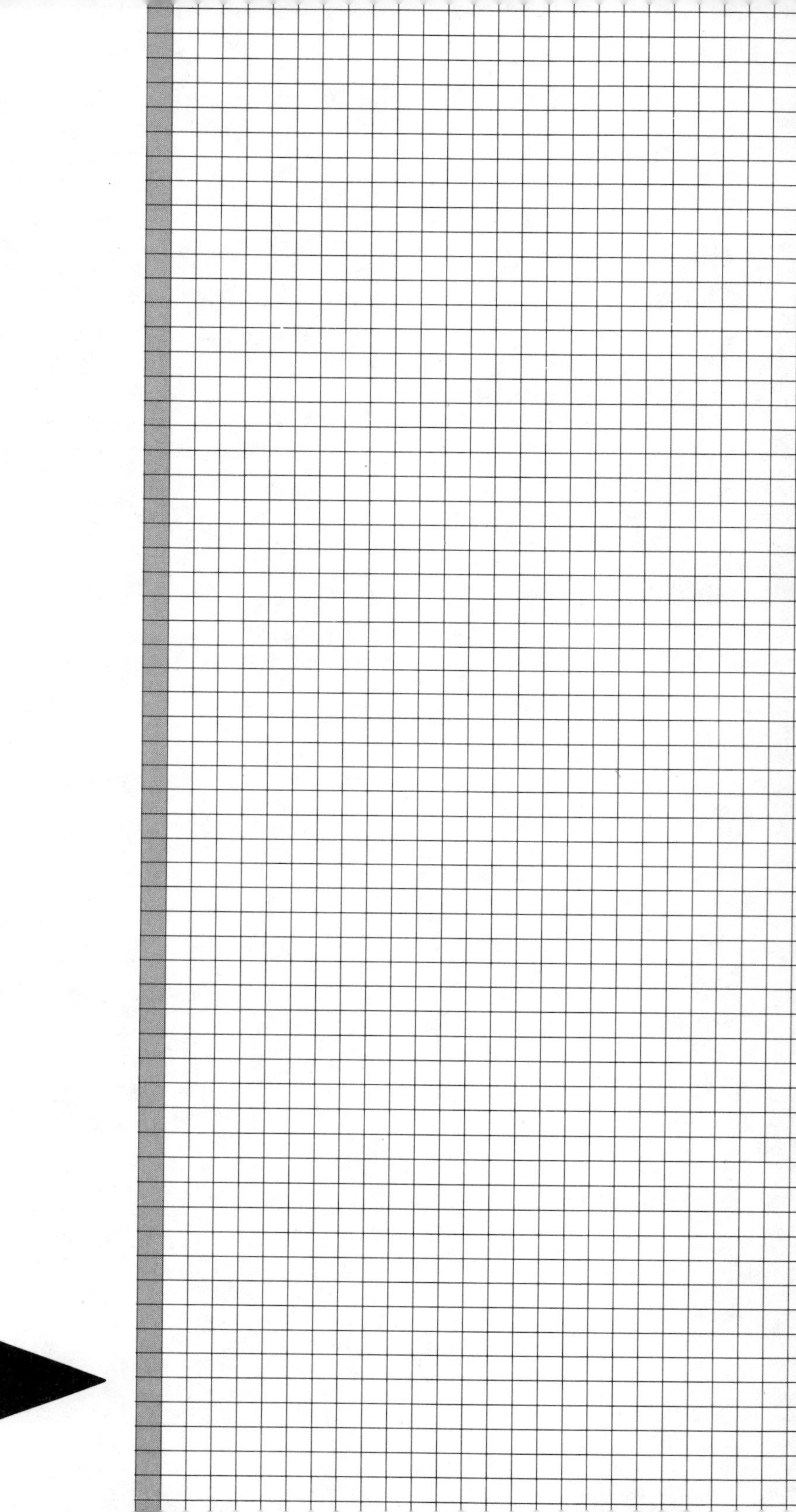

▶ 8 MAKING TEXT CHANGES

To insert text within a text block, 154

select the text tool, position the I-beam at the insertion point, click the mouse button, and start typing.

To highlight text, 156

select the text tool, position the I-beam in front of the text, click and hold down the mouse button, and drag the I-beam along the text until it is highlighted.

To replace existing text, 156

use the text tool to highlight the text you want to replace, then type in the new text.

To create special typesetting characters, 157

select the text tool, position the I-beam in the place you want the character to appear, and type in special keystroke combinations.

To move text using the Clipboard, 159

use the "Cut" command from the Edit menu to move the highlighted text to the Clipboard. Select an insertion point, then use the "Paste" command from the Edit menu to paste the text into a new location.

To replace text using the Clipboard, 161

highlight the text to be replaced and use the "Paste" command from the Edit menu to replace the highlighted text with text in the Clipboard.

To delete text, 162

highlight the text to be deleted, and use the "Clear" command from the Edit menu.

To place text outside of a text block, 163

create the text in the pasteboard and place it on the page outside of the text handles of any text already on the page.

To set the type specifications, 165

highlight the text and use the "Define styles" or "Type specs" command from the Type menu.

To enhance text with type style options, 169

highlight the text and select the "Style" option from the Type menu.

To select paragraph specifications, 173

highlight the text and select the "Paragraph" option from the Type menu.

To adjust the word spacing in ragged text, 178

select "Auto hyphenation" from the Paragraph Specifications dialog box. Click on the "Spacing" command from the Type menu to see the Spacing Attributes dialog box. Fill in a hyphenation zone value in the hyphenation zone text box.

To use the style sheet from your word processor, 183

match the name of the style in your word processed file with the name of the style in the PageMaker 3.0 style sheet.

To export text to your word processor, 184

select the text and choose the "Export" command from the File menu.

In this chapter, you will learn how to use PageMaker's text tool to add to or change the text you place into PageMaker. You will also learn how to designate the type specifications you've decided upon for your publication and how to set up paragraph specifications such as the space between paragraphs, hyphenation, indents, and more. You should have already made many of these decisions during the preliminary planning sessions in Chapter 4. Now you will learn how to implement them.

► EDITING TEXT WITHIN A TEXT BLOCK

Text within text blocks can be edited in two ways. You can use the text tool to insert, modify, or delete text within a text block. The second method, called cut and paste, allows you to move text around. You used this method in the last chapter when you cut text from a text block, moved it to the Clipboard, and pasted it into your PageMaker layout in a new location.

► USING THE TEXT TOOL FOR EDITING

PageMaker's text tool works best for creating small bits of text for your publication, such as mastheads, headings, or section titles. You can use the text tool either to make changes or additions inside a text block, or to type outside the handles of an already placed text block, as you will do later in this chapter.

The best way to add text to your publication with the PageMaker text tool is to type the text in the pasteboard area, make any necessary changes to it, and then place it in your publication. Otherwise, as you know, making changes to text within a text block affects all the threaded text blocks. For this reason, it is best to make changes to your text in the pasteboard area so that you can paste it into a text block in one step and make any subsequent adjustments to the threaded text blocks only once.

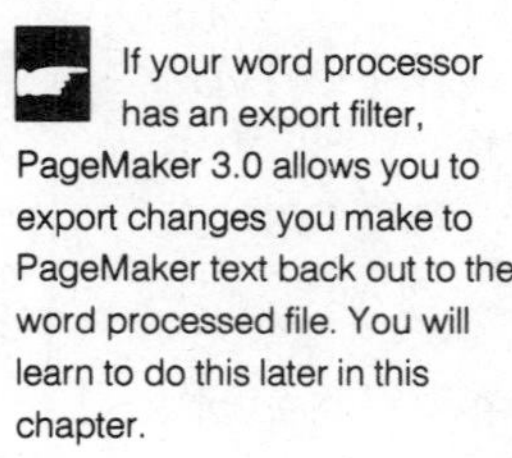
If your word processor has an export filter, PageMaker 3.0 allows you to export changes you make to PageMaker text back out to the word processed file. You will learn to do this later in this chapter.

Remember, if you type text within a block of text that you already placed in PageMaker from your word processor, the new text will only appear in the PageMaker publication, not in your word processed file.

Inserting Text with the Text Tool

Let's practice inserting text into our newsletter. If you closed the file after the last chapter, use the "Open" command from the File menu to select the newsletter. Let's insert a sentence into the first article we placed in the newsletter. If you used the short article file we created in Chapter 2, insert the sentence used in the following exercise. If you inserted a different short article, use the same procedure to insert a sentence of your own.

Now let's insert the sentence. Be sure page 1 is positioned in the publication window. If necessary, click on the page 1 icon.

1. Click on the text tool icon in the Toolbox.
2. Position the I-beam in the last paragraph in the first column on page 1.
3. Click the right mouse button to switch to the Fit-in-window view.
4. Position the I-beam between the two sentences in the last paragraph. Click the mouse button to position the flashing cursor, as shown in Figure 8.1.
5. Type the following sentence:

   Figure 1 illustrates one of the new features of PageMaker 3.0, templates.

The sentence is now inserted into the text block. It is threaded to the text block and acts just like all other text within the block. Notice, when you insert text within a column, that the new text conforms to the column guides, as shown in Figure 8.2. If you make a typing error, use either the backspace key to go back a space and correct the error, or use the replace text method explained later in this chapter.

As a text block fills with new text, the bottom handle will change from a number symbol to a plus symbol if the text that was pushed along by the inserted text needs to be placed. Whenever you insert text, be sure to check the bottom handle of the text block and place the additional text if necessary.

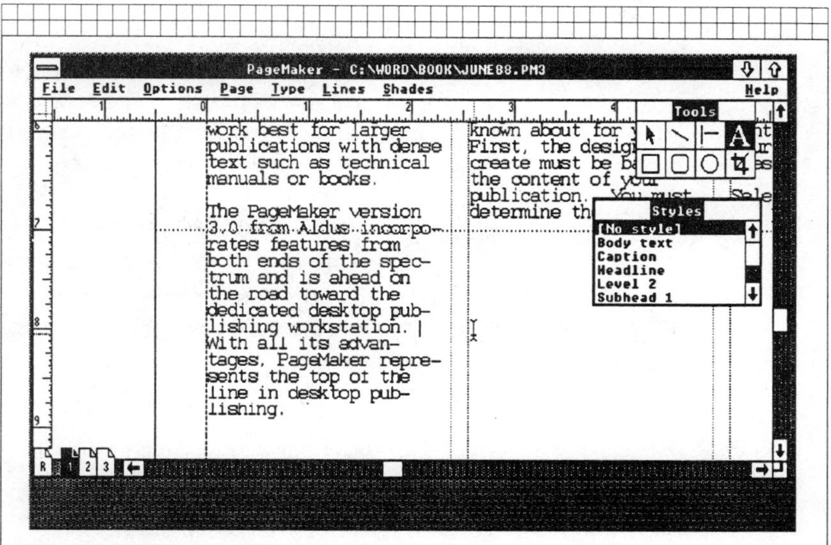

Figure 8.1: Inserting a sentence

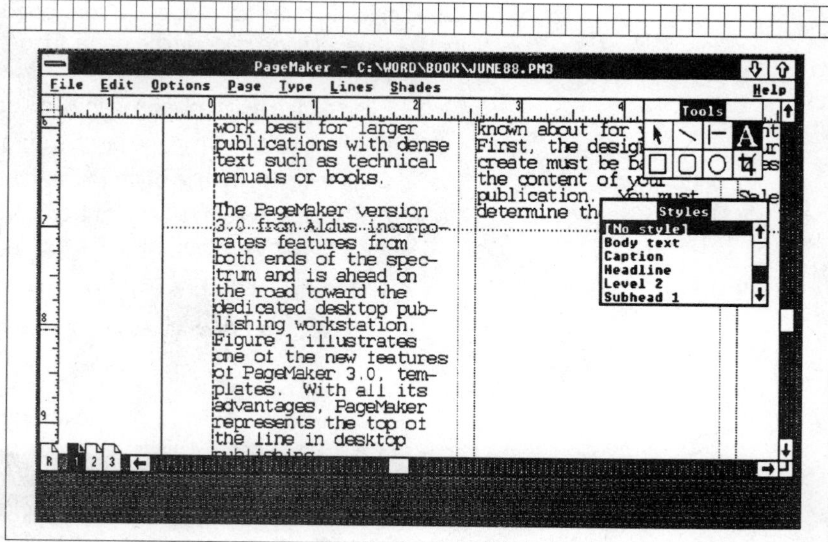

Figure 8.2: Text inserted within a text block

Replacing Text with the Text Tool

Occasionally you may want to make changes within a text block by replacing existing text with new text. This may be necessary if you discover a spelling error, or if you just decide to do some editing.

Let's practice replacing text by changing a sentence in the second paragraph of the second article on page 1. The sentence begins, ''You can avoid the pitfalls by sticking to ...'' The first step in replacing existing text is to highlight the text that needs to be replaced. To highlight text:

1. Select the text tool from the Toolbox.
2. Position the text tool at the beginning of the sentence. Click and hold down the mouse button.
3. Drag the I-beam across the sentence, highlighting the following portion of the sentence:

   You can avoid the pitfalls by sticking to

4. Release the mouse button and the text remains highlighted, as shown in Figure 8.3.

Once the text is highlighted, type in the new text to make the highlighted text disappear.

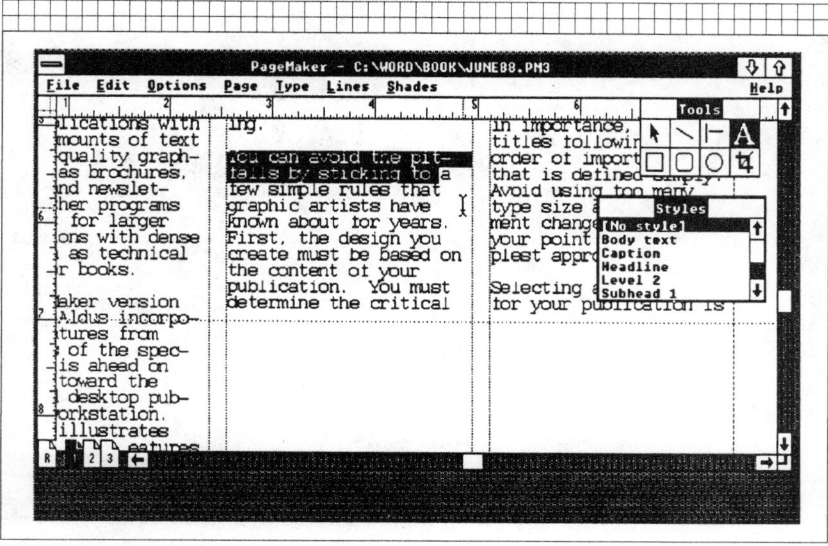

Figure 8.3: Highlighting text with the text tool

5. Type in the following new text:

    Let's discuss

The highlighted text is replaced with the new text, as shown in Figure 8.4. The sentence now reads

Let's discuss a few simple rules that graphic artists have know about for years.

► CREATING SPECIAL CHARACTERS

The text tool is also helpful for including special characters in your publication that are not available from your word processor. Table 8.1 lists the special characters you can create and the keystrokes used to create them.

Try inserting one of these special characters in your publication. For this example, we are going to insert a registration mark in the first article on page 1. The last sentence in the article talks about PageMaker. Since PageMaker is a registered trademark of Aldus, we will place a registration mark next to PageMaker in the article.

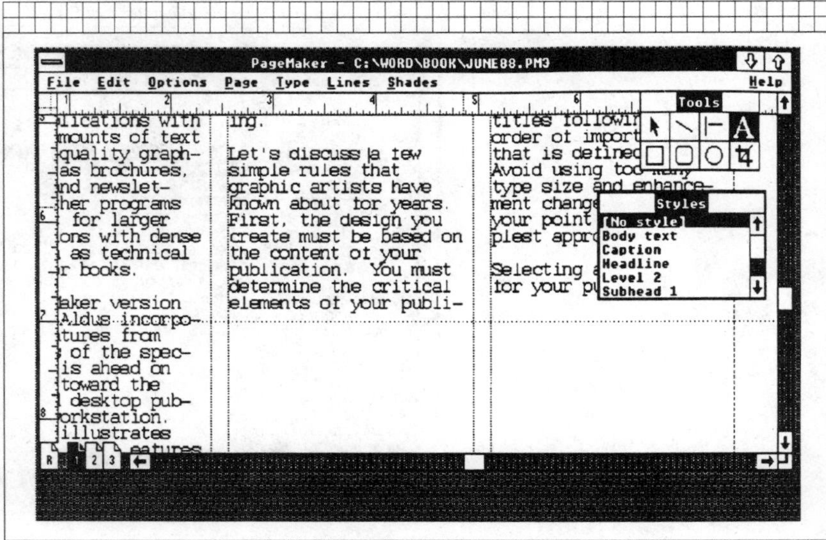

Figure 8.4: Replacing text

Be sure you are positioned on page 1.

1. Select a view that allows you to read and insert text easily, like the Actual Size view.
2. Click on the text tool from the Toolbox.
3. Position the I-beam in column one, just after the word *PageMaker* in the first sentence of the last paragraph in the article.
4. Click the mouse button and the flashing cursor will appear in the text.
5. Press the key combination for a registration mark:

   Ctrl Shift R

The registration mark is now inserted, as shown in Figure 8.5.

► CUTTING AND PASTING TEXT

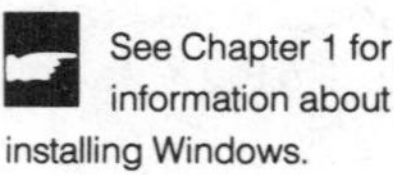

See Chapter 1 for information about installing Windows.

As you've learned, cutting and pasting text involves moving text to the Clipboard. Once the text is in the Clipboard, you can paste it to a new location in the same publication, into a new publication, or to an entirely different Windows application if you installed Windows separately from the PageMaker Install program. PageMaker's cut and paste method is similar to the Move or Copy command in

Special character	Keystrokes
Opening double quote (“)	Ctrl Shift [
Closing double quote (”)	Ctrl Shift]
Opening single quote (‘)	Ctrl [
Closing single quote (’)	Ctrl]
Em dash (—)	Ctrl Shift =
En dash (–)	Ctrl =
Em space (Point size)	Ctrl Shift M
En space (1/2 point size)	Ctrl Shift N
Bullet (•)	Ctrl Shift 8
Registration mark (®)	Ctrl Shift R
Copyright mark (©)	Ctrl Shift C
Paragraph mark (¶)	Ctrl Shift 7
Section mark (§)	Ctrl Shift 6
Fixed space (depends on font)	Ctrl Spacebar
Thin space (1/4 point size)	Ctrl Shift T

Table 8.1: Special-Character Keystrokes

your word processor. But PageMaker works with text blocks differently than a word processor does, so moving text around between threaded text blocks requires you to first move the text to a holding area, the Clipboard. From there, you can paste the text into a new location. You already know how to move text to the Clipboard using the ''Cut'' and ''Copy'' command options in the Edit menu. Remember, the ''Copy'' command both leaves the text block intact in your publication and places a copy of it in the Clipboard. The ''Cut'' command removes the text block from your publication and places it in the Clipboard.

Moving Text with the Cut and Paste Method

Let's practice moving text using the cut and paste method.

1. Use the text tool to highlight the third and fourth sentences in paragraph one of the second article, as shown in Figure 8.6.

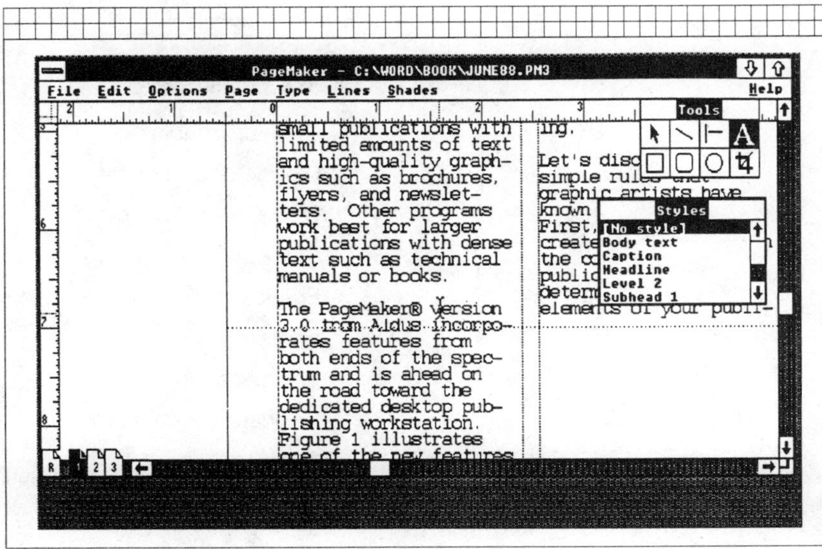

Figure 8.5: Inserted registration mark

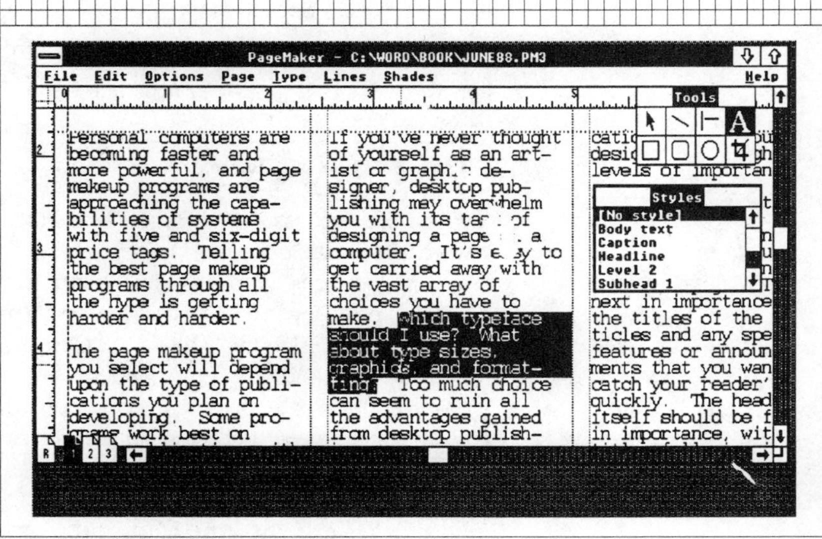

Figure 8.6: Highlighted text

2. Select the "Cut" command from the Edit menu. This moves the text to the Clipboard.
3. With the text cut to the Clipboard, use the text tool to select an insertion

point after the word *computer* in the first sentence of the second article.

4. Choose the "Paste" command option from the Edit menu.

The text from the Clipboard is inserted into the text block in a new place, as shown in Figure 8.7. Notice that it automatically conforms to the existing column or margin guides.

Replacing Text with the Cut and Paste Method

You can also use the cut and paste method to replace text. First you use the text tool to highlight text that you want to replace in a text block. You then replace the highlighted text by pasting in text from the Clipboard.

To do this, point the text tool on the first character of the text you want to replace. Click and hold the mouse button down while you drag the text tool across the text you want to replace. This highlights the text. Release the mouse button. Always be sure you've highlighted the correct text. Now choose the "Paste" command option from the Edit menu and the text in the Clipboard will replace the highlighted text.

This method of replacing text is useful when you want to replace text in the publication with a large block of text in the Clipboard. When you want to replace a small text block, type the text directly on the page without using the Clipboard.

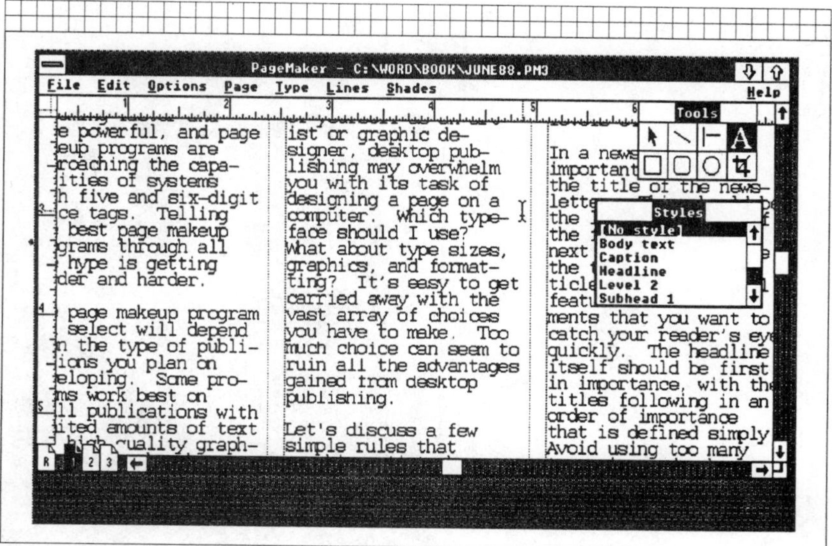

Figure 8.7: Moved text

▶ DELETING TEXT

You have already learned that one way to delete text is to move it to the Clipboard. However, this method has one disadvantage—the Clipboard only holds the last item placed in it. You may want to delete text without moving it to the Clipboard and destroying whatever contents are already there. Remember that once you delete text, it is not recoverable.

To delete text without using the Clipboard, first you must highlight it the same way you would highlight text for replacement. In this case we will delete the last sentence in the first paragraph of our long article. This sentence, shown in Figure 8.8, begins, "Too much choice ..."

1. Use the text tool to point to the first character of the text you want to delete.
2. Click and hold the mouse button while dragging the text tool until all the text you want to delete is highlighted.
3. Release the mouse button.

Remember that this text cannot be recovered once it is deleted, so double check to make sure you highlighted only the text you want to delete.

4. Select the "Clear" command option from the Edit menu, or press the Del key. The text is deleted and the space is automatically closed up, as shown in Figure 8.9.

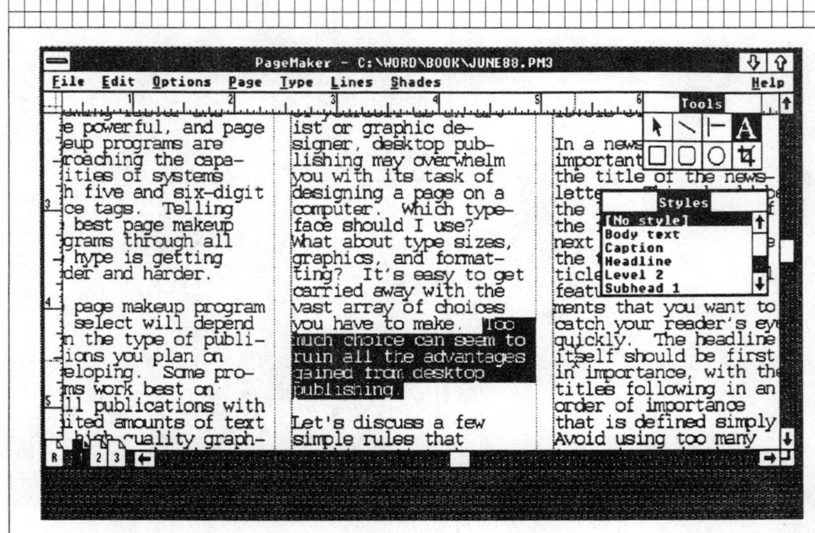

Figure 8.8: Highlighted text for deletion

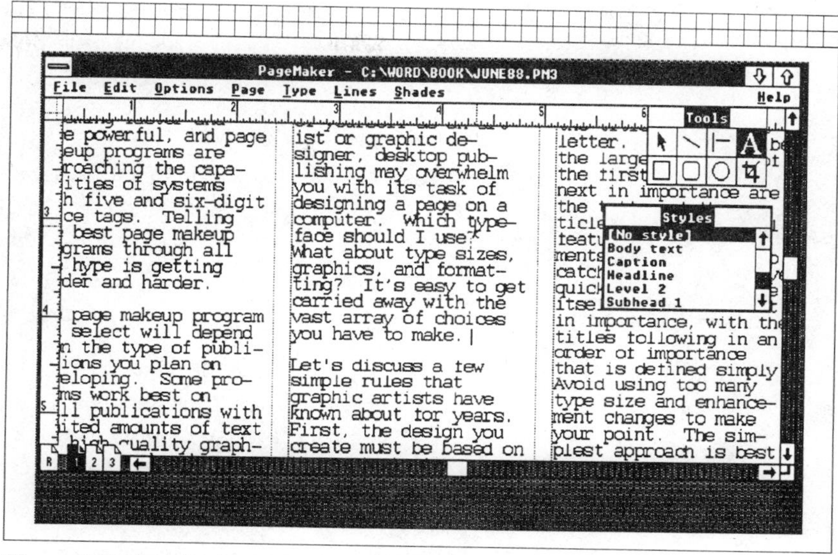

Figure 8.9: Text block with highlighted text deleted

You can also delete small amounts of text by using the backspace key to delete one character at a time. Just use the text tool to point to the text within your publication and click the mouse button. Each time you press the backspace key, the character preceding the text tool will be deleted.

▸ INSERTING TEXT OUTSIDE OF A TEXT BLOCK

A continuation line tells the reader the page on which the story is continued.

You can also insert text into your layout by placing it outside of existing text blocks. This works well for indicating the continuation line for an article, as well as for headlines, figure captions, and more. Text placed outside a text block is not affected when you make changes to the existing text blocks.

So far, we've placed three articles in our newsletter. Before we forget where we placed each threaded text block of the articles, let's insert continuation lines. To do so, we will place the the continuation lines outside of the existing text blocks. This way, if we decide later to make changes to the articles, the continuation lines will not be affected.

To create text blocks outside of the existing text blocks in the newsletter layout, we must create the text in the pasteboard area, then place it in our layout. The first article is all on page 1, so we do not need a continuation line for it. Let's start with the second article, which begins on page 1 and continues on page 3.

1. Use the scroll bars to position a blank area of the pasteboard in the middle of your screen.
2. Select the text tool from the Toolbox.
3. Move the I-beam into the blank area of the pasteboard and click the mouse button to position the flashing cursor.
4. Type

    cont. on pg. 3

5. To place the text on the page, click on the pointer tool from the Toolbox.
6. Point on the text in the pasteboard. Click and hold down the mouse button.
7. Slide the text onto page 1. Position the text at the bottom of the third column, as shown in Figure 8.10. Be sure the text is outside the handles of the article.

Now you have inserted a text block—a continuation line—indicating where the second article is continued. Because this text block is outside the second article, any changes you make to the article will not affect the inserted text block.

8. Repeat these steps to insert a continuation line on page 2 for the third article, which is also continued on page 3.

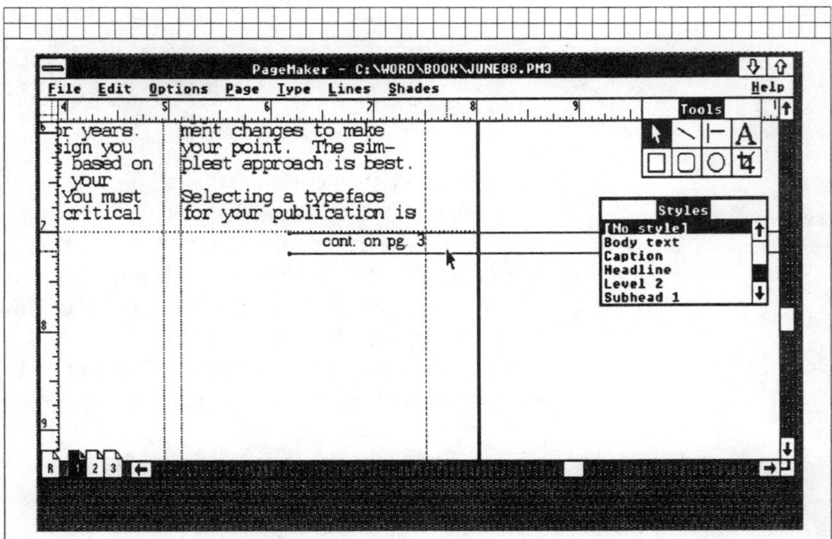

Figure 8.10: Inserting text outside of text blocks

▸ ENHANCING THE APPEARANCE OF YOUR TEXT

Now that you have placed your text into PageMaker and have altered it with the text tool to make it read as you want, it's time to specify your type and add text enhancements. In other words, now that your publication reads correctly, it's time to concentrate on its appearance. We already set a few type specifications using the "Define styles" command, and you may have already set many type specifications with your word processor as well. However, if you placed ASCII (text-only) files into PageMaker, PageMaker used its own default type specifications, so you must change these specifications.

In this section, you will learn how to make type specifications, then include text enhancements, such as boldface, italic, underline, and strikethrough, if they are not already in your word processed file. You will then learn how to make sure that your publication is printed with the correct font, the correct leading, and the correct type size.

▸ MAKING TYPE SPECIFICATIONS

Let's learn about type specifications by working with the headings to the articles. It's best to create the headings in the pasteboard first, then move them onto the page. Let's create a heading for the first article.

1. Use the scroll bars to position a blank area of the pasteboard in the middle of your screen.
2. Click on the text tool icon in the Toolbox.
3. Position the I-beam in the blank area of the pasteboard and click the mouse button to display the flashing cursor.
4. Type the following heading:

   PageMaker 3.0

To make your type specifications, the text must be highlighted. Be sure the text tool is still selected. To highlight text using PageMaker 3.0:

1. Position the text tool on the headline.
2. Triple-click the mouse button and the text is highlighted.

To highlight text using earlier versions of PageMaker:

1. Position the I-beam in front of the first letter of the headline.
2. Click and hold down the mouse button.

3. Drag the I-beam across the text.
4. When all the text is highlighted, release the mouse button.

With the text highlighted, you are ready to make the necessary type specifications. If you are using PageMaker 3.0, you already made the necessary type specifications using the "Define styles" command from the Type menu.

Using PageMaker 3.0:

1. Position the pointer tool in the Styles palette.
2. If necessary, use the scroll bars in the Styles palette to display the Headline style.
3. Click on the Headline style.

The highlighted text is changed to include the type specifications included in our Headline style.

If you are using an earlier version of PageMaker, you need to make type specifications each time you insert a headline. With the text highlighted:

1. Click on the Type menu and select the "Type specs" command. The Type Specifications dialog box, shown in Figure 8.11, is displayed. This box has many options for choosing type specifications. In the "Adding Text Enhancements" section of this chapter you will look closely at all these choices. For now, we'll choose a font and type size.

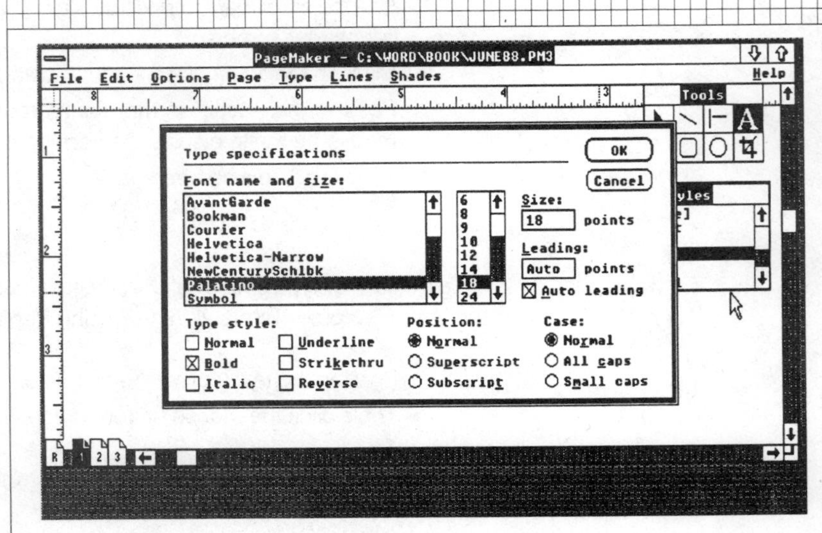

Figure 8.11: Type Specifications dialog box

2. Make the following selections: Palatino, 18 point, bold
3. Click OK.

The headline changes to include the new type specifications. You are now ready to place the headline in the newsletter.

1. Select the pointer tool from the Toolbox.
2. Point on the headline in the pasteboard. Click and hold down the mouse button.
3. Drag the headline onto the page and position it at the top of the first column of text on page 1, as shown in Figure 8.12.

Your first headline is now positioned on the page. Let's go ahead and place the headline for the second article on page 1. The headline for the second article is

Learning To Make Type Specifications

Type the headline in a blank area of the pasteboard. Select the same type specifications as you did for the heading of our first article.

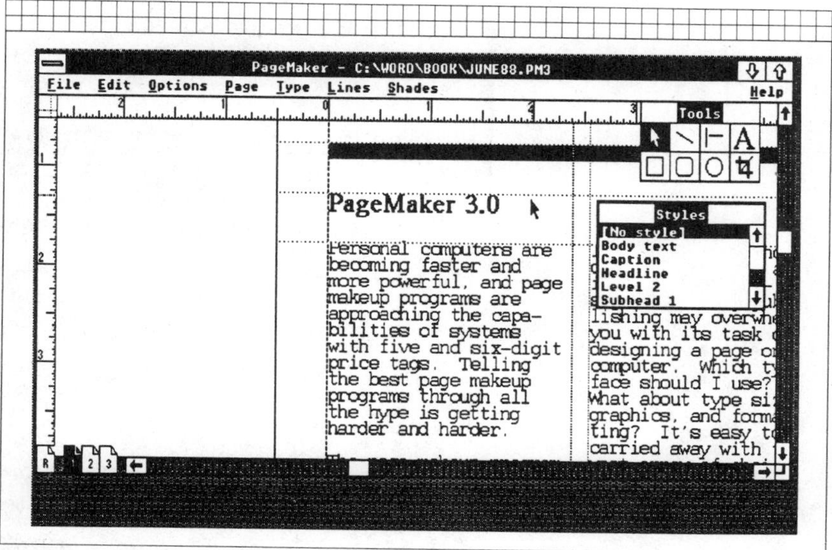

Figure 8.12: Placed headline

The second article covers two columns on the first page of our newsletter. Let's position the headline to span across the top of both columns.

1. Select the pointer tool from the Toolbox.
2. Click on the headline in the pasteboard to display the text handles.
3. Click on the top windowshade handle to load the text page icon with the headline text.
4. Position the corner of the text page icon at the intersection of the 1.75 inch ruler guide and the right margin.
5. Click and hold down the mouse button.
6. Drag the text page icon to the left until it is positioned at the intersection of the 1.25 ruler guide and the left column guide of the second column. Notice that a box is formed by the text page icon, as shown in Figure 8.13. This box indicates where the text will flow.
7. Release the mouse button.

The headline flows into the box. This method of flowing text across column guides can be used anytime to redefine where you want text to flow onto a page. If you were using a three-column format and you wanted text to flow across two of the columns, you could use the text icon to create a box across both columns. You can make text flow across column guide boundaries whenever you want.

Use the skills you just learned to place a headline on page 2 at the top of the third article in the newsletter. Create an appropriate headline in the pasteboard.

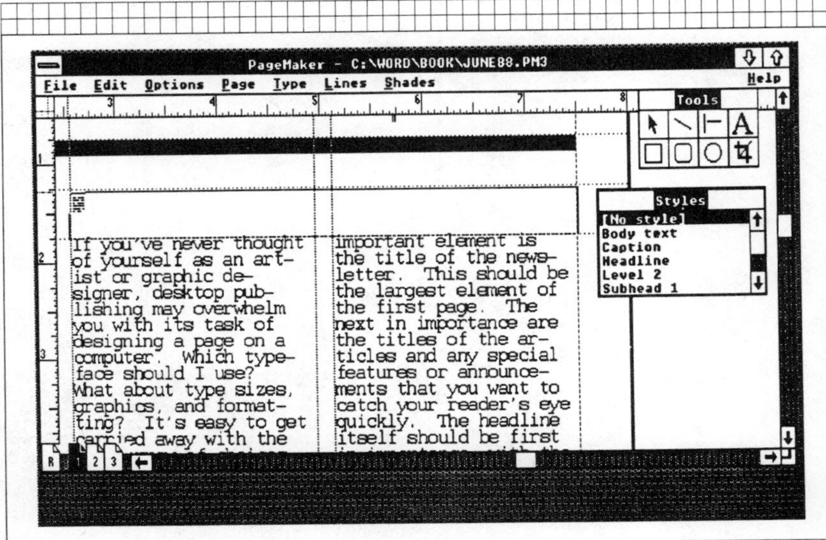

Figure 8.13: The text page icon boundary box

Select the same type specifications as the other two headlines in the newsletter. Place the headline at the top of the article on page 2. The third article covers all three columns on page 2, so you can span the headline across all three columns if you want to.

► ADDING TEXT ENHANCEMENTS

Text enhancements include bolding, italics, underline, strikethrough, and more. Whether you placed a text-only file with no text enhancements or you simply want to add a new enhancement, you can add them after your articles have been placed in your layout. Let's practice enhancing some text.

1. Select the text tool from the Toolbox.
2. Highlight the text you want to enhance. For our example, let's highlight the first mention of PageMaker version 3.0 in the first article. This occurs in the third paragraph.
3. Click on the Type menu.
4. Click on the "Bold" command.

A check mark appears next to the "Bold" option and the highlighted text is now bold, as shown in Figure 8.14. (To cancel or change your selection, just point to it again and click the mouse button to make the check mark disappear.) The dialog box also includes other enhancements such as italics, underlining, superscript, and subscript.

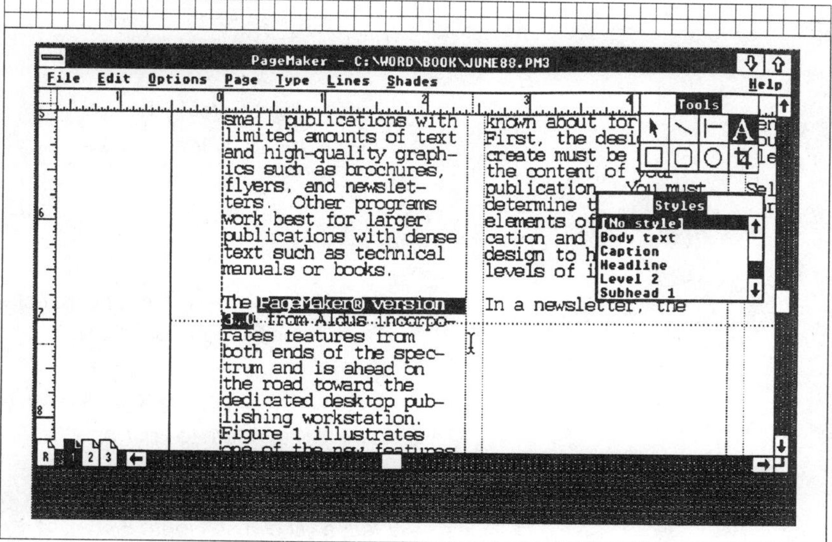

Figure 8.14: Bolded text

► SELECTING TYPE SPECIFICATIONS

At this point in the production of your newsletter you must refer to the design decisions you made about typestyles, leading, and fonts in Chapter 4. Let's begin with type. To make type on your screen match your design plans, begin by highlighting the text with the text tool. You must highlight text for which you want to change type specifications. If you want to change the type specifications for a multiple page publication, highlight the text one page at a time, or use the "Select all" command from the Edit menu. When you have highlighted the text you want to change, use the text tool to select the "Type specs" command option from the Type menu, or use the "Define styles" option if you are using PageMaker 3.0.

Let's select type specifications for the main body of text in each article. The first step is to select the text. Let's highlight the text in the first article.

1. Select the text tool from the Toolbox.
2. Position the I-beam anywhere in the first article.
3. Click the mouse button to select an insertion point in the article. The flashing cursor should now be positioned in the article.
4. Click on the Edit menu and choose the "Select all" command.

All the text in the article is highlighted. You are now ready to make your type specifications. You previously used the "Define styles" command from the Type menu to define your type specifications for the main body of text. If you are using PageMaker 3.0, select the style from the Styles palette to make the highlighted text include these type specifications.

Using PageMaker 3.0:

1. Position the pointer in the Styles palette.
2. Point to the body text style and click the mouse button.

If you are using an earlier version of PageMaker, you must make your type specifications each time. Using PageMaker 1.0 or 1.0a:

1. Click on the Type menu and select the "Type specs" command. The Type Specifications dialog box, shown earlier in Figure 8.11, is displayed.
2. Make the following selections: Palatino, 12 point
3. Click OK to return to your publication.

The highlighted text in the first article has changed to the type specifications you just selected, as shown in Figure 8.15. Use your skills to change the type specifications for the body text in the other two articles of your newsletter.

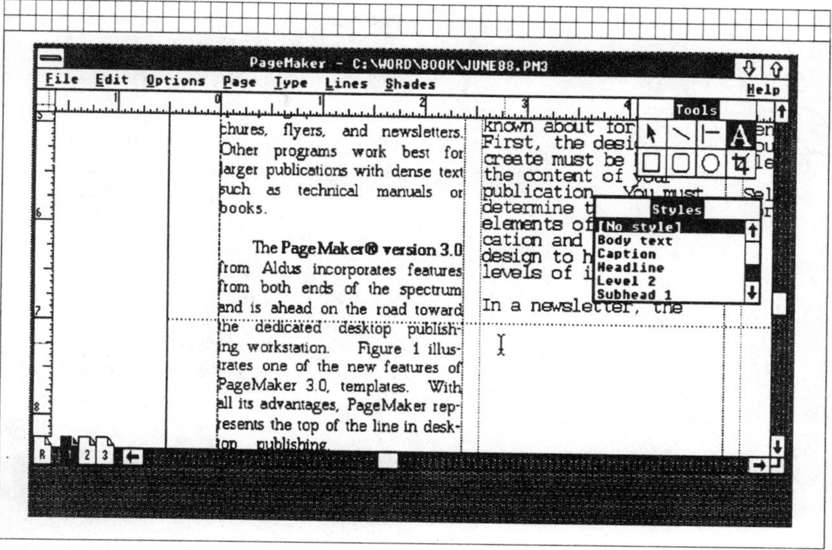

Figure 8.15: Changing the font

Now that you've worked a little with PageMaker's type specifications, let's discuss each element of the Type Specifications dialog box in more detail.

Selecting a Font

The box on the left side of the dialog box contains font names. As you learned in Chapter 4, a font is the complete set of characters, including enhancements, for a particular typeface. Use the scroll bar on the right side of the font box to reveal more fonts. All the fonts available on your target printer will be listed.

To choose a font, point to the font you want and click the mouse button. In the previous example, Palatino is the font you chose for the main body of text. You can see that the text on your screen has changed to Palatino. In some cases, though, PageMaker cannot produce a screen version of the font you chose. In these cases, an on-screen substitution is made for the font you selected. However, at print time, the font you selected will be printed.

Selecting a Type Size

The box to the right of the font box in the Type Specifications dialog box contains different type sizes. This box, called the *size scroll box,* has a scroll bar to reveal more type sizes. To select a type size, point to the size you want and click the mouse button. The small Size box to the right of the size scroll box displays the text size you selected. Another way to choose type size is to enter the size directly in this box. Simply position the text tool in the box, click the mouse button, and type in the type size you want. PageMaker will match the type in your publication to the type size you specify. PageMaker accepts text from 4 to 127 points, and all half-point sizes in between. The text size for your main body of text should probably be 10 to 12 points. If you select a size that is not available on your target printer, PageMaker automatically assigns the next available, smaller size.

Selecting the Leading

The next box in the Type Specifications dialog box concerns leading. As you learned in Chapter 4, leading is the vertical distance between two successive lines of text. It is measured in points from the top of the capital letters in one line to the top of the capital letters in the next one. Until you become more familiar with how to define type specifications, you would probably do better to stick with PageMaker's automatic leading selection. The automatic option calculates leading at 120% of point size. So, for 10-point text, the leading is 12 points. Leading is calculated to the nearest half point.

When you select the "Auto leading" option, an X-mark appears in the box marked "Auto leading." To select your own leading, point to the "Points" option in the Leading box. Click the mouse button and type in the leading you want, from .5 points to 127 points.

Selecting the Type Style

The Type Specifications dialog box also contains the type style options. As you've seen, type style may be independently selected from the Type menu, or here along with the other type specifications. You can use normal type, or you can enhance the type with boldface, italics, underline, or strikethrough. To select a type style, simply point to the box next to the style you want and click the mouse button. An X-mark will appear in the box next to the type style you selected. You can also select more than one type style at once—bold and italic type, for example.

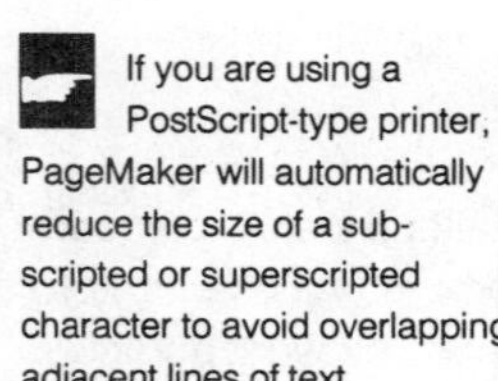

If you are using a PostScript-type printer, PageMaker will automatically reduce the size of a subscripted or superscripted character to avoid overlapping adjacent lines of text.

Positioning the Text

The position option buttons allow you to position text with relation to the baseline. The baseline is the imaginary line on which the characters of a line rest. Text may be positioned directly on the baseline, superscripted slightly above the line, or subscripted slightly below the line.

Selecting the Text Case

The last set of option buttons in the Type Specifications dialog box have to do with the case of the text. Normal text appears in a variety of upper- and lowercase letters, but the "Small caps" option, available on PostScript printers, changes all text to capitals that are about 70% as big as full-size capital letters. The "All caps" option changes all text to full-size capital letters. Select the option you want by pointing to the corresponding option button and clicking the mouse. The option button selected is the one containing the highlighted circle.

► MAKING PARAGRAPH SPECIFICATIONS

Paragraph specifications refer to the alignment of paragraphs, the spacing between paragraphs, and formatting elements such as indents and tabs.

If you are using earlier versions of PageMaker, let's make paragraph specifications for the main body of text in our newsletter articles, then we'll look in detail at each option. As with type specifications, designating paragraph specifications requires the text to be highlighted.

1. Click on the Type menu and select the "Paragraph" command. The Paragraph Specifications dialog box, shown in Figure 8.16, is displayed.

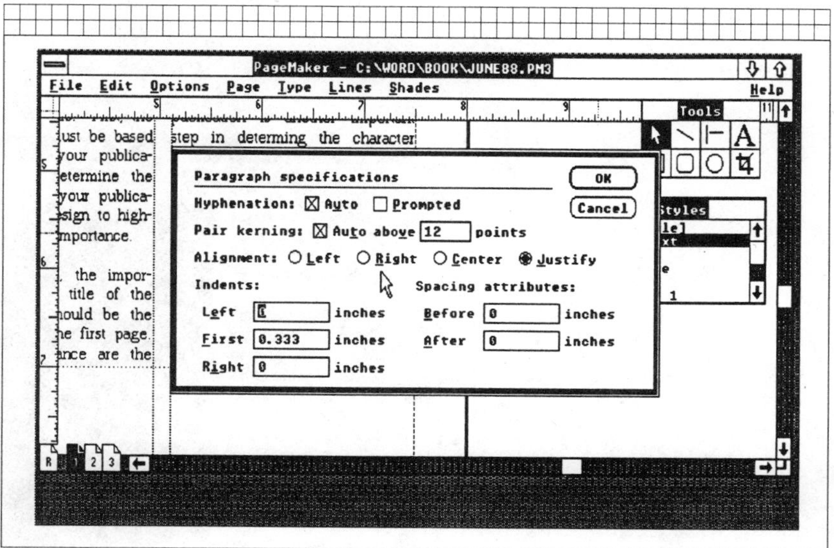

Figure 8.16: Paragraph Specifications dialog box

This box lets you determine how PageMaker will handle paragraph alignment, hyphenation, pair kerning, indenting (left, first, or right), and spacing before and after paragraphs. For now, let's select paragraph alignment and indentation.

2. Make the following selections: Justify; First line indent = 0.333
3. Click OK. The highlighted text quickly accommodates the new paragraph specifications, as shown in Figure 8.17.
4. Use the above steps to select the same paragraph specifications for all the articles included in the newsletter.

Let's continue working with paragraph formatting. This time we'll use the Type menu to adjust paragraph alignment.

► SETTING PARAGRAPH ALIGNMENT

You can set the paragraph alignment directly from the Type menu. Click on the Type menu and you will see the following options: left alignment, center, right, and justified. Left alignment creates a flush left margin and a ragged right one. Center alignment centers the text between the margins or column guides. Right alignment leaves a ragged left margin and a flush right one. Justified aligns the text flush on both the right and left sides, but small spaces have to be inserted between words to make the left and right margins line up.

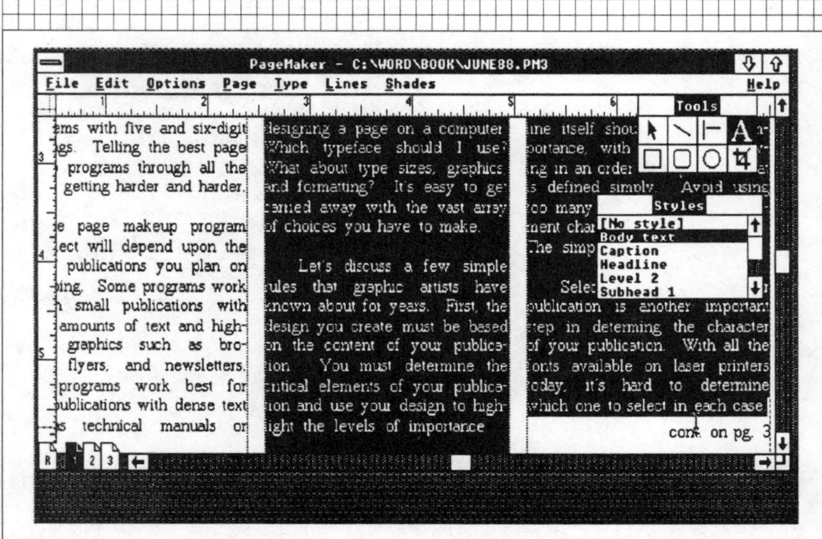

Figure 8.17: Setting paragraph alignment and first-line indent

To make adjustments to paragraph alignment, select the text tool from the Toolbox. Next, select a paragraph to align, either by highlighting all the text in the paragraph, or by using the flashing cursor to put an insertion point in the paragraph you want to select. Use the "Select all" command from the Edit menu if you want to realign all paragraphs. Next, use the text tool to select the Type menu. The Type menu displays the specifications of the selected text. If you click on the Type menu before you have selected any text, PageMaker will display its default alignment specifications. If none of the specification options are checked, that means you can select center, right, left, or justified alignment. To select an option, point to the alignment option you want and click the mouse button. A check mark will appear next to the option you selected. When you release the mouse button, the paragraphs you selected will automatically align to the new specification.

Another way to select paragraph alignment is to highlight the text and then choose the "Paragraph" option from the Type menu. The Paragraph Specifications dialog box, shown in Figure 8.16, will be displayed on your screen. From this dialog box, you can adjust paragraph alignment just as you did directly from the Type menu.

► CHANGING THE INDENT VALUE

You specify indents for your text from the Paragraph Specifications dialog box. The "Left" and "Right" options determine how far text should be indented from the left or right edges of a text block as specified in positive numbers. The "First" option determines how far to indent the first line of a paragraph. This indent, when specified in positive numbers, creates a first-line indent to the right of the following lines in the paragraph. The paragraphs in this book, for example, have positive indentations. When an indentation is specified in the negative, it means that the first line is indented to the left of the following lines. This is called a *hanging indent.* The first indent, however, cannot be larger than the left indent. All three indents cannot extend beyond the edges of the text blocks.

See Chapter 5 for details on how to select a measuring system and how to override it.

To select the indentation you want to use, choose the "Paragraph" option from the Type menu, point the text tool in one of the indent text boxes and click the mouse button. Type in the indentation you want. (In the previous example, we selected a first line indent of .333 inches.) The number you type in will be listed in the measurement system you selected.

► CHANGING THE SPACING BETWEEN PARAGRAPHS

Determining paragraph spacing is similar to selecting the leading between lines, except you are selecting the leading between paragraphs. The space between paragraphs is a function of two elements—the spacing before and the spacing after each paragraph. Each paragraph can be specified separately, but to maintain consistent spacing between paragraphs, it is best to specify either the spacing before or after, but not both.

Once you select your paragraph spacing, PageMaker will automatically leave blank spaces each time you press ↵ in your word processed file. For this reason, paragraphs at the beginning and end of text blocks are not spaced. Adjust the paragraph spacing either page by page by highlighting the text on a page, or set it for an entire article by using the "Select all" command from the Edit menu. Point to the Before text box in the Paragraph Specifications dialog box and click the mouse button to select it. You can now enter the spacing you want. Specify either the Before or After spacing to ensure you will have consistent spacing between paragraphs. If you don't set paragraph spacing and you are using an ASCII file, your paragraphs will not have spacing between them. If you are using a compatible word processor, you will probably not have to make adjustments.

The remaining two paragraph specification features in this dialog box are hyphenation and pair kerning. Both of these features are a bit more complicated; hyphenation is discussed in the next section, and pair kerning is explained in Chapter 9.

► HYPHENATING WORDS IN PAGEMAKER

When PageMaker flows text between column guides or margin guides, the lines are broken down automatically between words. When a word that you have not manually hyphenated is too big for a line, it is automatically dropped down to the next line, and this can create gaps in the text. However, PageMaker provides you with some options to prevent this—automatic hyphenation and prompted hyphenation.

If you use automatic hyphenation, words are broken according to PageMaker's dictionary and the supplemental dictionary you create. If you use prompted hyphenation, lines are broken between words and at hyphenation points you create when prompted. But prompted hyphenation only applies to selected paragraphs, not all paragraphs. If you use both automatic and prompted hyphenation, PageMaker can hyphenate words according to its dictionaries or according to your hyphenation when prompted.

You can select automatic hyphenation, prompted hyphenation, neither, or both. If you do not use any of the hyphenation features of PageMaker, lines will be broken at the ends of words or where you manually inserted a hyphen.

To specify the hyphenation you want to use, select the "Paragraph" command option from the Type menu. The Paragraph Specifications dialog box, shown earlier in Figure 8.16, is displayed on your screen. Use the text tool to choose the type of hyphenation you want: Auto, Prompted, neither, or both. Once you've made your selection, click OK. For practice, let's select prompted hyphenation. Remember, if you select prompted hyphenation, it will only work on those paragraphs you have asked PageMaker to prompt you about. To select a paragraph, either position the flashing text bar inside it, or highlight it. For practice, select any paragraph in the newsletter.

When PageMaker finds a word that needs hyphenation, it displays the Prompted Hyphenation dialog box, shown in Figure 8.18. A word requiring hyphenation will appear in the text box beside a few words of the preceding and following text. Use the text tool to point to the location in the word where you want to place the hyphen and click the mouse button. You may select more than one location for a hyphen in a word. Click "Next" when you have decided where to put the hyphen.

If the word is a specialized one that does not appear in PageMaker's dictionary, click on a check mark in the Add to User Dictionary box to add the word to your supplementary dictionary. This way, PageMaker will know where to hyphenate the word next time it appears when you are using automatic hyphenation. If the box is already clicked on and you don't want PageMaker to add the word to your supplementary dictionary, click the check mark off.

Once you have finished hyphenating a word in the text box, click "Next" to display the next word requiring hyphenation. You can double-click the mouse button to indicate the hyphenation point and move on to the next word in one step. When you are ready to turn off the prompted hyphenation feature, click "Stop."

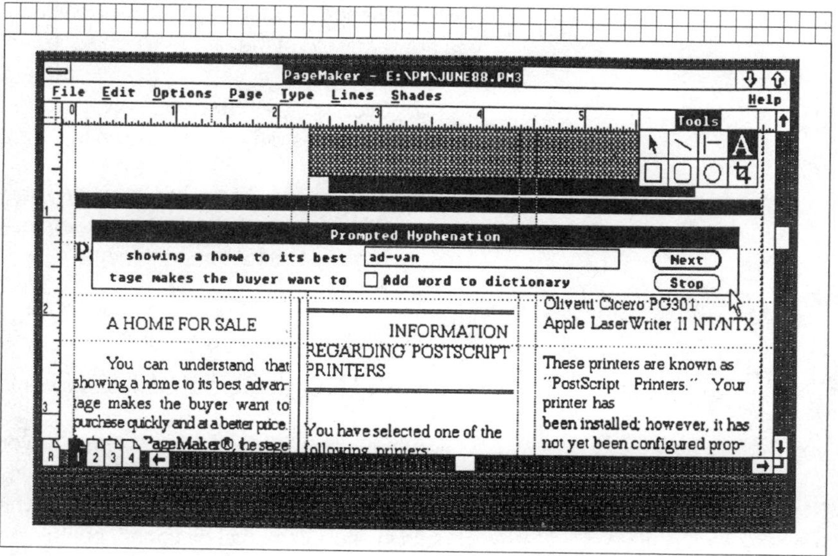

Figure 8.18: Prompted Hyphenation dialog box

► USING THE HYPHENATION ZONE

Besides automatic and prompted hyphenation, you can control hyphenation by setting the hyphenation zone. The hyphenation zone sets a range for hyphenating unjustified text. The smaller you set this zone, the more often PageMaker may be forced to hyphenate words. If the hyphenation zone is too large, the text may appear more ragged than necessary. PageMaker recognizes the hyphenation zone only when you are using automatic or prompted hyphenation.

It may happen that PageMaker will violate the hyphenation zone setting you specify. This happens because PageMaker is only able to hyphenate the words in its 110,000-word dictionary and the words you created using discretionary hyphen settings.

Let's use PageMaker's hyphenation controls to improve the look of line breaks in unjustified text. First, select an insertion point or an entire article of ragged text that you want to adjust. Next, turn the automatic hyphenation feature on.

1. Select the "Paragraph" command from the Type menu. The Paragraph Specifications dialog box, shown earlier in Figure 8.16, is displayed.
2. An X-mark in the "Auto" option indicates that automatic hyphenation is turned on. Automatic hyphenation is the PageMaker default. If necessary, click on the "Auto" option.
3. Click OK.

With an insertion point selected and the automatic hyphenation feature active, you are ready to set the hyphenation zone.

4. Click on the "Spacing" command from the Type menu. The Spacing Attributes dialog box, shown in Figure 8.19, is displayed.
5. Type in the desired hyphenation zone in the Hyphenation Zone text box. Setting the zone at .25, for example, limits the white space at the end of ragged text to a quarter inch.
6. Click OK.

► CREATING A SUPPLEMENTAL DICTIONARY

You may often use specialized terms in your publications. When PageMaker 3.0 wants to hyphenate a word, it checks its own built-in dictionary of 110,000 words (90,000 for earlier versions) to see where the hyphen should go. Next, it checks the supplemental dictionary containing specialized words you've added.

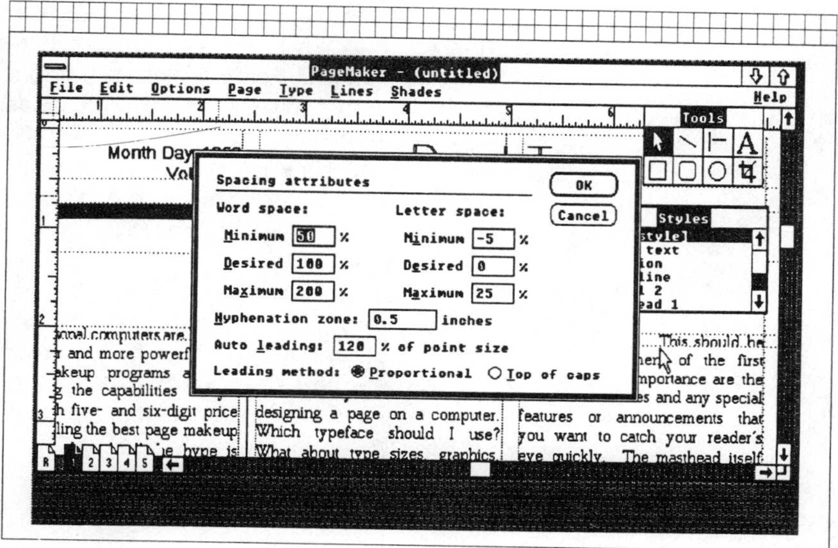

Figure 8.19: The Spacing Attributes dialog box

There are two ways to add words to the supplemental dictionary. You've already seen how to add words to the supplemental dictionary when PageMaker prompts you for hyphenation. You can also create your own dictionary.

To create your own dictionary, create a text-only file using a text editor or a word processor that can create text-only files. Call the file PMUSUSER.TXT. This is the dictionary file name PageMaker recognizes. In the file, type the words you want in the dictionary. Be sure to type in hyphens in the correct places in each word. Next, edit the file to add or delete words, or to make corrections. Save the file. Now make sure the file is in the same directory as the PageMaker application. If it is in another directory, move it to the PageMaker directory using MS-DOS commands. The next time PageMaker's hyphenation feature checks the dictionaries, it will check this file, too.

► USING DISCRETIONARY HYPHENS

A *discretionary hyphen* is a hyphen that you type in when you type the word. A discretionary hyphen lets PageMaker know where to break a word at the end of a line. It does not show on the screen unless the word appears at the end of a line and requires a hyphen, in which case, PageMaker hyphenates the word where you inserted the discretionary hyphen. Use this hyphenation option if you want to avoid using PageMaker's hyphenation features, or if you think a word isn't included in either the supplemental dictionary or PageMaker's dictionary.

You can insert discretionary hyphens wherever you like in your PageMaker layout. For instance, you may find a line that appears too short in a column because a long word at the end of the line had to be dropped down to the next line. Inserting a discretionary hyphen in the long word divides it between the two lines.

To type a discretionary hyphen, point the text tool to where you want the hyphen to appear in the word. Press and hold the Ctrl key and press the hyphen key (-). The hyphen is displayed on the screen only if PageMaker needs to hyphenate the word at the end of a line. You can insert more than one discretionary hyphen in a word.

To delete a discretionary hyphen when it appears at the end of a line, use the text tool to point to the hyphen. Press the backspace key. PageMaker will break the word again if you inserted another discretionary hyphen, otherwise it will drop it down to the next line. To delete a discretionary hyphen that isn't currently showing, use the text tool to select the entire word or at least the characters on both sides of the hyphen. Now retype the text you selected, leaving out the hyphen.

As you can see, PageMaker provides a number of different ways for hyphenating text. You can use automatic hyphenation, prompted hyphenation, neither, or both. You can create your own supplemental dictionary for hyphens, and you can add discretionary hyphens. You may find one method that works better for you, or you may find that a combination works best under specific circumstances.

► USING TABS AND LEADERS

You already learned how to set left, right, and first line indents. PageMaker provides one more paragraph specification feature—tab stops. Use tab stops to create the tables and lists within your publication that you did not create using your word processor. Use the tab stops to align text you created using your word processor as well. PageMaker's default tabs are positioned at every half inch, but you can change this setting and align the tabs in four different ways: left, right, center, or decimal.

In addition, you can specify five kinds of leaders. A *leader* is a pattern that fills the space between tab stops. Leader characters draw the reader's eye across the page. You often see leaders used in tables because they make such information easier to read. For example, you may want to use leaders for a listing of contents with page numbers, as in this example:

Software news..Page 2
Recent releases..Page 4
Conferences...Page 4

You can choose to have no leader between tab stops, choose from one of three leaders provided by PageMaker, or customize your own. After you set a tab stop, you can change or delete it, but you can't adjust the alignment or leader designation. If you want to adjust either one of these features, you can always delete the tab stop and create another one.

► INSERTING TAB STOPS

In this section you'll set two tab stops and a leader pattern. Before you begin, use the text tool to select the text or paragraph in which you want to insert a tab stop.

1. Choose the "Indents/tabs" option from the Type menu. PageMaker displays the Indents/Tabs dialog box, shown in Figure 8.20.

To help you select tab stops, PageMaker displays a special ruler in the dialog box. You can set up to 20 tab stops, depending on the increments on the ruler. This ruler matches the horizontal ruler guide even though it appears to be unaligned in the middle of the screen. The zero mark of the dialog box ruler is lined up with the left edge of the page. The markers already in the ruler show the existing PageMaker default tabs, the first line indent, any left or right indents, and the left margin. If you selected more than one paragraph, and they have different settings, then no marks are displayed on the rulers of the Indents/Tab dialog box.

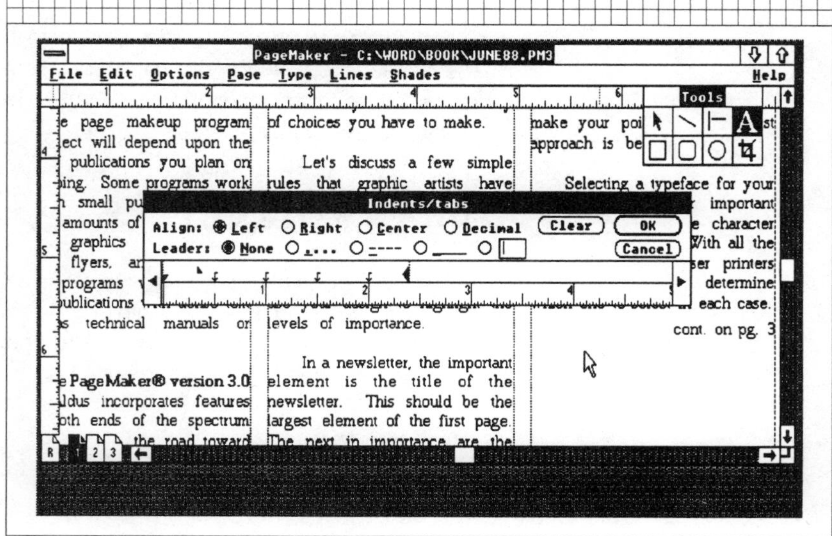

Figure 8.20: Indents/Tabs dialog box

The ruler itself is wider than the one in the dialog box. Point to the arrows on either side of the scroll box and click the mouse button to see the rest of the ruler. If you need to reposition the ruler, point on the title bar of the dialog box, click and hold the mouse button. Then move the box to the location you want and release the mouse button.

2. Click the option button indicating which type of alignment you want. Let's select "Left."

A left tab stop is the kind most of us are used to from our typewriter days. It aligns text to the right of the tab mark. A right tab stop aligns text to the left of the tab mark. A center tab stop centers text around the tab mark. And a decimal tab stop, useful when you are working with dollar-and-cents figures, lines up a decimal point on the tab mark.

3. Next, click on the leader pattern you want to use, or create your own pattern. To create your own leader, you would point the text tool in the text box and type the one or two characters you want PageMaker to repeat as a leader. But let's select the dot pattern.
4. Point to the bar just above the ruler where you want the tab stop to appear and click the mouse. Let's create our tab stops at .5 and 1.5 on the ruler.
5. When you have made your tab and indent selections, click OK.

With the tab stops set, point the text tool to the left of the text you want to align at the next tab stop. Now if you want to align columns of data, you can use the tab stops. To move to a tab stop, press the Tab key on your keyboard. The cursor is quickly aligned with the tab stop.

► REPLACING AND DELETING TAB STOPS

To replace an already existing tab stop, just click over it. To delete a tab stop, click on the tab stop and drag it into the ruler. You can also reposition a tab stop or an indent by clicking on it and moving it to a new location. To clear all the tab stops at once, click the "Clear" button on the dialog box.

► MORE ABOUT PAGEMAKER 3.0 STYLE FEATURES

The PageMaker 3.0 style features allow you to perform many time-saving tasks. You can use style sheets from your word processor. And if your word processor doesn't have a style sheet feature, PageMaker 3.0 can read style tags from your word processed file as long as they match the names in the Styles palette.

In addition, you can rename, remove, or edit a style in your Styles palette. If you created a style sheet that you are no longer using, you can delete it from your palette. Or, you can change the specifications in an existing style sheet.

▶ USING STYLE SHEETS WITH YOUR WORD PROCESSED FILE

PageMaker 3.0 allows you to quickly apply styles to text imported from your word processor. If you are using a word processor with style sheets, you can import those style specifications as long as the style name in the style sheet matches the style name in PageMaker's Styles palette.

If you are using a word processor that doesn't have style sheets, PageMaker still lets you include styles from your word processed file as long as they have tags. The tag must be placed at the beginning of each paragraph or group of paragraphs you want to insert in PageMaker. All style name tags must match style name tags in PageMaker's Styles palette. Suppose you want to insert a headline from your word processor. You would write the style name *<headline>* in enclosed brackets, then you would write the headline itself in your word processed file.

▶ EDITING A PAGEMAKER STYLE SHEET

If you want to delete a style sheet from your palette, you must start with the Define Styles dialog box. However, if you want to rename or edit a style sheet, you can start with the Edit Style dialog box.

To remove a style sheet, select the "Define styles" command from the Type menu. In the Style scroll box, select the name of the style you want to remove. Click "Remove," then click OK. The style will be removed from the Styles palette.

To rename a style sheet, you can skip the Define Styles dialog box, and begin with the second dialog box, Edit Style. To display the Edit Style dialog box directly, the Styles palette must be displayed in the publication window. With the pointer in the Styles palette, hold down the Ctrl key and click on the style name you want to change. In the Name text box, type in the new name of the style. Click OK and the style is renamed, keeping all the specifications that were originally designated.

Editing a style also begins with the Edit Style dialog box. Display the Edit Style dialog box from the Styles palette. Click on the command button you want and make the necessary changes to the style specifications. When you are finished, click OK. The old style name with the new specifications is complete.

► OVERRIDING STYLES

Once you've set the style for a block of text, you may decide you want to override or change some of the specifications. When a style is overridden, PageMaker places a plus sign next to the style name in the Styles palette.

PageMaker 3.0 allows you to permanently or temporarily override a specification in a style sheet. A permanent override is created by changing a type style command, either directly from the Type menu, or from the Type Specifications dialog box in the Type menu. Remember, type style options are text enhancements such as bold, italics, normal, underline, strikethrough, reverse, all caps and small caps, superscript and subscript. A permanent override makes the style change stand out from the rest of the text, even if the entire style sheet is later changed to match the override. For example, let's say you bold some text in a style sheet. A plus sign will appear next to the style name in the Styles palette. But if you later change the entire style sheet to bold text, the plus sign will remain, and the overridden style will reverse itself and become normal type. Since PageMaker recorded the change as a permanent override, the text will continue to stand out from the rest of the style.

A temporary override is created by changing Type menu commands in the Type Specifications dialog box. A temporary override will disappear if the entire style sheet is changed to include the override. For example, if you change the left indent for a paragraph to .5, a temporary override is created. But if you later change the style sheet to set the left paragraph indent at .4 for all paragraphs, the temporary override will conform to the new style.

► EXPORTING TEXT WITH PAGEMAKER 3.0

PageMaker 3.0 allows you to export text from your PageMaker publication to a text-only or word processed file. Any format changes you made to text within PageMaker can be exported as long as the new format is recognized by your word processor. As you've noticed, we've made many changes to our word processed articles since we placed them in our PageMaker layout. These changes can be exported and used by your word processor as a word processed file.

In the future, export filters for other word processors will become available from Aldus.

Text can be exported to your word processor as either a formatted file or a text-only file. A text-only file does not include formatting commands, but does include any changes to written text. To export formatted text, you must use an *export filter* that is compatible with your word processor. An export filter is a program that can translate PageMaker's formatting commands into commands your word processor can work with. PageMaker 3.0 has a built-in filter compatible with Microsoft Word files and text-only files. Text-only files can be used by any word processor, but the formatting commands are lost. Keep in mind that exporting text means just that—the *text* is exported to a word processed file; any graphics included in a PageMaker file cannot be exported.

If your word processor has an export filter, PageMaker can export a formatted file, even if the filter was installed separately from PageMaker. If your application supports style sheets, PageMaker will automatically supply style tags in the exported file. The style tags will include all formatting commands used by your word processor. Any formatting commands that are not used by your word processor will disappear in the exported text.

Exporting a file as text-only allows your word processor to read the text, but the formatting you used in your PageMaker file is lost. However, you can use your word processor to replace any formatting commands that were lost when you changed to text-only. The advantage of text-only files is they can be transferred to other computer systems. This gives you the flexibility of moving text from your PageMaker files to completely different computer systems.

Although PageMaker 3.0 comes with an export filter for Microsoft Word files, some formatting commands used by Microsoft Word are not recognized by PageMaker. This means that these formatting commands are dropped when the file is imported into PageMaker. However, when the file is exported from PageMaker to Microsoft, the original Microsoft formatting commands are reapplied to the file.

For example, Microsoft Word comes with graphics capabilities for placing boxes around text. When a file with one of these boxes is imported into PageMaker, the box is not displayed. However, the box will reappear when the file is exported back out using the Microsoft Word export filter.

In addition, Word has an underlining feature that underlines words without underlining the spaces between them. When a Word file is imported into PageMaker, the words as well as the spaces between them are underlined. But, once again, exporting the file back to Microsoft Word reestablishes Word's underlining function.

Now that you know a little about PageMaker's exporting ability, let's practice exporting one of the articles we placed in our newsletter. We made some text changes to the first article in our newsletter, so let's export this file. The first step is to select the article. You can choose portions of the article for export, or select the entire article.

1. Select the text tool from the Toolbox.
2. Click an insertion point anywhere in the first article in the first column of page 1.

The article now contains an insertion point—a flashing cursor—indicating which article is selected. You are ready to export the file.

1. Click on the File menu and select the "Export" command. The Export to File dialog box, shown in Figure 8.21, is displayed.

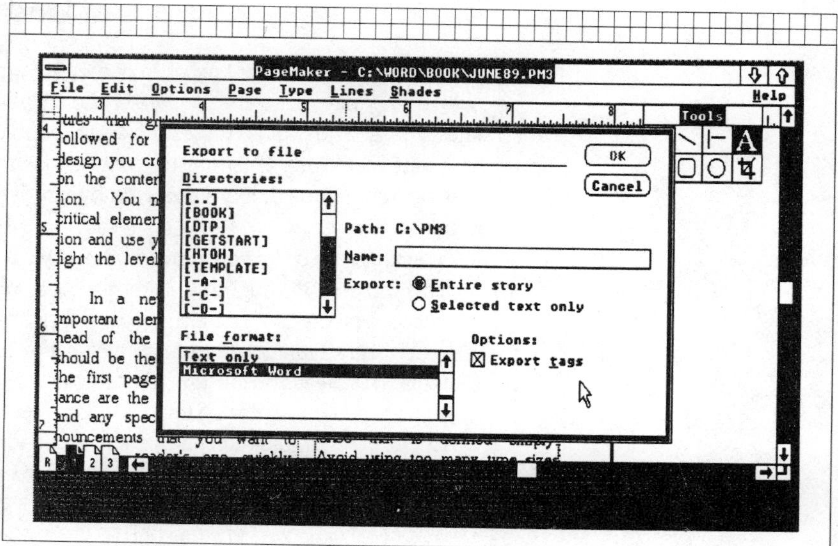

Figure 8.21: The Export to File dialog box

2. In the Directories scroll box, click on the drive where you want the file to reside.
3. Type in a name for the exported file in the Name text box.
4. To export the entire article, click on the "Entire story" option button. You can also export a portion of the article by selecting the text and clicking on the "Selected text only" option button.
5. To export tags to a style sheet, click on the "Export tags" option.
6. Click on the export file format you want to use in the File Format scroll box. The scroll box lists PageMaker's export filters and any filters you installed separately.
7. Click OK.

Now the selected story is exported under the name you indicated in the dialog box. If the file name already exists, PageMaker prompts you. You can then replace the old file with the new exported file, or select a new file name.

► SUMMARY

In this chapter, you used PageMaker's text tool to add, modify, and delete text. You also learned how to indicate font, size, and spacing of text and how to align, indent, and space your paragraphs. Using PageMaker 3.0, you learned how to use the Style options and file export features. In the next chapter, you will use PageMaker's text typography features to make text adjustments that used to be available only to professional printers.

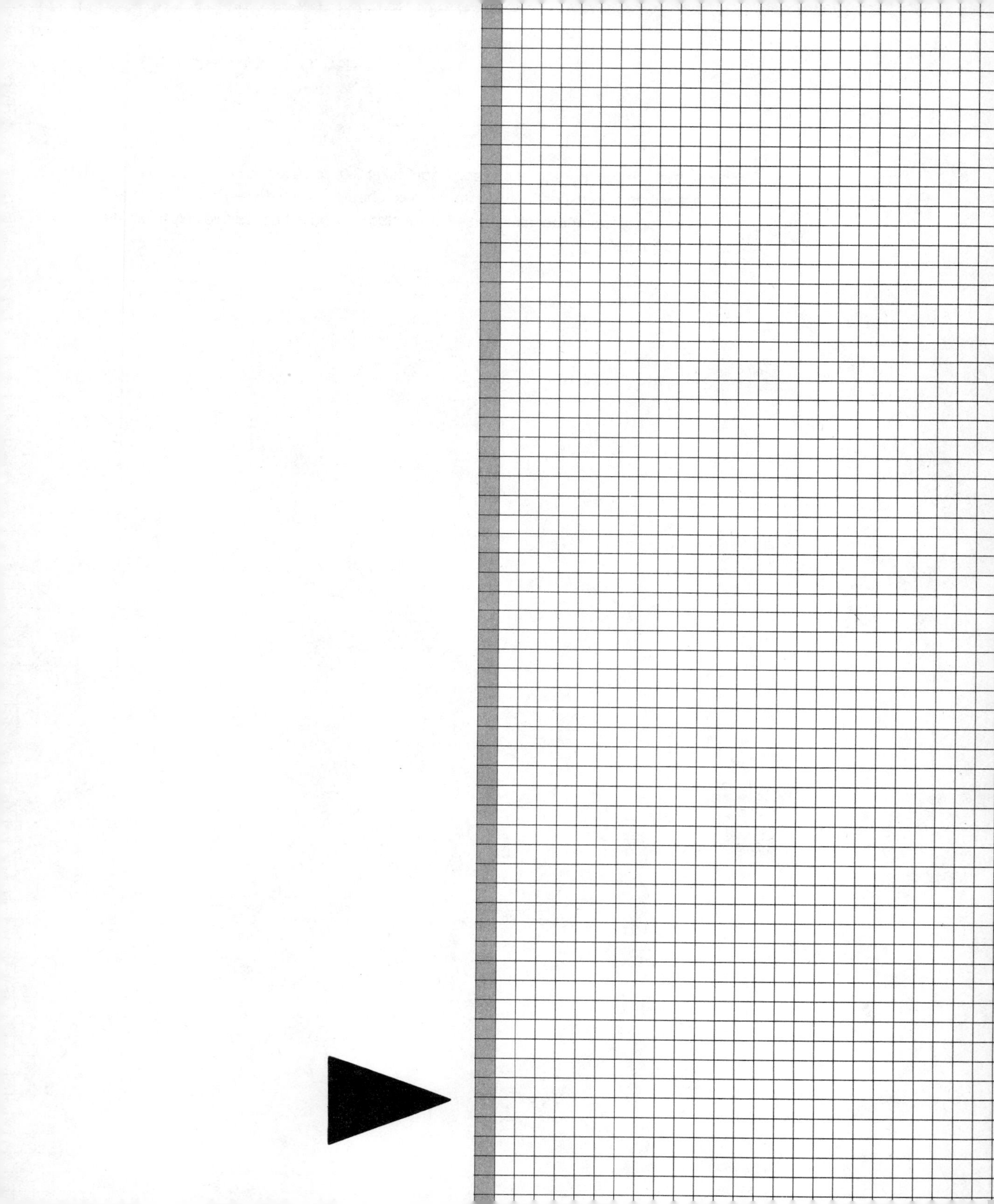

9 ENHANCING YOUR PUBLICATION WITH TEXT TYPOGRAPHY

To kern text automatically, 192

click on the "Paragraph" command from the Type menu to display the Paragraph Specifications dialog box. Click on the "Auto above" option in the Pair Kerning field.

To kern text manually, 194

insert the text cursor between the pair of letters you want to kern. Hold down the Ctrl key to tighten the spacing, or press the Ctrl and Shift keys to add space. Press the backspace key for each increment of space you want to delete or add.

To adjust the spacing between words, 195

click on an insertion point in the text and choose the "Select all" command from the Edit menu. Choose the "Spacing" command from the Type menu to see the Spacing Attributes dialog box. Fill in the range of values in the Word Space text boxes.

To adjust the spacing between letters, 196

click on an insertion point in a paragraph. Choose the "Spacing" command from the Type menu to see the Spacing Attributes dialog box. Fill in the range of values in the Letter Space text boxes.

You can also change the look of your publication by manipulating the leading between lines of text and between paragraphs. In addition, you can insert blank lines before and/or after each paragraph.

The term *typography* can mean various things in publishing. Sometimes it refers to the overall book design, but a more encompassing definition refers to the appearance or arrangement of type on a page. In this chapter, we deal with two aspects of typography—kerning and text justification. Kerning concerns spacing between select pairs of letters, and justification involves spacing between letters and words, and the alignment of your text in relation to the margins.

With PageMaker, you can adjust these typographical elements. Controlling the spacing between words and letters in a word gives you flexibility in the way your text appears.

In this chapter, you'll kern some character pairs in the final newsletter article, using both automatic and manual kerning methods. Then you'll adjust the spacing between words and letters in the article.

► KERNING TEXT

Each font has specific, built-in spacing between characters. For this reason, certain sets of characters may look like they are spaced too far apart or too close. For example, the space between the *Y* and the *o* in *You* may appear too wide because the top part of the capital letter takes up extra space. Likewise, space between letters may appear too close, like the *f* and the *e* in *fee*, for example. PageMaker lets you adjust the spacing between letters. This process is called *kerning* or *pair kerning.*

PageMaker provides two ways for you to kern text: automatically and manually. Check your printer manual to see if your printer can kern text. If it can, you can use PageMaker's automatic pair kerning feature. Automatic kerning applies only to the character pairs specified by the font manufacturer. If your printer can't kern text, you can use manual kerning. Manual kerning allows you to increase or decrease the space between character pairs. Manual kerning can be done while automatic kerning is activated.

The benefits of pair kerning text are most noticeable at point sizes of 12 or larger. In addition, pair kerning requires the constant recomposition of text, adding to the time it takes PageMaker to compose a page. For this reason, try to kern text only when the benefits outweigh the drawbacks.

► USING AUTOMATIC KERNING

If your printer does kern text, it is already set up to kern specific pairs of characters. Most kerning-capable printers kern the following character pairs: Yo, We, To, Tr, Ta, Wo, Tu, Tw, Ya, Te, P., Ty, Wa, yo, we, T., Y., TA, PA, and WA. Some printers also kern the following character pairs: OV, OY, VA, YO, Av, Wt, and Wm.

PageMaker's default setting kerns character pairs that are over 12 points in size. Let's use the automatic kerning feature to kern the character pairs in the first paragraph of the first article in our newsletter. To do this, we will have to change the pair kerning default setting to 8 points.

1. Select the text tool from the Toolbox.
2. Click on an insertion point anywhere in the first paragraph in the first column on page 1.
3. Click on the "Paragraph" command in the Type menu. The Paragraph Specifications dialog box, shown in Figure 9.1, is displayed.
4. An X-mark automatically appears in the "Auto above" box option in the Pair Kerning field, indicating automatic pair kerning is selected. Leave the default set. (Clicking on the box would turn off the font's automatic pair kerning function.)
5. Change the default setting in the Pair Kerning Points text box to 8 points.
6. Click OK.

The spacing between the kerning pairs in the first paragraph has now been adjusted, though you may not notice any difference —the text size of the newsletter is too small.

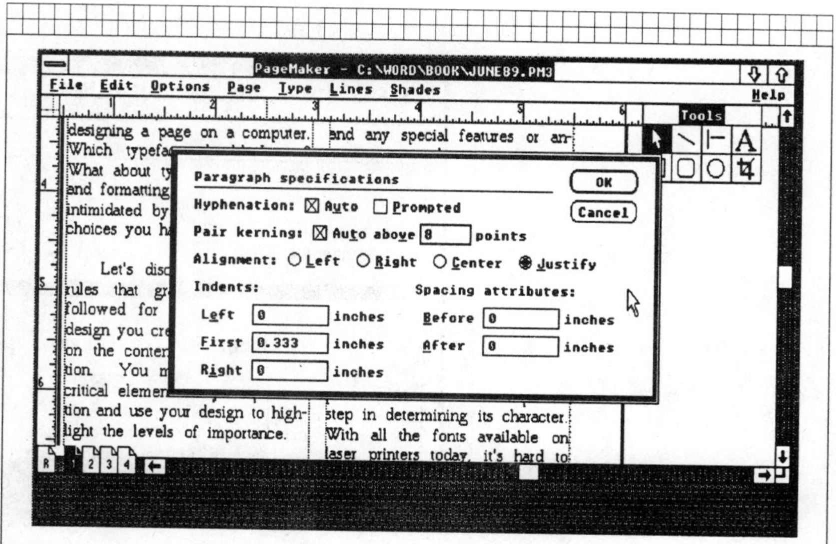

Figure 9.1: Paragraph Specifications dialog box

▶ USING MANUAL KERNING

An em space is a typographic measurement that is equal to the point size of the designated type. For example, the em space for 12-point type is .5 point, or one character wide.

PageMaker also provides a method for you to kern character pairs manually. This method works with any printer. You can insert or delete space between characters at about 1/24 of an em space.

In our newsletter title, *DeskTop News,* the space between the *T* and *o* in *DeskTop* needs to be tightened up. Let's use the manual kerning feature to tighten up this space in the masthead title of our newsletter. Since 36-point type was used in the title, this time you will be able to see the benefits of pair kerning. To use PageMaker's manual kerning feature:

1. Select the text tool from the Toolbox.
2. Position the I-beam between the two characters in the pair (the *T* and the *o*) and click the mouse button. This selects the insertion point, as shown in Figure 9.2.
3. We are tightening, or deleting, space between the two characters. To tighten space, hold down the Ctrl key. (To add space, hold down the Ctrl and Shift keys.)
4. Now press the backspace key for each increment of space you want to delete. Pressing the backspace key twice (which in this point size is about 1/12 of an em space) is probably enough.

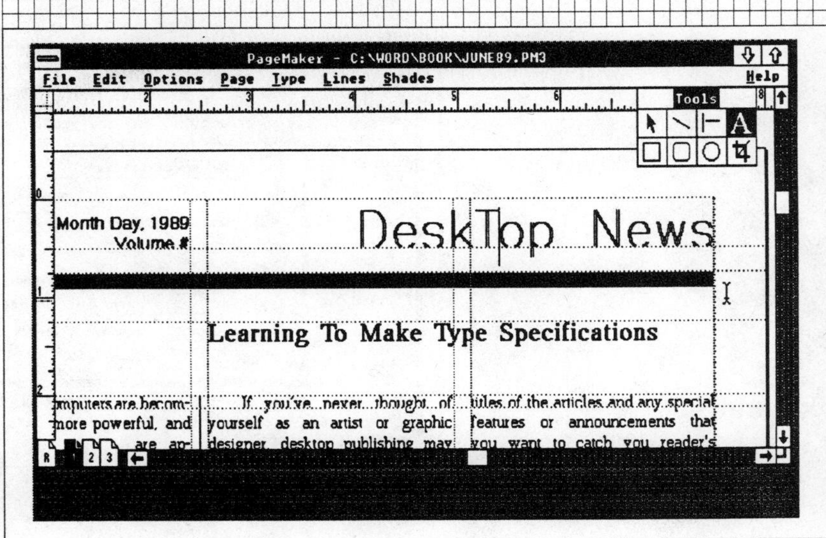

Figure 9.2: Insertion point for manual kerning

The space between the *T* and the *o* in our newsletter title has been tightened up. You may choose to repeat the procedure and tighten the space between the last two characters, *o* and *p*. Again, the kerning may not show up on your screen—it depends on the resolution of your monitor—but the kerning will show when you print your page.

▸ JUSTIFIED TEXT COMPOSITION

As you learned in the previous chapter, justified text is aligned flush on the right margin and on the left one. When you select "Justify" from the Type menu, PageMaker justifies text by adjusting the amount of space between the characters within a word, and the amount of space between the words themselves. PageMaker gives you some control over how the space is adjusted when you justify text. You can control both the spacing between words and the spacing between letters.

▸ ADJUSTING THE SPACE BETWEEN WORDS

PageMaker measures the space between words as a percentage of the standard word spacing built into the particular font you are using. The standard spacing is 100%. The default settings allow a minimum spacing of 50% (half the usual distance between words in the font) and a maximum spacing of 200% (twice the usual distance between words in the font). PageMaker's standard spacing is always the font manufacturer's predefined spacing. (PageMaker refers to this as the *Desired* spacing.) This 50%–200% range enables PageMaker to vary the space between words so that a justified line looks evenly spaced.

A wide range of spacing may produce large gaps between some words and small gaps between others. A narrow range of spacing limits the amount of space PageMaker can add or delete between words, and this may cause a lot of hyphens to appear in your text. Therefore, it's important to make sure that automatic hyphenation is turned on for justified text formats. If your columns are narrow, PageMaker may hyphenate more often than you want it to. When this happens, you may have to adjust the letter or word spacing, make the hyphenation zone narrower, or select an alignment other than justified.

Try to select a range of word spacing to give PageMaker some leeway to make the necessary adjustments to justify text. For the first article of our newsletter, let's select 80% as a minimum, 100% as a Desired setting (to remain within the font's standard whenever possible), and 110% as a maximum. This 80%–110% range will provide consistency in spacing, while providing PageMaker with enough flexibility to justify text.

To adjust the spacing between words in the first article of the newsletter:

1. Select the text tool from the Toolbox.
2. Click on an insertion point anywhere in the first article.
3. Choose the "Select all" command from the Edit menu to select the entire article.
4. Click on the "Spacing" command from the Type menu. The Spacing Attributes dialog box, shown in Figure 9.3, is displayed.
5. Fill in the Word Space text boxes with the following values: Minimum: 80%, Desired: 100%, Maximum: 110%
6. Click OK.

Now the space between words is adjusted to the 80%–110% range you indicated. Since the adjustments are small, you may not notice the difference on your screen, but you will see them at print time.

▶ ADJUSTING THE SPACE BETWEEN LETTERS

PageMaker measures letter spacing differently than word spacing. The Desired letter spacing built into the font you are using is measured at 0%. Enter 0% in the Minimum letter space box if you want to keep the font's standard spacing

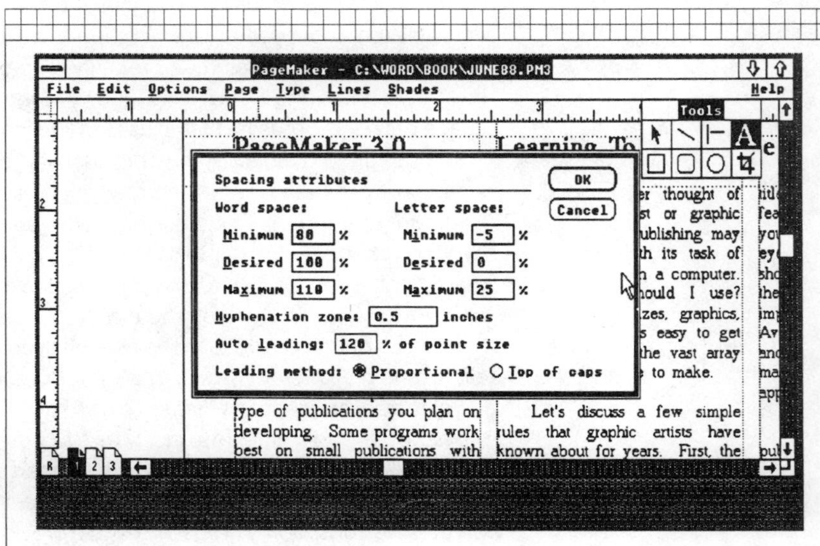

Figure 9.3: Spacing Attributes dialog box

between letters. To make the spacing between letters smaller than the font's standard, enter a negative number in the Minimum letter space box. Increase the range of spacing between letters by entering a positive number in the Maximum letter space box. For example, if you enter 25%, that means PageMaker can add up to 25% more space to the standard font space between letters. PageMaker lets you set the Maximum letter spacing between 0% and 200%, and the Minimum letter spacing between −200% and 0%. The Desired letter spacing value must be greater than or equal to the Minimum setting, and less than or equal to the Maximum setting.

The greater the range you set between the Minimum and Maximum letter spacing, the more flexibility PageMaker has for adjusting the space between letters. PageMaker's default settings work best in most instances. Adjusting the letter spacing comes in handy when you need to pull up an extra line of text, or when you just want to make some changes to the spacing between letters.

> An *orphan* is a single word at the end of a sentence that sits alone at the top of a column or the bottom of a paragraph.

Let's adjust PageMaker's letter spacing to tighten up the space between words. Figure 9.4 shows a portion of the first article of your newsletter. You can see how the word *books* is an orphan on a line by itself. By adjusting the letter spacing, we can bring *books* up into the previous line of text.

1. Select the text tool from the Toolbox.
2. Click an insertion point anywhere in the second paragraph of the first article.

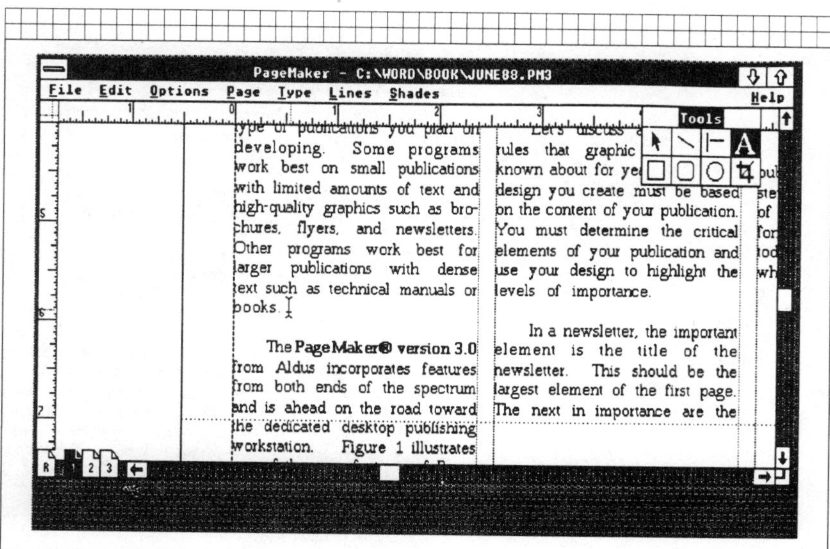

Figure 9.4: Orphaned text

3. Choose the "Spacing" command from the Type menu. The Spacing Attributes dialog box, shown earlier in Figure 9.3, is displayed.
4. Fill in the Letter Space text boxes with the following values: Minimum: –25%, Desired: 0%, Maximum: 0%
5. Click OK.

The word in the last line of the paragraph now is included in the previous line of text, as shown in Figure 9.5.

▶ UNJUSTIFIED TEXT COMPOSITION

Unjustified text is either flush on the left margin, the right margin, or centered between the margin or column guides. Whether or not you use unjustified lines is largely an aesthetic decision. Though the trend is to use justified text, unjustified is often preferable because it has more even word spacing and fewer hyphenated words, making it more readable.

PageMaker cannot control the letter spacing of unjustified text. It uses the standard letter spacing of the font you are using. But you can control the word spacing of unjustified text the same way you control the word spacing for justified text—with the Spacing Attributes dialog box. A good standard to use with unjustified text is to set word spacing somewhere in the range of 50% to 200%.

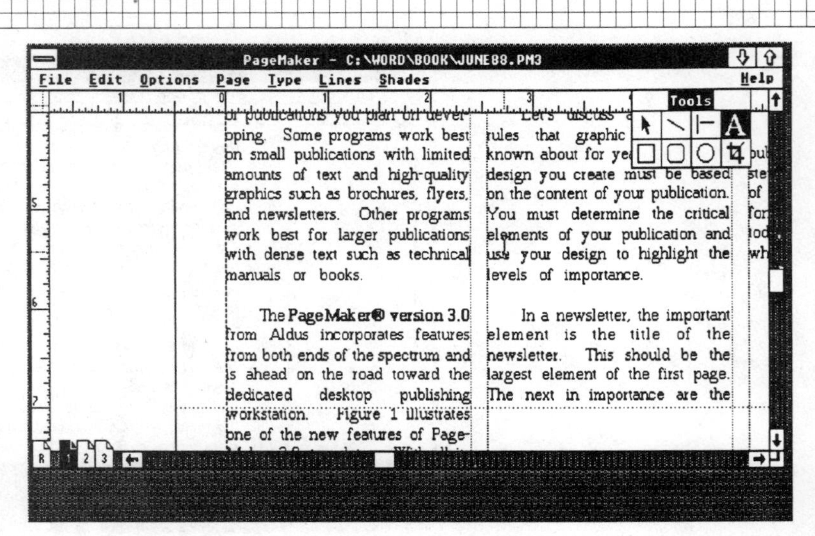

Figure 9.5: Adjusting letter spacing to eliminate orphans

See Chapter 8 for a full discussion of PageMaker's hyphenation methods.

In addition to controlling the word spacing for unjustified text, you can clean up the look of ragged text by controlling hyphenation at the end of the lines. PageMaker breaks a line of unjustified text in one of four ways: between words, at the discretionary hyphens you set, at the regular hyphens you typed in, or by automatic or prompted hyphenation. Essentially, controlling hyphenation adjusts the amount of white space at the end of a line of unjustified text. If you find after recomposition that the text is too ragged for your liking, go back and make the hyphenation zone smaller. On the other hand, if you find that the recomposed text is hyphenated more than you like, go back and make the hyphenation zone larger. Another way to clean up the look of unjustified text is to use the prompted or discretionary hyphens you learned about in the last chapter.

SUMMARY

As you can see, PageMaker provides you with a variety of ways to control the composition of text in your publication. You can change the spacing your word processor injects into text. And you can even adjust how ragged, unjustified text looks. These kinds of changes may not seem to matter at first, but they can make all the difference between a professional- and an unprofessional-looking publication.

► PART IV:

WORKING WITH GRAPHICS

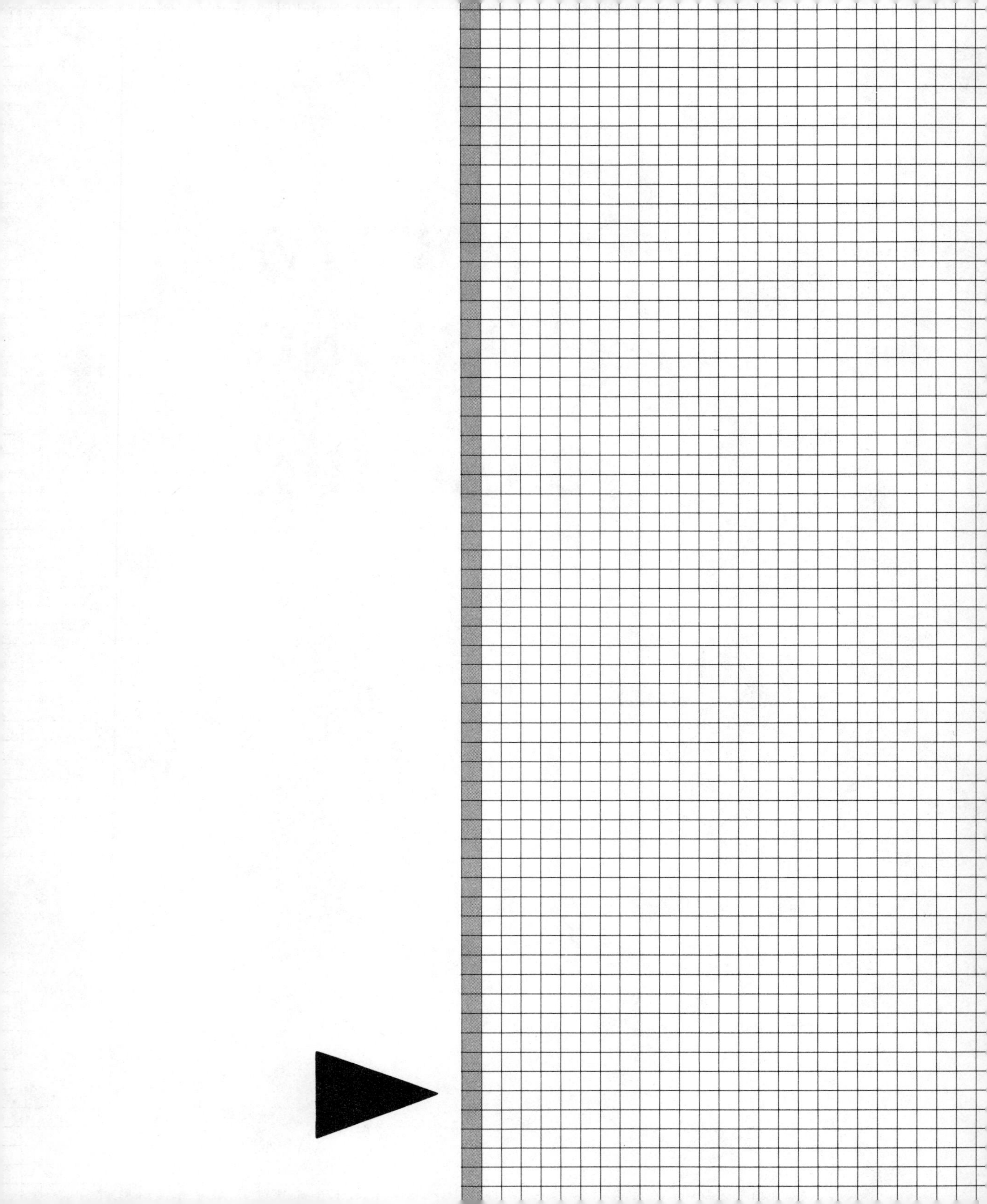

10 BRINGING GRAPHICS INTO YOUR PUBLICATION

To run a Windows program in background mode, **206**

point to the black area at the top of the screen, click and drag the program's icon down to the bottom of the page, then release the mouse button.

To bring up a program running in background mode, **206**

double-click on the program's icon.

To place a graphic on the pasteboard, **210**

select the "Place" command from the File menu. In the Place File dialog box, highlight the file name of the graphic you want to place and click OK. Your icon is loaded with the graphic. Position the icon on the PageMaker pasteboard and click the mouse.

To copy or cut a graphic in PageMaker to the Clipboard, **212**

select the graphic and use the "Copy" or "Cut" command from the Edit menu.

To move a graphic from the pasteboard to a publication, **213**

use the pointer tool to point on the graphic, click and hold down the mouse button, and drag the graphic to the new position.

To delete a graphic from the pasteboard, **214**

select the graphic and use the "Clear" command from the Edit menu, or press the Shift and Del keys simultaneously.

To resize a graphic, 215

click on a handle, then hold down the mouse button and drag the graphic out to its new size.

To resize a graphic proportionally, 215

hold down the Ctrl key as you resize it.

To restore a graphic to its original proportions, 218

select the graphic, hold down the Shift key, and click on a handle of the graphic.

To trim a graphic, 218

position the cropping tool from the Toolbox on a handle of the selected graphic. Click and hold down the mouse button. The cropping tool turns into a double-headed arrow. Move the mouse until the parts you don't want are trimmed and release the mouse button.

PageMaker allows you to place graphics created with a separate graphics software application into your PageMaker publication. Although PageMaker has a few draw capabilities of its own for creating graphics, these capabilities are limited, and you should try to create most of your graphics outside PageMaker using your own graphics software.

Placing graphics from another application is very simple when you take full advantage of the Windows operating environment. If you installed a full version of Windows, you can split your screen into separate windows. You can create a graphic on one half of the screen using your graphics software, and place it into PageMaker running on the other half of your screen. This way, you can see both applications running on the screen at the same time, or you can run one application in the background of the other. A program running in background mode is not displayed on your screen; it is kept running behind the program in the foreground. The background program is accessed by double-clicking on the program's icon. Keep in mind that running screens side by side only works with Windows-compatible graphics programs. Placing graphics into your PageMaker layout is just as simple when you are using a runtime version of Windows. Graphics are imported into PageMaker using the "Place" command, the same command you used to import text from your word processor.

► RUNNING TWO PROGRAMS AT ONCE

Let's run the Windows Paint program in background mode so you can create graphics and place them in PageMaker.

1. With PageMaker running, point to the black area at the top of the screen.
2. Click and hold the mouse button. The pointer turns into the PageMaker icon.
3. Drag the icon down until it is next to the Windows disk icon at the bottom of the screen. This is the MS-DOS Executive disk icon. Release the mouse button.

PageMaker is now in the background, as shown in Figure 10.1. Notice the PageMaker icon in the lower-left corner. When you want to return to PageMaker, double-click on the PageMaker icon.

Let's now bring up the Windows MS-DOS Executive screen so you can select the Paint program.

4. Point to the MS-DOS disk icon and click and hold the mouse button.
5. Drag the icon to the middle of the screen and release the mouse button. The MS-DOS Executive screen is displayed, as shown in Figure 10.2.

Figure 10.1: The PageMaker icon with PageMaker in the background

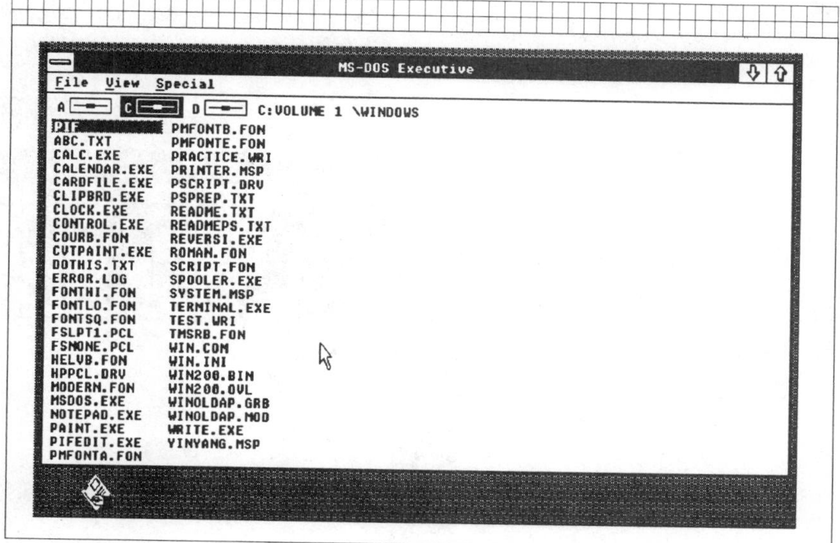

Figure 10.2: The MS-DOS Executive screen and the PageMaker icon

You will see a list of files in alphabetical order. Notice too that the PageMaker icon is still displayed. This is because PageMaker is running in the background. You can bring PageMaker to the foreground at any time by dragging the icon into the middle of the screen.

You are almost ready to start up the Paint program. But first, switch to the Windows directory.

6. Select the "Change directory" command from the Special menu and type in the name of the Windows directory, WINDOWS.
7. Click OK.
8. Point to the PAINT.EXE file and double-click the mouse button. The Paint program is displayed on your screen, as shown in Figure 10.3.

Notice that the PageMaker icon is still present. You can now create a graphic in Paint, copy it to the Clipboard, and paste it into PageMaker without having to enter and exit either program. You will learn how to do this later in this chapter.

If you want to run both programs on your screen at once, you can split the screen into two screens, as shown in Figure 10.4. Refer to your Windows manual for details on splitting windows.

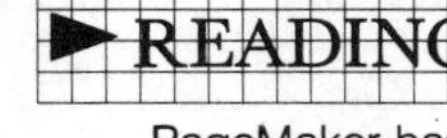

► READING GRAPHICS

For more information about graphics programs and how they work with PageMaker, see Chapter 1.

PageMaker has no trouble reading most graphics directly from disk. Bit-mapped graphics produced by paint programs can be easily read, and so can object-oriented draw files. A *bit-mapped* graphic means that the image is formed by a series of dots

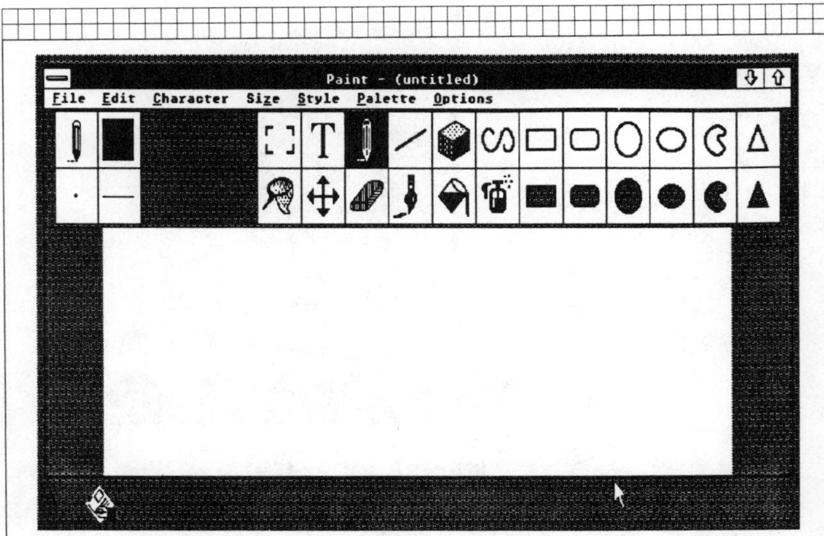

Figure 10.3: The Windows Paint program

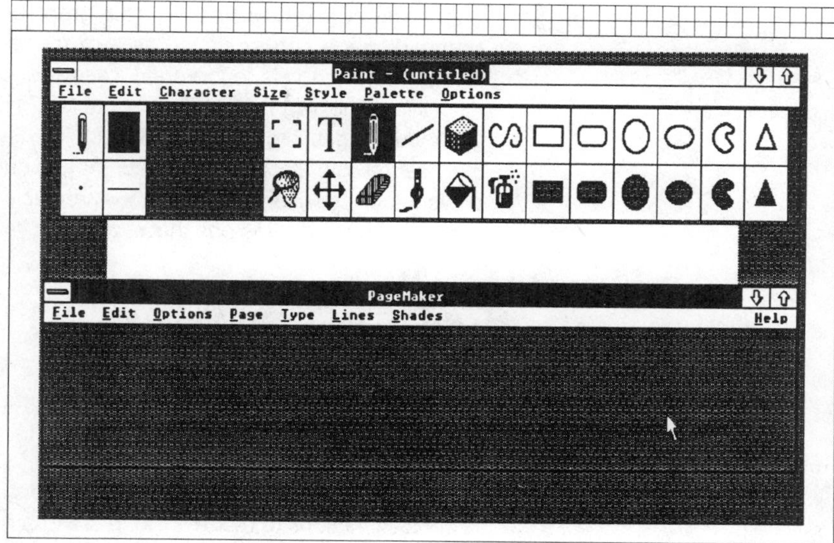

Figure 10.4: A split screen

called pixels. An *object-oriented* draw graphic is created by a sequence of draw commands such as straight-edge and arc. Encapsulated PostScript (EPS) graphics created by writing a PostScript program or by using a PostScript graphics program can be read by PageMaker. PageMaker can also read scanned images.

Paint programs let you create graphics using traditional sketching and painting tools. A paint program creates bit-mapped images, with each bit corresponding to a particular number of pixels. Since pixel size varies among computer systems and printers, a graphic created on one computer system, then used on a different computer system with PageMaker, may create a distorted graphic. You can compensate for these changes using PageMaker's proportional reductions and enlargements.

Draw programs work best for creating precision graphics—lines, geometrical shapes, mechanical drawings, and charts. Since PageMaker works with drawing commands, graphics created with draw programs translate easily when printed.

EPS graphics can have two parts. The first part is the PostScript code used to print the graphic using a PostScript printer. The other is an optional screen image that creates a draw-type graphic to display on your screen. If you create an EPS graphic without an accompanying screen image, a box will appear in place of the graphic on your PageMaker screen. At print time, the EPS graphic is printed in place of the box.

A scanned image is created using a device that electronically enters a picture or graphic into the computer. Scanners read photographs and artwork directly from paper and convert the image into a graphics file that PageMaker can use. A scanned image can be saved as a bit-mapped image or a gray-scale image. A *gray-scale image* is rendered in a series of shades of gray by dots of differing intensities. The Tag Image File Format (TIFF) is a format standard that converts scanned images into bit-mapped graphics. Saving the image in TIFF gives you the best results. Because scanned images can be quite large, PageMaker displays a low resolution version of the scanned image on your screen but the high resolution version is the one that is printed.

► PLACING GRAPHICS

When PageMaker places a graphic in a publication, the graphic remains the same size it was when you created it with your graphics software. Keep this in mind when you are creating graphics. Try to scale your original graphics to the size you want them to be in your publication. When this is not possible, and PageMaker places a graphic that is too big or too small, you can still use PageMaker's graphics functions to resize it, but resizing a graphic can affect the clarity of the image. For example, shrinking a very detailed graphic will blur the image.

You place graphics in your publication much the same way as you place text from your word processor. Use the column guides and the ruler guides to line up your graphics in your layout. The difference between placing text and placing a graphic is, when a graphic is placed in a column, the text does not flow around it. Each graphic is an independent block. It does not become part of the text block in which it was placed. So the best approach is to place your graphic first, then flow the text around it using the PageMaker 3.0 text wrap feature. (You'll learn about text wrapping in Chapter 12.)

For the exercises in this chapter, you will need to create a practice graphic using your graphics software. It must be a box-shaped graphic with corners. When your practice graphic is ready, save it.

In Chapter 8, we inserted a sentence in the first article that referred to Figure 1 on the page. It's time to place Figure 1 in our newsletter. For the example in this book, Figure 1 is a graphic of a template included with PageMaker 3.0. You will substitute your own practice graphic.

If you no longer have the newsletter displayed on your screen, bring it up using the "Open" command from the File menu. To place the graphic:

1. Select the "Place" command from the File menu. The Place File dialog box, shown in Figure 10.5, is displayed.
2. If necessary, move to the directory where your practice graphics file is located and highlight the file name.
3. Click OK or "Place as new graphic."

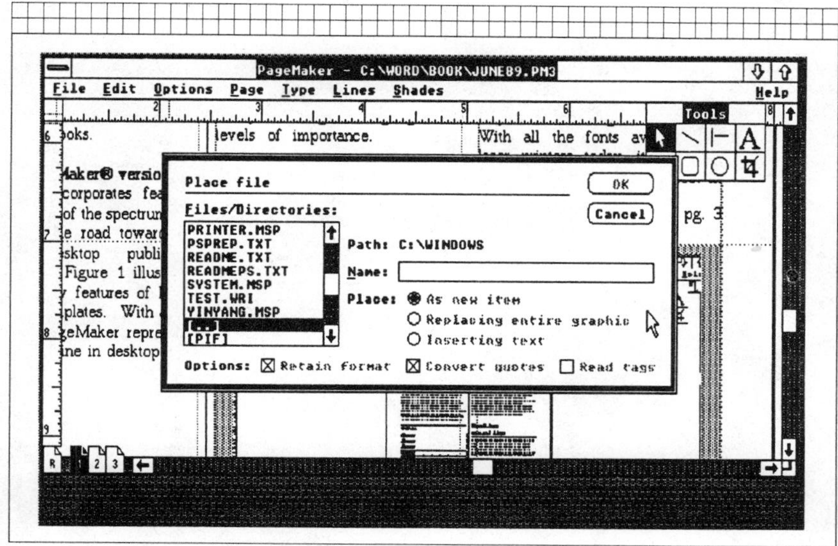

Figure 10.5: The Place File dialog box

The pointer icon is loaded up with your graphics file. If you created your graphic with a paint-type program, the icon turns into the paintbrush icon. If you used a draw program, the icon turns into the pencil icon. An EPS graphic displays a PostScript icon, and a scanned image using TIFF displays a TIFF icon. In our example, the paintbrush icon is displayed.

Let's first position the graphic in the pasteboard.

1. Use the gray scroll bars to position a blank area of the pasteboard in the middle of your screen.
2. Position the icon in the pasteboard and click the mouse button. The graphic flows into the pasteboard area, as shown in Figure 10.6.

Notice the eight small rectangles surrounding the graphic. These are handles—when they are showing it means the graphic is selected. These handles, similar to text block handles, help you resize or crop graphics as necessary. Keep the graphic in the pasteboard—in a moment you'll move it to the Clipboard.

► REPLACING A GRAPHIC

PageMaker 3.0 lets you replace a graphic in your publication with a new one. You can replace both the graphics you imported from your draw and paint programs, and the graphics you made with PageMaker's drawing tools. (PageMaker drawing tools are covered in the next chapter.) If the new graphic is the same size

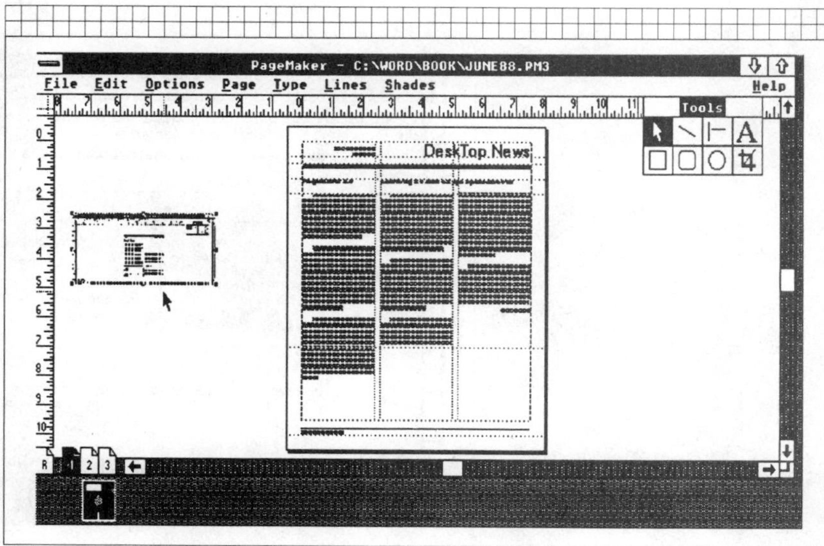

Figure 10.6: The graphic flowed into the pasteboard

as the replaced one, PageMaker automatically scales and crops it for you in the same way. But if the new graphic is a different size, PageMaker will reproportion it automatically to fit the space occupied by the replaced graphic.

To replace a graphic you imported from a paint or draw program, use the pointer tool to select the graphic you want to replace. With the graphic selected, click on the "Place" command from the File menu. The Place File dialog box (Figure 10.5) is displayed. Click on the "Replacing entire graphic" option button. The new graphic will appear in place of the selected one. Pressing the Shift key and clicking on a handle makes the graphic revert to its original size. Pressing the Ctrl key and clicking on a handle returns the graphic to the size of the one it replaced.

► WORKING WITH GRAPHICS AND THE CLIPBOARD

The Clipboard in the Windows environment allows you to temporarily store the text or graphic you last copied or cut. Use the Clipboard when you want to retain an original copy of a graphic before you start making changes to it, or when you want to store a graphic in order to move it somewhere new in your publication. The first step is to cut the graphic to the Clipboard. From there, you can paste it in a new location, or in a new publication altogether. In the case of a new publication, once the graphic is in the Clipboard, bring up the new publication and paste the graphic where you want it.

Refer to the manual that came with your Windows-compatible graphics software to learn more about moving graphics to the Clipboard.

Lastly, you can use the Clipboard to transfer a graphic from a Windows-compatible graphics program to PageMaker. First you create a graphic in another window with your graphics software, then you copy it to the Clipboard. Next, place the graphic in your PageMaker publication.

In Chapter 7 you learned that the Clipboard can only hold one item at a time. Remember, each time you copy or cut text or a graphic to the Clipboard, the last item in the Clipboard is erased and is replaced by the new item. The new item will remain there until the next time you copy or cut something to the Clipboard, or you exit the Windows environment.

To copy a graphic placed in PageMaker to the Clipboard, be sure the graphic is selected. You'll know a graphic is selected when its eight handles are showing.

1. Select the practice graphic you placed earlier on PageMaker's pasteboard. If the handles are not showing, point anywhere on the graphic with the pointer tool and click the mouse button.
2. Choose the "Copy" command from the Edit menu.
3. A copy of the practice graphic is moved to the Clipboard, and the practice graphic in the pasteboard is still there.

Your screen won't look any different. Later you will use the "Paste" command option from the Edit menu to place the second copy of the practice graphic back on the pasteboard. The "Cut" command in the Edit menu removes a graphic from the publication and puts it in the Clipboard. The Del key may also be used to cut a graphic to the Clipboard.

► ADJUSTING GRAPHICS

Once you place a graphic in the publication, you can use PageMaker to make changes to it. You can move the graphic anywhere on the page. You can also move it to another page in the publication by moving it to the pasteboard area, then displaying the page where you want to place the graphic in the publication window, and moving the graphic from the pasteboard onto the page. You can reduce or enlarge a graphic and later restore it to its original proportions. You can also crop a graphic to edit out the parts you don't want.

► MOVING A GRAPHIC ONTO THE PAGE

PageMaker allows you to select an individual graphic or a group of graphics to move together in a publication.

Let's position your practice graphic on the page.

1. Be sure page 1 is displayed. If not, click on the page 1 icon.
2. The pointer tool should already be selected. If not, select the pointer tool from the Toolbox.
3. Point anywhere on the graphic except on the handles. Pointing on the handles may cause the graphic to resize and look distorted.
4. Click and hold down the mouse button.
5. Drag the graphic into position on the page, in the blank space at the bottom of columns 2 and 3, as shown in Figure 10.7. Use the column guides to accurately place the graphic, then release the mouse button.

If your graphic does not fit well into the space, don't worry about it. Later in this chapter you will learn how to resize and shape a graphic to make it fit better.

If you want to move a graphic in only one direction, either horizontally or vertically, release the mouse button and hold down the Shift key while you move the graphic with the pointer tool. This limits the direction that the mouse can drag the graphic on the page.

► ERASING A GRAPHIC

Using the PageMaker commands, you can delete a graphic completely. Let's paste the graphic from the Clipboard into the publication window so we can practice deleting a graphic.

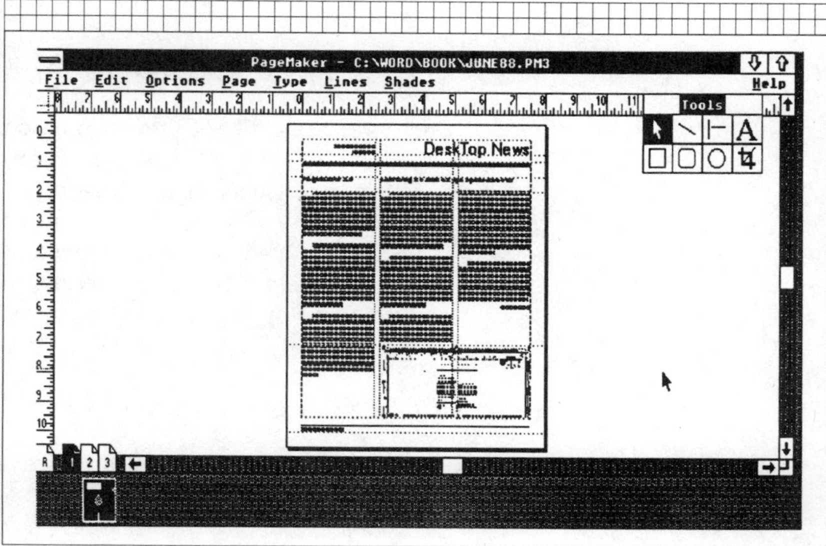

Figure 10.7: The placed graphic

1. Use the "Paste" command from the Edit menu to paste the graphic in the Clipboard to the pasteboard.
2. The pasted graphic appears in the middle of the screen. Use the pointer tool to move the graphic into a blank area of the pasteboard.
3. Point and click on the graphic to select it.

Remember, a graphic is selected when the eight rectangular box handles are displayed. You can delete more than one graphic at a time by holding down the Shift key as you select the graphics. Be sure the graphic in the pasteboard, not the one on page 1, is selected.

4. Once you're sure that the graphic you want to delete is selected, point to the Edit menu. Now you must select either the "Cut" or "Clear" command from the list of command options.

If you select the "Cut" option, the graphic will be moved back to the Clipboard again. To retrieve it, you can use the "Paste" command. If you select "Clear," the graphic will be deleted permanently from the pasteboard. Another way to delete a selected graphic is to press the Shift and Del keys simultaneously.

5. Select either the "Cut" or "Clear" command. Your graphic disappears.

► RESIZING A GRAPHIC

PageMaker allows you to enlarge or reduce the size of a graphic. You can keep the original proportions, or you can stretch or compress the graphic in order to make it a new size. If your graphic looks distorted after you've resized it, you can always return it to its original, undistorted state.

When you create a graphic using your paint program, the resolution of the graphic may be different from the resolution on your screen. When you resize a graphic, it may blur on the screen but print out fine. Or it may look fine on the screen but look blurred on the printed copy. You can avoid these problems by using PageMaker's standard reductions and enlargements. Do this by holding down the Ctrl key as you enlarge or reduce the graphic.

Changing the Proportions

With the pointer, select a graphic that you want to resize. You can resize the graphic on page 1, or you can resize another graphic, as I will do. Unlike using cutting and pasting, you can only resize one graphic at a time. If you want to maintain the original proportions in a graphic as you resize it, hold down the Ctrl key.

Otherwise, the graphic will distort as you resize it. PageMaker lets you resize a graphic in four ways:

- To resize a graphic and keep the original proportions, point on any handle and hold down the Ctrl key.
- To resize a graphic both horizontally and vertically at the same time, point on a corner handle.
- To resize a graphic horizontally (which widens it), point on a left-side or right-side middle handle.
- To resize a graphic vertically (which elongates it), point on a top or bottom middle handle.

For practice, try holding down the Ctrl key to resize proportionally, then try it with distortion. Notice the different results. Figure 10.8 shows the graphic before any changes were made. Figure 10.9 shows the graphic proportionally enlarged in size. Figure 10.10 shows the graphic enlarged in size, but distorted because the Ctrl key was not used.

To use the PageMaker reduction feature, press and hold down the main mouse button. The pointer turns into a double-headed arrow. Then press and hold the Ctrl key. Move the pointer until the graphic is the size you want it. If you are holding

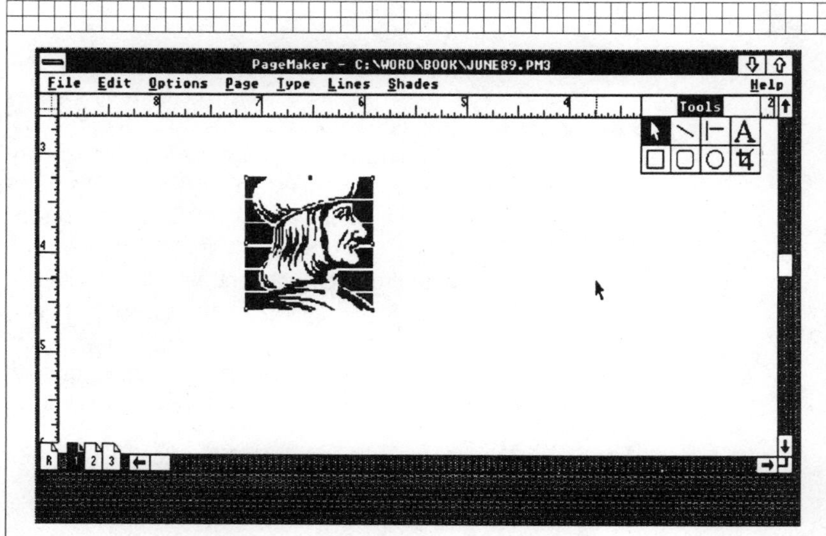

Figure 10.8: Graphic before any changes have been made

the Ctrl key to get a standard reduction, move the pointer to the standard reduction line you want to use. When the graphic is the size you want, release the mouse button and Ctrl key.

Figure 10.9: Proportionally enlarged graphic

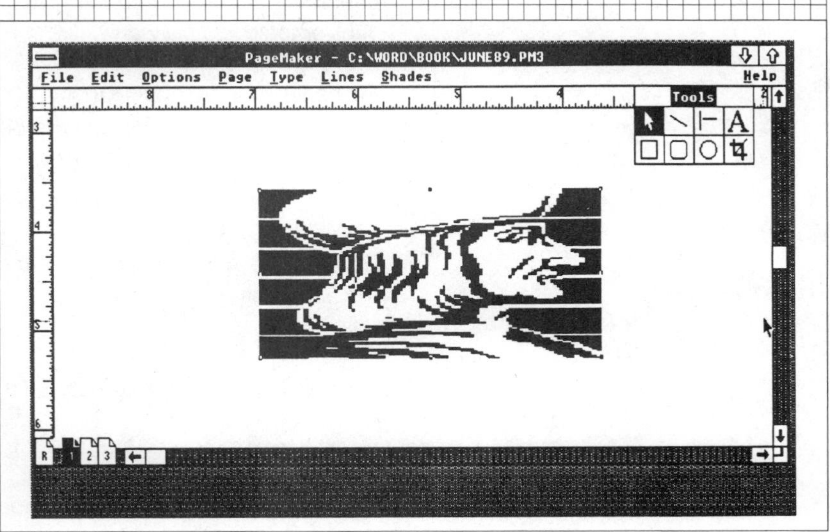

Figure 10.10: Distorted enlarged graphic

Restoring a Graphic to its Original Proportions

If you did not hold down the Ctrl key as you resized your graphic, it probably distorted in order to fit into its new size. You can restore a graphic to its original dimensions. First, select the distorted graphic. Press and hold down the Shift key. Point to any handle on the graphic and click the mouse button. The graphic is restored to its original dimensions, although its original size is not necessarily recovered.

► TRIMMING A GRAPHIC

You can use the PageMaker cropping tool to delete any part of a graphic. With the cropping tool, you can trim, or crop, the unwanted part without changing the rest of the graphic, as if you were using scissors. As a result, the overall size of the graphic will be reduced, but the size of the uncropped portion will remain the same.

Let's crop the graphic we just enlarged.

1. Select the graphic.
2. Select the cropping tool from the Toolbox, which is the one you see highlighted in Figure 10.11. The pointer will change to the cropping tool icon.
3. Position the cropping tool on a handle of your selected graphic. Corner handles are used to trim the graphic vertically or horizontally. To trim your graphic vertically only, select a top or bottom handle. To trim horizontally only, select a side handle. Make sure the handle shows through the center of the cropping tool.
4. Click and hold down the main mouse button. The cropping tool icon turns into a double-headed arrow.
5. Move the mouse until the parts you don't want are trimmed away, as shown in Figure 10.11.
6. Release the mouse button and the untrimmed parts of the graphic remain intact.

► ADJUSTING THE BORDERS OF A GRAPHIC

After you crop, you may need to adjust the borders of the graphic to make it fit the space it occupied before you cropped it. You can use the cropping tool to do this. When you use this tool, PageMaker automatically creates a frame, or border, to show you the borders of the graphic so you can see where you are cutting away. The frame then disappears after you have made the adjustment.

Let's adjust the borders of the graphic you just cropped.

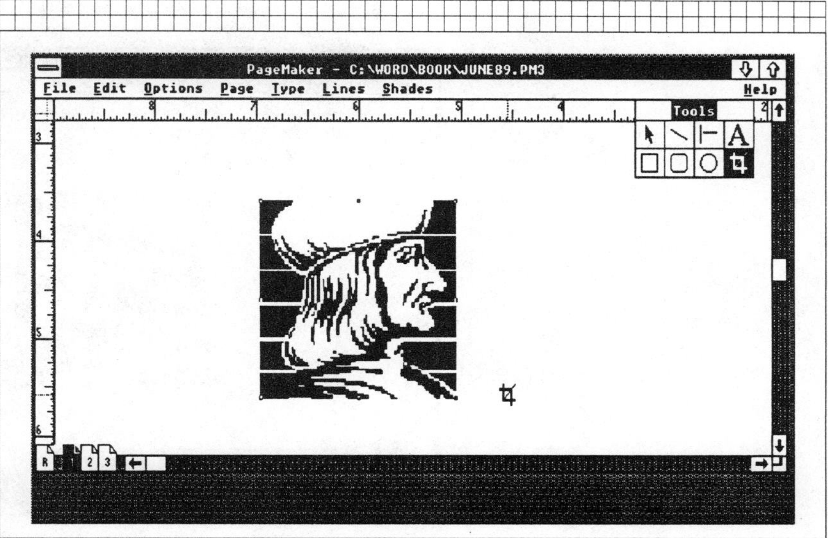

Figure 10.11: Cropping a graphic

1. Select the graphic with the cropping tool (if it is not still selected) by positioning the cropping tool on a handle of the graphic. Make sure the handle shows through the middle of the cropping tool.
2. Click and hold the mouse button and the cropping tool turns into a double-headed arrow.
3. Now slide the mouse around until the parts of the graphic you want are showing, as if you were making a frame around the graphic, as shown in Figure 10.12. You can make this "frame" smaller or larger as you like by dragging the mouse until the frame is the size you want. Release the mouse button when the graphic you want is framed.

If you want to adjust what part of the graphic is within this frame, point the cropping tool in the center of the cropped graphic. Click and hold the main mouse button to make the grabber hand appear. Now slide the mouse around in any direction until the parts you want are displayed in the frame of the cropped graphic. Once the graphic is positioned as you want it, release the mouse button.

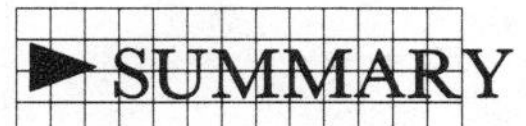

► SUMMARY

As you've learned, there are many ways to manipulate a graphic you created with your graphics software after you've placed the graphic in PageMaker.

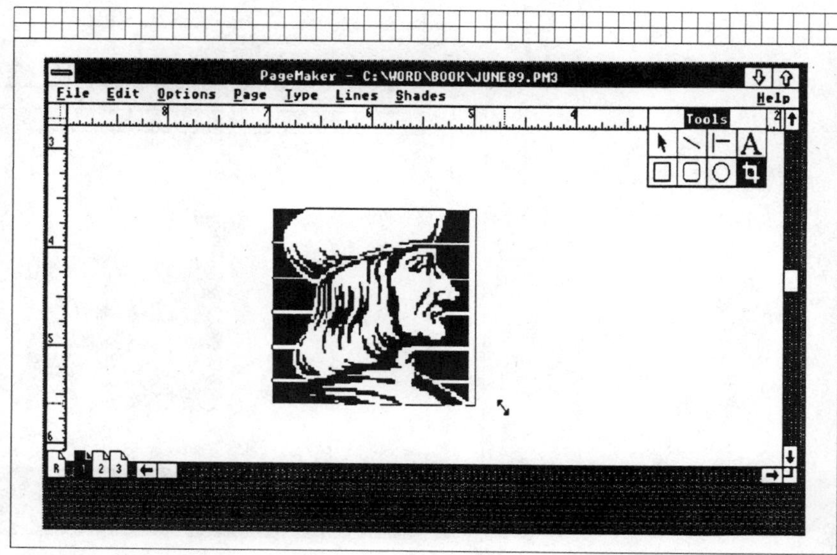

Figure 10.12: Framing a graphic

You've probably noticed that the more accurately you create your graphic outside of PageMaker, the easier it is to place in your publication. In the next chapter, you will learn how to use PageMaker's own graphics capabilities to enhance your graphics and the entire design of your publication.

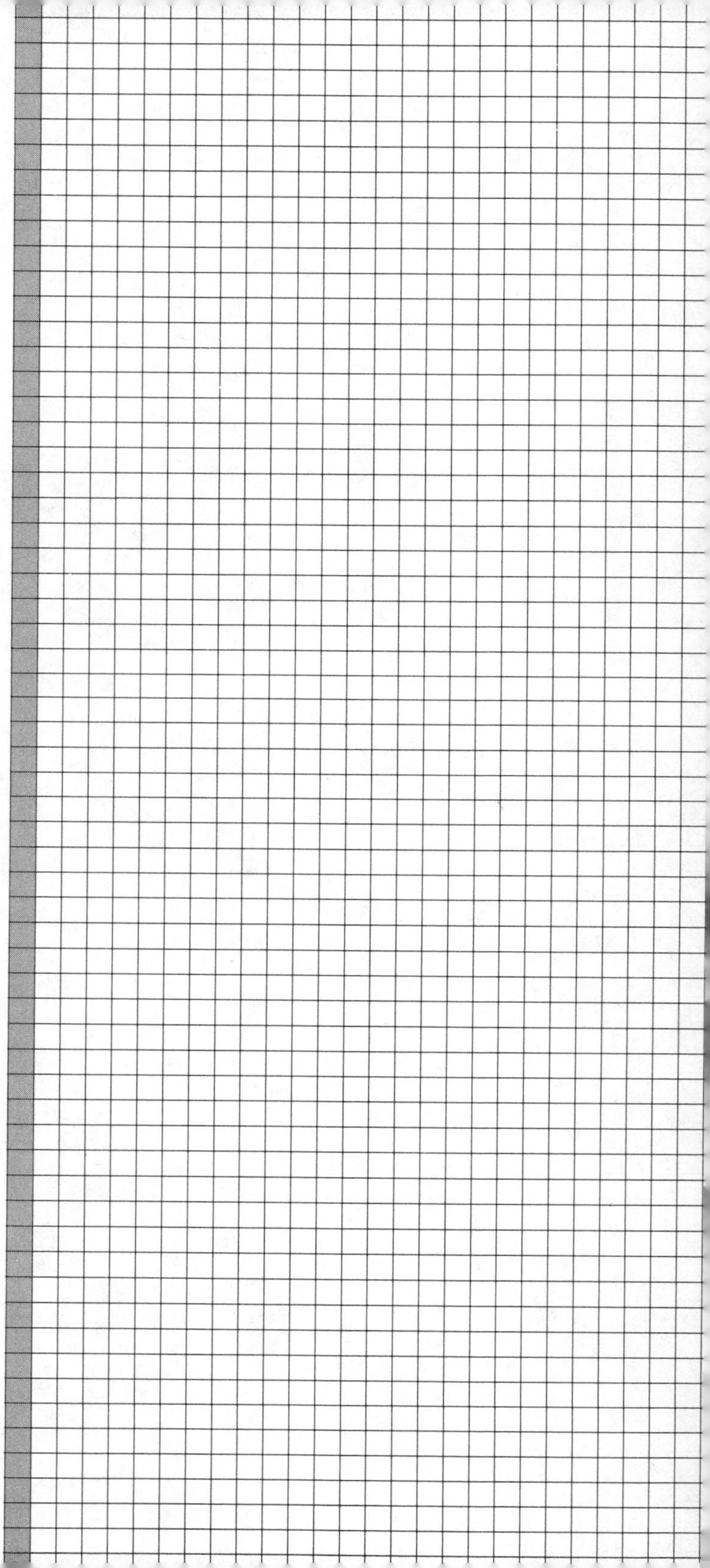

11 CREATING GRAPHICS WITH PAGEMAKER

To draw a line, 226

select the diagonal or perpendicular line tool from the Toolbox, click on the Lines menu, then select the type of line you want to use. Click and hold down the mouse button and glide the crossbar to draw the line. When you've finished drawing, release the mouse button.

To draw a box around a graphic, 227

select either the square- or round-corner box tool from the Toolbox. The tool changes into a crossbar. Position the crossbar at one corner of the graphic, click and hold down the mouse button. Drag the crossbar to the opposite corner and release the mouse button.

To change a rectangle to a square, 227

hold down the Shift key and click on a handle of the rectangle.

To draw a circle or oval, 229

select the circle tool from the Toolbox. Click and hold down the mouse button while sliding the crossbar in any direction.

To change an oval into a circle, 229

hold down the Shift key and click on a handle of the oval.

To change the length and direction of a line, 232

click on a handle of the line, and move the handle in the new direction to the length you want.

To add shading or a pattern to a PageMaker graphic, 232

click on the Shades menu and select the shade or pattern you want.

To add a color to your Colors palette, 237

select the "Define color" command from the Options menu. In the Define Colors dialog box, click on "New" to see the Edit Color dialog box. In this box, type in the name of the color you want to add to the Colors palette. Click on the color model you want to use and create the color with the slider bars.

To add spot color to text or to a graphic, 241

select the text or graphic and click on the color you want in the Colors palette.

To control the lightness, contrast, and screen pattern 243

in paint-type or scanned images, select the "Image control" option from the Options menu.

PageMaker has four different drawing tools to help you enhance the look of the graphics you place in PageMaker and embellish the look of your page layout. You can also choose the style and point size of the lines in your graphics, select from a variety of shade patterns, customize the corners of your PageMaker-created boxes, and more.

In this chapter you'll learn to use these tools to draw lines, squares, rectangles, circles, and ovals. You'll also learn to add shading and colors to your graphics, and to adjust the size, contrast, degree of lightness and darkness, and screen pattern of graphics.

► DRAWING STRAIGHT LINES

PageMaker has two line tools in the Toolbox to help you draw a line on your page in any direction: the perpendicular line tool, which draws lines at 45-degree increments, and the diagonal line tool, which draws lines in any direction. The diagonal tool can be made to work like the perpendicular tool—simply hold down the Shift key while the diagonal tool is selected. This way, you can draw 45-degree lines whenever you need to without switching tools.

Both tools, after they have been selected, are represented on the screen by a crossbar. When you draw, the line begins at the intersection of the crossbar. Diagonal lines centered on the crossbar can be rotated 45 degrees by sliding the crossbar in the direction in which you want the lines to rotate.

You have already used one of the line tools to create a rule across the top and bottom of your publication. Let's practice using the line tool to create a hairline between columns. (A hairline is a very fine line between page columns that helps guide the reader's eye down the column.)

Let's practice drawing a hairline.

1. Select the perpendicular line tool from the Toolbox or use the diagonal line tool with the Shift key. The pointer turns into the crossbar icon.
2. Click on the Lines menu and select the "Hairline" option. A check mark will appear next to the option to show you've selected it.
3. Check the Options menu to see if the "Snap to guides" feature is selected. Since we want to draw between the column guides, "Snap to guides" must be off.
4. Position the crossbar on the 1.75-inch horizontal guide, between the column guides separating the first and second column.
5. Click and hold down the mouse button.
6. Slide the crossbar down the column guides and position it on the bottom margin guide.
7. Release the mouse button.

A hairline should now exist between the first and second columns, as shown in Figure 11.1. This hairline will help the reader distinguish between the short article in column 1 and the long article in columns 2 and 3.

Like text blocks and graphics, lines also have handles, as shown in Figure 11.1. Line handles rest at each end so you can reposition the line if necessary. Later in this chapter you will learn how to use these handles to make adjustments to lines you've drawn with PageMaker.

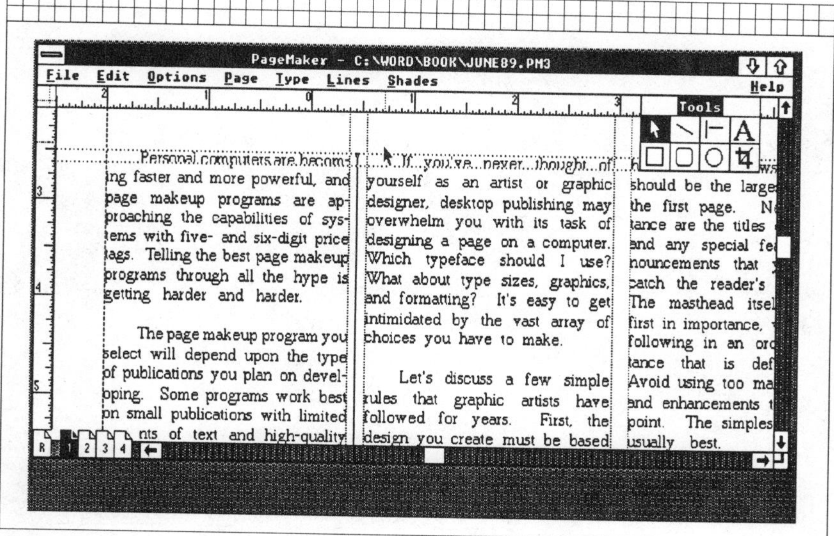

Figure 11.1: Drawing a hairline

► DRAWING GEOMETRIC SHAPES

PageMaker also provides tools to draw rectangles, squares, circles, and ovals. In addition, you can select from six rounded corner styles for squares and rectangles. Once a graphic is drawn, you can also make adjustments to its position, and you can change a rectangle into a square or an oval into a circle.

► DRAWING RECTANGLES AND SQUARES

Just as there are two line tools, there are two tools for drawing squares and rectangles: one for drawing rounded corners and one for square corners. You can use these tools to enhance your graphics by framing them in boxes on the page. Both tools draw rectangles, and either can be used to draw squares by pressing the Shift key while you use the tool.

Let's practice using these tools by framing the graphic on page 1.

Whenever you select a drawing tool, the pointer changes into a crossbar.

1. Select either box tool from the Toolbox. The pointer changes into a crossbar.
2. Position the crossbar at one corner of the graphic.
3. Click and hold down the mouse button.
3. Drag the crossbar diagonally to the opposite corner of the graphic.
4. When the crossbar is positioned, release the mouse button.

You have now created a box to frame the graphic on page 1, as shown in Figure 11.2.

To select a tool, click on the one you want from the Toolbox.

If you used the rounded-corner tool to frame the graphic on page 1, you can now choose from six styles of rounded corners to put around the graphic. If you did not use the rounded-corner tool, go back and frame the graphic on page 1 with the rounded-corner tool so you have something to practice with. To add rounded corners to the framed graphic on page 1:

1. Be sure the box on page 1 is selected. You can select several boxes at a time by pressing the Shift key each time you select a graphic.
2. Choose the "Rounded corners" option from the Options menu. The Rounded Corners dialog box, shown in Figure 11.3, is displayed.

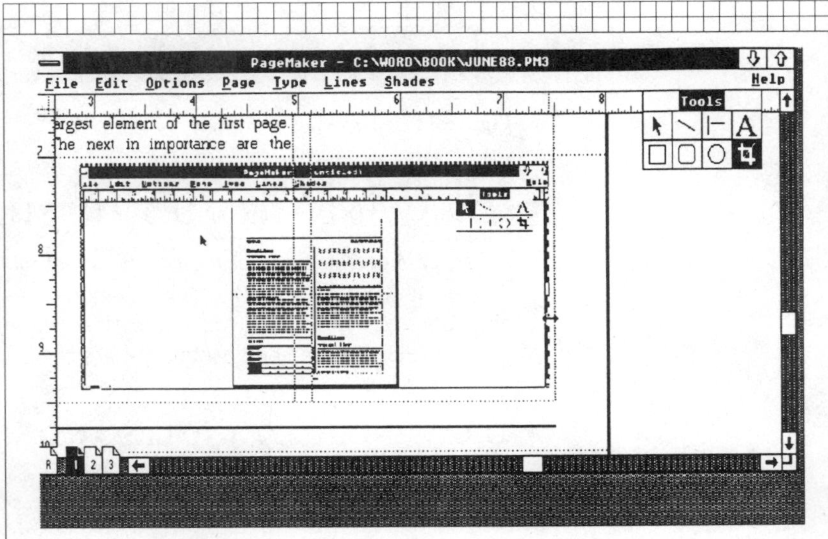

Figure 11.2: Graphic framed with box

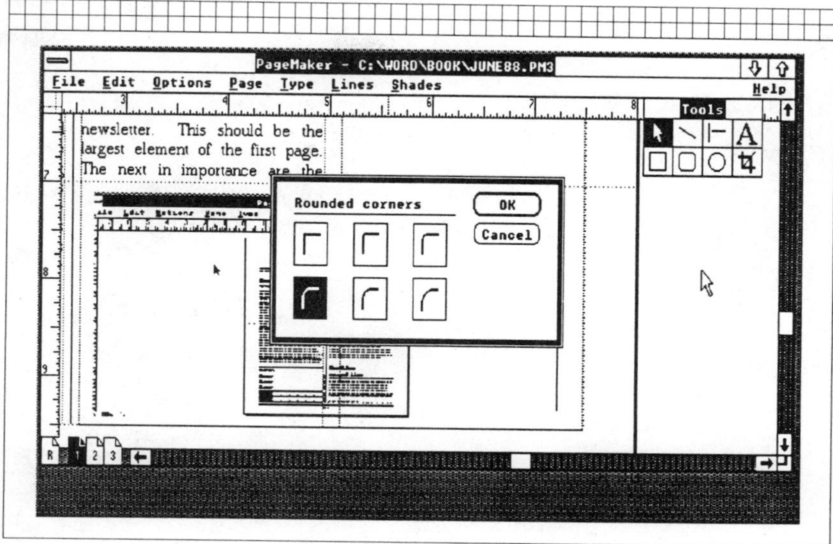

Figure 11.3: Rounded Corners dialog box

There are six corner styles in the dialog box. You have to choose one at a time. The currently selected corner style is highlighted. Let's select a new corner style.

3. Point to the option button corresponding to the rounded corner you want to use, click the mouse button, then click OK.
4. The box on page 1 now contains the corner style you chose.

If you want to change a rectangle into a square, you can do it quickly without having to redraw. First, make sure the rectangle you want to change is selected. Remember, a graphic is selected when its handles are visible. Hold down the Shift key and point on any rectangle handle. Click the mouse button and the rectangle quickly changes to a square. Remember that when you resize a graphic, text or other graphics may get covered up.

► DRAWING OVALS AND CIRCLES

Let's practice drawing some circles and ovals. If you are running out of room on the page, click on a new page or use the pasteboard area for practice. First we'll draw an oval, then we'll change it into a circle.

1. Select the circle tool from the Toolbox.

2. Position the center of the crossbar where you want to start drawing the oval. Click and hold the mouse button while sliding the crossbar in any direction.
3. When the oval is positioned and sized as you want it, release the mouse button and the oval is created, as shown in Figure 11.4.

If you wanted to make a perfect circle, you would follow the same procedure, except you would hold down the Shift key while sliding the crossbar.

Let's change the oval to a circle. First, be sure the oval you just drew is selected.

4. Hold down the Shift key and point to any handle on the oval.
5. Click the mouse button and the oval quickly changes to a circle.

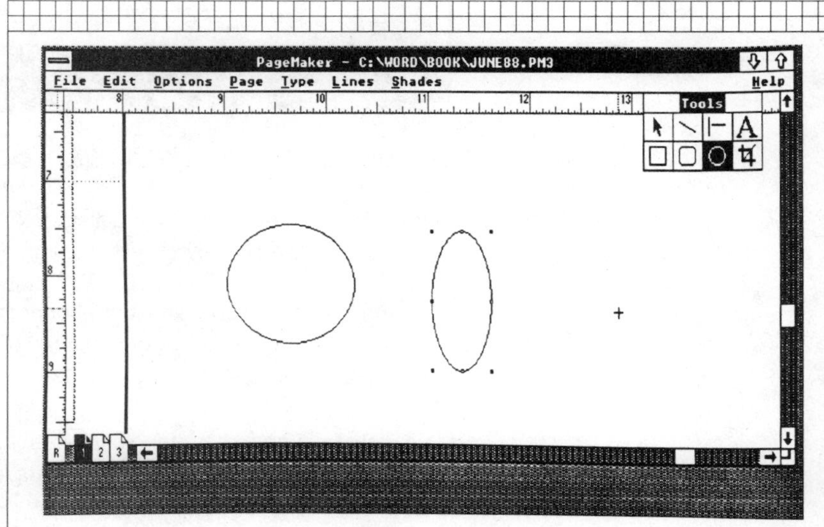

Figure 11.4: A circle and oval drawn with PageMaker

► ADJUSTING AND ENHANCING PAGEMAKER'S GRAPHICS

There are several adjustments or enhancements you can make to the graphics you draw with PageMaker's graphics tools. You can select from ten different line styles as well as several point sizes. In addition, you can fill graphics with a variety of shade patterns. You can also make adjustments to the size of graphics and to the length and direction of lines.

► CHOOSING THE LINE WIDTH AND STYLE

You can adjust the width and style of a line in your PageMaker graphics. Figure 11.5 shows the 18 sizes and styles you can choose from. The 1-point through 12-point line size samples in the Lines menu are shown at their actual size. (The .5-point line looks the same as the 1-point line on the screen because it is too small to show at actual size.) The hairline size is not shown. Choose the "None" option when you want to erase a selected line. The "Reverse line" option creates a white line on a dark background. It will be discussed later.

The variety of patterns and widths enables you to provide interest to your publication by adding a creative touch to your graphics. However, remember that simplicity is one of the basic design principles.

Let's select a 1-point line size for the box framing the graphic on page 1.

1. Select the box surrounding the graphic. Remember, the box is selected when its handles are displayed.
2. Click on the Lines menu, shown in Figure 11.5, and select the "1pt" option. The lines of the box will now be 1-point lines.

Depending on the resolution of your screen, and the view you are using, the new line point size you select may not look different than the old line. Try changing to a larger view, such as Actual Size, to get a better idea of how the new line will

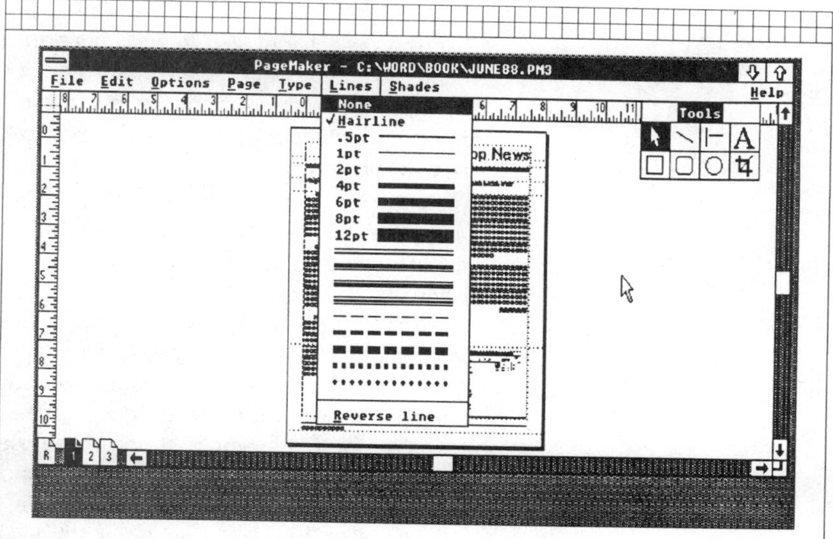

Figure 11.5: The Lines menu showing the sizes and styles of lines

look at print time. The width of a line at print time also depends on the resolution of your printer. If you select a hairline, the smallest line option, your printer must have a resolution of 288 pixels per inch or more in order for the line to print accurately. Otherwise, the line will print wider on the page.

For practice, choose another line style by pointing to it and clicking the mouse button. Again, the lines of the box surrounding the graphic on page 1 are quickly changed.

► CHANGING THE LINE LENGTH AND DIRECTION

You can lengthen or change the direction of a line drawn with PageMaker. First, use the pointer tool to select a line. Next, click on either handle of the line and hold the mouse button until the pointer turns into a crossbar. Now move the handle in any direction until the line is the length you want and the direction you want. Release the mouse button and the line is placed in its new position on the page.

Often you will want to change the length of a line without inadvertently altering its orientation. If the line is currently horizontal or vertical, or it is at an exact 45-degree angle, you can "freeze" its orientation by holding down the Shift key while you use the pointer to lengthen the line or make it shorter.

► USING SHADING AND PATTERNS

You can select from 14 different shades and patterns to enhance the geometric shapes you create with PageMaker's graphics tools. Though these shading patterns are frequently used to fill in geometric shapes, they can also be used to create many other design effects. For example, Figure 11.6 shows our newsletter title with shading over the text. Figure 11.7 illustrates how shading can be used to create a box without borders. In this case, the boxes are bullets for a list of items. Or, you can combine shading with lines to create an effect such as that in Figure 11.8. The running heads on each page of this book are also examples of how a pattern can be used with text.

The Shades menu (Figure 11.9) shows the shading and patterns available. The percentage options indicate the various shades of gray. The "Paper" and "Solid" options can be used to block out unwanted parts of a graphic. PageMaker doesn't provide a way to erase a part of a graphic, but these options can be used like an eraser. For example, suppose you used PageMaker to place text over a graphic you created in another graphics application, but want to black out the parts of the graphic that touch the text in order to make the text easier to read (see Figure 11.10). You first would place the text over the graphic, then use the "Paper" option to block out a portion of the graphic, as shown in Figure 11.10.

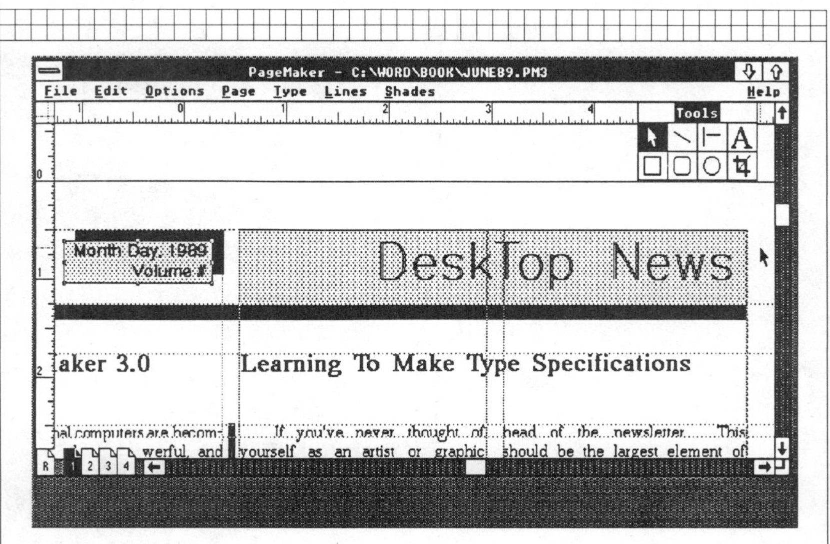

Figure 11.6: The newsletter title enhanced with shading

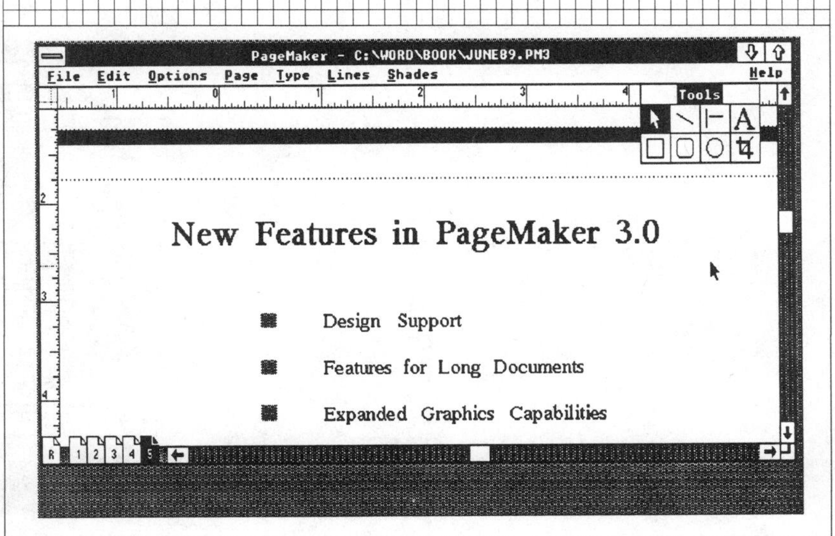

Figure 11.7: Using shading as a box without borders

Let's select a shade as a background to the graphic we framed in a box on page 1.

Figure 11.8: Combining two graphic enhancements—shading and rules—with text

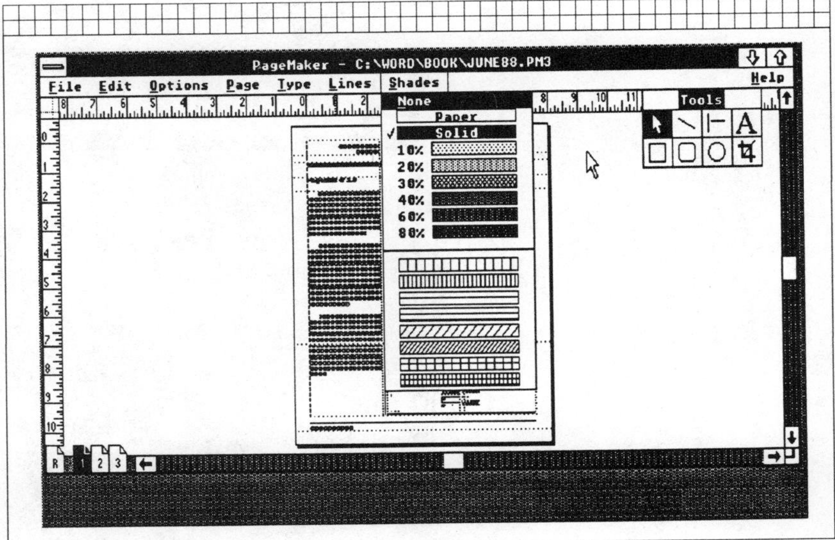

Figure 11.9: The Shades menu

1. Select the page 1 graphic with the pointer tool. Make sure all handles are displayed.
2. Click on the Shades menu, shown in Figure 11.9.

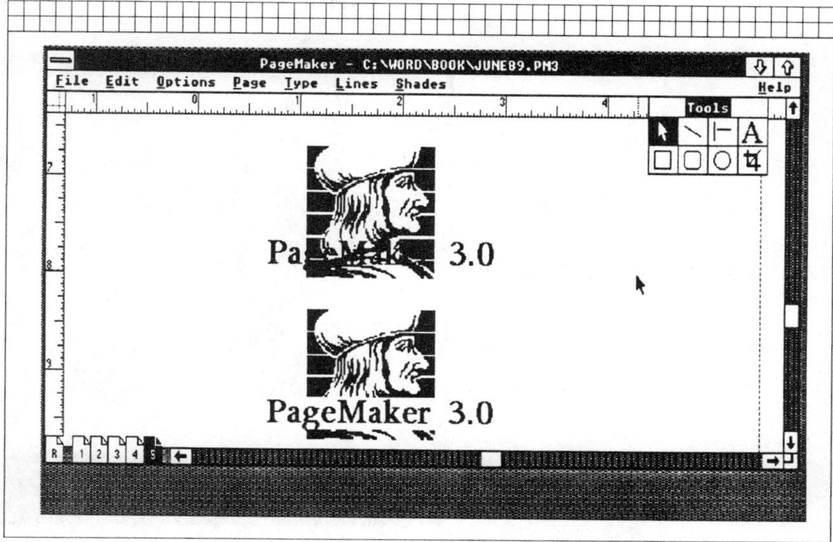

Figure 11.10: The "Paper" option on the Shades menu used to erase part of a graphic

3. Select the "40% shade" option. A check mark appears next to the selected option, and the box is covered with the 40% gray shade. Notice how the shade covers the graphic—the graphic is now in the background, and the shaded box is in the foreground.

When two graphics overlap like this, you can switch them, moving one to the background and the other to the foreground. We need to switch the two overlapping graphics on page 1 and put the original graphic in the foreground and the shaded PageMaker box in the background. To do this:

1. Use the pointer tool to select the graphic. The selected graphic, in this case, the shaded box, is the one in the foreground.
2. Click on the Edit menu.
3. Select the "Send to back" option from the menu.

Now the selected graphic, the shaded box, is sent to the background and the original graphic is in the foreground, as shown in Figure 11.11. The shaded box has become a backdrop to help the original graphic stand out.

Regardless of the view you take of the publication window, the shades you see on your screen are the same hue as the ones you select from the Shades menu. But shade patterns, like the resolution of your graphics, vary depending on the print resolution you are able to get from your printer.

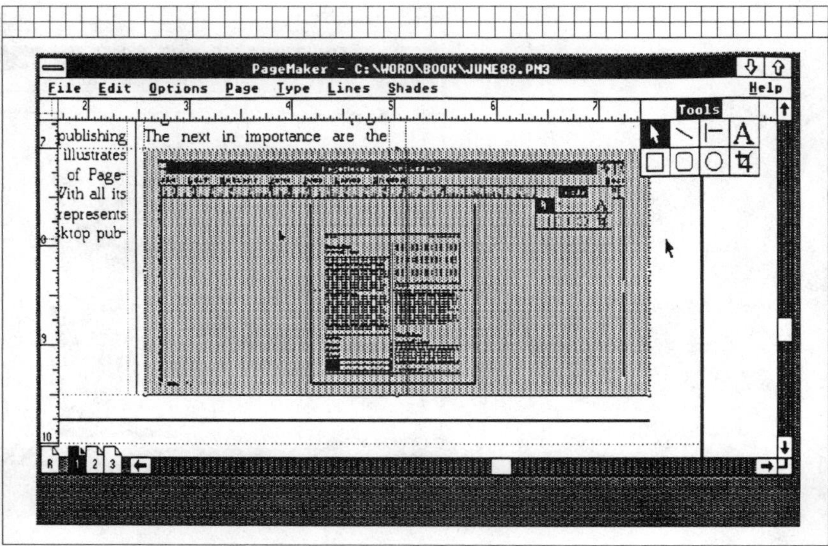

Figure 11.11: Graphic with shaded backdrop

► RESIZING YOUR PAGEMAKER GRAPHICS

Any graphic you draw using PageMaker graphics tools can be resized. You can keep the same proportions as you resize, or you can allow the graphic to distort when you enlarge or reduce it. When you resize a graphic, PageMaker anchors one corner on the page while the rest of the graphic is made smaller or larger.

You already resized a placed graphic—one you made outside of PageMaker—in the last chapter. Let's practice resizing one of PageMaker's graphics using the same method.

1. Use the pointer tool to select the circle you created earlier. If you want to retain the original proportions, hold down the Shift key.
2. Point on a handle of the circle and click and hold the mouse button. The pointer changes to a double-headed arrow. Choose a corner handle if you want to stretch or compress the graphic both horizontally and vertically. Choose a middle handle if you want to resize the graphic in only one direction.
3. Move the arrow around on the page until the graphic is resized the way you want it and release the mouse button.

▸ USING SPOT COLOR

PageMaker 3.0 lets you apply spot color to the foreground of any part of a publication, including text and graphics. However, to use this enhancement, your printer must be able to print in color. Used sparingly, spot color can enhance the look of your publications. You can use a monochrome monitor to do this, except with a monochrome monitor, spot color appears as shades of gray.

Even with a color monitor, PageMaker can only show an approximation of the colors you will print. Sometimes the color on your screen does not match the colors your printer is able to print. This problem arose because desktop publishing brings many different fields together. As a desktop publisher, you are learning how to do several jobs at once—computer operator, graphic artist, writer, and professional printer. Unfortunately, the people who work in these fields each have a different way of defining color in a publication. But PageMaker lets you choose among three standard color models so you can use the one most familiar to you.

The color model you may be most familiar with is the Red, Green, Blue, or RGB model, used in computer displays. The Hue, Lightness, Saturation, or HLS model, is often used in graphic design. The third model is the CMYK, or Cyan, Magenta, Yellow, Black. It is used in a four-color printing process.

PageMaker lets you define the colors for your publication in much the same way you defined style sheets for text. Currently, a Styles palette for defining text is displayed on your screen. Let's put the Styles palette away and display the Colors palette instead.

1. Click on the Options menu.
2. The "Styles palette" option has a check mark next to it. Click on the "Styles palette" option to unselect it, and the Styles palette will disappear from the publication window.
3. Click on the Options menu again.
4. Click on the "Colors palette" option.

The publication window now displays the Colors palette, as shown in Figure 11.12. The Styles palette is not displayed, but it can be brought back at any time by selecting the "Styles palette" option.

If you have a color monitor, blue, green, and red also appear by default on the Colors palette.

Notice that the Colors palette already contains some colors, even though we haven't defined any yet. The three choices, Paper, Black, and Registration, are PageMaker default values. Black refers to all text; Paper means white, although you can change it to a new color; and Registration is black. To this list, you can add up to 65,000 colors, although the number of colors available depends on the hardware you are using.

Let's define a new color to use in our publication.

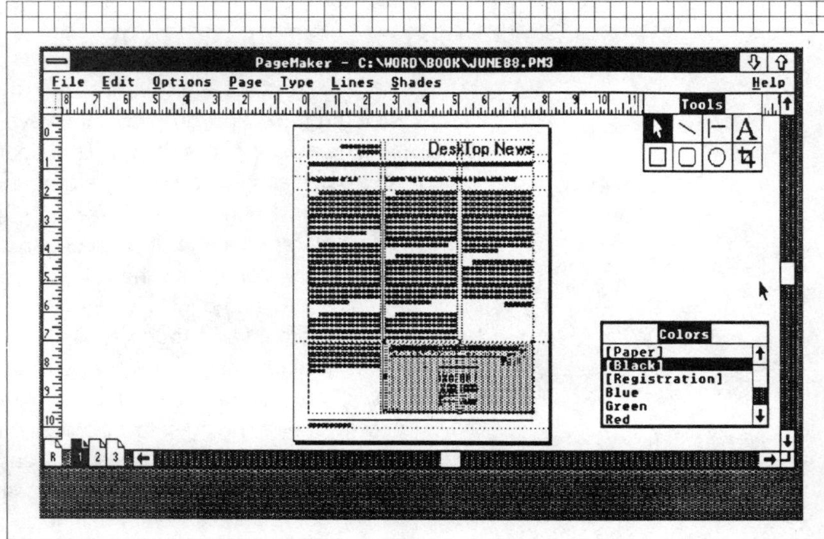

Figure 11.12: The Colors palette

1. Select the "Define colors" command from the Options menu. The Define Colors dialog box, shown in Figure 11.13, is displayed.
2. Click on the "New" option. The Edit Color dialog box (Figure 11.14) is displayed.
3. Let's add a shade of blue, aqua, to our publication. In the Name dialog box, type *aqua*.
4. Click on the color model you want to use. If you select "RGB," the Edit Color dialog box displays three slider bars for adjusting red, green, and blue color shades; selecting "HLS" displays three slider bars for adjusting hue, lightness, and saturation (Figure 11.15); "CMYK" displays four slider bars for adjusting cyan, magenta, yellow, and black (Figure 11.16).
5. In the "RGB" Edit Color dialog box (Figure 11.14), click on the slider bars in the Blue box until you find the aqua shade. You could also type in a percentage value in the Blue text box. The box to the right of the slider bars shows the original color value on top, and the adjusted color value on the bottom.
6. Click OK. You are returned to the Define Colors dialog box.

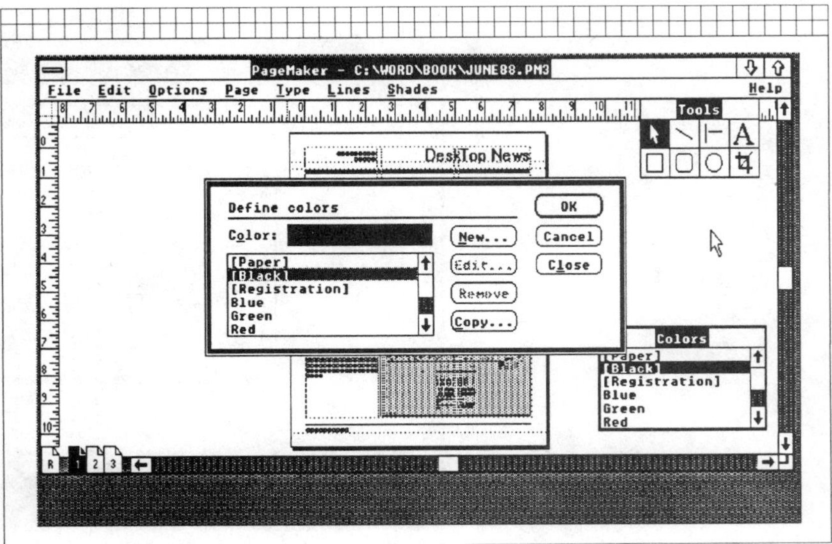

Figure 11.13: The Define Colors dialog box

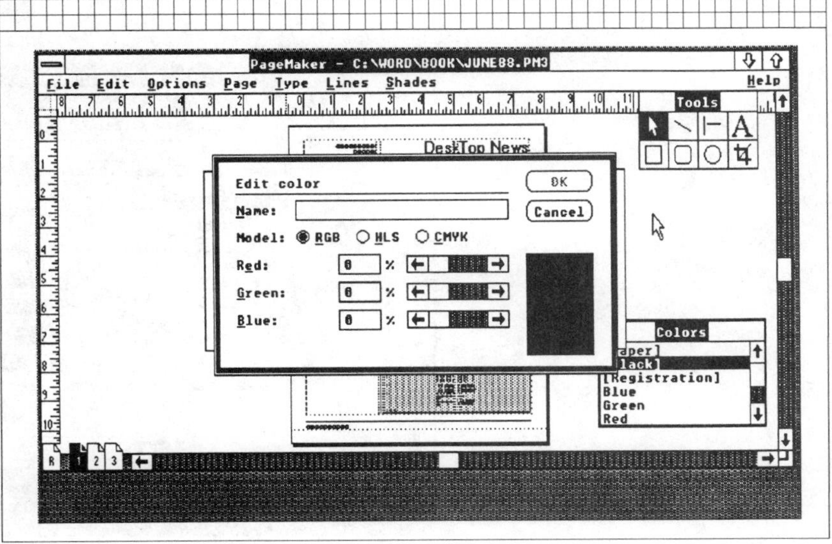

Figure 11.14: The Edit Color dialog box with "RGB" selected

7. Click "Close" to save the color definition. (Clicking Cancel does not save the changes.)

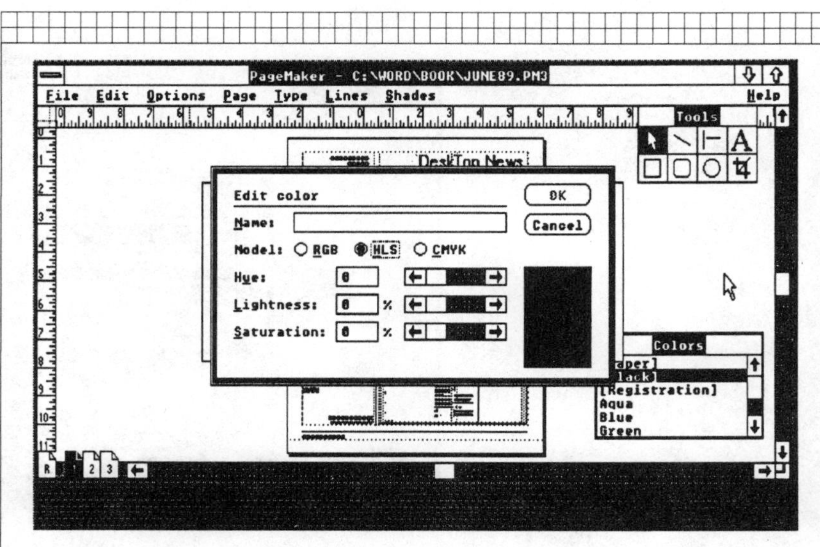

Figure 11.15: The Edit Color dialog box with "HLS" selected

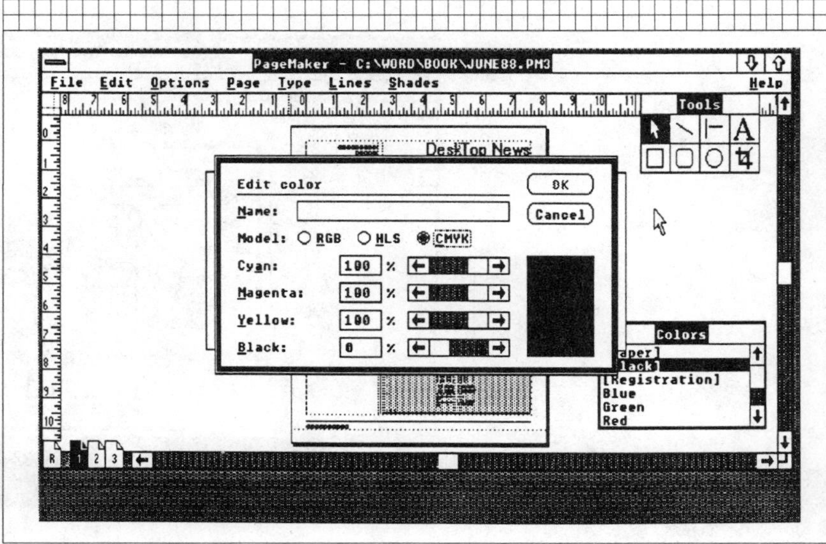

Figure 11.16: The Edit Color dialog box with "CYMK" selected

▸ APPLYING COLOR TO A PUBLICATION

You have now defined a new color, aqua, in the Colors palette. The next step is to apply this color to your publication. Let's change one of the rules in the newsletter to aqua.

1. Click on the master page icon to display the master page on which the 12-point rule at the top of the page was originally placed.
2. Use the pointer tool to display the handles on the rule.
3. Click on the "Aqua" option in the Colors palette.

The 12-point line changes from black to aqua. If you are using a monochrome monitor, you won't see this change on your screen, but at print time your color printer will print the rule in aqua.

You can add colors to your publication by choosing them directly from the Colors palette, or you can create a color with the Define Colors dialog box (Figure 11.13). You can apply color to text as well as graphics. For example, you can spot color text by first highlighting the text, then defining the color. You also can apply color to a part of a graphic that would otherwise be black. Or you can make a shade or shade pattern change colors.

▸ EDITING AND COPYING COLORS

When you want to edit a color, select the "Edit" option from the Define Colors dialog box. This displays the Edit Color dialog box (Figures 11.14 through 11.16). Define the new color as you did in the previous exercise and click OK. If the color is new to the color sheet, PageMaker will add it to the Colors palette. If the color is already in the Colors palette, a dialog box like the one in Figure 11.17 will ask if you want to change the old color definition to mean the new color. Click on the "Remove" option from the Define Colors dialog box (Figure 11.17) if you want to remove a previously defined color.

PageMaker has a feature for copying a color from one publication to another. First, select the "Copy" option from the Define Colors dialog box. This displays the Copy Colors dialog box, shown in Figure 11.18. In the Files/Directories scroll box, find which publication you wish to copy from, and type the name of the publication in the text box. Click OK and the publication's entire color sheet is copied to the publication you have been working on.

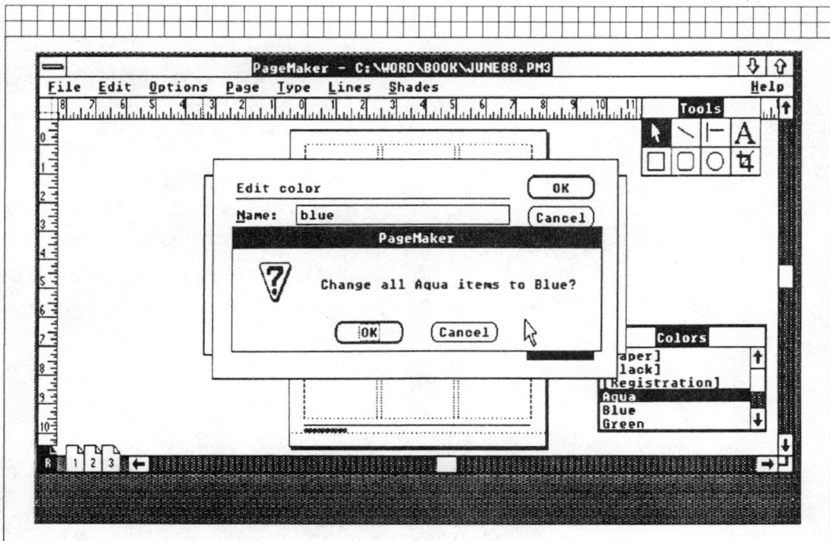

Figure 11.17: The Change Color dialog box

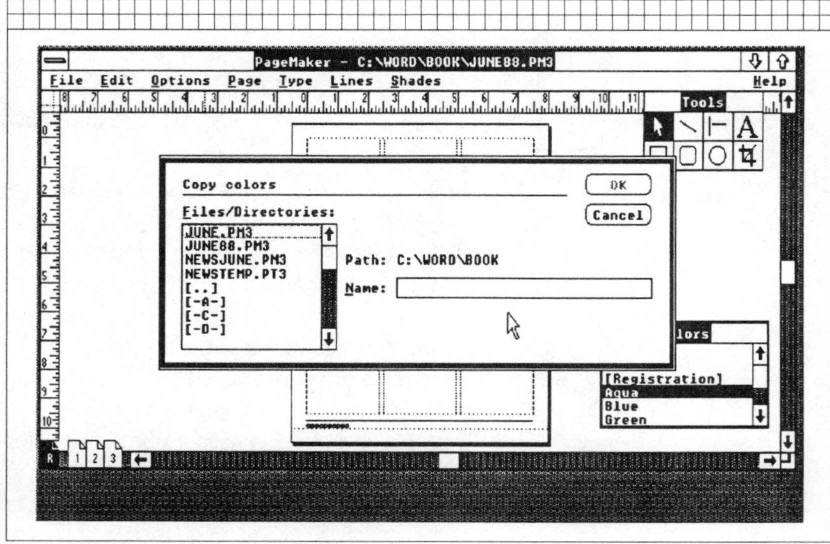

Figure 11.18: The Copy Colors dialog box

▸ USING IMAGE CONTROL TO ADJUST THE LOOK OF YOUR GRAPHICS

Image control will not work with draw or EPS graphics.

PageMaker 3.0 has added the image control feature to give you more control over the look of your paint and scanned images. You can adjust the lightness, contrast, and screen pattern of your graphics. To see these options, click on the Options menu and select the "Image control" command. The Image Control dialog box, shown in Figure 11.19, is displayed.

Lightness refers to the levels of light and dark for the entire graphic. If you select a high percentage of lightness, the darker parts of your graphic will look gray. Contrast refers to the difference between the light and dark portions of a graphic. A high percentage of contrast makes the dark portions of a graphic darker and the light portions lighter. A low percentage of contrast makes the differences between the light and dark portions smaller. Figure 11.20 illustrates the different effects you can create in a graphic by changing the lightness and contrast. The graphic at the top was produced with 0% lightness and 50% contrast, PageMaker's defaults; the one in the middle was produced with 50% lightness and 50% contrast; and the one at the bottom was produced at 0% lightness and –50% contrast.

To change the screen pattern of a graphic, select one of the patterns from the Screen options in the Image Control dialog box. To change the angle of the lines or dots in a screen pattern, type in an angle value in the Screen Angle text box. To

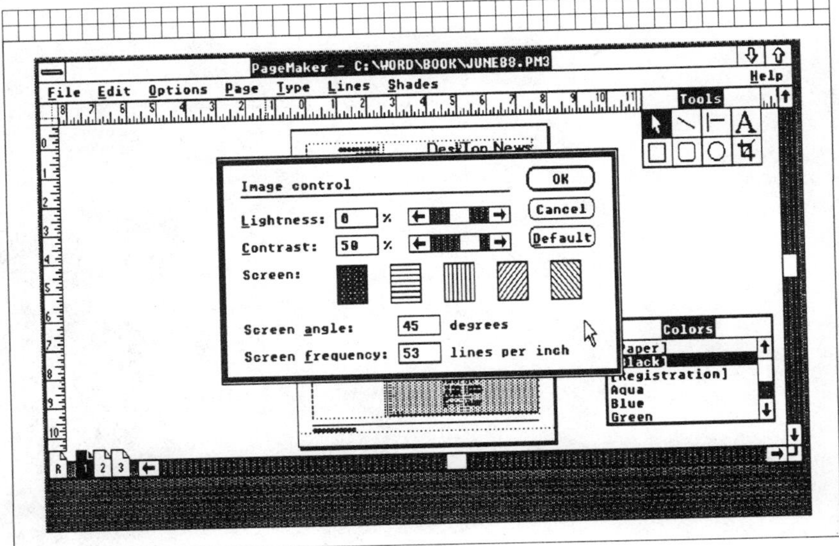

Figure 11.19: The Image Control dialog box

Figure 11.20: The same graphic at 0% lightness and 50% contrast; at 50% lightness and 50% contrast; and 0% lightness and –50% contrast.

change the number of lines or dots per inch, type a value in the Screen Frequency text box.

Let's adjust the graphic we placed on page 1 of our publication.

1. Click on page 1 of the newsletter.
2. Use the pointer tool to select the graphic on the first page.
3. Click on the Options menu and select the "Image control" command. The Image Control dialog box, shown in Figure 11.19, is displayed.
4. To change the lightness, click in the Lightness slider bar or type in a percentage value in the text box. To change the contrast, click in the Contrast slider bar, or type in a percentage value in the text box.
5. Click OK.

The graphic on page 1 changes to accommodate your new image definitions. Experiment with these image controls to see how they work.

► SUMMARY

As you can see, PageMaker's graphics capabilities can be used for a variety of functions. Keep in mind, however, that the capabilities are simple. You'll want to develop complicated graphics with other graphics software and then bring them into your PageMaker publication. Use PageMaker's graphic tools for touching up and enhancing graphics, not for creating graphics.

► PART V:

THE TOTAL EFFECT

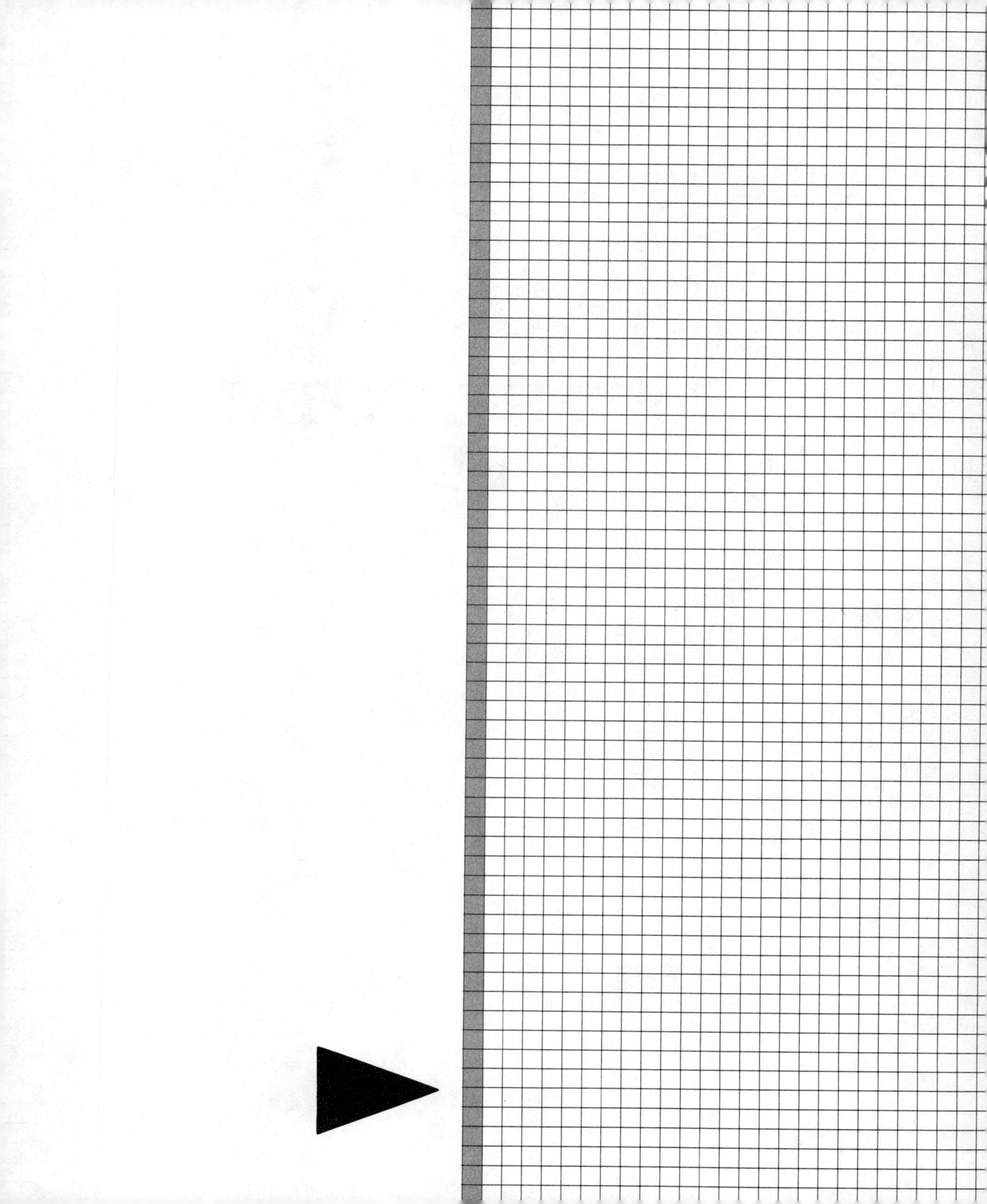

12 BRINGING TEXT AND GRAPHICS TOGETHER FOR A PROFESSIONAL-LOOKING PUBLICATION

To add a blank page at the end of your publication, **252**

click on the page icon for the last page, then click on the "Insert pages" command from the Page menu. In the Insert Pages dialog box, make sure a 1 is in the text box. Click on the "After current page" option button.

To use PageMaker 3.0's automatic text wrap features, **255**

click on the "Text wrap" command from the Options menu and fill in the Text Wrap dialog box.

To flow text across a graphic, **256**

click on the None icon (the left-most icon) in the Wrap Option box in the Text Wrap dialog box.

To stop text flow at a graphic, **257**

click on the rectangular wrap icon and the column break text flow icon in the Text Wrap dialog box.

To wrap text around the sides of a graphic, **260**

click on the rectangular wrap boundary icon and the wrap-around text flow icon in the Text Wrap dialog box.

To reshape a graphic boundary, **260**

click on the dotted graphics boundary where you want new handles to appear. Click on and drag the boundary handles to new positions around the graphic.

To manually wrap text around a rectangular graphic, **265**

create text blocks on the top, side, and bottom of the graphic. Flow text down the column, on top of the graphic, to the side, and below the graphic.

To manually wrap text around a graphic with an irregular shape, **267**

flow text into text blocks you've created on the top, side, and bottom of the graphic. Use the Return or Tab keys to adjust the text to the shape of the graphic.

To position an enlarged capital letter in the text, **270**

enlarge the letter using the Type menu, then cut it to the Clipboard to create its own text block. Paste the letter back and position it next to the text.

To reverse type, **275**

create a dark background on which to place the type. Highlight the type and select the "Reverse type" option from the Type menu.

To reverse a line, **276**

create a dark background on which to place the line. Select the line and choose the "Reverse lines" option from the Lines menu.

To create a drop shadow, **277**

create a graphic the same size and shape as the one you want to put the drop shadow behind. Overlap the two graphics, placing the shadow box over the original box, and select the "Send to back" command from the Edit menu to move the shadow behind the original box.

You have now learned most of the skills you need to create professional-looking publications. You know how to import word processed files into PageMaker, how to adjust the text to fit into your PageMaker layout, and how to bring graphics into your publications and create visual enhancements using PageMaker's graphics. In this chapter you bring all these skills together. You will learn to use PageMaker's text wrapping features, and you also will learn additional design effects such as reversing type, enlarging the initial letter in a paragraph, and more.

▶ INSERTING A PAGE IN YOUR NEWSLETTER

Before you practice using these new features, you need to insert a fourth and final page in the newsletter. Figure 12.1 shows the final, printed version of page 4.

1. Click on the page 3 icon to display the last page of the newsletter in the publication window.
2. Click on the Page menu.
3. Select the "Insert pages" command. The Insert Pages dialog box, shown in Figure 12.2, is displayed.

PageMaker lets you create publications that are up to 128 pages in size. You may use the options in the Insert Pages dialog box to insert pages before or after the current page, or between two pages when facing pages are displayed. You can use the Remove Page dialog box, which is also in the Page menu, to remove pages from your publication.

4. The text box should contain a 1. If not, type in 1.
5. Click on the "After current page" option button.
6. Click OK.

A fourth page is inserted in the newsletter, and you are automatically positioned on the new page. Notice that all the master page elements are in place.

We are going to include some information about a desktop publishing conference on page 4 of our newsletter. The page will have a lightly shaded graphic in the background, and information about the conference in the foreground. Before we begin, you need to prepare two graphics to practice with. Use either a draw or paint program to create a lightly shaded graphic that can be used as a backdrop for text, and an irregularly shaped one so you can practice contouring a graphics boundary.

Let's place the first graphic as a backdrop. Use the skills you learned in the last two chapters to place your graphic. Adjust the size of the graphic so that it occupies the top third of the page, as shown in Figure 12.3.

DeskTop News
presents the
First Annual Desktop Publishing Conference

May 14 - 16, 1989

The First Annual Desktop Publishing Conference is geared towards people working in all aspects of the printed communications industry. If you are a graphic artist or typesetter, this conference will help you get started in desktop publishing. If you have been using desktop publishing on your job, this conference will show you all the latest in graphics and layout design for desktop publishers. The workshops are varied enough to give you exactly what you're looking for, answers to your questions.

All the workshops on the first day of the conference are geared towards enhancing your design skills and familiarizing you with all the hardware and software associated with desktop publishing.

Fees: Weekend (includes Friday night keynote speaker, Saturday and Sunday conference): $395.00
One-day only: $225.00

Registration: Please register in advance by mail. Limited one-day only registration will be available each day of the conference. Include your name, your company, and your job title. Indicate if you are registering for the entire conference or for one day only.

Bring your confirmation of registration to the registration table before 9 a.m. on the day you are attending.

Send your completed registration and a check or money order made payable to:

DeskTop Publishing Conference
133 East 78th Street
New York, NY 10013

DeskTop News 4

Figure 12.1: The printed final version of page 4 of the newsletter

With the graphic in place, let's practice using some of PageMaker's text wrap features.

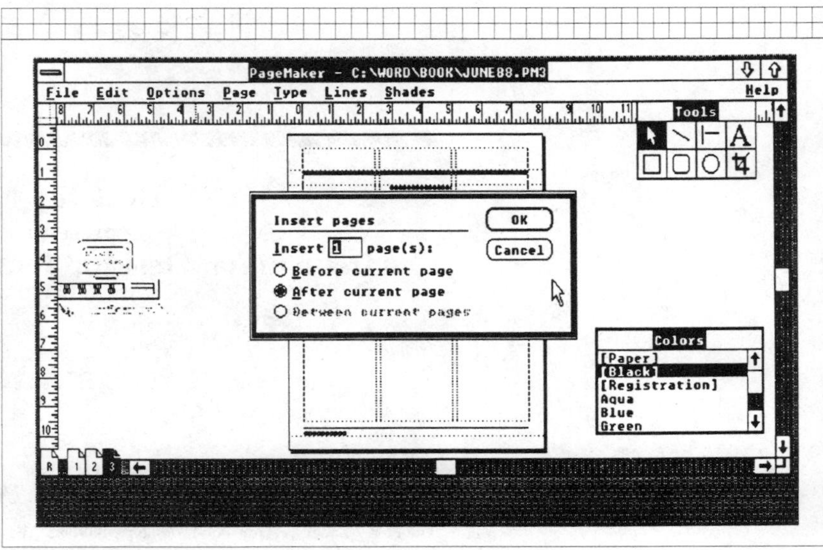

Figure 12.2: The Insert Pages dialog box

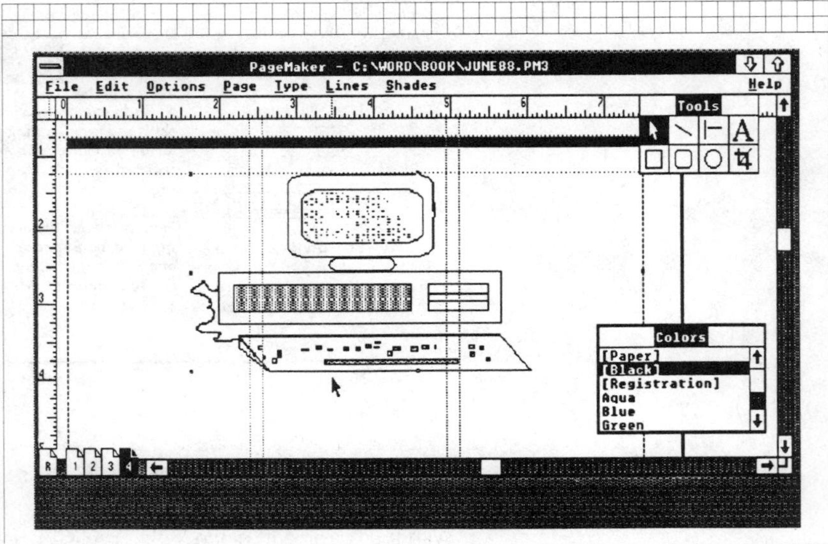

Figure 12.3: Graphic on page 4

► USING PAGEMAKER'S TEXT WRAP FEATURES

In version 3.0, when the automatic text wrap feature is turned off, manual text wrap becomes the default.

PageMaker 3.0 lets you wrap text either manually or automatically. However, earlier versions of PageMaker require you to wrap text around graphics manually. If you are using PageMaker 1.0 or 1.0a, skip ahead to the section "Wrapping Text Manually." PageMaker 3.0 users should complete the exercises in both the next section and the section on wrapping text manually. Before you continue, though, all users should type in the following text, which you will wrap around the graphics you created at the beginning of this chapter. When you've finished entering the text, save the file.

> The First Annual Desktop Publishing Conference is geared towards people working in all aspects of the printed communications industry. If you are a graphic artist or typesetter, this conference will help you get started in desktop publishing. If you have been using desktop publishing on your job, this conference will show you all the latest in graphics and layout design for desktop publishers. The workshops are varied enough to give you exactly what you're looking for, answers to your questions.
>
> All the workshops on the first day of the conference are geared towards enhancing your design skills and familiarizing you with all the hardware and software associated with desktop publishing.
>
> *Fees:* Weekend (includes Friday night keynote speaker, Saturday and Sunday conference): $395.00
> One-day only: $225.00
>
> *Registration:* Please register in advance by mail. Limited one-day only registration will be available each day of the conference. Include your name, your company, and your job title. Indicate if you are registering for the entire conference or for one day only.
>
> Bring your confirmation of registration to the registration table before 9 a.m. on the day you are attending.
>
> Send your completed registration and a check or money order made payable to:
>
> Desktop Publishing Conference
> 133 East 78th Street
> New York, NY 10013

► AUTOMATIC TEXT WRAP

The automatic text wrap feature of PageMaker 3.0 lets you wrap text around a graphic, flow text across a graphic, or make text jump over a graphic. You can wrap text around a graphic with a box shape or one with irregular edges. You also can tell PageMaker to wrap text the same way for each graphic, or you can customize text wrap for each graphic.

When text flows automatically around a graphic, it flows according to how you set the text wrap boundaries and the paragraph, indent, and alignment attributes. PageMaker inserts a line space before and after consecutive paragraphs, but disregards this line space when text or a graphic falls between two paragraphs. Instead, the text flows immediately after the graphic, without a line space in between.

Flowing Text Across a Graphic

Flowing text across or over a graphic creates an interesting effect. A lightly shaded graphic behind the text on a page is attractive and catches your reader's attention.

Let's flow text across the lightly shaded graphic on page 4. To do this, you first need to eliminate the graphics boundary. (You'll learn about the graphics boundary in the next section.)

1. If necessary, select the pointer tool from the Toolbox and select the graphic on page 4.
2. Click on the Options menu and select the "Text wrap" command. The Text Wrap dialog box, shown in Figure 12.4, is displayed.

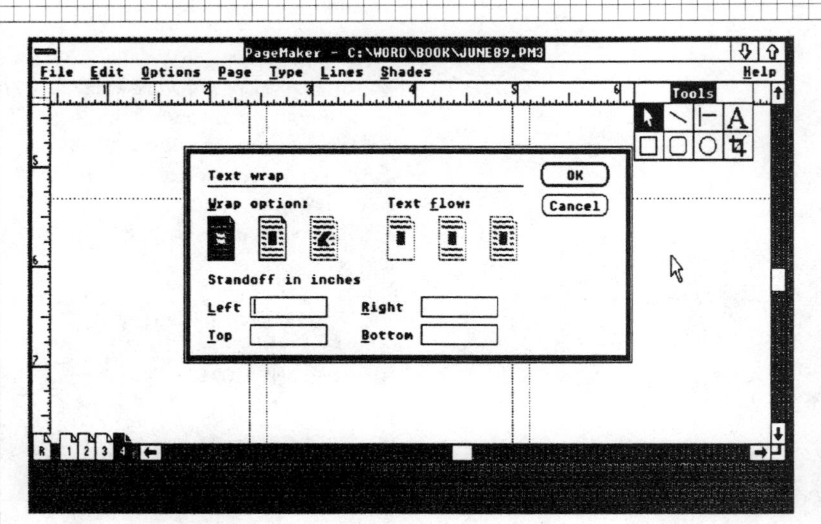

Figure 12.4: The Text Wrap dialog box

There are three sections to the dialog box: the Wrap Option and Text Flow sections with three page-description icons each, and the Standoff in Inches section. You will learn about these features shortly. Meantime, we need to remove the boundary so the text will flow across our graphic, not wrap around it.

3. Under the Wrap options, click on the None icon, the one furthest to the left. This is the icon for flowing text across a graphic; in effect, it removes the graphic boundary.
4. Click OK.

Chapter 6 discusses how to flow text across column guides.

Now the graphic has no boundary. Text placed on the page will flow across the graphic as if it wasn't there. Now let's flow some text about the desktop publishing conference across the graphic.

5. Using your word processor, type in the following four-line heading about a desktop publishing conference.

   DeskTop News
   presents the
   First Annual Desktop Publishing Conference
   May 14–16, 1989

6. Save the file.
7. Use the skills you've learned so far to flow the text across the column guides on the page. Page 4 of your newsletter should look like the example in Figure 12.5.

Flowing Text Around a Graphic

Besides flowing text across a graphic, you can also make text skip over a graphic. PageMaker has a Text Wrap feature that makes the flow of text stop when it encounters a graphic in a column.

To practice using this feature, let's place a smaller copy of the graphic on page 4 just below the middle of column 1, and flow text around it. Go ahead and place the graphic. Page 4 of your newsletter should now look like Figure 12.6. Make sure the new graphic is selected, then follow the directions below to set the Text Wrap options for the graphic.

1. Click on the Options menu and select the "Text wrap" command. The Text Wrap dialog box, shown earlier in Figure 12.4, is displayed.

Look at the three page-shaped icons under the Wrap Option section of the dialog box. The first Wrap option flows text across a graphic. The second icon flows text around a graphic. The third flows text around a graphic with irregular edges.

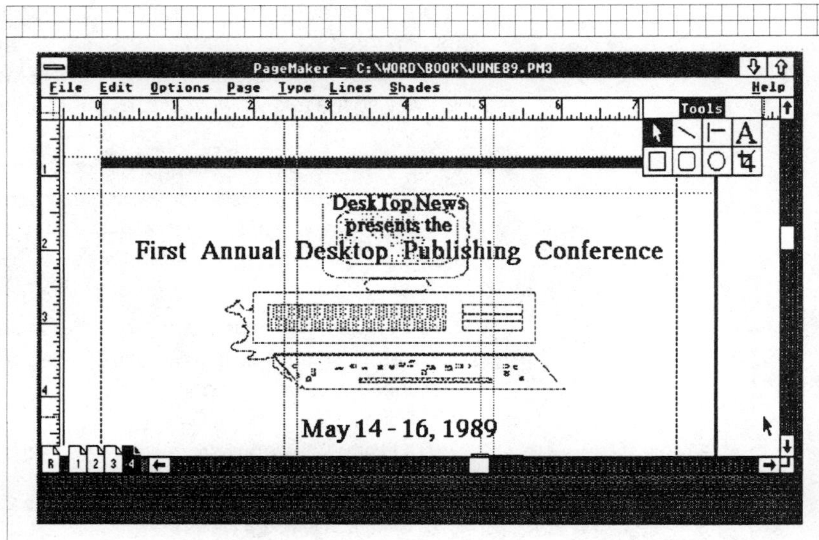

Figure 12.5: Flowing text across a graphic

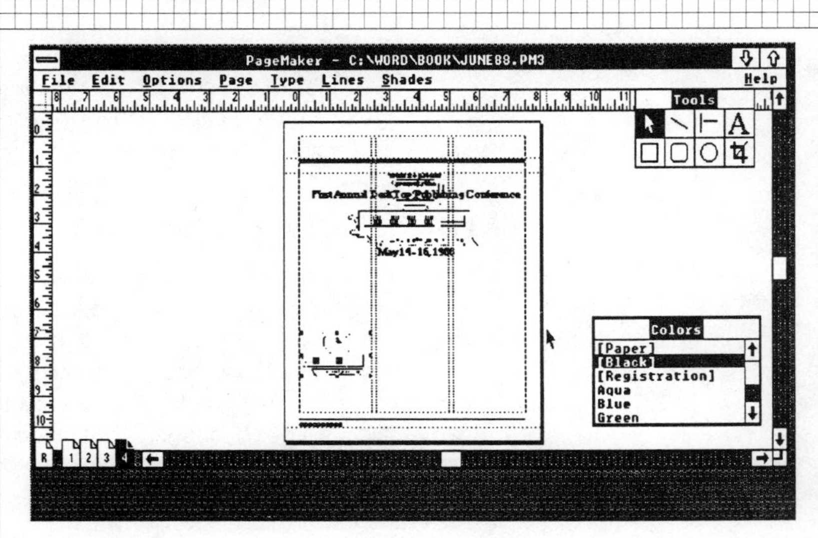

Figure 12.6: Second graphic placed in column 1

Now look at the three icons under the Text Flow section. The first icon stops the flow of text entirely when a graphic is encountered. The second icon stops the flow of text above a graphic and continues flowing text below it. The third flows text down the sides of a graphic.

2. In the Wrap Option section, click on the middle icon, the rectangular boundary icon. This is the one with a rectangle in the center.

In all versions of PageMaker, each graphic has handles that allow you to make changes to a graphic. PageMaker 3.0 adds a *graphics boundary.* PageMaker displays the graphics boundary when you select automatic text wrap. This boundary determines how text will flow around your graphic. It surrounds the graphic and appears as a dotted line with handles.

You can stick with a rectangular graphics boundary, or make the shape of the boundary conform to the contours of the graphic. The graphics boundary enables you to include figure captions within the boundary of a graphic without having to worry that changes made to the text around the graphic will affect the figure caption.

Now look just below the Wrap Option icons at the Standoff in Inches text boxes. These boxes are used for sizing the rectangular boundary around a graphic.

3. Type in .25 in the Top text box to make the text stop flowing a quarter inch above the graphic. Since our graphic will force a column break, you only need to make an entry in the Top text box. You would type a negative number in this box if you wanted text to overlap a part of the graphic.

Now choose the way you want text to flow by selecting one of the Text Flow options.

4. Under the Text Flow options, click on the column break icon, the first one on the left.
5. Click OK.

A rectangular graphics boundary is displayed around the graphic. It includes a column break below the graphic.

6. Now flow the text you typed earlier, about the desktop publishing conference, into the first column. The text will flow until it reaches the graphics boundary, as shown in Figure 12.7.

See Chapter 8 for an explanation of the Autoflow feature and how it works.

At this point, if you are flowing text with the ''Autoflow'' option, the text will jump automatically to the beginning of the next column. If a graphic is in that column too, the text will skip over the second graphic and jump to the next column. But if you are not using the Autoflow feature to flow text, the text will stop flowing when it reaches a graphic, and you will have to place the remaining text on your own.

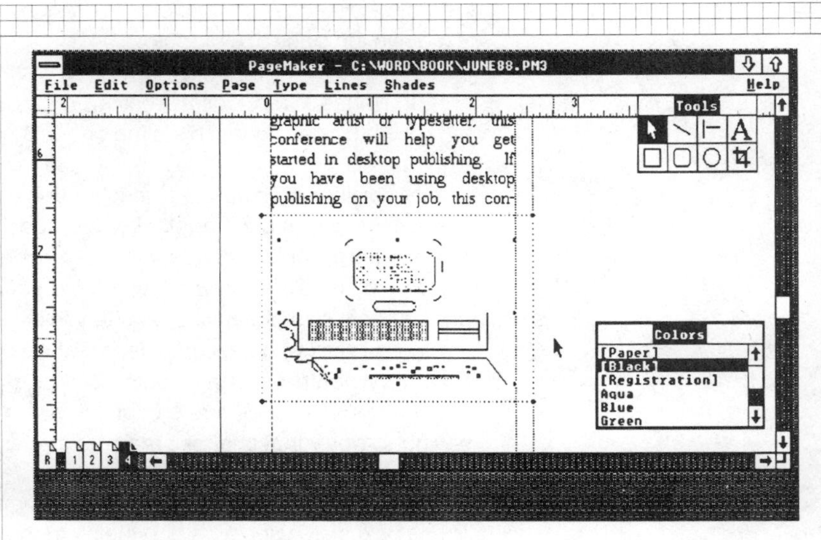

Figure 12.7: Stopping text flow at a graphic

Wrapping Text Around the Sides of a Graphic

PageMaker's Text Wrap features also let you flow text around the sides of a graphic. You can either flow the text around a rectangular graphics boundary, or around a customized graphics boundary that conforms to the shape of your graphic.

For practice, let's use the graphic with irregular edges that you created at the beginning of this chapter. Use the "Place" command from the File menu to place the graphic on page 4, overlapping columns 2 and 3, as shown in Figure 12.8. Since our graphic is in both columns, we will have the text in column 2 wrap around the left side of the graphic, and the text in column 3 wrap around the right side. In order for text to wrap around the side of a graphic, the graphic must run up against, or overlap, a column guide. To increase the distance between a graphic and a column guide, increase the standoff around the graphic. (Besides increasing the standoff, you also could move the graphic away from the column guide. Be careful though, because the standoff also works to keep text away from a graphic, so moving the graphic manually away from a column will also affect text flow in the column.)

With the graphic in place, we are ready to wrap the text around the sides of the graphic. Be sure to select the graphic first.

1. Click on the Options menu and select the "Text wrap" command. The Text Wrap dialog box (Figure 12.4) is displayed.

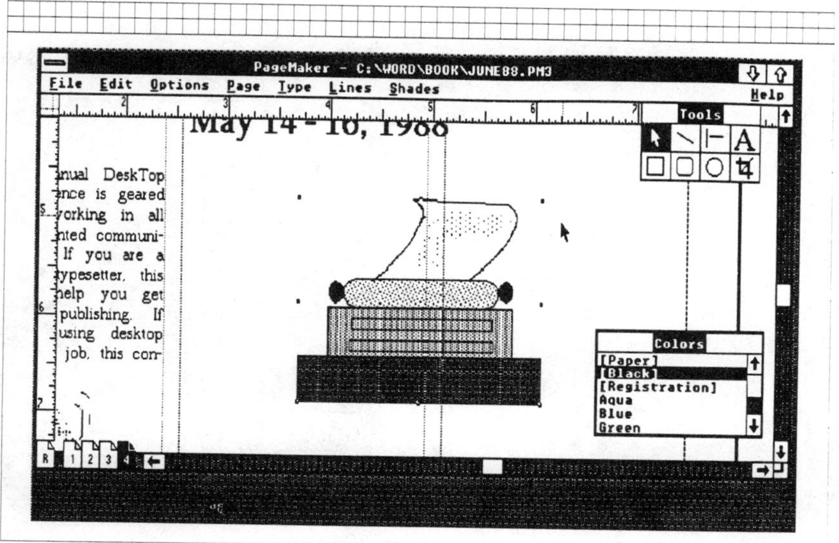

Figure 12.8: The third graphic placed on page 4

2. Under the Wrap options, click on the middle icon, the rectangular graphics boundary icon. (This one has a rectangle in the center.)
3. Under the Text Flow options, click on the wrap-around icon, the third icon.
4. Click OK.

The text automatically flows around the sides of the graphics boundary. However, because we selected the rectangular boundary icon, and because our graphic has irregular edges and is not rectangular, the graphic boundary does not conform to the shape of the graphic. Let's change the size of the rectangular boundary.

5. Point on a segment of the boundary line. Click the mouse button and drag the line out to create a larger boundary, as shown in Figure 12.9. The text reflows around the new boundary line.

Now let's customize the graphics boundary to make it conform to the shape of our graphic. First, though, let's see what the changes we just made to the rectangular boundary have done to the selections in the Text Wrap dialog box.

1. Click on the Options menu and select the "Text wrap" command. The dialog box (Figure 12.4) is displayed.

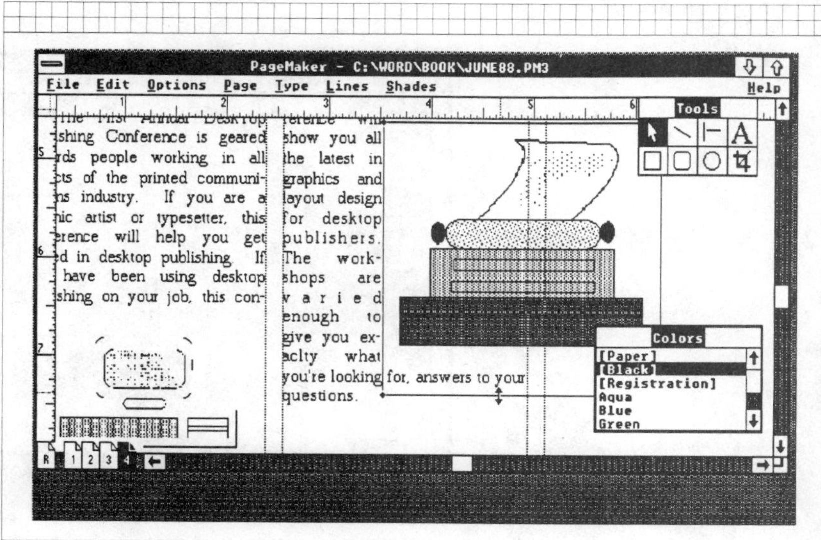

Figure 12.9: Reshaping a boundary line

2. Under the Wrap options, the custom-wrap boundary icon is now highlighted.
3. Click OK.

Our graphics boundary is customized, but it is still in a rectangular shape. We need to change the shape of the graphics boundary, but to do this we must create handles on the boundary line where we want boundary movement to occur. A graphics boundary must have a minimum of three handles. If you try to use fewer than three, PageMaker displays a warning. PageMaker also has a minimum distance that is required between the handles on a boundary line. If you try to add a handle within this minimum distance, PageMaker will not create the handle. If you make a mistake and need to delete a handle, use the pointer tool to point on the handle, then click and hold down the mouse button. Drag the unwanted handle over one you want to keep, then release the mouse button. The handle will disappear.

Let's add some handles to our graphics boundary. How many handles you add depends on the shape of your graphic. To create a handle:

4. Click on the pointer tool from the Toolbox.
5. Point to the dotted line of the graphics boundary where you want a new handle to be.
6. Click the mouse button.

A diamond-shaped handle appears where you clicked the pointer on the graphic boundary. Repeat this process until you have placed a handle at each point where you want to reshape the graphics boundary. The boundary line and new handles should look like the example in Figure 12.10.

Once the handles are in place, you can use them to reshape the graphics boundary. To reshape the boundary line:

1. Point on a handle on the graphics boundary.
2. Click and hold down the mouse button.
3. Drag the handle to a new position.
4. Release the mouse button.

Now you can make the boundary line conform to the shape of your irregular graphic. To stop movement in a handle that's in line with two adjacent handles, hold down the Shift key while you reposition an adjacent handle. Once you've created the new boundary line, the text will flow around the shape of the boundary, as shown in Figure 12.11.

► WRAPPING TEXT MANUALLY

All PageMaker versions let you wrap text manually around or across a graphic. You can wrap text around graphics with even or irregular edges. Both techniques

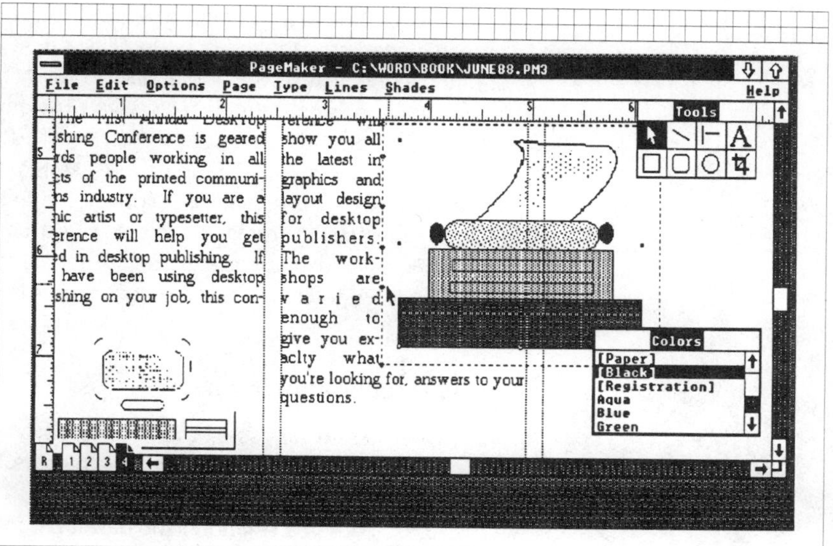

Figure 12.10: New handles on a graphics boundary

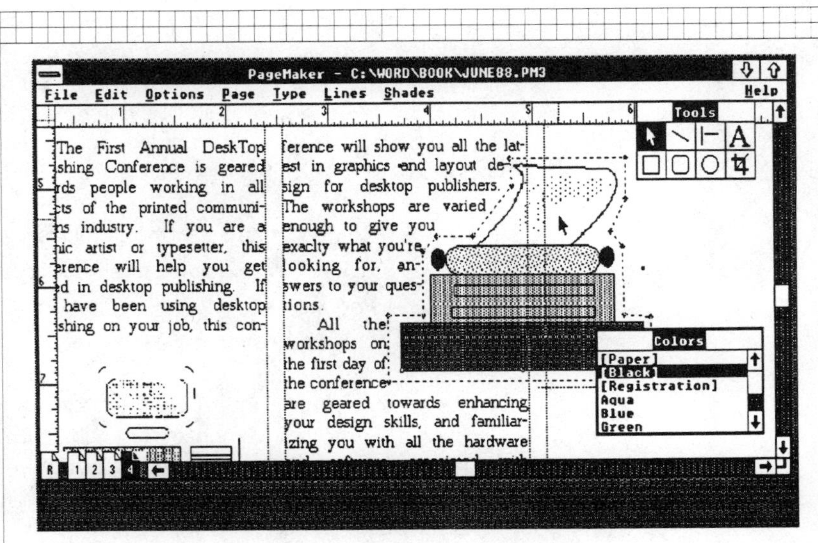

Figure 12.11: Flowing text around a custom boundary line

are similar, except that when you wrap text around an irregular edge, you can't use auto text flow to place your text.

If you are using PageMaker 1.0 or 1.0a, you will use the text about the desktop publishing conference that you typed earlier to practice manual text wrapping. However, before you begin wrapping text, place a smaller copy of the graphic you placed near the top of page 4 just below the middle of column 1. Then continue to the next section, "Manually Flowing Text Across a Graphic."

If you are using PageMaker 3.0, you just learned how to wrap text automatically around a graphic. Since page 4 is now filled, use the "Insert pages" command from the Page menu to bring up the Insert Pages dialog box and add a fifth page to practice on. Next, place a graphic in the first column of the page. A box created using the box tool from the Toolbox will do just fine. Skip the next section ("Manually Flowing Text Across a Graphic") and go to "Manually Wrapping Text Around an Even Edge" to learn to flow text manually onto your practice page.

Manually Flowing Text Across a Graphic

Flowing text across or over a graphic creates an interesting effect. A lightly shaded graphic behind the text on a page is attractive and catches your reader's attention.

Let's flow some text about the desktop publishing conference across the lightly shaded graphic at the top of page 4.

1. Using your word processor, type in the following four-line heading about a desktop publishing conference.

   DeskTop news
   presents the
   First Annual Desktop Publishing Conference
   May 14–16, 1989

2. Save the file.
3. Click on the "Place" command from the File menu and select the file you just created with your word processor.
4. Click on the OK command button.
5. Use the skills you've learned so far to flow the text onto page 4.
6. Use the corner handles of the text block to adjust the text to lay over the graphic, as shown in Figure 12.5.

Manually Wrapping Text Around an Even Edge

When you wrap text around an even edge, you are essentially resizing one text block and creating three: one on top of the graphic, one to the side of the graphic, and one below the graphic. In this chapter, the examples refer to wrapping text around graphics. However, you can use the same methods you'll learn here to wrap text around another text block.

Now that your graphic in the first column of page 4 (for 3.0 users, page 5) is in place, use the "Place" command from the File menu to flow the text about the desktop publishing conference into the column. Beginning at the top left-hand corner of the column, flow the text into the column containing the box, so that the text stops flowing when it reaches the box, as shown in Figure 12.12.

The plus sign on the bottom handle of the text block means there is more text to flow in. Point to the plus sign and click the mouse button. The pointer turns into the text icon. Point the text icon just below the box, flush with the left side of the column. Now click the mouse button. The remaining text flows into the column just below the box, leaving a blank area next to the box, as shown in Figure 12.13.

Now let's use the skills you learned in Chapter 7 to resize the text block. Point on the top handle of the text block that you placed below the box. Click and hold the mouse button. Now drag the text block up until it is just below the preceding text block and release the mouse button. The graphic is covered with the text, as shown in Figure 12.14.

Now you have to move the text off the graphic. To do this, point to the upper left-hand corner handle of the lower text block. (If you had positioned the graphic on the right side of the column and you wanted to flow text down the left side, you would select the bottom right-hand corner handle of the text block instead.) Click

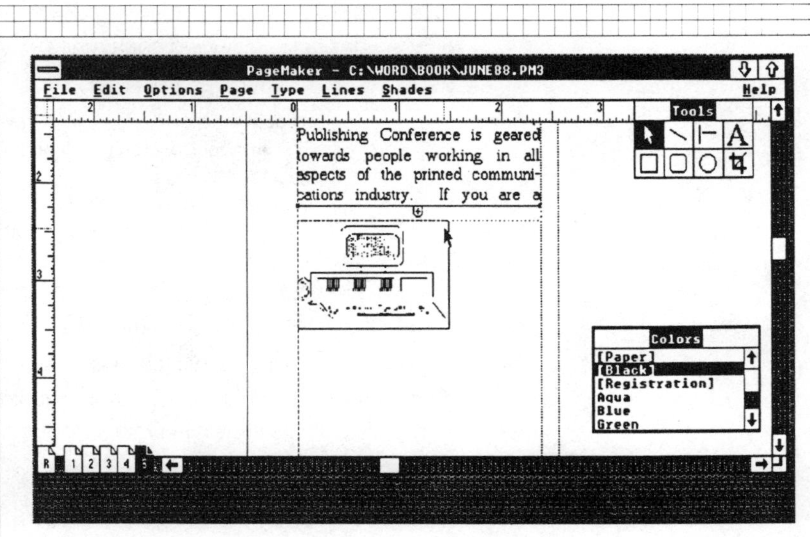

Figure 12.12: Flowing text in a column

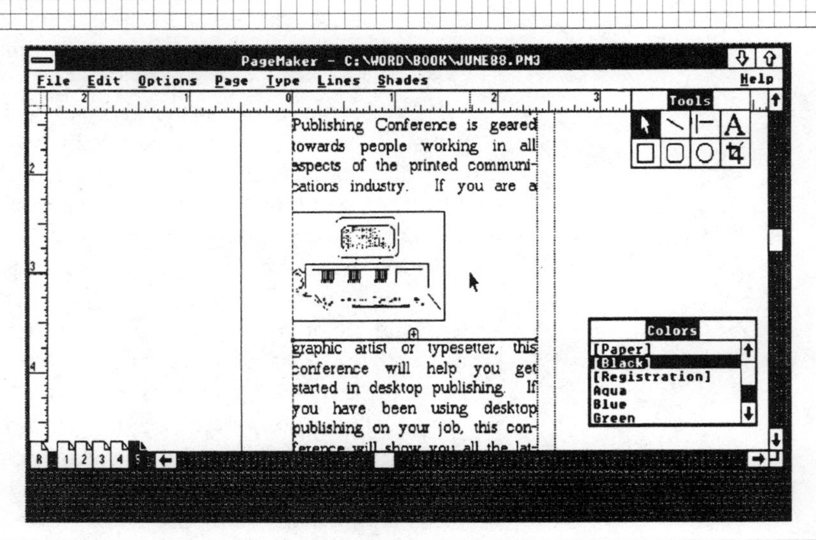

Figure 12.13: Flowing text below the box

and hold the mouse button. Drag the text block until it becomes narrower and it makes room for the graphic. The right side and top of the text block remain

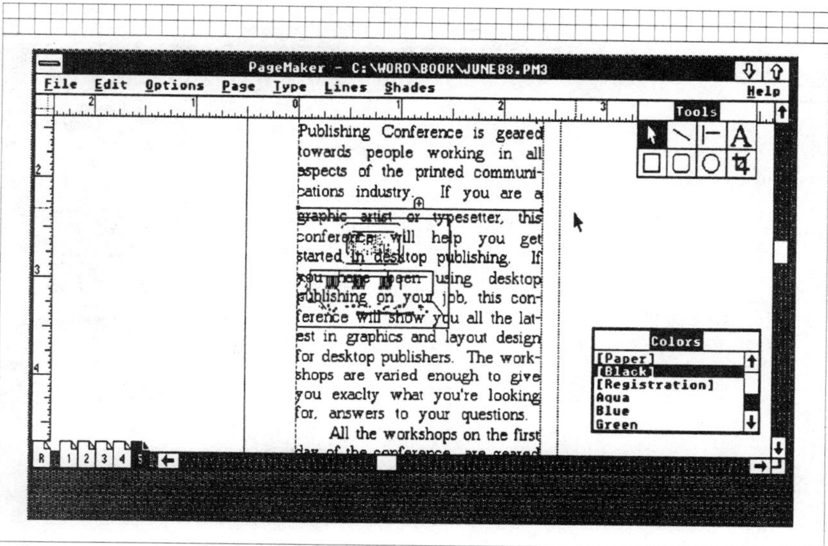

Figure 12.14: Text covering a graphic

anchored, but when you release the mouse button, the text block should have narrowed to expose the graphic on the left side of the column, as in Figure 12.15.

Notice that the text block is narrow not just to the right of the graphic, but down the right side of the column as well. To fix this, we have to shorten the narrowed text block first. To shorten it, point to the plus symbol in the bottom handle of the block. Click and hold the mouse button while you drag the handle up the column until the text block is positioned next to the graphic. Release the mouse button. The narrowed text block should look like the one shown in Figure 12.16.

Now click on the plus sign at the bottom of the narrowed text block to make the pointer turn into the text icon. Point the text icon below the graphic box and flush with the left side of the column. Click the mouse button and the text flows down the column as shown in Figure 12.17. If necessary, you can go back and align the text blocks using the skills you learned in Chapter 7.

Manually Wrapping Text Around an Irregular Edge

You can also wrap text around the irregular edge of a graphic. There are a few different ways of doing it, depending on how your graphic is situated. You may choose to wrap your text by using multiline text blocks, or tab stops and carriage returns.

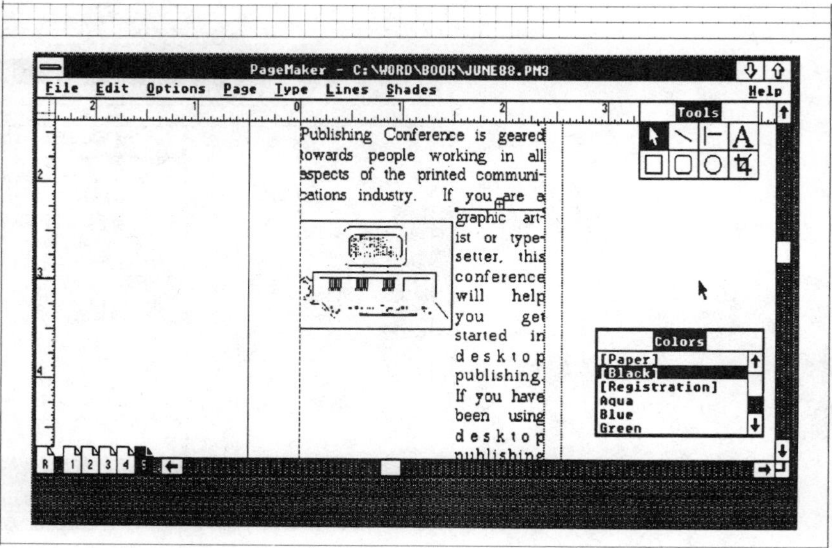

Figure 12.15: Narrowed text block

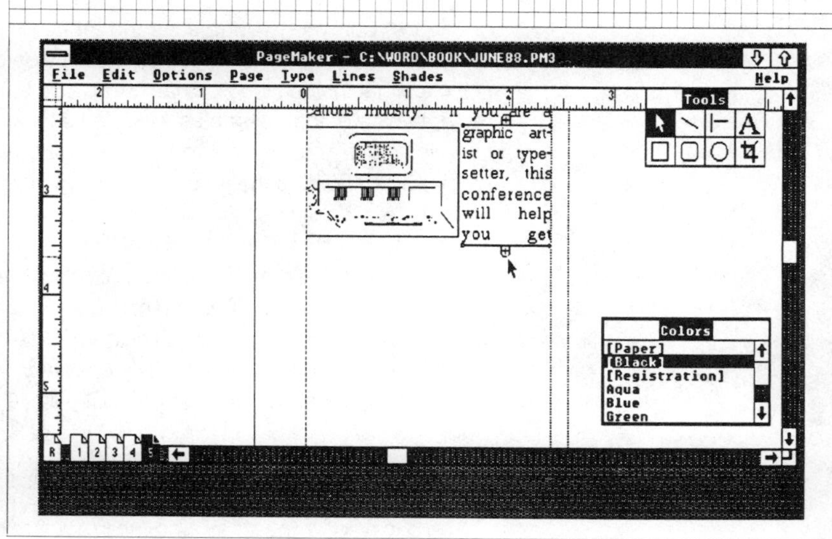

Figure 12.16: Shortened narrow text block

To practice, we need to place a graphic with an irregular edge the page. Version 1.0 and 1.0a users can use the graphic you created at the beginning of this chapter. Now, place the graphic on page 4, flush with the right edge of the first

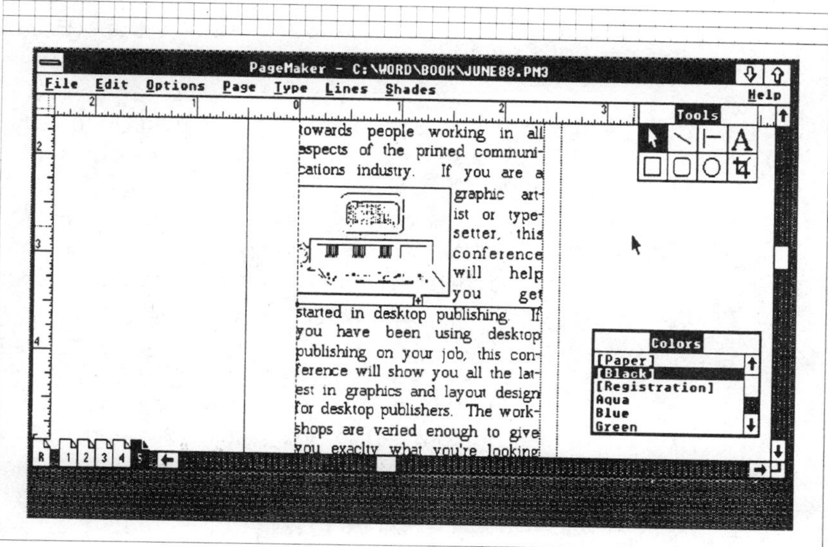

Figure 12.17: Text flowed around a graphic box

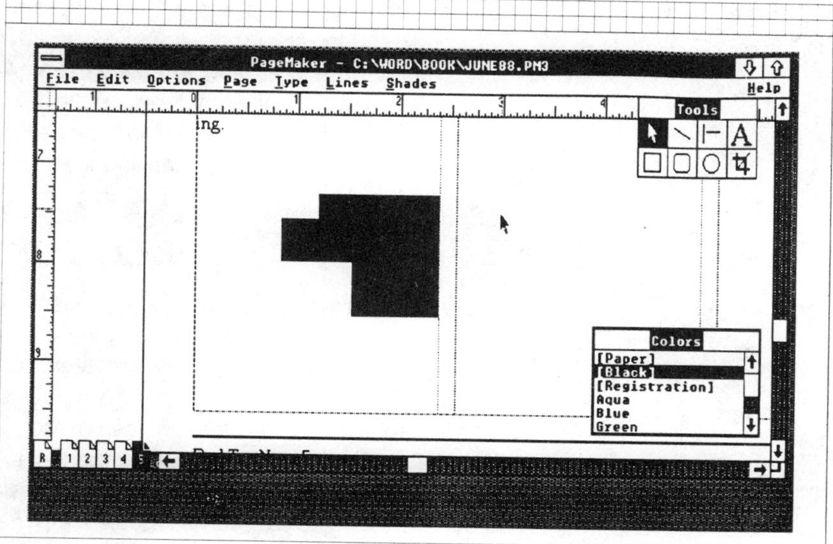

Figure 12.18: A shaded graphic with an irregular edge

column, as shown in Figure 12.18. Version 3.0 users can create shaded boxes of varying sizes. Use the Shades menu options to shade in the boxes and make them easier to work with.

You are now ready to flow in the text. Use the "Place" option from the File menu. Place the text at the top of the column and flow it in. The text will stop flowing automatically when it reaches the graphic you just placed. Click on the bottom handle of the text block and drag it down to the bottom of the column. Release the mouse button and the text fills the column, covering the graphic, as in Figure 12.19.

In this case, the best way to wrap the text is simply to insert carriage returns. Point to the text tool in the Toolbox and click the mouse button. Position the text tool after the last word in the line before the graphic. Click the mouse button and the text bar appears. Press the Return key to end the line at the insertion point. Repeat this procedure for each line that overlaps the graphic. When you are finished, your screen should look something like Figure 12.20.

If your graphic was flush with the left side of your column, you would use tab stops instead of carriage returns to wrap your text. Simply use the "Tab/indent" command from the Type menu to create tab stops after a graphic that is flush left. Once the tab stops are there, position the text tool at the start of each text line—it doesn't matter that the text is covered by the graphic—and press the Tab key. The text will align itself with the tab stop, just past the graphic.

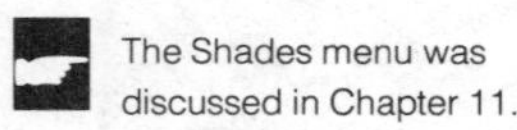

The Shades menu was discussed in Chapter 11.

If your graphic is irregular on the left and right sides, you can wrap the text around one side of the graphic at a time, in which case the text will read down one side and then down the other, or you can use the Tab key to move the overlapped text outside of the graphic. In this case, your text will read from left to right on either side.

To insert a graphic in the middle of a text block, shorten the text block by clicking on the bottom handle. Next, place the graphic in the space opened up by the shortened text block. Then you can flow the text around the graphic.

► USING SPECIAL DESIGN EFFECTS

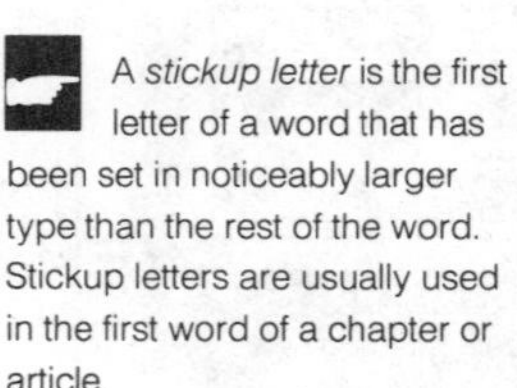

A *stickup letter* is the first letter of a word that has been set in noticeably larger type than the rest of the word. Stickup letters are usually used in the first word of a chapter or article.

PageMaker gives you special design effects for enhancing your publication and making information stand out on the page. To enhance text, you can use stickup letters, make headlines cross several columns, or create reverse type. To enhance graphics, you can create drop shadows or reverse lines, superimpose text on graphics, or use color. You can even mix the number of columns on a single page. Remember, though, it's important to choose design enhancements carefully. Cluttering the page with too many design enhancements can make it harder to communicate with your audience. When you add a design effect, be sure you have a good reason for doing so.

► MAKING STICKUP LETTERS

You've probably noticed in some publications that the first letter of a chapter or section is sometimes enlarged. This first letter is called a *stickup letter*. Stickup letters help capture the reader's eye and mark off the beginning of a new section or

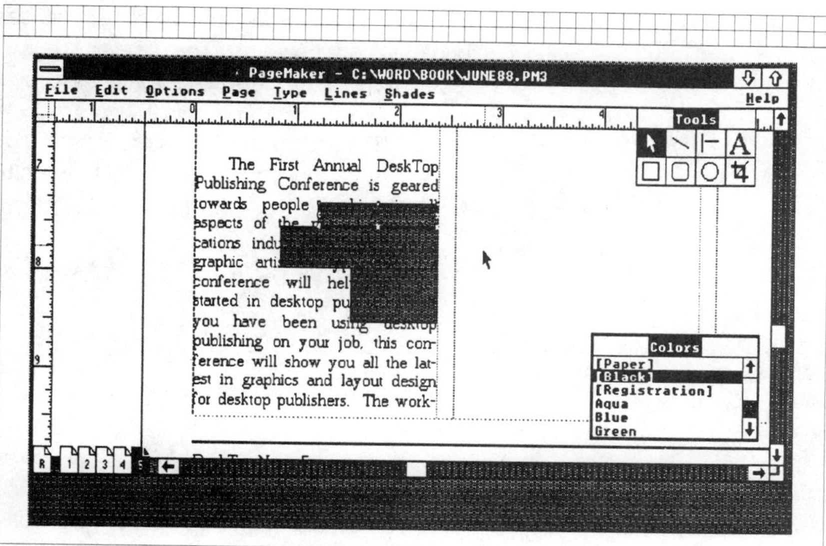

Figure 12.19: Flowing the text block

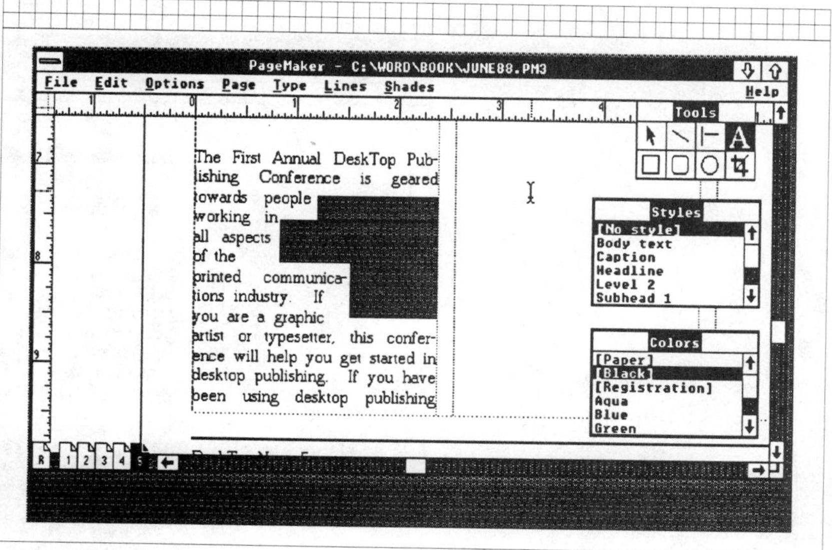

Figure 12.20: Wrapping text around an irregular graphic

chapter. In your newsletter, you'll use this design element to clearly indicate the beginning of a new story. The remaining text will be continued after the stickup letter or wrapped around it. To create a stickup letter:

1. Point to the top of the first column in page 1 of the newsletter and click the right mouse button to select the Actual Size view.
2. Select the text tool from the Toolbox and point to the first letter of the story in column 1.
3. Click and hold the mouse button, dragging the text bar over the letter to select it.

Making type specifications was discussed in Chapter 8.

Let's select a larger point size for this letter using the "Type specs" option from the Type menu.

4. Point to the Type menu. Select the "Type specs" option and indicate a larger point size (you could try a size 2–4 points larger). The initial letter is now larger than the rest of the text. Its baseline is even with the rest of the line, and PageMaker has automatically adjusted the leading between the first line and the second one to accommodate the enlarged letter, as in Figure 12.21.

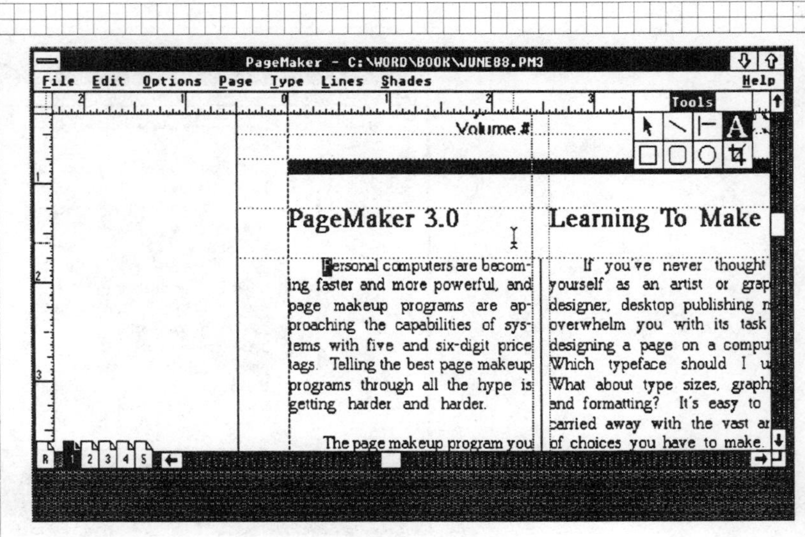

Figure 12.21: An enlarged stickup letter

Now that the stickup letter is highlighted, wrap the other text in the paragraph around it. To do so, you must first remove the stickup letter from the paragraph so you can make adjustments to it without disturbing other text.

1. Make sure the stickup letter is still selected. Use the text tool to select the "Cut" option from the Edit menu.
2. Click the text tool on the pasteboard to select an insertion point outside the publication.
3. Use the text tool to select the "Paste" option from the Edit menu. The stickup letter is placed into the pasteboard where you indicated.
4. Select the pointer tool from the Toolbox and select the letter from the pasteboard using the pointer. Drag the stickup letter into the publication and place it exactly where you want it, as shown in Figure 12.22. (Notice that if you change the view, the stickup letter looks larger.)

The stickup letter has been placed directly over the text. Now treat the paragraph text as a new text block and wrap it around the stickup letter.

5. Click on the bottom-left corner handle of the column 1 text block and move the text block to the right so that the stickup letter is no longer covering anything.

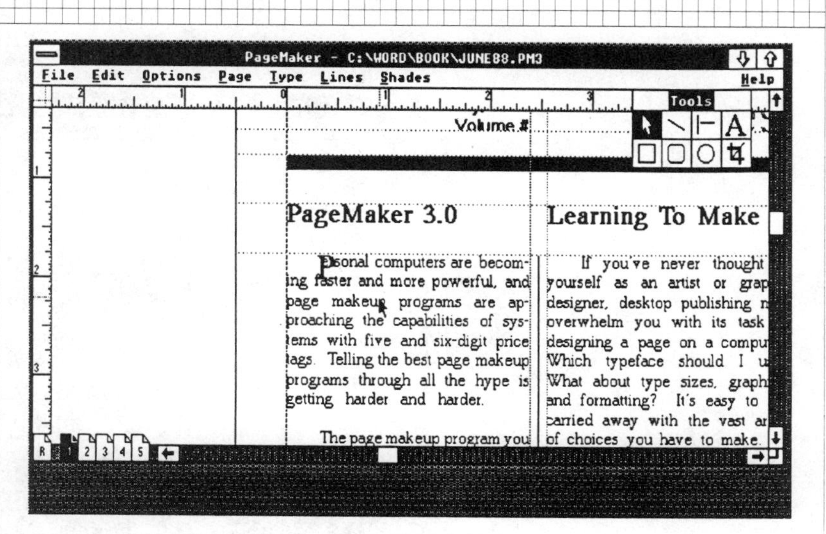

Figure 12.22: Dragging the stickup letter over text

6. Shorten the text block so that it is only as long as the bottom of the stickup letter.
7. Click on the plus sign at the bottom of the shortened text block. Place the text icon flush with the left column, below the stickup letter, and click the mouse button.
8. The text flows underneath the stickup letter, as shown in Figure 12.23.

► SPREADING A HEADLINE

You already had some practice spanning a headline across columns when you placed the headline for the second article of the newsletter. Spreading a headline is a little different from spanning a headline. To spread a headline, insert spaces between the letters. Use the space bar to manually insert the spaces, or the "Spacing" command from the Type menu to calculate extra spaces between letters. Remember, to spread a headline, the headline must be its own text block.

For practice, let's use the title of our newsletter on page 1.

1. Position the text tool between the letters in the headline one at a time, and press the space bar. In effect, as you add spaces between the letters, you are making each letter of the headline into a separate word.
2. Add two spaces between the words *DeskTop* and *News,* as shown in Figure 12.24.

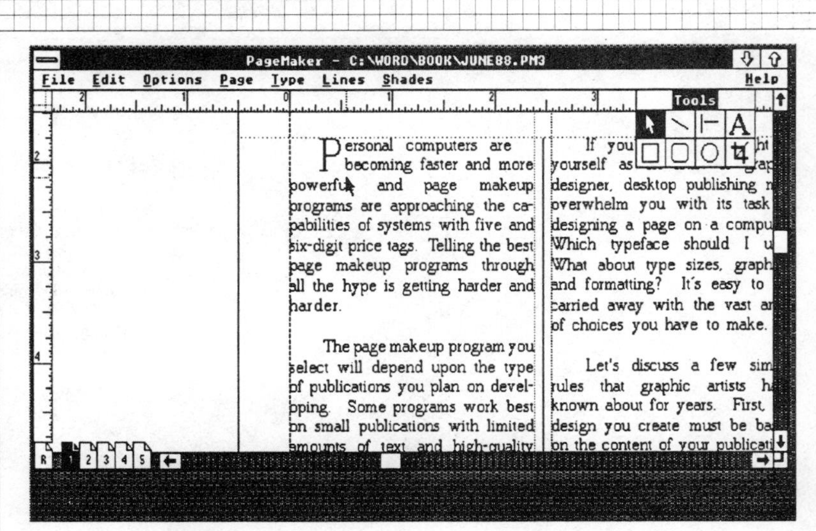

Figure 12.23: Text wrapped around a stickup letter

Now you must insert a nonbreaking space at the end of the line. PageMaker will not separate a line that ends with a nonbreaking space, and because you want your headline to be a single line, inserting a nonbreaking space ensures that PageMaker doesn't split the headline in two.

3. Position the text bar after the last letter of the headline.
4. To create nonbreaking spaces, hold down the Ctrl key and press the space bar. Insert as many nonbreaking spaces as it takes to reach the end of the line.
5. Select the text block by putting the text tool on the headline.
6. Choose the "Justified" option from the Type menu. PageMaker automatically makes the necessary adjustments to letter spacing to give you an evenly spaced headline.

► REVERSING TYPE

Your printer must be able to "print" white type in order to use this feature.

Most of the time, you will be using black type on white paper. However, reverse type is an effective way to enhance a title or even a word. Reverse type means that you reverse colors, with the white letters "printed" against a shaded or solid black background.

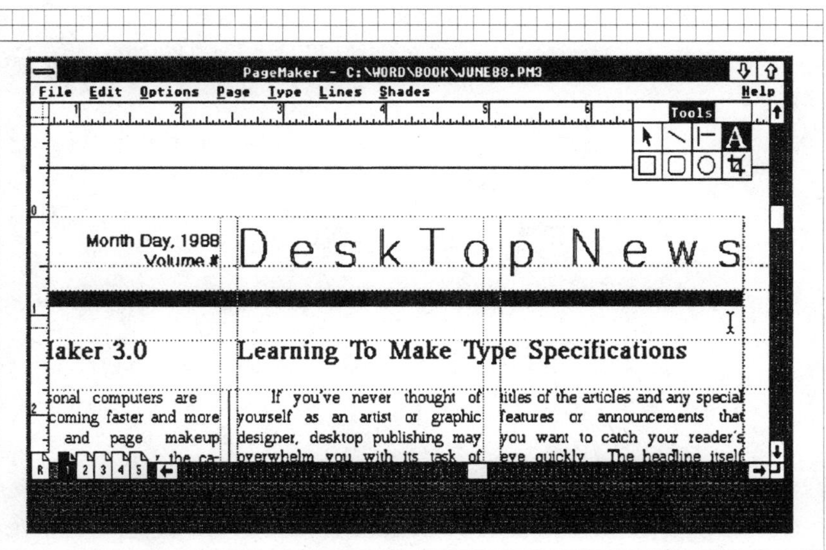

Figure 12.24: Spreading a headline

Creating boxes and shading them is discussed in Chapter 11.

To reverse type, you have to create a shaded box first. Select the box tool from the Toolbox. Create a box on the page where you want the reverse type to appear. With the box selected, choose a shade from the Shades menu. Remember to use the "Bring to front" and "Send to back" commands from the Edit menu as you need them. Use the text tool to select the text you want to reverse in the shaded box. Remember, text is selected when it is highlighted on the screen. Next, choose the "Reverse type" option from the Type menu. Choosing this option places a check mark next to it, which means that the text you selected is now reversed. If you choose the option again, the type will be restored to its original color.

If you reverse type without positioning a shaded box over it first, the reversed type will appear white on a white background and it won't be visible. In order to see reversed type, it must appear over a contrasting background. If you cannot find your reversed type, be sure the text block containing it is selected. Then drag the text block onto a dark background and the reversed type will become visible.

► REVERSING LINES

If your printer can produce "white type," you can reverse lines as well as reverse type. All lines you create using PageMaker can be reversed—black lines can become white and white lines can become black. The space between double and triple lines also reverses. Reversing lines works with any line style in the Lines menu.

As with text, the first thing you must do to reverse lines is create a contrasting background.

1. Use the box drawing tool to create a rectangle in a blank space of your publication. Use the Shades menu to shade in the rectangle.
2. Make sure the graphic is not selected. In fact, make sure nothing is selected on the page.

You are now ready to select a line style from the Lines menu.

3. Point to the Lines menu and choose a line style.
4. Choose "Reverse lines" from the Lines menu.
5. Use one of the drawing tools to draw inside the shaded rectangle you just made.

You will see a white line like the one in Figure 12.25 developing inside the shaded rectangle. To reverse a line you already placed on the page, select it and choose the "Reverse lines" option from the Lines menu.

► USING DROP SHADOWS

A drop shadow adds a new dimension to a graphic. A *drop shadow* is a shaded or black duplication of a graphic placed slightly askew of the original. The effect makes the graphic look three-dimensional. In this section, you'll create the drop shadow shown in Figure 12.26.

In order to make a drop shadow, you must have created a graphic the same size and shape as the one you want to place the drop shadow behind. For practice, let's use the month, day, year, and volume number box in the masthead. Use the box graphics tool from the Toolbox to create a box around this part of the masthead, as in Figure 12.26. Now you must create a copy of this box.

1. Be sure the box is selected. Since you created the box with PageMaker, choose the ''Copy'' option from the Edit menu. A copy of the box is moved to the Clipboard.
2. Choose the ''Paste'' option from the Edit menu and paste a copy of the box into the pasteboard area.
3. Drag this copy onto the page and place it where you want the drop shadow effect to be. For the best results, you should place the shadow slightly askew of the original.
4. With the shadow covering most of the original box, choose the ''Send to back'' option from the Edit menu. This moves the shadow behind the graphic.

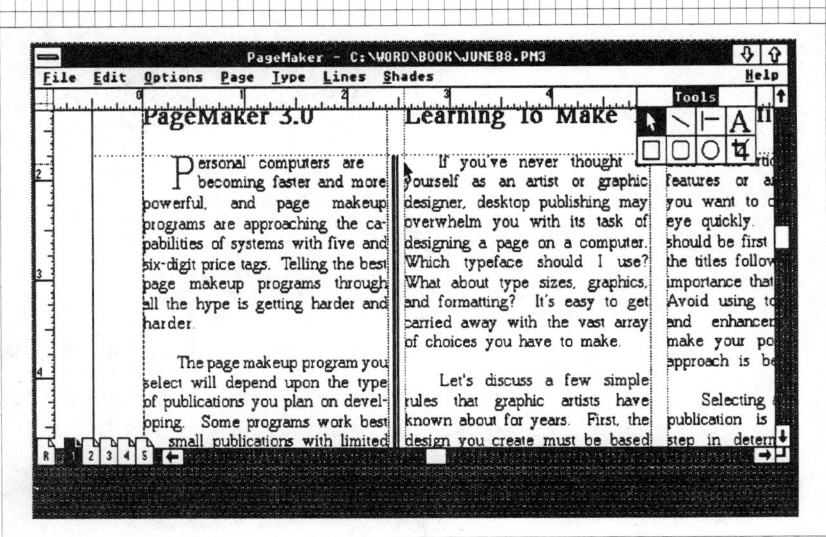

Figure 12.25: Reversed line

The effect should look similar to the graphic in Figure 12.26. You can make changes to the shading of the graphic by selecting a different shade from the Shades menu. You can always drag the original graphic around until you are satisfied with its placement in relation to the drop shadow. If you don't want the shadow to have a border, select the "None" option from the Lines menu. Again, before you make any changes to a graphic, be sure the graphic is selected. If necessary, use the "Send to Back" and "Bring to Front" commands from the Edit menu to reverse the order of the boxed graphics and send the one in the foreground to the background.

► ADDING TEXT TO GRAPHICS

So far, you've treated text blocks and graphics separately, but PageMaker lets you combine text blocks and graphics on a page. For example, you would do this to enhance a stickup letter by placing a shaded box around it. Adding text to graphics requires you to work in layers, stacking one layer over another. The only thing you have to keep in mind is the shading—make sure the text is readable when it is placed over a graphic.

Let's practice by placing text inside a shaded box with a drop shadow. Create a new box with a drop shadow like the one in Figure 12.27 on a practice page. Shade the box at about 40% so the text will be visible through the shading. Next, use the text tool to create a small bit of text in the pasteboard. For this example, create a boxed headline with the label *NEWS*.

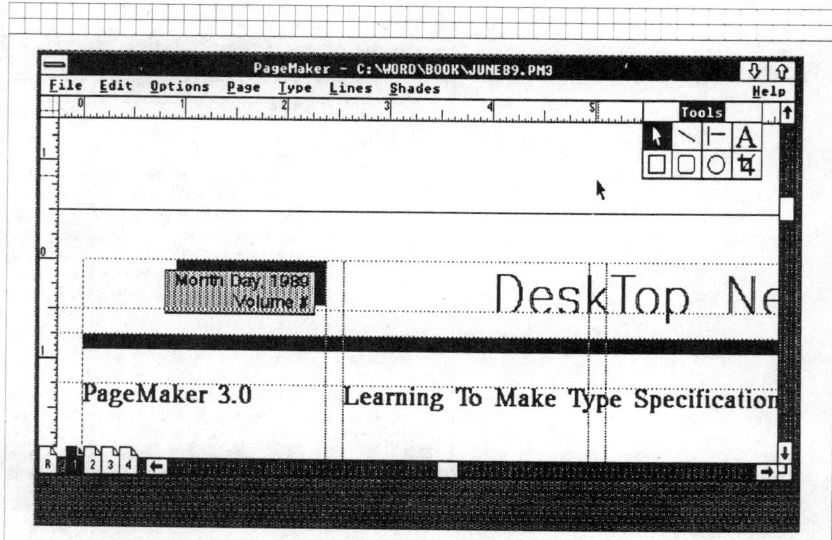

Figure 12.26: A drop shadow enhancing the date and volume box

Use the pointer tool to place the text on top of the drop shadow graphic. The text should now be placed within the graphic box and look something like the text and graphic shown in Figure 12.27. Make sure the text is legible. If necessary, you can change the stacking order of the text and graphics using the "Send to back" or "Bring to front" options from the Edit menu.

► USING DIFFERENT COLUMN FORMATS ON THE SAME PAGE

You may want to create a publication layout that has two or more column formats per page. For example, suppose you decide to split your page so that the top half has a two-column format, and the bottom half has a three-column format. This is actually much simpler to do than it sounds.

Let's practice setting up a page with two different column formats. On the top third of the page we will create a two-column format, and on the bottom two-thirds we will create a three-column format.

1. Add a blank page to your newsletter and turn off the master page format to eliminate all column guides on the page.
2. Click on the "Display master items" command from the Page menu. The page should not have any guides other than the margin guides.

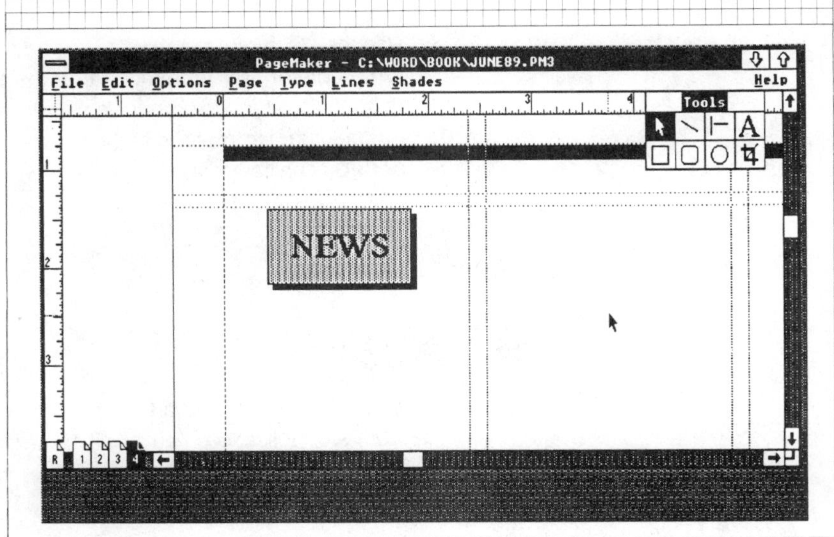

Figure 12.27: Text and graphic layering

3. Use the "Column guides" command from the Options menu and set up a two-column format.
4. With the new column guides in place, select either one of the line tools from the Toolbox.
5. Use this line tool to draw a horizontal line across the page where you want to separate the top two-column format from the bottom three-column format. Draw the line about one-third of the way down the page.

This straight line across the page will stop text from flowing into the lower two-thirds of the page where the three-column format will be.

6. Use the "Place" command from the File menu to select a practice text file and flow some text into the upper third of the page. Start at the upper left-hand corner of the first column. Notice that text flow stops at the line you drew.
7. Click on the plus symbol in the handle and flow more text into the second column starting at the top of the page. You should now see text in both columns above the line you drew.
8. Point to the line you drew and select it. With the line handles showing, delete the line by selecting the "Clear" command from the Edit menu.

Now you are ready to set up a three-column format for the bottom half of the page.

9. Use the "Column guides" command from the Options menu to set up a three-column format. Notice that the text on the top half of the page remains in a two-column format even though the column guides for the three-column format run to the top of the page. Your page is now set up and you can flow text into the lower two-thirds using the three-column format, as shown in Figure 12.28.

SUMMARY

In this chapter, you learned a few tricks for creating special design effects in your PageMaker publication. You might not use all of these features in your publications. Still, as you become more familiar with PageMaker, you'll find more ways to use these advanced design techniques.

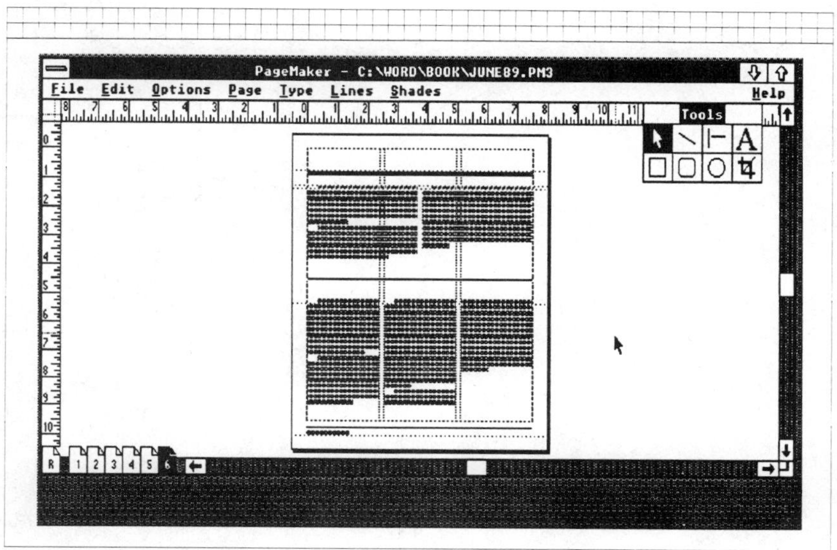

Figure 12.28: Two different column formats on the same page

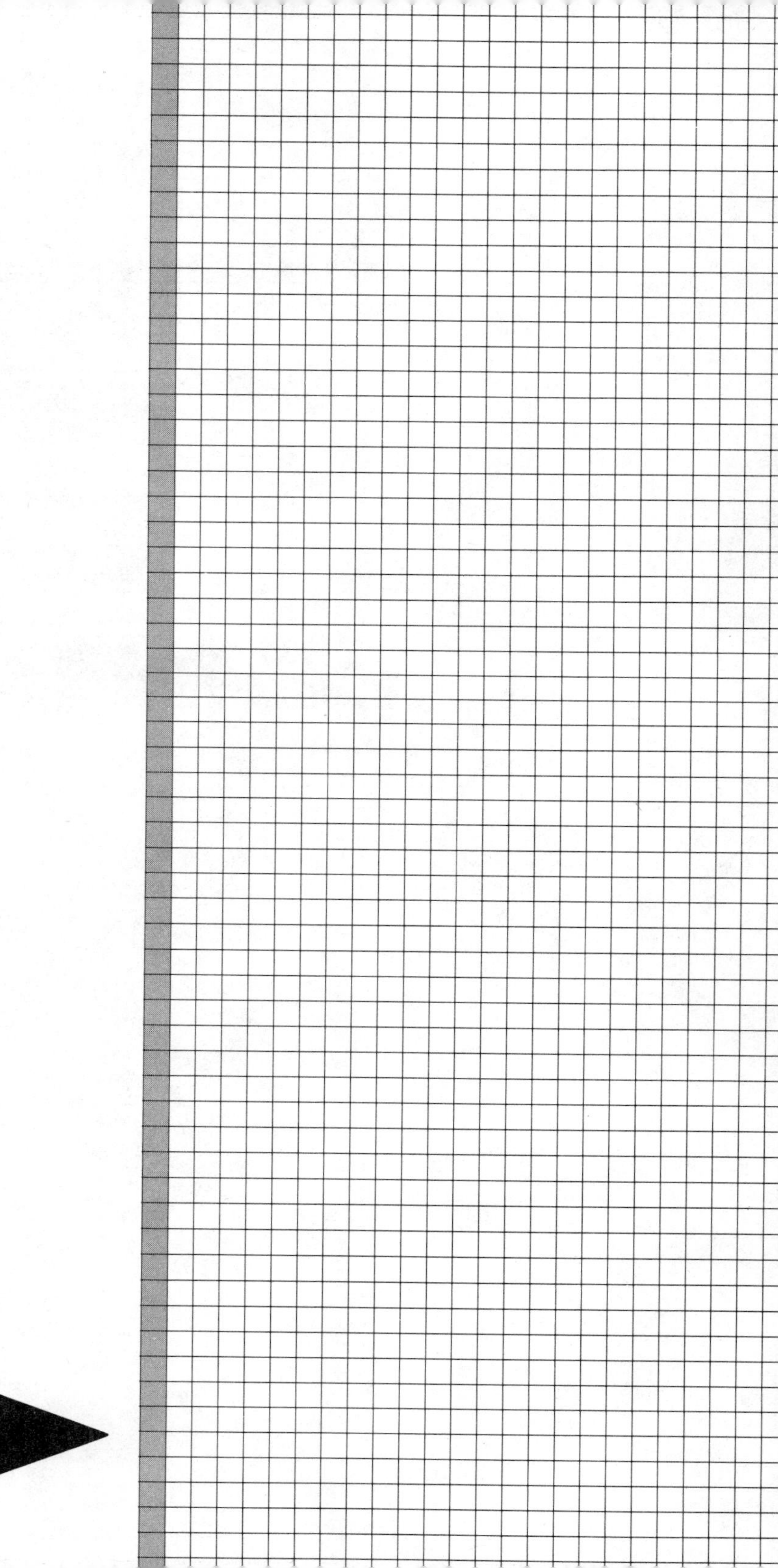

13 PRINTING YOUR PUBLICATION

To change the point size at which text is greeked, 287

click on the "Preferences" command from the Edit menu and change the pixel value in the Greek Text Below box.

To make text more visible on your screen, 288

stretch out a font size by clicking on the Preferences dialog box and changing the value in the Stretch Text Above box.

To specify when to substitute vector fonts for screen fonts, 288

click on the "Preferences" command from the Edit menu and set the point size in the Vector Text Above box in the Preferences dialog box.

To add PCL soft fonts to your system, 290

click on the "Printer setup" command from the File menu. Click on the "PCL" option and the "Setup" button. Click on the "Fonts" option in the PCL Printer dialog box. Insert the software in drive A and click on the "Add fonts" button.

To print your publication, 296

click on the "Print" command from the File menu and fill in the options in the Print dialog box.

To use bit-mapped smoothing with paint-type graphics, 296

click an X-mark in the Bit-mapped Smoothing box of the Print dialog box.

To speed up the printing of line art, 296

use Fast Rules with PCL Printers. Bring up the Print dialog box and click an X-mark in the Fast Rules box.

To print crop marks on the page, 296

bring up the Print dialog box, and click an X-mark in the Crop Marks box.

To print thumbnails using a PostScript printer, 298

bring up the Print dialog box from the File menu and specify which pages you want to see in thumbnail. Click an X-mark in the Thumbnails box and select a printer.

To enlarge or reduce the page size of your printed publication, 299

display the Print dialog box. Click an X-mark in the Scaling box and then type in a percentage for the amount you want to enlarge or reduce the page.

To use Spot Color overlays, 304

click an X-mark in the Spot Color Overlays box of the Print dialog box.

To control printing speed, 305

click on the "Spooler" command from Windows Control menu. In the Spooler window, click on the Priority menu and select the "High" or "Low" command.

To print a publication to disk, 307

edit the WIN.INI Windows file in your word processor or Notepad application to include the printer port, OUTPUT.PRN.

As you develop your publication, it is helpful to print it periodically so you can get an idea of what the final printed page will look like. Printing with PageMaker is quite easy. You can choose from a host of print specifications, and you can change them to your liking each time you want to print your publication.

In this chapter you will learn how to install fonts on your printer to use in printing your publications. A *font* is a complete set of typeface characters. Some fonts may be available immediately on your printer, and others may be downloaded from a floppy diskette. PageMaker gives you several options for changing the look and design of the fonts you use; you will learn how to make these changes so the font will give you just the look you want for your publication.

As you know, PageMaker supports a variety of printers. The target printer that you specify when you begin your publication determines the type specifications available to you as you develop it. When you are ready to print, these specifications will appear in your publication as long as you are using your target printer. If you print on a different printer without changing the target printer designation, PageMaker will adjust the type specifications automatically to make them conform to the parameters of the new printer's capabilities. Changes in type specifications can sometimes affect the look of your publication, so you may find it necessary to go back through the publication and make minor adjustments.

If your printer uses a page description language such as PostScript, you can scale, reduce, or enlarge the image. In this chapter, you will learn how to print thumbnails, or miniatures, oversize copies, and, of course, regular size pages. You'll also learn about color printing, how to use the Spooler (a Windows application that stores files sent to be printed), and how to print to your disk.

▶ USING SCREEN VERSIONS OF FONTS

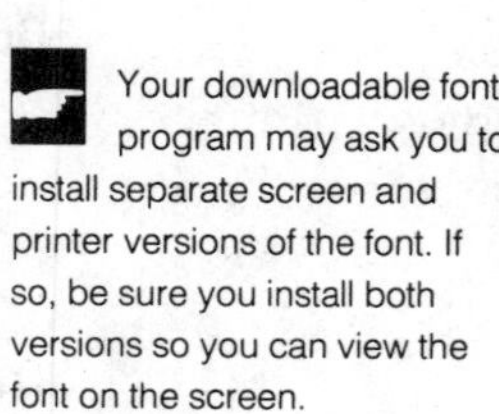

Your downloadable fonts program may ask you to install separate screen and printer versions of the font. If so, be sure you install both versions so you can view the font on the screen.

PageMaker tries to be a WYSIWYG page-composition program. (WYSIWYG is an acronym for *What You See Is What You Get.*) When you designate type specifications, PageMaker looks for a matching screen version of the font, size, and style you specified. If your font has a screen version, PageMaker displays it on your screen exactly as it will appear when you print it. However, PageMaker cannot always find an exact match between screen fonts and printout fonts, and it has different ways of dealing with this problem.

If PageMaker can find a matching screen version of the font but can't size it on the screen properly, it substitutes the next smaller point size of the font. This does not affect your printout—text in the publication is sized exactly as you specified.

If PageMaker can't find a matching screen version of the font, it automatically substitutes a generic Windows-based font on the screen. (Again, the final printed version will show the font you specified for the target printer.) PageMaker substitutes the closest match for the unavailable screen font with one of five generic fonts—Times Roman, Helvetica, Roman, Modern, and Script.

Proportional spacing means that the spacing between letters is tightened to adjust for differences in letter size. Proportional text looks tighter and requires less kerning.

Times Roman is substituted for proportionally spaced serif fonts such as Times, Palatino, and Century Schoolbook, and Helvetica is substituted for proportionally spaced sans serif fonts such as Avant Garde. Both of these substitution fonts are bit-mapped fonts measured in screen pixels. They are available in the following sizes: 6, 7, 8, 9, 10, 11, 12, 14, 16, 18, and 24 pixels. If your screen has a vertical resolution of 72 dots per inch, then the pixel sizes are the same as point sizes. Check the manual that came with your computer system to find out what the vertical resolution of your screen is. If your screen does not have a vertical resolution of 72 dots per inch, PageMaker can display fonts in multiples of the available sizes. This is done by scaling a version of a generic font. For example, a point size of 36 is possible because it is a multiple of 12 (12 × 3). If a scaled version is not possible, PageMaker displays the next smaller point size on the screen. Remember that the font size displayed on your screen also depends on the page view you select.

The Roman, Modern, and Script generic screen fonts are slightly different than the Times Roman and Helvetica fonts because they are vector fonts. *Vector fonts* are draw-type fonts that PageMaker can scale to any size. All three generic vector fonts are on the list of printer fonts in the Type Specs dialog box, but it is not a good idea to use a vector font for printing because it produces a ragged looking type. Even when the screen font is available, PageMaker substitutes a vector font if the text on your screen is larger than 24 pixels. The 24-pixel mark is the PageMaker default value. In the next section, you will learn how to change this default.

▸ CHANGING THE WAY FONTS DISPLAY

You now know that PageMaker displays screen fonts that match the font that will be printed, or if it cannot match the font, it chooses a generic font. Though PageMaker makes these choices automatically, there are some ways to manipulate the way text is displayed on your screen.

Greeking Text

Whenever possible, you should use matching screen fonts to display your main body of text between the type sizes of 8 and 12 points. However, if you use a point size that is too small to display on the screen, PageMaker substitutes unreadable, or *greeked*, text. You probably noticed that PageMaker takes a few seconds to display text on the screen. Greeked text takes less time to display. Of course, you cannot make changes to greeked text on the screen. To read greeked text you have to select a larger view from the Page menu.

To find out what greeked text looks like, click on the "Preferences" command from the Edit menu. The Preferences dialog box is displayed. By default, PageMaker greeks all text below 6 pixels. Change this value by entering 12 in the

Greek Text Below text box and click OK. Now change to the Actual Size view. Notice that all text smaller than 12 pixels has been greeked, but text larger than 12 pixels is still displayed on the screen, as shown in Figure 13.1. Be sure and change back to 6 pixels (PageMaker's default value) in the Preferences dialog box so you can read your text.

Stretching Fonts

PageMaker will stretch your screen fonts to make them display at larger point sizes so they will match the type size you specified for printing. To see the effect of stretching a screen font, click on the "Preferences" command from the Edit menu. The Preferences dialog box is displayed. Lower the value in the Stretch Text Above text box to below 24 pixels, PageMaker's default, and click OK. PageMaker will stretch screen fonts above the size you just indicated in the text box.

The more a screen font is stretched, the more distorted it looks on the screen. If stretched text begins to look too distorted, you can substitute a screen font that displays at a larger point size.

Using Vector Fonts

You can determine the font size at which PageMaker starts substituting vector fonts—Roman, Modern, and Script—in place of screen fonts. Vector fonts require

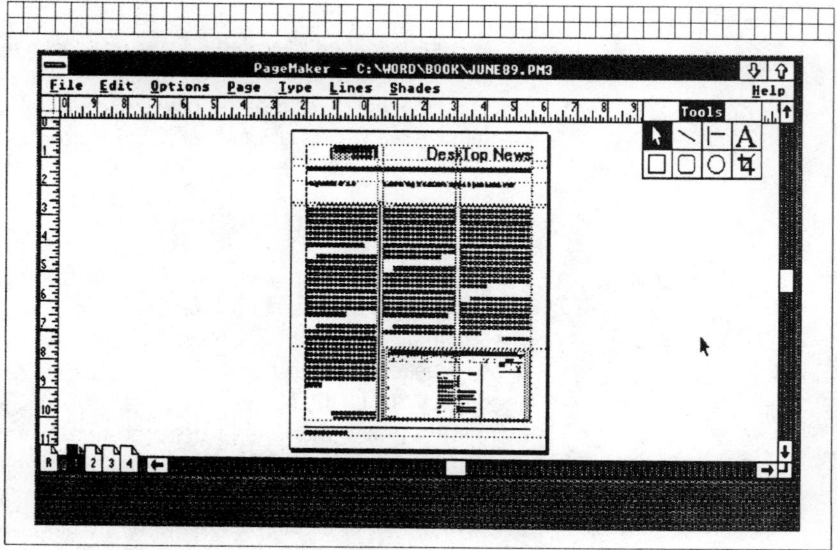

Figure 13.1: Greeked text

less memory to display than screen fonts do, but they also take longer to display than it would take if you simply stretched out your screen fonts.

PageMaker starts making vector text substitutions beginning at 24 pixels. Again, you can change this default by selecting the "Preferences" command from the Edit menu. Next, in the Preferences dialog box, put a lower value than 24 pixels in the Vector Text Above text box, and click OK. Now any text with a larger point size than the value you just entered will be displayed in a generic vector font. If you have a screen font that can display in large point sizes, increase the default value in the Vector Text Above box. A screen font that displays well at a large point size does not need a generic substitution.

► VISUAL DISCREPANCIES

Resolution is the number of dots used to construct the image, either on your screen or on your printed copy. It is measured in dots per inch; the higher the number of dots per inch, the clearer your image's appearance.

What you see on the screen may not match the printed version for other reasons as well. If the resolution on your screen and the resolution on your printer are different, it can result in discrepancies between what you see on your screen and what comes out of your printer. Because PageMaker lets you set up your publication for a variety of printers, these discrepancies can sometimes be quite large.

Both the Hewlett-Packard LaserJet+ and the Apple LaserWriter have resolutions of 300 dots per inch (dpi). The IBM PagePrinter 3812 has a resolution of 240 dpi, and some PostScript typesetters have resolutions of 1200–2400 dpi or more. Often, these resolutions will be slightly different from the resolution of your screen. As a result, fonts and character spacing may look different on your screen than they do when printed. The measuring of distance on a screen that uses 640 dpi is different from the final output printed at 1200 dpi on a typesetter. Therefore, the spacing of text on your screen may look different than the printed version. However, discrepancies between the screen version of text and the printed version are easy to get accustomed to once you've worked with PageMaker and your printer on a few publications.

PageMaker does try to compensate to make the screen version look just like the printed version. PageMaker may insert or delete spacing between the characters of a generic font in order to make the screen and printer line length match. This way, the line length on your screen will always be the same as the line length when you print.

► WORKING WITH SOFT FONTS

There are three ways for your computer system to use fonts. *Resident fonts* are built into the memory of your printer. The number of resident fonts varies among printers. Check your printer's user manual to find out how many resident fonts it

When you use the PageMaker Install program (discussed in Appendix A), you have to provide information about the built-in or cartridge fonts on your printer.

has. *Cartridge fonts* are contained in a cartridge that you insert into your printer. Cartridge fonts are used by laser printers that have a page language such as Printer Command Language (PCL). Laser printers use a page language to help interpret the information for printing a document. Some laser printers use PCL, others use the PostScript page description language. To use cartridge fonts, click on the "Printer setup" command from the File menu to bring up a dialog box and let PageMaker know they are installed. *Soft fonts* are fonts that you copy from a diskette onto your computer. *Downloadable fonts* are soft fonts that are available from third-party vendors. They allow you to add new fonts to your system without having to change cartridges for each new font. If you want to install downloadable fonts, use the instructions that came with the font package.

Depending on the target printer you select, PageMaker makes specific fonts available to you. As you enter your type specifications, PageMaker allows you to choose only the fonts available on your target printer.

► USING PCL PRINTER FONTS

Hewlett-Packard LaserJets and PCL-compatible printers use PCL. The following PCL printers are supported by PageMaker:

Apricot Laser	HP LaserJet Series II
Epson GQ-3500	Kyocera F-1010 Laser
HP LaserJet	Okidata LaserLine 6
HP LaserJet 500 Plus	Quadram QuadLaser 1
HP LaserJet 2000	Tandy LP-1000
HP LaserJet Plus	Tegra Genesis

A PCL font contains all the characters with a specific point size, type style, and orientation. PCL printers can use resident, cartridge, and soft fonts. However, not all printers can use soft fonts, so check your user manual to see if yours can use them. Soft fonts must be installed on your system before you can use them, and many soft fonts have their own installation programs. If you are using one of these programs, be sure to install the software for the Windows environment too. Most soft fonts include the following sets of files:

- The Printer Font file, which contains the actual font.
- The Printer Font Metrics file (PFM), which is required for Windows applications. If this file is not included with your soft font, a generic PFM file is generated during installation.

- The Screen Font file, which provides the screen representation of the printed font. If your soft font does not include a screen font file, PageMaker substitutes a generic screen font.

Each font is loaded on your system as either a temporary or a permanent font. Permanent fonts are stored in your printer's memory and they print much faster than temporary fonts. The drawback of permanent fonts is that they take up space in your printer's memory—space that is needed for printing complex layouts and graphics. Temporary fonts are copied to the printer at print time.

PageMaker 3.0 includes a built-in Soft Font Installer. The Installer can be used to load temporary or permanent fonts, move fonts between printer ports on your system, remove fonts, and edit font names.

The Soft Font Installer dialog box can be displayed from either the Windows Control menu or the PageMaker File menu. (To display the Soft Font Installer dialog box from the Control menu, select the Control Panel command.)

1. Click on the "Printer setup" command from the File menu. The Printer Setup dialog box, shown in Figure 13.2, is displayed.
2. Click on the "PCL printer" option in the scroll box.
3. Click on the "Setup" button. The PCL Printer dialog box, shown in Figure 13.3, is displayed.

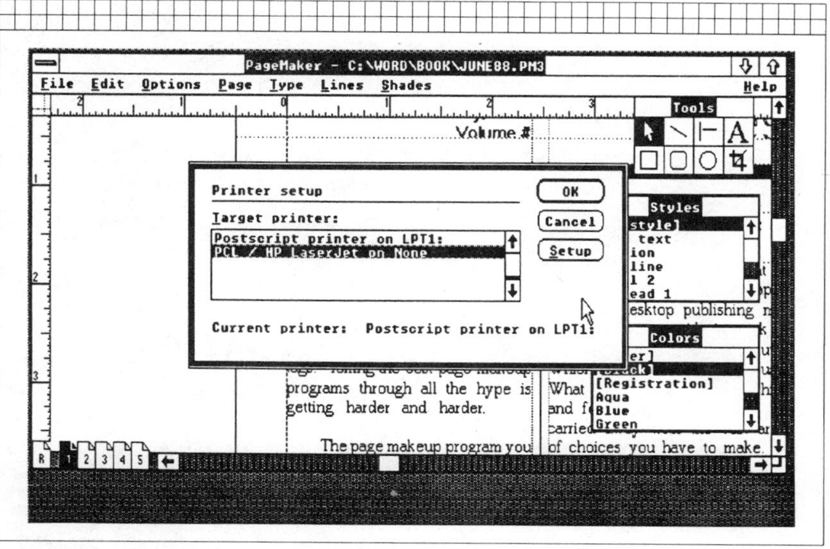

Figure 13.2: Printer Setup dialog box

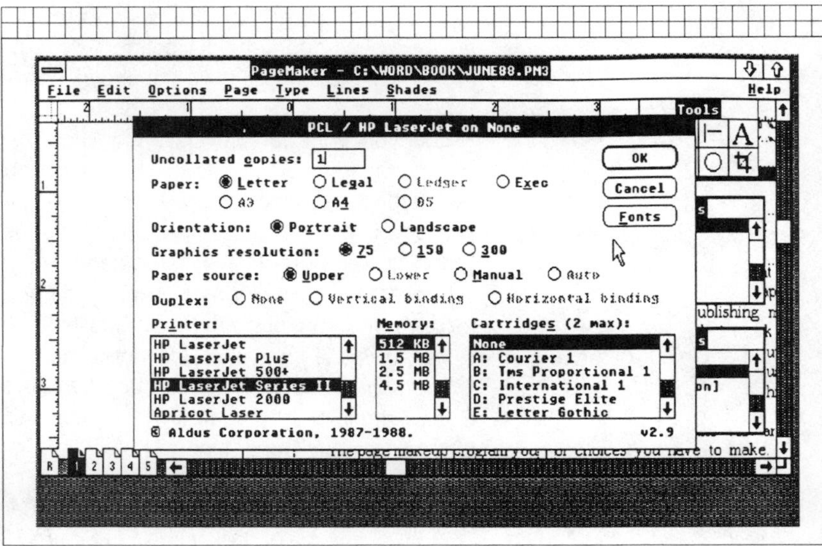

Figure 13.3: PCL Printer dialog box

4. Click on the "Fonts" button. The Soft Font Installer dialog box, shown in Figure 13.4, is displayed.
5. Insert the software diskette in drive A.
6. Click on the "Add fonts" button.
7. Hold down the Shift key and click on the fonts you want to add. To select all the fonts, hold down Ctrl and Shift keys.
8. Click on the "Add fonts" button again. The Add Fonts dialog box, shown in Figure 13.5, is displayed.
9. Enter the drive and directory name where you want the fonts to reside. The default is C:\PCLFONTS.
10. Click OK. The font is added.

At this point, one of two things will happen, depending on whether or not PageMaker recognizes the font name you just added. If the name of the font is recognized, you are returned to the Soft Font Installer dialog box. But if the name of the font is not recognized, the Font Metrics dialog box is displayed.

11. In the Font Metrics dialog box, enter the font name in the Name text box. Click on the "Font family" option button.
12. Click OK and you are returned to the Soft Font Installer dialog box.

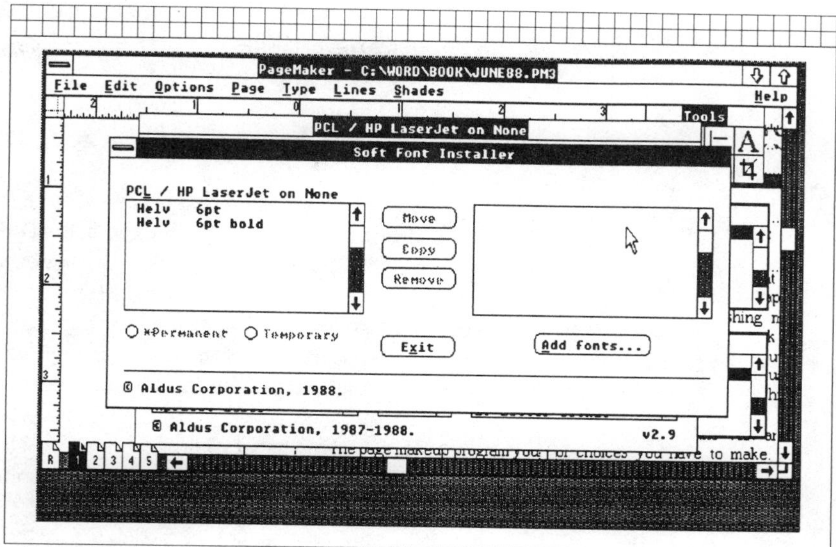

Figure 13.4: Soft Font Installer dialog box

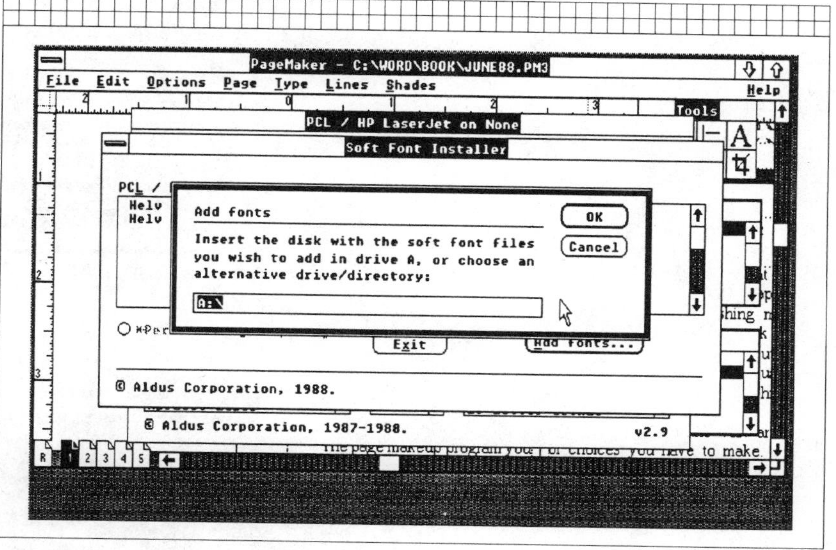

Figure 13.5: Add Fonts dialog box

Now you must decide if you want to install the font permanently or temporarily. If you choose to install the font permanently:

13. Select the font by clicking on it.
14. Click on the "Permanent" option button and click "Exit."

If you do not specify a font as permanent, PageMaker adds it as a temporary font. If you specify a font as permanent, the Download Options dialog box, shown in Figure 13.6, is displayed. The "Download now" and "Download at startup" options both contain a check mark. The "Download now" option downloads the fonts for use immediately. The "Download at startup" option will automatically download the fonts each time you turn on your computer. If you plan on using these downloadable fonts again and again, select the "Download at startup" option to make the fonts readily available to you every time you turn on your computer. However, to save time when you start up your computer, select the "Download now" option if you don't plan on using these fonts often.

15. Make a selection and click OK. When the Print dialog box is displayed, click OK again to return to the publication window.

Your soft fonts are now installed on your system. The Soft Font Installer dialog box also lets you copy or move fonts from one printer port to another, remove installed fonts, or edit a font name. To copy, move, or remove a font, click on the

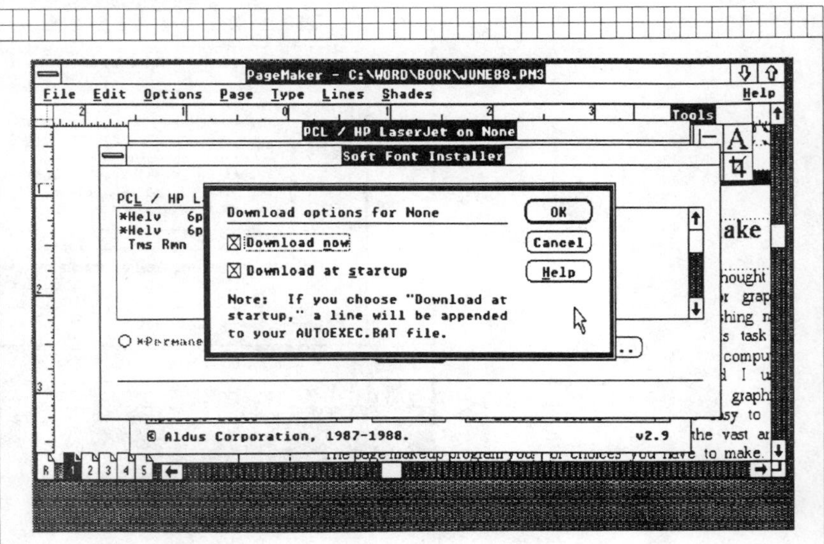

Figure 13.6: Download Options dialog box

appropriate button in the Soft Font Installer dialog box (Figure 13.4). To edit a font name, click on the "Enable edit" button from the soft font installer Control menu. This adds an "Edit" option button to the Soft Font Installer dialog box.

▶ USING FONTS WITH POSTSCRIPT

PostScript is a page description language used by many laser printers and typesetters. PageMaker has a printer driver for PostScript that supports the following printers:

Agfa P400PS	IBM Personal Pageprinter
AST PS-R4081	Linotronic 100/300/500
Apple LaserWriter	NEC SilentWriter LC-890
Apple LaserWriter Plus	QMS-PS 800/800A/800 Plus
Dataproducts LZR 2665	TI OmniLaser
Digital LN03R ScriptPrinter	VariTyper VT-600
Digital LPS Print Server 40	Wang LCS15-DSK

PostScript works with fonts differently than PCL. PostScript produces fonts mathematically, scaling sizes from 4 to 127 points.

Printers that use PostScript have many resident fonts, though fonts vary from printer to printer. For example, the following fonts are resident on an AST PS-R4081:

Courier	ITC Zapf Chancery Medium Italic
Gothic	ITC Zapf Dingbats
Helvetica	New Century Schoolbook
Helvetica Condensed	Palatino
ITC Avant Garde	Symbol
ITC Bookman	Times

Printers with PostScript can also use soft fonts, but PageMaker does not include an installer for PostScript downloadable soft fonts. To see if you can install PostScript fonts, refer to the user manual that came with your font software.

▶ SIZING YOUR PUBLICATION FOR PRINTING

PageMaker lets you print your publication in a variety of sizes. With a PostScript printer you can print thumbnails. A thumbnail is a miniature version of a page; you can see up to 16 thumbnails on one printed page. Thumbnails enable you to preview your layout design before printing. In addition, if you are using a printer with a page description language such as PostScript, PageMaker lets you scale your publications to print enlarged or reduced versions of them. You can also print oversize pages. An oversize page means that your page is too large to fit on your printer, so you have to divide the page into sections, or tiles, and later assemble them manually. This feature will be explained later.

A regular size page is the same size or smaller than the paper you are printing on. In other words, the paper size you selected when you began the publication must be the same size or smaller than the paper in your printer.

► PRINTING REGULAR SIZE PAGES

It's time to print our newsletter.

1. Click on the "Print" command from the File menu. The Print dialog box, shown in Figure 13.7, is displayed on your screen. Either the printer you last used or the target printer is highlighted in the Printer box at the bottom of the dialog box.
2. Enter the number of copies you want to produce in the Copies text box. You can print up to 99 copies at a time. For practice, we'll just print one copy of our newsletter, so choose the default of 1.

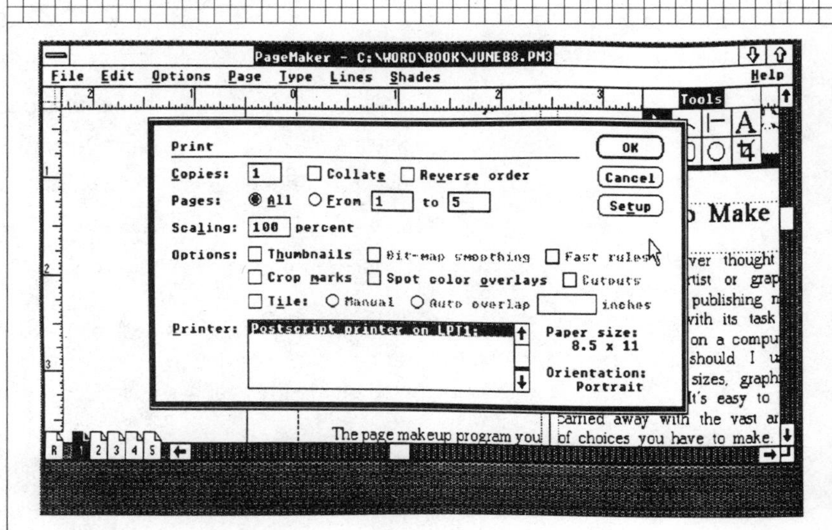

Figure 13.7: The Print dialog box

You can choose to have these copies collated or printed in reverse order. To specify collating, click an X-mark in the Collate box. Your printer is not collating if it stacks the pages in the output tray face up. If this is the case, click an X-mark in the Reverse Order box to reverse the order in which the pages are printed.

If you are printing multiple copies and you select Collate, PageMaker will print one complete copy of the entire range of pages, then print the next copy. If you are printing multiple copies and select Reverse Order, PageMaker will print all the copies of page 1 before moving on to page 2. Collated copies can take a long time to print if you are using a laser printer.

3. For now, use the PageMaker default.

Next, select the pages you want to print. The two option buttons allow you to print the entire publication or specific pages.

4. Click the "All" option button to print the entire publication.

If you wanted to specify certain pages for printing, you would click the "From" option button and enter a page range in the text boxes. Entering page numbers in either of the text boxes automatically selects the "From" option button.

The Scaling box is used to enlarge or reduce your page size. Right now, we are printing regular size pages, so we'll use 100% scaling.

5. Click in the Scaling box and type in 100.

Printing thumbnails and oversize pages is explained later in this chapter.

The next set of options in the Print dialog box refers to page sizing. PageMaker 3.0 includes a bit-map smoothing feature. Click an X-mark in the Bit-map Smoothing option box and PageMaker will smooth out any paint-type graphics you included in your newsletter. Smoothing cleans up ragged edges by adding dots to the filled-in areas of a paint-type graphic. However, smoothing slows down the printing process and can darken an image. Leave the box blank for now.

See the section "Color Printing" for details on the "Spot color overlays" and "Cutouts" options.

If you are printing to a PCL printer, you can also use the "Fast rules" option. "Fast rules" speeds up the printing of line art by sending the dimensions of a line to the printer instead of a bit-mapped image. Do not use "Fast rules" if you are printing spot color overlays with cutouts.

6. Since we are printing regular size pages at this time, click the X-mark off in the Thumbnails box if needed.

The next option box is the Crop Marks box. Crop marks are trim lines that mark where the edges of the page size you selected appear on the page. You would use the "Crop marks" option if the paper you were printing on was larger than the paper size you specified in the Page Setup dialog box and you wanted crop marks displayed to show where to cut the pages. For now, leave the Crop Marks box blank and use the defaults in the Tile box.

Now you must specify the printer you want to use. In most cases, you will print to your target printer so that the specifications you indicated throughout your publication carry over to the printed version. If you do not specify the printer, PageMaker prints to the printer you last used. This can be a printer you used with PageMaker, or a printer you used with another Windows application. PageMaker gives you the chance to specify the printer each time you print so you can print draft copies, for example, to another printer you installed on your system.

If you select a printer different from the target printer you designated when you began the publication, PageMaker will substitute the fonts, styles, and sizes available on the new printer that most closely approximate your original specifications.

7. To change the printer selection, highlight the printer you want by pointing and clicking the mouse button on it. If the printer you want is not showing, click in the scroll bar until you see it. Then highlight the printer by clicking on it.
8. With your print specifications established, click OK to begin printing, or click "Cancel" if you decide that you do not want to start printing. This is your last chance to cancel the print process before it starts. As soon as OK is clicked, the publication is sent to the printer—unless you changed the target printer. In this case, you will be asked if you want to recompose the entire publication. Click OK if you want to recompose the publication before sending it to the printer.

All four pages of your newsletter should begin to print. If you decide to stop the printing process, click "Cancel" after PageMaker indicates that printing is in progress. However, a page or two may print before the process is finally cancelled.

► PRINTING THUMBNAILS

Your printer must use a page description language such as PostScript in order to print thumbnails. Refer to the manual that came with your printer to see if it uses a page description language. If it does, you can print up to 16 thumbnails on one piece of paper. Thumbnails take a long time to print because each page is so dense; one printed page can take as long as a few minutes.

To print thumbnails, select the "Print" option from the File menu. The Print dialog box is again displayed. Go ahead and specify the number of copies you want and the pages you want to see in thumbnail. Next, click an X-mark in the box marked Thumbnails. Select your printer and click OK when you are ready.

The thumbnails will begin printing. Notice the highlighted page icon at the bottom of the publication window. This indicates which page is currently printing.

► PRINTING ENLARGED OR REDUCED PAGES

You can enlarge or reduce the printed image of a page, but again you have to have a printer that uses a page description language such as PostScript. Specify whatever scaling you want in the Scaling text box. For example, scale at 67% to print a page that is one-third smaller vertically and horizontally, or scale at 300% to print a page three times larger. If you want to enlarge your page to a size bigger than your printer can handle on one page, you'll have to print an oversize page, which is explained in the next section. Figures 13.8, 13.9, and 13.10 show a newsletter page at regular size, at 67% scaling, and at 300% scaling.

Meanwhile, to print an enlarged or reduced page, choose the "Print" command from the File menu. The Print dialog box is again displayed. Point to the Scaling box and fill in the size of the enlargement or reduction you want to make. Remember, you are entering the percentage that indicates the sizing change. When you've completed the dialog box, click OK.

The scaled pages will start printing. Enlarged or reduced pages may take a little longer to print than the originals. Again, the page icon at the bottom of the publication window indicates which page is currently printing.

► PRINTING OVERSIZE PAGES USING THE TILING OPTION

PageMaker defines an oversize page as one that is larger than the paper you are printing on. For example, suppose you choose to enlarge a page by 200%, but the enlarged image is too large to fit on the paper you are printing on. Or suppose you decide to print on smaller paper than you indicated in the Page Setup dialog box when you began your publication. In each case you would need to print an oversize page.

When you print an oversize page you must divide your page into sections or *tiles.* Each tile is then printed on its own page. It's up to you to reassemble the printed pages by hand on a pasteup board. PageMaker also provides an overlap feature so that you can print to the edge of a page.

If you want to control what is printed on each tile, you can specify where each section or tile starts, but if you do not care how each tile is split, you can choose the automatic default and PageMaker will do it for you.

Let's practice printing in sections. Make sure the first page of the publication you want to print is showing on the screen.

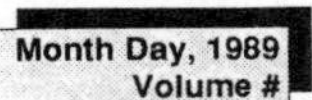

DeskTop News

PageMaker 3.0

Learning To Make Type Specifications

Personal computers are becoming faster and more powerful, and page makeup programs are approaching the capabilities of systems with five- and six-digit price tags. Telling the best page makeup programs through all the hype is getting harder and harder.

The page makeup program you select will depend upon the type of publications you plan on developing. Some programs work best on small publications with limited amounts of text and high-quality graphics such as brochures, flyers, and newsletters. Other programs work best for larger publications with dense text such as technical manuals or books.

The PageMaker® version 3.0 from Aldus incorporates features from both ends of the spectrum and is ahead on the road toward the dedicated desktop publishing workstation. Figure 1 illustrates one of the new features of PageMaker 3.0, templates. With all its advantages, PageMaker represents the top of the line in desktop publishing.

If you've never thought of yourself as an artist or graphic designer, desktop publishing may overwhelm you with its task of designing a page on a computer. Which typeface should I use? What about type sizes, graphics, and formatting? It's easy to get intimidated by the vast array of choices you have to make.

Let's discuss a few simple rules that graphic artists have followed for years. First, the design you create must be based on the content of your publication. You must determine the critical elements of your publication and use your design to highlight the levels of importance.

In a newsletter, the most important element is the masthead of the newsletter. This should be the largest element of the first page. Next in importance are the titles of the articles and any special features or announcements that you want to catch the reader's eye quickly. The masthead itself should be first in importance, with the titles following in an order of importance that is defined simply. Avoid using too many type sizes and enhancements to make your point. The simplest approach is usually best.

Selecting a typeface for your publication is another important step in determining its character. With all the fonts available on laser printers today, it's hard to determine which one to select in each case.

cont. on pg. 3

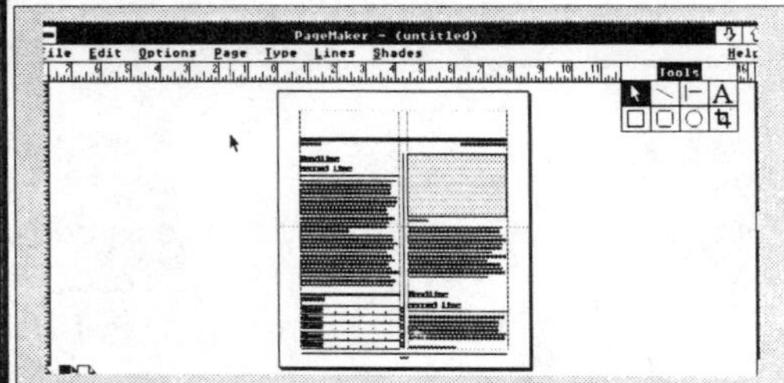

Figure 1: PageMaker 3.0 Newsletter Template

DeskTop News 1

Figure 13.8: A newsletter page at regular size

1. To choose where to start printing a file, select the "Rulers" option from the Options menu if it is not on already. If the zero point is set at the intersection of the top and left margin, move the ruler's zero point to the upper-left corner of the page itself.

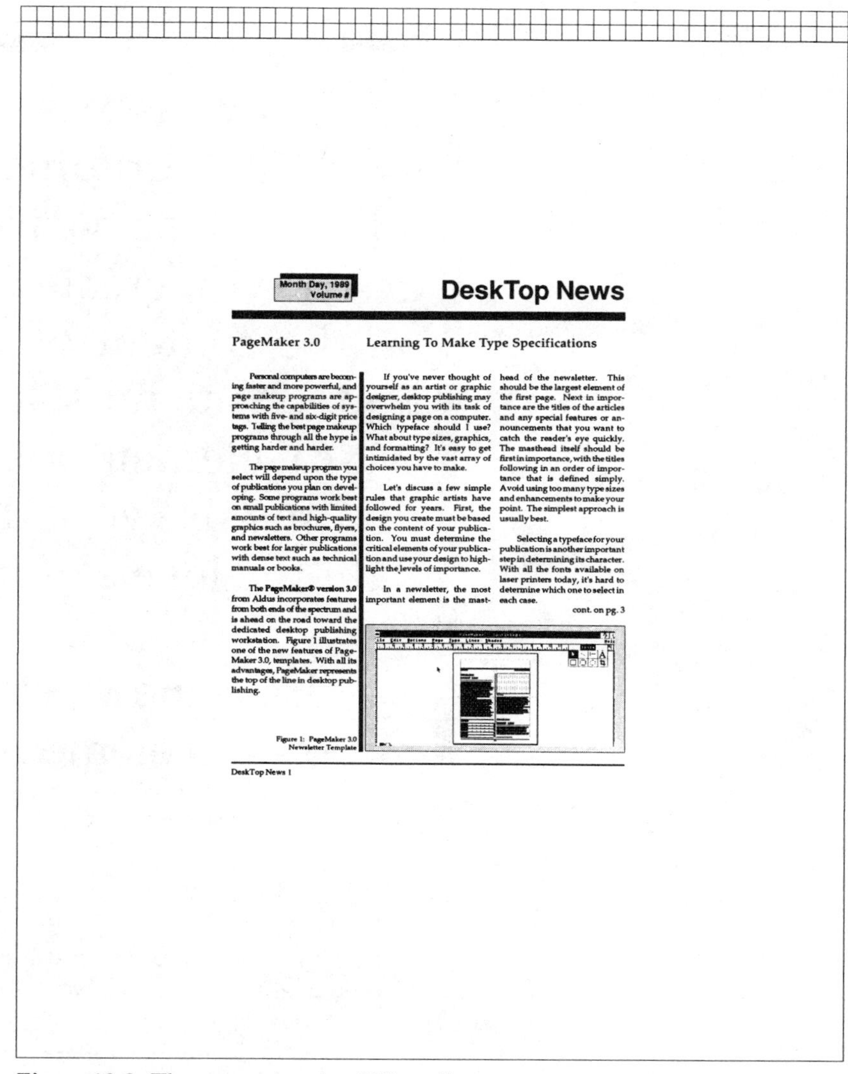

Month Day, 1989
Volume #

DeskTop News

PageMaker 3.0

Personal computers are becoming faster and more powerful, and page makeup programs are approaching the capabilities of systems with five- and six-digit price tags. Telling the best page makeup programs through all the hype is getting harder and harder.

The page makeup program you select will depend upon the type of publications you plan on developing. Some programs work best on small publications with limited amounts of text and high-quality graphics such as brochures, flyers, and newsletters. Other programs work best for larger publications with dense text such as technical manuals or books.

The PageMaker® version 3.0 from Aldus incorporates features from both ends of the spectrum and is ahead on the road toward the dedicated desktop publishing workstation. Figure 1 illustrates one of the new features of PageMaker 3.0, templates. With all its advantages, PageMaker represents the top of the line in desktop publishing.

Figure 1: PageMaker 3.0 Newsletter Template

Learning To Make Type Specifications

If you've never thought of yourself as an artist or graphic designer, desktop publishing may overwhelm you with its task of designing a page on a computer. Which typeface should I use? What about type sizes, graphics, and formatting? It's easy to get intimidated by the vast array of choices you have to make.

Let's discuss a few simple rules that graphic artists have followed for years. First, the design you create must be based on the content of your publication. You must determine the critical elements of your publication and use your design to highlight the levels of importance.

In a newsletter, the most important element is the masthead of the newsletter. This should be the largest element of the first page. Next in importance are the titles of the articles and any special features or announcements that you want to catch the reader's eye quickly. The masthead itself should be first in importance, with the titles following in an order of importance that is defined simply. Avoid using too many type sizes and enhancements to make your point. The simplest approach is usually best.

Selecting a typeface for your publication is another important step in determining its character. With all the fonts available on laser printers today, it's hard to determine which one to select in each case.

cont. on pg. 3

DeskTop News 1

Figure 13.9: The page reduced at 67% scaling

2. Choose the "Print" option from the File menu to bring up the Print dialog box (Figure 13.7).
3. Point to the Pages box and specify a page range of 1 to 1. Specify scaling at 300%.
4. Highlight the Tile box. Highlight the "Manual" option button.

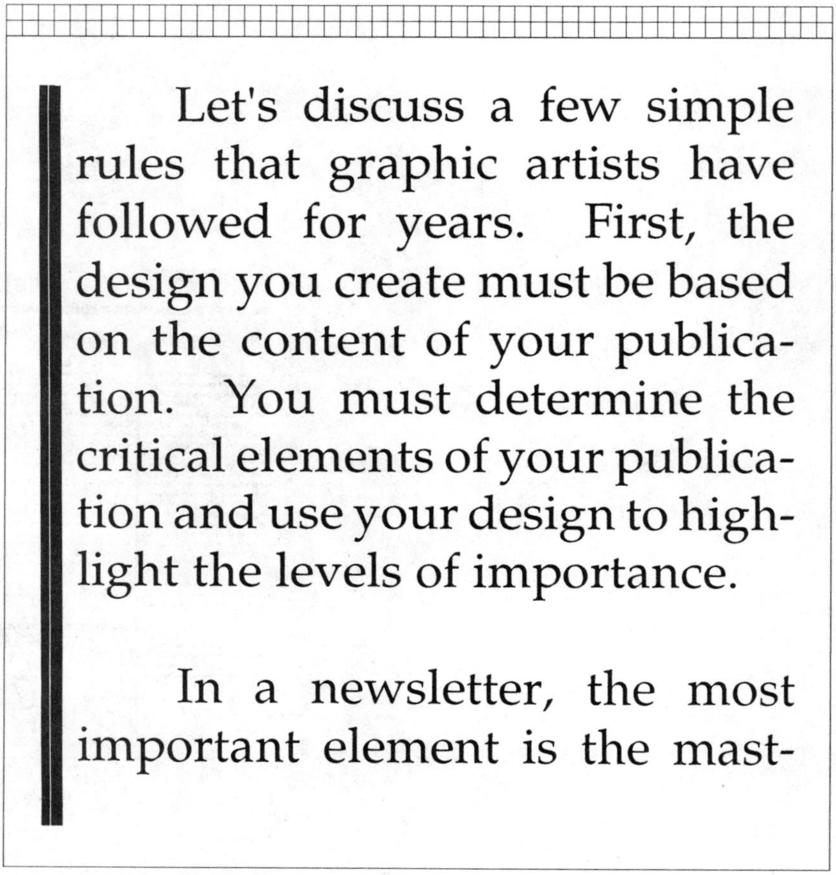

Let's discuss a few simple rules that graphic artists have followed for years. First, the design you create must be based on the content of your publication. You must determine the critical elements of your publication and use your design to highlight the levels of importance.

In a newsletter, the most important element is the mast-

Figure 13.10: The page enlarged at 300% scaling

Try manual tiling first so that you can select the tile portions yourself and control the break-up of pages. For example, if you had a complex graphic you wouldn't want to split it at a location with a lot of detail, so you would select manual tiling to break up the page in a blank area and make cutting and pasting on a layout board easier. Select a tile manually by sectioning off a part of the page with the zero marker. Do this by setting a zero point at the upper-left corner of the area of the page being sectioned off as a tile.

5. With the zero point marker in the upper-left corner of the newsletter page, click OK. Your screen and printed tile should look like the examples in Figure 13.11.

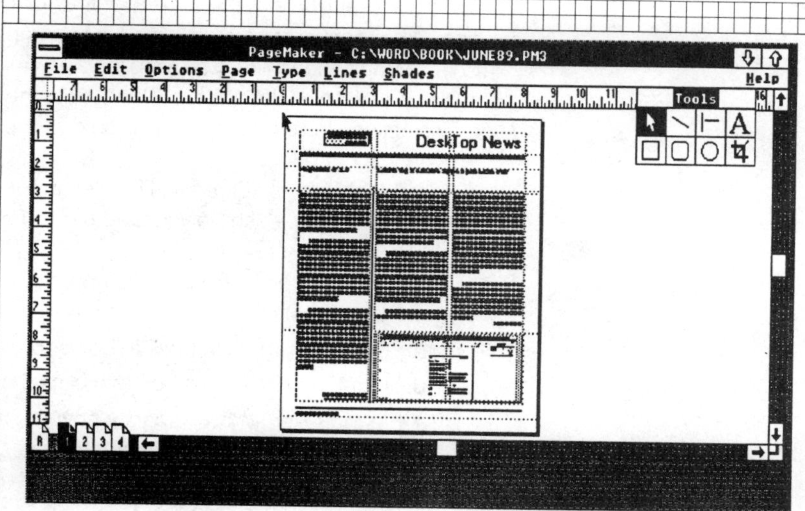

Month Day, 1989
Volume #

PageMaker 3.0

Personal computers are becor
ing faster and more powerful, ar

Figure 13.11: A tile selected manually with the zero point at the upper-left corner of a 300% enlarged page; the printed tile is at the bottom

PageMaker prints all the copies for the first tile before moving on to the second one. When the printing of the first tile is completed, you must select the starting point for the second tile by moving the zero point on the ruler to the upper-left corner of the next tile. Next select "Print" from the File menu and make the appropriate selections from the Print dialog box. This process must be repeated for each tile you want to print.

Use PageMaker's automatic tiling feature when you do not need to select the beginning point for each tile yourself. To use PageMaker's automatic tiling option:

1. Select "Print" from the File menu. Again, the Print dialog box (Figure 13.7) is displayed.
2. Click an X-mark in the Tile box and the "Auto" option button.
3. Point to the Overlap box and click the mouse button.
4. In the Overlap box, specify how much overlap you want between tiles. Be sure to make the overlap area larger than the edge of the page that your printer can't reach. One-quarter to one-half of an inch is a good overlap size to select.
5. Select your other printing specifications and click OK when you are ready to print.

The page icon at the bottom of the publication window indicates which page is currently printing. When PageMaker has printed the sections of your page, you will have to paste them together manually on a pasteboard. Experiment with PageMaker's tiling feature and soon you will get a feel for how it works.

► COLOR PRINTING

You can print your publication in color using a desktop color printer, or at a commercial print shop, using several types of printing devices: dot-matrix printers, plotters, thermal transfer printers, ink jet printers, and film recorders.

If you plan to print your publication at a commercial print shop, you must print a separate page for each color in your publication. The shop will then make a color overlay for each of these pages before printing the publication. For example, if you used blue and red color on page 1, you would print two copies of that page—the printer would use one page for an overlay that would contain only the areas to be printed in red, and the other page for an overlay that would contain only the areas to be printed in blue.

Once the overlays are made, the printer places the overlays one on top of the other. The printer must be able to line up the colors on each overlay precisely, so you must include registration marks on the pages that will need overlays. These registration marks are guides for the printer, and are positioned at exactly the same place on each page at the top, bottom, and both sides of the page.

PageMaker 3.0 can be used to automatically add the registration marks on every page. Adding registration marks automatically is done at print time. To print the registration marks and the name of the overlay's color outside the printing area of the page, the page size must be smaller than the size of the paper. Here's how to add registration marks automatically.

1. Click on the "Print" command from the File menu. The Print dialog box (Figure 13.7) is displayed.
2. Click an X-mark in the "Spot color overlays" box.
3. Make your other selections in the dialog box. If your page size is smaller than your paper size, you should use crop marks.
4. Click OK. The pages are printed with the registration marks in place.

PageMaker offers another print option for color printing—the "Cutouts" option. When you use overlays, there are spots where the colors overlap. The "Cutouts" option will create a blank spot, or will "cut out" this overlapping area. However, since the registration is usually not 100 percent accurate (creating "tight" or "loose" registration), the printer may need to change the cutouts you provide to adjust for registration irregularities. Because of this, you may want to let your printer handle the overlapping colors for you.

► QUEUEING FILES AND INTERRUPTING PRINTING WITH THE SPOOLER

The Spooler is a Windows application for storing files that were sent to the printer. The Spooler's job is to send files to the printer in the order they were received so you can keep on working while you are printing. The Spooler also lets you interrupt or cancel printing. In addition, you can select the speed at which the Spooler sends files to the printer.

► CHANGING THE SPEED OF THE SPOOLER

Speeding up the Spooler will slow down your work speed while a file is printing. This happens because PageMaker has to dedicate more of its memory to printing. On the other hand, slowing down the Spooler makes your PageMaker work go faster. To change the speed of the Spooler, click on the "Spooler" command from the Windows Control menu. (If Windows was installed separately, run the SPOOLER.EXE application from the Windows MS-DOS Executive window.) The

Spooler window, shown in Figure 13.12, is displayed. Click on the Priority menu and select the "High" or "Low" command. "High" increases the speed of the Spooler, and "Low" decreases the speed.

► INTERRUPTING AND CANCELING PRINTING

You can interrupt or cancel a print job through the Spooler window. To interrupt the printing process:

1. Click on the "Spooler" command from the Control menu. The Spooler window is displayed.
2. Click on the name of the file you want to interrupt.
3. Click on the "Pause" command from the Queue menu.
4. When you are ready to resume printing, click on the "Resume" command from the Queue menu. Printing is resumed where it left off.

To cancel printing:

1. Click on the "Spooler" command from the Control menu. The Spooler window is displayed.
2. Click on the name of the file you want to cancel.

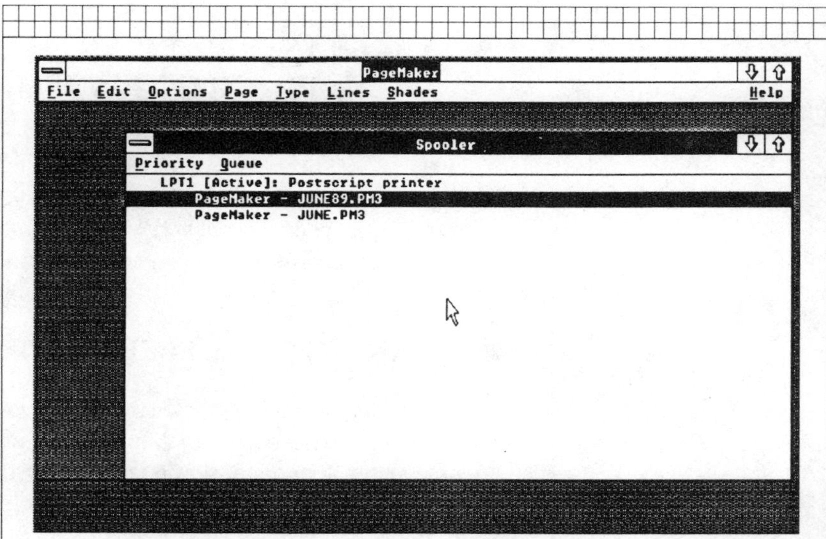

Figure 13.12: Spooler with files queued

3. Click on the "Terminate" command from the Queue menu.
4. Click OK to stop printing.

Once you cancel printing, the next file in the print queue is sent to the printer. Remember, when you cancel a print job in the middle, you may have to reset your printer for the next file.

When you cancel a print job, PageMaker automatically creates a temporary file (_SPL_.TMP) on your hard disk. Go to the directory where you are storing temporary files when you want to remove one. The SET TEMP statement in your AUTOEXEC.BAT file indicates where these files are stored.

► PRINTING TO DISK

Printing a publication to a diskette copies all the associated graphics files, including fonts, into the publication. The publication can then be printed from the diskette using MS-DOS commands; you won't need to use a system with PageMaker to print it. Printing a publication to disk allows you to send the publication over a modem, or move to another system that has the printer you want.

Printing a file to disk copies all the temporary fonts used in the publication. Permanent fonts must be downloaded separately to the printer before print time.

To print a file to disk, you must edit a Windows file called WIN.INI to add a printer port called OUTPUT.PRN. At print time, you must assign your target printer to the OUTPUT.PRN port. This port is actually a file on your hard disk. The file can then be copied to a floppy diskette using the MS-DOS COPY command.

Let's edit the WIN.INI file to print our publication to disk. To edit the file, you can use the Notepad text editor included with Windows, or your own word processor.

1. Bring up the WIN.INI file in your word processor, or use the Notepad application.
2. Scroll down the numeric keypad to move to the section of the file that starts with *[ports]*.
3. Position the cursor at the end of the section.
4. Add the following to the file:

   OUTPUT.PRN =

5. Save your changes and close the file.

With WIN.INI edited to print to the OUTPUT.PRN port, you must set up your printer to print to the OUTPUT.PRN port.

1. Click on the "Control Panel" command from the Control menu. The Control Panel menu, shown in Figure 13.13, is displayed.

2. Click on the "Connections" command from the Setup menu. The Printer Connection dialog box, shown in Figure 13.14, is displayed.

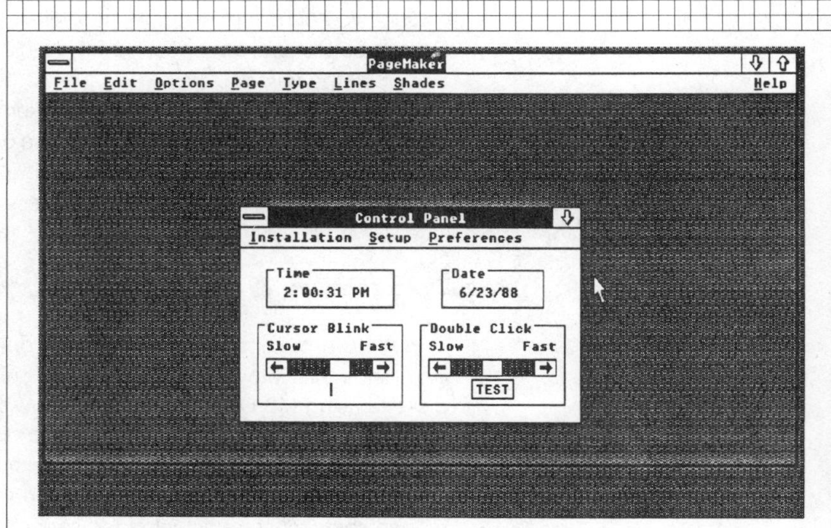

Figure 13.13: The Control Panel

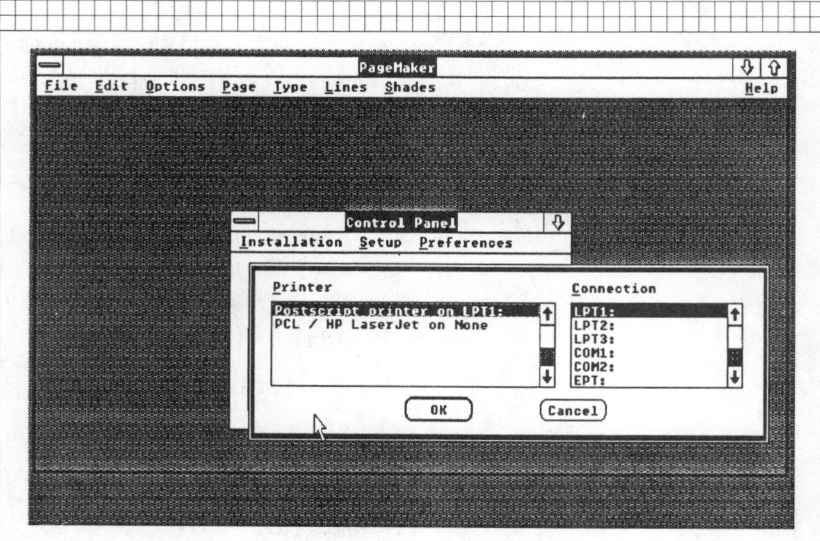

Figure 13.14: The Printer Connection dialog box

3. Click on the OUTPUT.PRN port in the Connection scroll box.
4. Click on the "Printer" command from the Setup menu. The Default Printer dialog box, shown in Figure 13.15, is displayed.
5. Click on the destination printer.
6. Click OK.

You are now ready to print your publication to disk. Follow the printing procedures you have just learned. Select the "Print" command from the File menu. Fill in the dialog box and send the file to the printer. Be sure to select the destination printer using port OUTPUT.PRN. The publication is printed to your hard disk. To transport the file to a different system, use the MS-DOS COPY command.

SUMMARY

As you can see, PageMaker offers you several ways to print your publication. For example, if your printer can print thumbnails, you can print thumbnails as you design your publications to evaluate your page layouts. Be sure you print often during publication development so that you can make any necessary adjustments to the final printed version early on.

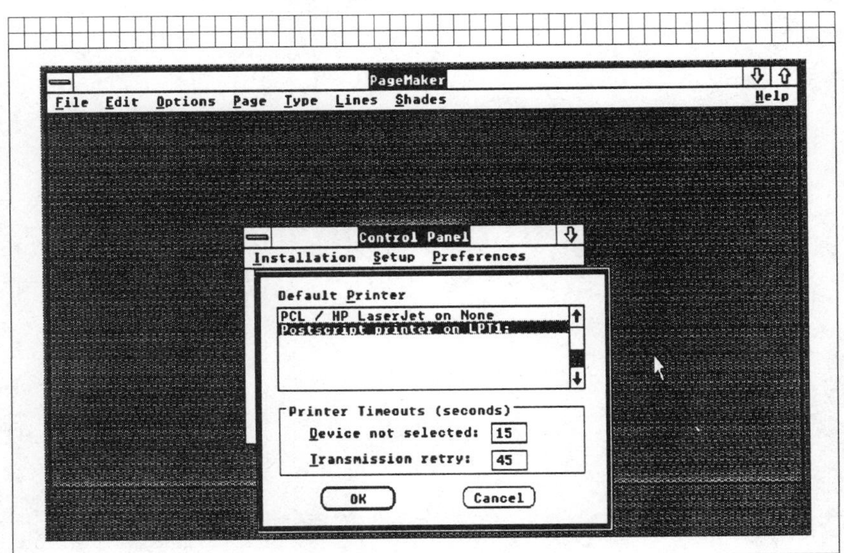

Figure 13.15: The Default Printer dialog box

▸ 14 CUSTOMIZING PAGEMAKER'S TEMPLATES

To use one of PageMaker's built-in templates, 314

double-click on the "Open" command from the File menu. Click on the [Template] subdirectory and select the template you want to use.

To recompose a PageMaker template, 315

click on the "Printer setup" command from the File menu. Click on the "Setup" command button and make your printer selections.

To change the style used in a template, 318

hold down the Ctrl key and click on the style sheet you want to change in the Styles palette.

To replace a placeholder in a template, 318

display the handles on the placeholder text or graphic. Click on the "Place" command from the File menu. Select the replacement text or graphic and click on the "Replace entire story" or "Replace entire graphic" option.

To save a PageMaker template under a new name, 324

click on the "Save as" command from the File menu. Type in a new file name in the text box and click on the OK command button.

Working with this book, you learned how to use PageMaker to create a template for your newsletter publications. PageMaker also provides 18 predesigned templates with your version 3.0 software. They are designed for a variety of publications, including newsletters, brochures, spec sheets, overheads and slides, name tags, reports, invitations, and more.

If publication design is still new to you, it's a good idea to start with some layouts that have already been designed for you. You can also edit PageMaker's templates with your own changes. The edited template can be saved under a new template name for use again.

In this chapter you will learn how to use PageMaker's templates. You will learn how to customize a template to better suit your needs by making changes to style sheets, editing placeholders, and even making adjustments to master pages.

► USING PAGEMAKER 3.0'S BUILT-IN TEMPLATES

PageMaker 3.0 includes several templates for developing a variety of publications. The PageMaker templates include text placeholders for mastheads, headlines, captions, and the main body of text. (A text placeholder holds a place on the page for you to plug in your text. A graphic placeholder holds an area for you to substitute your own graphics into the template.) Some templates also have style sheets. The following templates are included with PageMaker 3.0 (the ones marked with an asterisk have style sheets):

BROCHURE.PT3*	NAMETAG.PT3
BULLETIN.PT3*	NEWSLETR.PT3*
CALENDAR.PT3	OVERHDHZ.PT3*
DIRECTRY.PT3*	OVERHDVT.PT3
DSTRBUTE.PT3	PRICELST.PT3*
EXECSUMM.PT3*	REPORT.PT3*
FLYER.PT3	SLIDE.PT3
INVITE.PT3	SPECSHT.PT3*
MEMO.PT3	SPKRNOTE.PT3

Let's select a template to work with. To use one of PageMaker's templates, you first must locate the directory where the templates are stored.

1. Click on the "Open" command from the File menu.
2. Double-click on the [Template] subdirectory in the PM3 directory. The template files are displayed.

3. Double-click on the template titled BROCHURE.PT3. The template is displayed in the publication window, as shown in Figure 14.1.

► RECOMPOSING A PUBLICATION FOR YOUR PRINTER

To use one of these templates, you must recompose the publication for your printer. Let's recompose the template to use on your printer.

1. Click on the "Printer setup" command from the File menu. The Printer Setup dialog box, shown in Figure 14.2, is displayed.
2. Click on the name of the printer you are using as your target printer in the scroll box. (Refer to Appendix A for instructions on how to set up your printer.)
3. Click on the "Setup" command button. The Setup dialog box unique to your printer is displayed. An example of a Setup dialog box for a PostScript printer is shown in Figure 14.3.
4. The brochure template we chose uses a landscape orientation. Click on the "Landscape" option button.
5. Click OK. The Printer Setup dialog box is redisplayed.

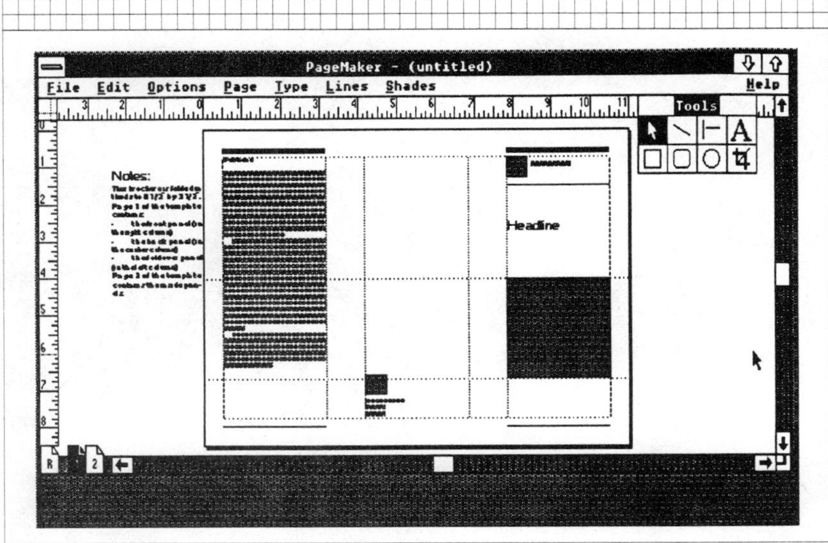

Figure 14.1: The PageMaker brochure template

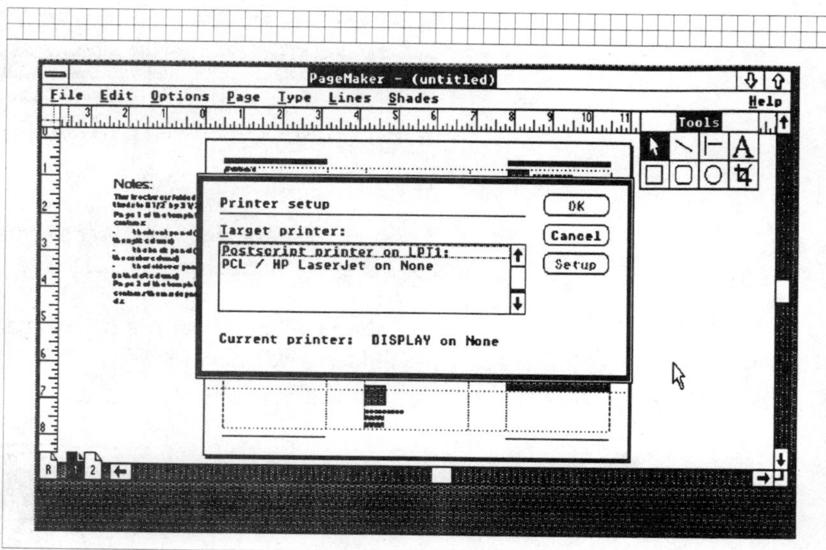

Figure 14.2: The Printer Setup dialog box

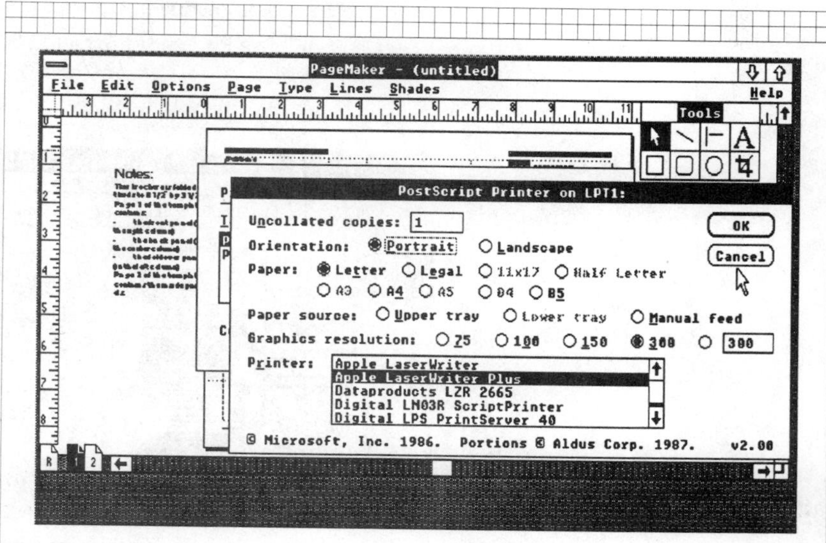

Figure 14.3: The Setup dialog box for a PostScript printer

6. Click OK again. The dialog box shown in Figure 14.4 asks if you want to recompose the template for the new printer. Click OK.

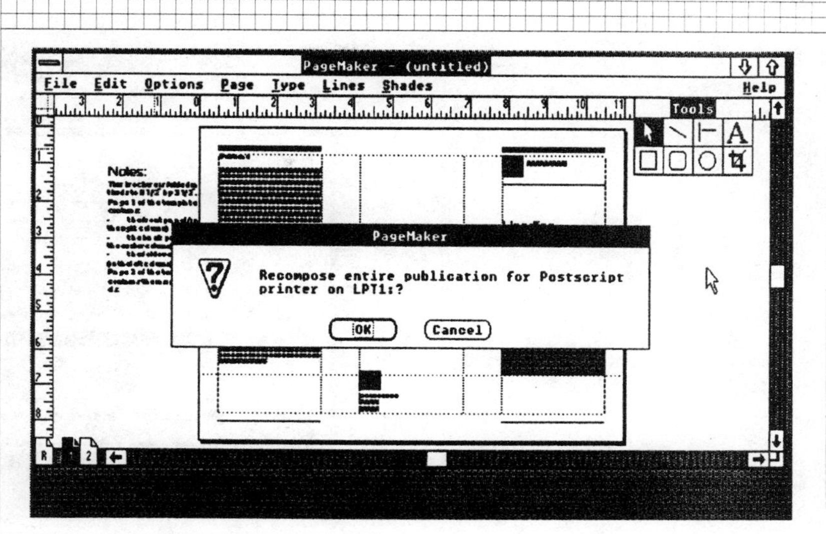

Figure 14.4: Query dialog box

It takes a few seconds for the template to recompose for the new printer. The templates are designed to use Times and Helvetica fonts. If you don't have fonts to match the template's fonts, PageMaker will substitute fonts for you.

► PRINTING A PAGEMAKER TEMPLATE

Let's print the template as Aldus has designed it. Then we can customize the design of the template for our own needs and tastes. To print the template:

1. Click on the "Print" command from the File menu.
2. The Print dialog box, shown in Figure 14.5, is displayed. Use the default values to print one copy of this two-page template, as shown in Figure 14.6.
3. Click OK to start printing.

Since items in the pasteboard don't print, you don't have to move the notes. Keep them there to remind you of the template's features.

Notice the simulated text placeholders used in PageMaker's templates. The text, called Lorem Ipsum text, includes style sheets that define the paragraph and type specifications. Also notice the notes that Aldus has included in the pasteboard area to help you use this template to create a brochure. The notes tell you that this brochure is to be folded in thirds for a finished size of 8.5" by 3.5", and what is included on each page of the template.

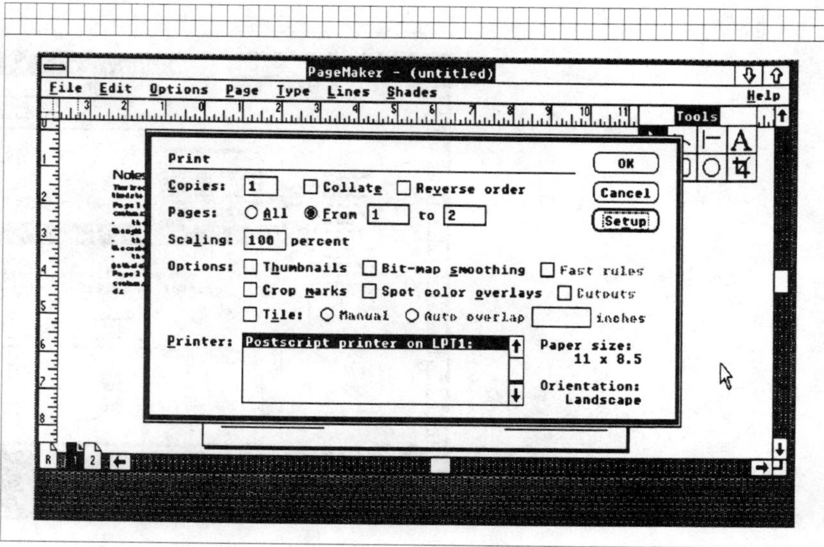

Figure 14.5: The Print dialog box

► EDITING STYLE SHEETS IN TEMPLATES

Let's look at the style sheets for this brochure template. Four style sheets are included: Body text, First Para, Headline, and Subhead. The body text is in 10-point Times Roman type. The text is justified with a first line indent set at 0.25''. The First Para style sheet refers to the first paragraph of the main body of text in the brochure. This first paragraph uses the same typography as the body of text without indenting the first line of text in the paragraph. The headline uses Helvetica type set at 24 points, and is flush left. The subhead also uses Helvetica, but at a smaller point size of 14 to indicate that it is less important than the headline.

Be sure any changes you make to the template enhance the design of the publication.

These are the specifications selected at Aldus for this brochure template. But suppose your printer can't print Helvetica and Times Roman type, or you have another reason for wanting to change the specifications of the brochure. It's possible to change the specifications in a template style sheet to suit your needs. As you learned in Chapter 4, you should have a good reason for changing PageMaker's specifications, since each specification serves a specific purpose. For example, the Helvetica type was selected for the heading and subheadings because its sans serif type stands out on a page.

Let's change the body text and first paragraph style sheets to use Courier type.

1. Click on the "Styles palette" option in the Options menu to display the Styles palette in the publication window.

Subhead

Quis nostrud exerci tation ullamcorper suscipit lobortis nisl ut aliquip ex ea commodo consequat. Duis autem vel eum iriure dolor in hendrerit in vulputate velit esse molestie consequat, vel illum dolore eu feugiat nulla facilisis at vero eros et accumsan et iusto odio dignissim qui blandit praesent luptatum zzril delenit augue duis dolore te feugait nulla facilisi. Lorem ipsum dolor sit amet, consectetuer adipiscing elit, sed diam nonummy nibh euismod tincidunt ut laoreet dolore magna aliquam erat volutpat.

Ut wisi enim ad minim veniam, quis nostrud exerci tation ullamcorper suscipit lobortis nisl ut aliquip ex ea commodo consequat. Duis autem vel eum iriure dolor in hendrerit in vulputate velit esse molestie consequat, vel illum dolore eu feugiat nulla facilisis at vero eros et accumsan et iusto odio dignissim qui blandit praesent luptatum zzril delenit augue duis dolore te feugait nulla facilisi. Lorem ipsum dolor sit amet, consectetuer adipiscing elit, sed diam nonummy nibh euismod tincidunt ut laoreet dolore magna aliquam erat volutpat. Ut wisi enim ad minim veniam, quis nostrud exerci tation ullamcorper suscipit lobortis nisl ut aliquip ex ea commodo consequat.

Duis autem vel eum iriure dolor in hendrerit in vulputate velit esse molestie consequat, vel illum dolore eu feugiat nulla facilisis at vero eros et accumsan et iusto odio dignissim qui blandit praesent luptatum zzril delenit augue duis dolore te feugait nulla facilisi.

Company name
Address
Address

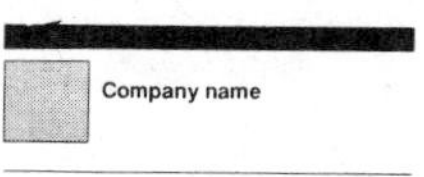

Headline

Headline

Subhead

Lorem ipsum dolor sit amet, consectetuer adipiscing elit, sed diam nonummy nibh euismod tincidunt ut laoreet dolore magna aliquam erat volutpat. Ut wisi enim ad minim veniam, quis nostrud exerci tation ullamcorper suscipit lobortis nisl ut aliquip ex ea commodo consequat. Duis autem vel eum iriure dolor in hendrerit in vulputate velit esse molestie consequat, vel illum dolore eu feugiat nulla facilisis at vero eros et accumsan et iusto odio dignissim qui blandit praesent luptatum zzril delenit augue duis dolore te feugait nulla facilisi.

Lorem ipsum dolor sit amet, consectetuer adipiscing elit, sed diam nonummy nibh euismod tincidunt ut laoreet dolore magna aliquam erat volutpat. Ut wisi enim ad minim veniam.

Subhead

Duis autem vel eum iriure dolor in hendrerit in vulputate velit esse molestie consequat, vel illum dolore eu feugiat nulla facilisis at vero eros et accumsan et iusto odio dignissim qui blandit praesent luptatum zzril delenit augue duis dolore te feugait nulla facilisi. Nam liber tempor cum soluta nobis eleifend option congue nihil imperdiet doming id quod mazim placerat facer possim assum. Lorem ipsum dolor sit amet, consectetuer adipiscing elit, sed diam nonummy nibh euismod tincidunt ut laoreet dolore magna aliquam erat volutpat. Ut wisi enim ad minim veniam, quis nostrud exerci tation ullamcorper suscipit lobortis .

Duis autem vel eum iriure dolor in hendrerit in vulputate velit esse molestie consequat, vel illum dolore eu feugiat nulla facilisis at vero eros et accumsan et iusto odio dignissim qui blandit praesent luptatum zzril delenit augue duis dolore te feugait nulla facilisi. Lorem ipsum dolor sit amet, consectetuer adipiscing elit, sed diam nonummy nibh euismod tincidunt ut laoreet dolore magna aliquam erat volutpat.

Ut wisi enim ad minim veniam, quis nostrud exerci tation ullamcorper suscipit lobortis nisl ut aliquip ex ea commodo consequat. Duis autem vel eum iriure dolor in hendrerit in vulputate velit esse molestie.

Subhead

Consequat, vel illum dolore eu feugiat nulla facilisis at vero eros et accumsan et iusto odio dignissim qui blandit praesent luptatum zzril delenit augue duis dolore te feugait nulla facilisi.

Lorem ipsum dolor sit amet, consectetuer adipiscing elit, sed diam nonummy nibh euismod tincidunt ut laoreet dolore magna aliquam erat volutpat. Ut wisi enim ad minim veniam, quis nostrud exerci tation ullamcorper suscipit lobortis nisl ut aliquip ex ea commodo consequat

Duis autem vel eum iriure dolor in hendrerit in vulputate velit esse molestie consequat, vel illum dolore eu feugiat nulla facilisis at vero eros et accumsan et iusto odio dignissim qui blandit praesent luptatum zzril delenit augue duis dolore te feugait nulla facilisi. Lorem ipsum dolor sit amet, consectetuer adipiscing elit, sed diam.

Subhead

Ullamcorper suscipit lobortis nisl ut aliquip ex ea commodo âconsequat. Duis autem vel eum iriure dolor in hendrerit in vulputate velit esse molestie consequat, vel illum dolore eu feugiat nulla facilisis at vero eros et accumsan et iusto odio dignissim qui blandit praesent luptatum zzril delenit augue duis dolore te feugait nulla facilisi. Lorem ipsum dolor sit amet, consectetuer adipiscing elit, sed diam nonummy nibh euismod tincidunt ut laoreet dolore magna aliquam erat volutpat. Ut wisi enim ad minim veniam, quis nostrud exerci tation ullamcorper suscipit lobortis nisl ut aliquip ex ea commodo consequat.

Autem vel eum iriure dolor in hendrerit in vulputate velit esse molestie consequat, vel illum dolore eu feugiat nulla facilisis at vero eros et accumsan et iusto odio dignissim qui blandit praesent luptatum zzril delenit augue duis dolore te feugait nulla facilisi.

Lorem ipsum dolor sit amet, consectetuer adipiscing elit, sed diam nonummy nibh euismod tincidunt ut laoreet dolore magna aliquam.

Subhead

Duis autem vel eum iriure dolor in hendrerit in vulputate velit esse molestie consequat, vel illum dolore eu feugiat nulla facilisis at vero eros et accumsan et iusto odio dignissim qui blandit praesent luptatum zzril delenit augue duis dolore te feugait nulla facilisi.

Nam liber tempor cum soluta nobis eleifend option congue nihil imperdiet doming id quod mazim placerat facer possim assum. Lorem ipsum dolor sit amet, consectetuer adipiscing elit, sed diam nonummy nibh euismod tincidunt ut laoreet dolore magna aliquam erat volutpat. Ut wisi enim ad minim veniam. Nam lobor tempore aliquam set amet dignissim feugit illum magna.

Figure 14.6: The printed brochure template

2. Hold down the Ctrl key. Click on the Body Text style sheet in the Styles palette. The Edit Style dialog box, shown in Figure 14.7, is displayed.
3. Click on the "Type" command button. The Type Specifications dialog box, shown in Figure 14.8, is displayed.
4. Click on "Courier" type in the scroll box.
5. Click OK. You are returned to the Edit Style dialog box.
6. Click OK again to return to the publication window. PageMaker is making your change in the style sheet. The body text is redisplayed with the changes included in the style sheet.

Let's continue with our changes. Suppose you intend to print with a color printer. You decide to use blue ink to help make the headline and subheadings stand out.

7. Hold down the Ctrl key. Click on the Headline style sheet in the Styles palette. The Edit Style dialog box (Figure 14.7) is displayed.
8. Click on the "Color" command button. The Define Colors dialog box, shown in Figure 14.9, is displayed.
9. Click on the "New" command button. The Edit Color dialog box, shown in Figure 14.10, is displayed.
10. Select the color model you want to work with—RGB, HLS, or CMYK. (You learned about color models in Chapter 11.)
11. Select "Blue." If you like, adjust the color.
12. Once you have the color selected and named, click OK. You are returned to the Define Colors dialog box.
13. Click OK again. Color has now been added to the Headline style sheet. Repeat this process to select the same color for the Subhead style sheet.

Let's make two more changes to help make Aldus's brochure template more useful to us. Suppose you work for a company that produces several different brochures for its different product lines each year. You want to maintain consistency to ensure that your publications are quickly recognizable as belonging to your company. Let's substitute your company name and logo for the placeholders in the brochure.

A style tag is the style sheet name surrounded by angle brackets, for example, <Subhead>. Style tags are discussed in Chapter 8.

To do this exercise, you will need two files to work with. First, create a word processed file that contains a fictitious company name. Since the company name is using the Subhead style sheet specifications, include a style tag in your word processed file. Remember, a style tag that corresponds to a style sheet defined in your PageMaker layout can be used in your word processed file. The style tag

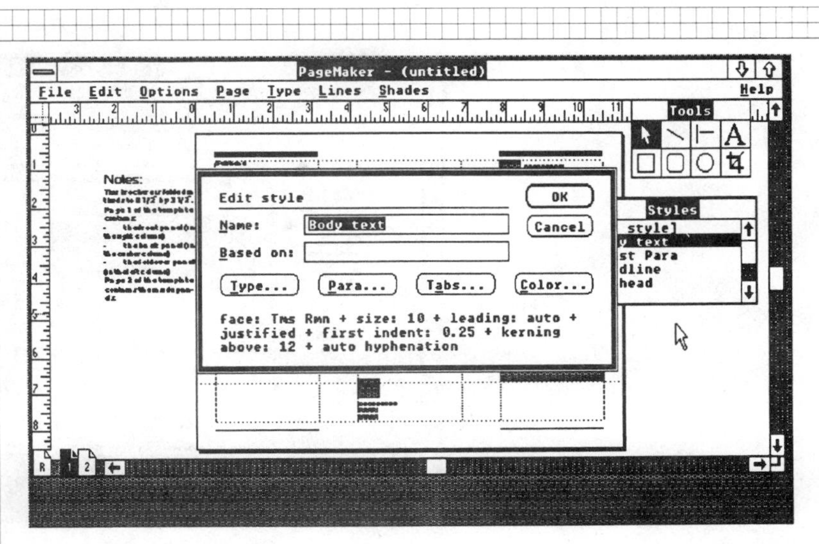

Figure 14.7: The Edit Style dialog box

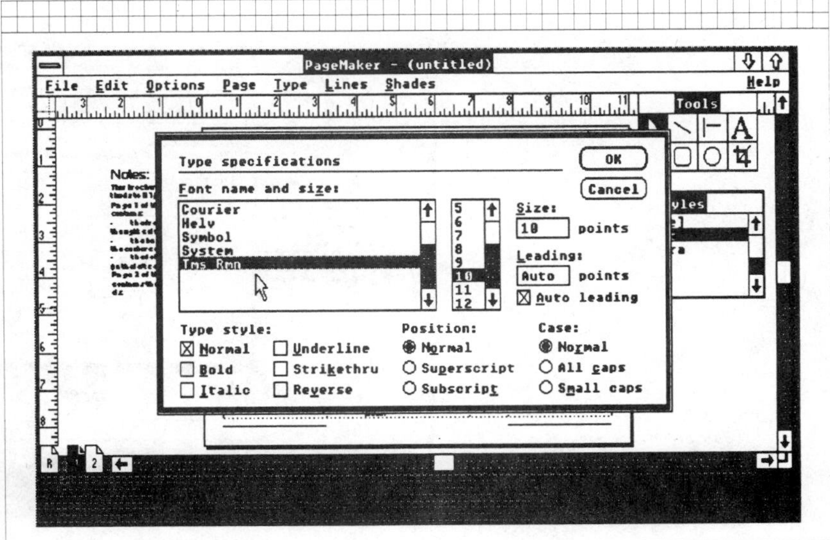

Figure 14.8: The Type Specifications dialog box

should be placed just after the company name in the word processed file. Second, create a graphics file that contains a simple graphic to be used as your company logo. You can create the graphic with a paint or draw program, or scan a graphic.

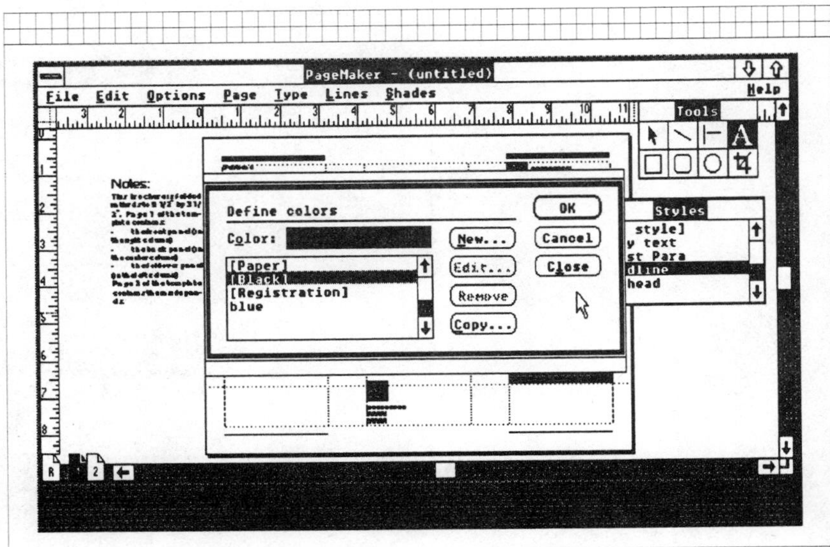

Figure 14.9: The Define Colors dialog box

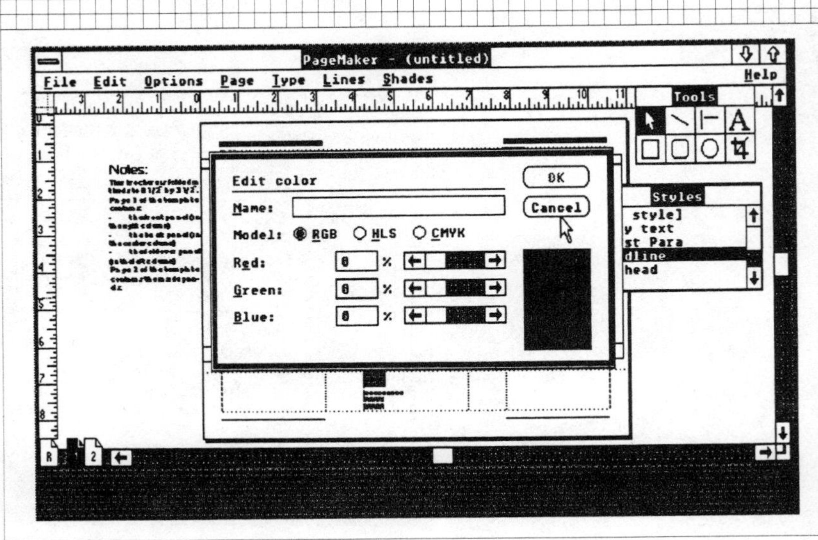

Figure 14.10: The Edit Color dialog box

Now let's place our company name into the brochure. Notice that the name appears in two locations—at the top of the third column on page 1 and at the bottom of the second column on the same page. We must replace them one at a time.

1. Select the text tool from the Toolbox.
2. Use the text tool to highlight the words *Company name* at the top of column 3 on page 1.
3. Click on the "Place" command from the File menu. The Place File dialog box, shown in Figure 14.11, is displayed.
4. Click on the name of the word processed file you created that contains the company name.
5. Click on the "Replace entire story" option (this option is available in 3.0 only). We are replacing the placeholder in the brochure with our unique company name.
6. Click on the "Read tags" option near the bottom of the dialog box (this option is available in version 3.0 only).
7. Click OK or "Place." The company name placeholder in the brochure is replaced with the company name you selected. The specifications used for the subheadings in the brochure are applied to the company name. Repeat this process to replace the company name placeholder at the bottom of column 3. Or, use the copy-and-paste method to place a copy of the logo in column 3 into column 2. Remember to remove the placeholder in column 2 first.

Let's now replace the logo placeholder in the brochure template with the company logo you created.

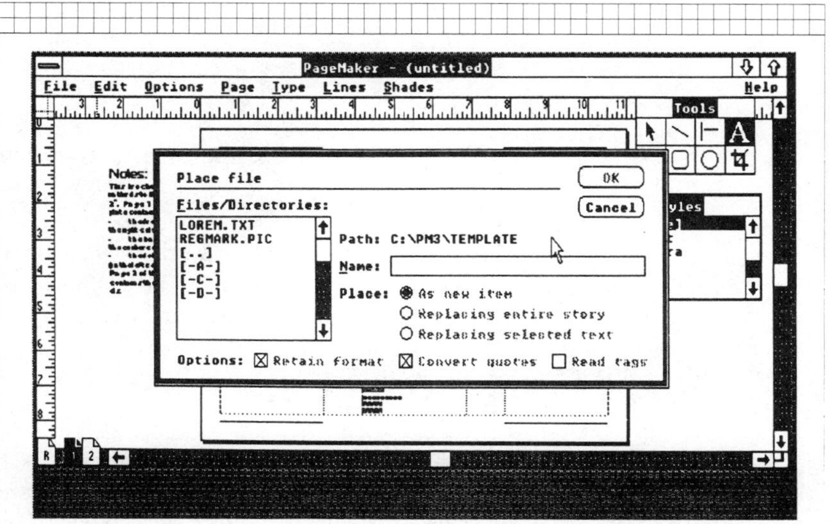

Figure 14.11: Place File dialog box

1. Select the pointer tool from the Toolbox.
2. Click the handles on the small shaded box placeholder next to the company name at the top of column 3.
3. Click on the "Place" command from the File menu. The Place File dialog box is displayed.
4. Click on the name of the graphics file you created that contains the company logo.
5. Click on the "Replace entire graphic" option.
6. Click OK. The graphic placeholder in column 3 is replaced with the logo you created using your graphics software. Use the pointer tool to adjust the size of the graphic to fit in the brochure if necessary. Remember to hold down the Shift key while you resize the graphic to prevent distortion of the original dimensions. Repeat this procedure, or use the copy-and-paste method to replace the placeholder in column 2.

▸ SAVING YOUR CHANGES TO PAGEMAKER'S TEMPLATES

You may find the templates provided with PageMaker 3.0 useful for many different publications. For this reason, it's important to save any changes you make to the templates under a new name. This way, anytime you want to use one of PageMaker's templates, it is available to you in its original form. Let's save our new template under a new name.

1. Click on the "Save as" command from the File menu.
2. In the text box, type in a unique name for this template.
3. Click on the "Template" option button.
4. Click OK.

Your template is now saved under a unique name. In the future, as you create your publications, you will be able to draw on PageMaker's built-in templates, as well as the ones you create and customize.

▸ SUMMARY

In this chapter you learned how to customize one of PageMaker's templates to make it better fit your needs. In the process, you were able to review many of the features you learned to use throughout this book. These same features can be applied when you create your own templates from scratch. Simply open a new file and add the elements for your new template, including placeholders for text and graphics, and a layout grid that can include column and ruler guides.

Remember to start with a simple layout that you can embellish later as your design skills develop. With a little practice, you too will be creating beautiful publications.

APPENDICES

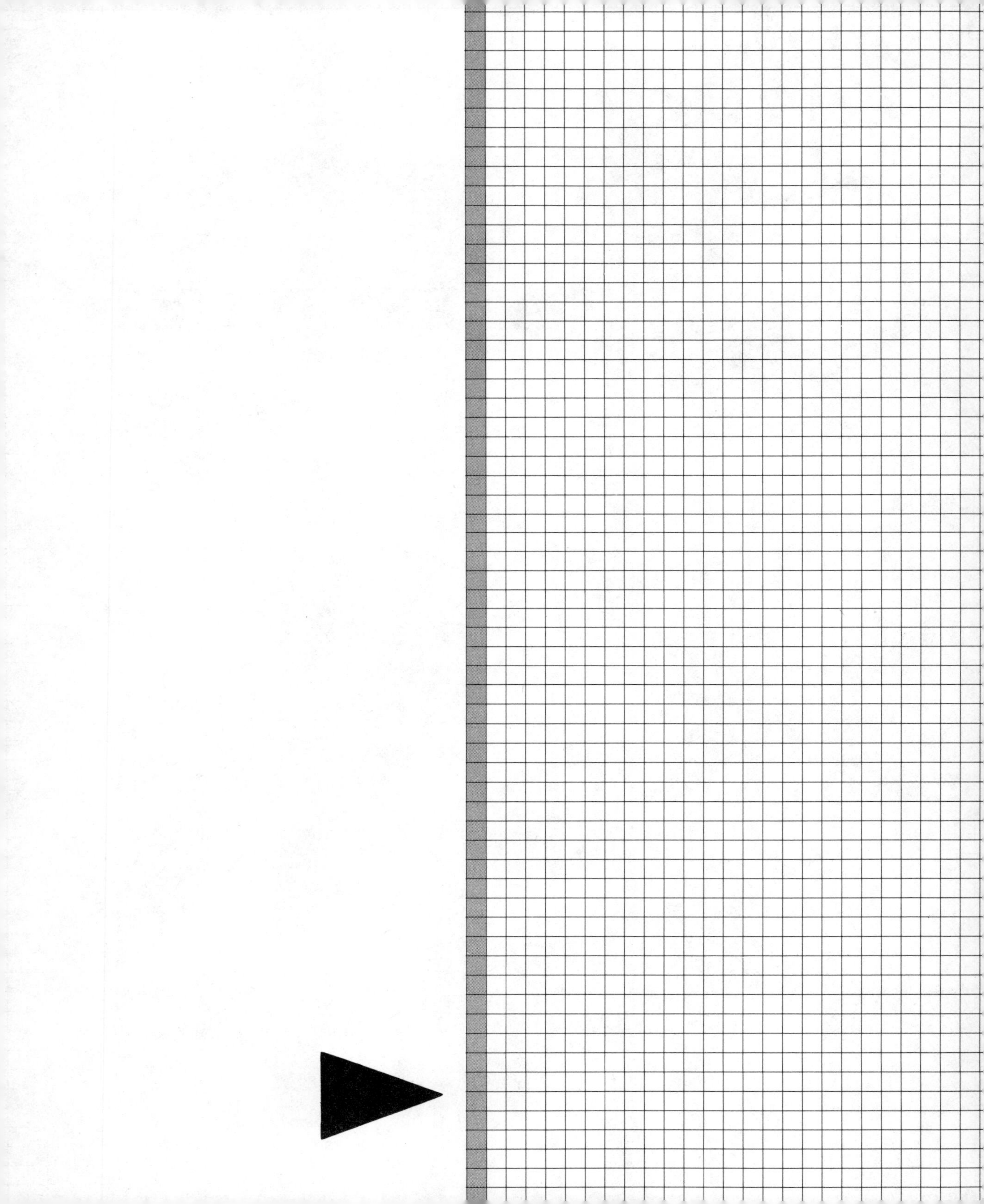

A INSTALLING PAGEMAKER

The following steps are necessary to install PageMaker on your system:

1. Make back-up copies of the PageMaker and Windows diskettes.
2. Install Windows (use version 2.0 with PageMaker 3.0).
3. Install PageMaker.
4. Install printer drivers.
5. Add downloadable software fonts.

Before you begin installing PageMaker, check to be sure you have the necessary diskettes. The version of Windows included with your PageMaker package is a runtime version. The runtime version lets you run PageMaker within the Windows operating environment, but does not allow you to run any other applications. The full version of Windows may be purchased separately from the PageMaker program. It allows you to run PageMaker and any other Windows-compatible applications. If you are installing a full version of Windows, install Windows separately. Refer to the users manual that came with your Windows software for installation instructions.

You need the following diskettes to install PageMaker 3.0 and Windows:

3½-inch diskettes:

PageMaker	**Windows**
Install	Setup/Build
Program/Dictionary	Displays
Drivers/Filters	Utilities
Templates	Fonts
Getting Started	

5¼-inch (1.2Mb) diskettes:

PageMaker	**Windows**
Install/Program/Dictionary	Setup/Build/Displays
Drivers/Filters/Templates	Utilities/Fonts
Getting Started	

You need the following diskettes to install PageMaker 3.0 and Windows:

PageMaker	**Windows**
Install	Setup

Program	Build
Dictionary	Utilities
Tutorial	Fonts
Driver	

► SYSTEM REQUIREMENTS

To run PageMaker and Windows, you need an IBM Personal System/2 (model 30, 50, 60, or 80), or an IBM PC AT (or a fully compatible) computer. The hard disk should be 20 megabytes (Mb) or larger. The floppy drive must be able to read double-sided 1.2Mb 5¼-inch diskettes or 720K 3½-inch diskettes. Running Windows 2.0 requires an MS-DOS version of 3.1 or later.

To install PageMaker alone, the hard disk must have at least 3.5Mb of space. To install Windows and PageMaker, the hard disk must have at least 4.5Mb of space. The computer must have a minimum of 640K of memory. To increase PageMaker's performance, use extended or expanded memory.

A Windows-compatible mouse is necessary to use PageMaker. You also need a Windows-compatible graphics adaptor along with a color or monochrome graphics monitor. A Windows-compatible printer is necessary for output. (Refer to "Installing Printer Drivers" later in this appendix and to Appendix F.)

► MAKING BACK-UP COPIES OF PAGEMAKER

Floppy diskettes are vulnerable to damage, so it's important to make back-up copies of each diskette before you begin the installation process.

Be sure to label your blank diskette so it matches the label of the original disk *before* you copy it.

To make back-up copies of your diskettes, use the MS-DOS DISKCOPY command. On a system with two identical floppy drives, use the DISKCOPY command to format the blank diskette and copy the PageMaker diskette in one step. Type this format for the DISKCOPY command:

```
DISKCOPY [A:] [B:]
```

On a system with two unmatching floppy drives, or only one floppy drive, use the DISKCOPY command by typing this format:

```
DISKCOPY [A:] [A:]
```

Do not copy a 5¼-inch diskette onto a 3½-inch diskette, or vice versa. This will disable the PageMaker Install program.

When you have copied your diskettes, put the originals in a safe place and use the copies to install and run your PageMaker program.

► USING DIRECTORIES TO ORGANIZE YOUR HARD DISK

Because so many applications and files are necessary for creating a desktop publication, it is important to organize your hard disk in a logical manner. When you create a publication using PageMaker, you create word processed files with a word processor. Next, you use a graphics application to create your graphics. Third, you combine these two files to create a publication using PageMaker. In doing so, you may use template publications or boilerplate designs.

In order to keep track of all these files, you should organize your hard disk into several directories. The first directory is called *Windows.* It holds the Windows program and all your Windows-compatible applications such as Microsoft Windows Write and Windows Paint. If you do not already have Windows installed on your hard disk, you can automatically install it when you run the PageMaker Install program, which is explained later in this appendix.

The second directory is called *PM3* for PageMaker 3.0, or *PM* for earlier versions of PageMaker. This directory holds the PageMaker program, any template publication designs, any boilerplate graphics or text that you will be using frequently, and also your publication, once it is created.

If you are using word processors and graphics programs that are not Windows compatible, create separate directories for each of these applications. Place the files created with each application in the respective directory.

The PageMaker Install program automatically creates the Windows and PageMaker directories. If you want to create a separate directory for your other applications or for storing your finished publications, use the MS-DOS command MKDIR. For example, to create a directory for your final newsletter publications, you may want to create a separate directory called NLTR. To create this directory on the C drive, type

```
md\nltr
```

at the C: prompt. The directory is created on your C drive. To log onto the directory from the C drive, type

```
cd\nltr
```

You can then use the MS-DOS COPY command to move files into a newly created directory.

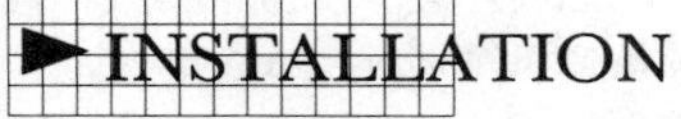

► INSTALLATION

This section provides installation procedures for installing Windows and PageMaker automatically, and for installing only PageMaker if you have previously installed Windows on your system. It also gives you instructions for installing printer drivers.

► INSTALLING WINDOWS AND PAGEMAKER AUTOMATICALLY

PageMaker provides an installation program that allows you to install both PageMaker and a runtime version of Windows by following step-by-step instructions displayed on your screen.

The PageMaker Drivers/Filters disk and the Windows Utilities disk hold the printer drivers that are available to you. During the Windows installation process, you will be asked to indicate your printer. If your printer is listed, be sure to select it. If you are installing Windows separately, or if you're using a printer that is not listed during the installation process, you must install your printer driver separately before using PageMaker. When you've installed PageMaker and Windows, go to the "Installing Printer Drivers" section of this appendix for instructions.

To install both PageMaker and Windows, first turn on your computer and be sure the C prompt is displayed.

1. To install Windows, insert the Windows Setup disk in drive A.
2. Log onto the A drive by typing

   a:

   and press Return (↵).
3. Type

   setup

   and press ↵.

The Setup program begins. Follow the on-screen instructions to install Windows. You will be prompted to insert the other Windows diskettes. After Windows is installed, you will be prompted to install PageMaker. Press *C* to install PageMaker after you have installed Windows. If you are installing PageMaker 3.0, you will be prompted to install the additional features of import/export filters, and the Getting Started and Templates files. The Getting Started files, used for the PageMaker tutorial, and the PageMaker templates are stored in their own subdirectories. You will be asked which import/export filters and templates you want to install. You can install all of them, or select only the ones you will be using frequently. Now go to the "Installing Printer Drivers" section to install your printer.

► INSTALLING PAGEMAKER ONLY

Use the following instructions to install PageMaker only:

1. Insert the PageMaker Install/Program disk in drive A.
2. Log onto drive A by typing

   a:

   and press Return (↵).
3. Type

   install

   and press ↵.

The installation program begins. Follow the on-screen instructions to install PageMaker. You will be asked to replace the installation disk in the A drive with the remaining PageMaker disks so that the Install program can automatically install all the PageMaker files onto your hard disk.

AUTOEXEC.BAT and CONFIG.SYS are MS-DOS files that are a part of your operating system. These files must be amended in order to run PageMaker.

The Install program also appends your AUTOEXEC.BAT and CONFIG.SYS files so that your system can run PageMaker. A PATH statement is automatically added to your AUTOEXEC.BAT file to allow you to run PageMaker from a directory other than the one in which it is installed. The FILES and BUFFERS sizes in your CONFIG.SYS file are automatically expanded to 20 to ensure that PageMaker responds quickly to your commands. Continue to the next section, "Installing Printer Drivers," to install your printer.

► INSTALLING PRINTER DRIVERS

Use the following instructions for installing a printer driver. (If you are updating a printer driver, use the "Delete printer" command from the Control Panel to remove the existing driver before you add the new driver.)

1. Click on the "Control panel" command from the Windows Control menu. The Control Panel, shown in Figure A.1, is displayed.
2. Click on the "Installation" command. You will see the Installation menu.
3. Select the "Add New Printer" command from the Installation menu. A dialog box asks you to indicate the pathname to locate the printer driver.
4. Insert the disk containing the printer driver you want to install in drive A, or indicate the directory that contains the printer driver on your hard disk.

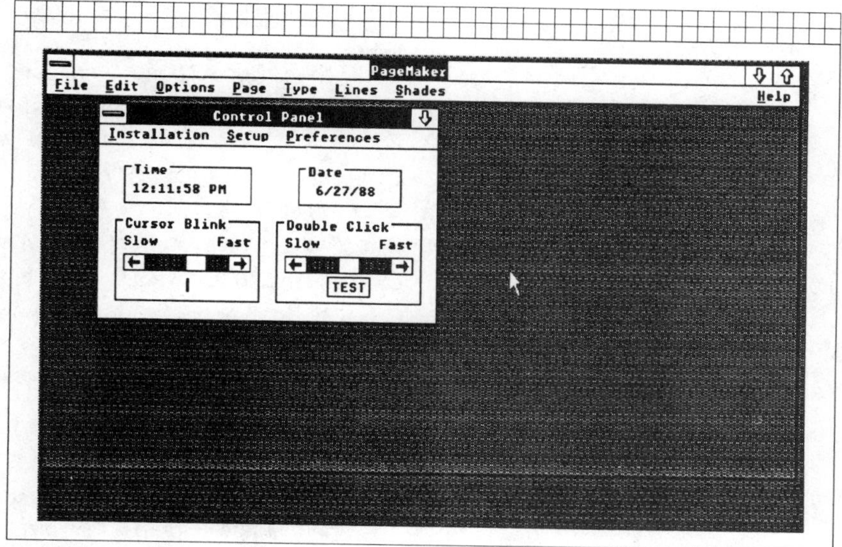

Figure A.1: The Control Panel

5. Click OK. A dialog box listing the available printers is displayed.
6. Highlight the printer driver you want by clicking on it.
7. Click on the "Add" command button. A new dialog box appears, asking you to indicate the pathname for the driver.
8. Select the directory in which Windows is installed.
9. Click on the "Yes" command button.

The printer driver is now installed in your system. To use your printer, it is still necessary to indicate the port on which the printer resides. The following ports are available to you:

LPT1	First parallel printer
LPT2	Second parallel printer
LPT3	Third parallel printer
COM1	First serial printer or communications port
COM2	Second serial printer or communications port
EPT	Port for the IBM Personal Pageprinter
OUTPUT.PRN	Port for printing a publication to disk

The Control Panel is also used to set the port for your printer.

1. Click on the "Control panel" command from the Windows Control menu. The Control Panel (Figure A.1) is displayed.
2. Click on the "Setup" command. You will see the Setup menu.
3. Click on the "Connections" command. You then will see the dialog box shown in Figure A.2.
4. Click on the printer you want to set up in the Printer scroll box.
5. Click on the port you want to use in the Connection scroll box.
6. Click OK.

If you are using a parallel port, you have completed the installation of your new printer driver with its associated port. If you are using a serial port, continue to indicate your communications port settings.

7. Click on the "Control panel" command from the Windows Control menu. The Control Panel (Figure A.1) is displayed.
8. Click on the "Setup" command. You will see the Setup menu.
9. Choose the "Communications Port" command from the Setup menu. The Communications Settings dialog box, shown in Figure A.3, is displayed.

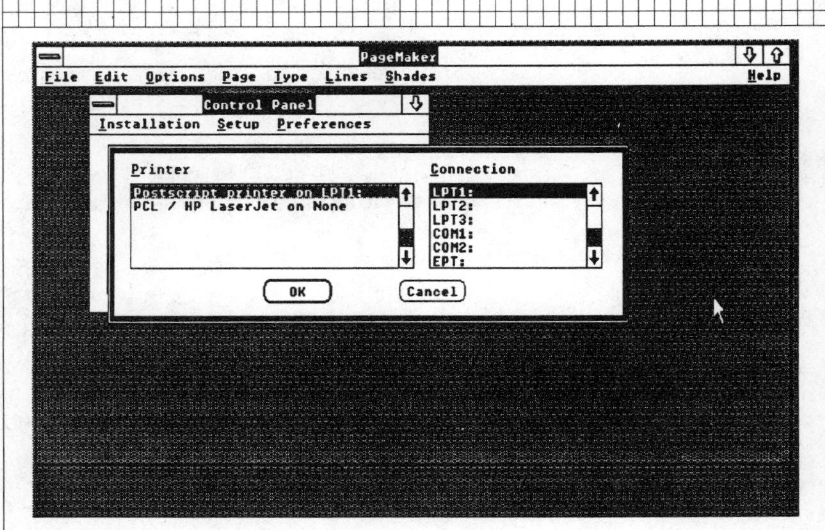

Figure A.2: The Printer/Connection dialog box

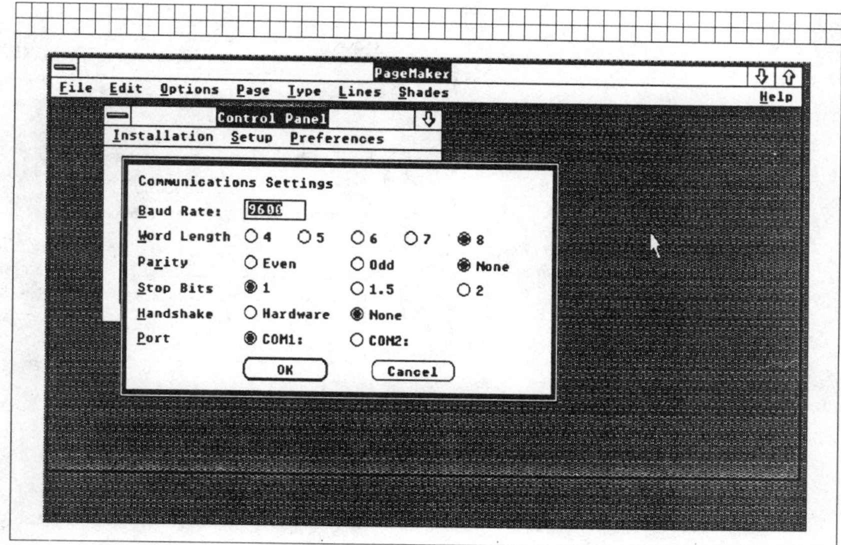

Figure A.3: The Communications Settings dialog box

10. You will see six boxes in which to indicate your communications port settings. Refer to the users manual that came with your printer. In most cases, you will want to use these settings:

    Baud Rate: 9600

    Word Length: 8

    Parity: None

    Stop Bits: 1

    Handshake: Hardware

11. Click OK.

Your printer installation is now complete. All that's left is for you to select the default printer. The default printer is the one you select to print your publication. You may change this default if you decide to use a different printer for your output; the new selection then becomes your default.

1. Click on the "Control panel" command from the Windows Control menu. The Control Panel (Figure A.1) is displayed.
2. Click on "Setup," then choose the "Printer" command from the Setup menu. The Default Printer dialog box, shown in Figure A.4, is displayed.

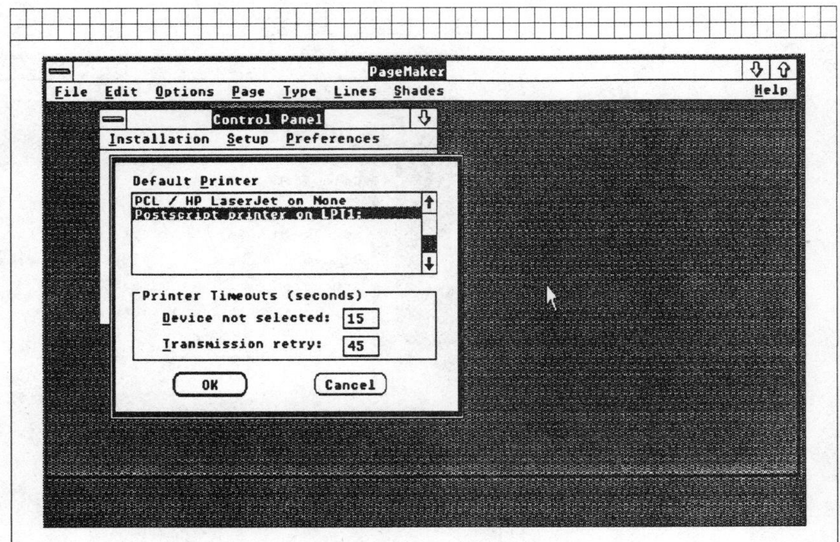

Figure A.4: The Default Printer dialog box

3. Click on the name of your printer to highlight it in the scroll box.
4. Indicate your printer timeout settings in the text boxes. "Device not selected" controls the length of time your system should use trying to connect to a printer. "Transmission entry" refers to how long your system should try to print if the printer is busy. Figure A.4 shows the PageMaker defaults for these settings.
5. Click OK. A dialog box appears displaying the default settings for this printer.
6. Click OK.

Any changes you want to make to the printer defaults must be done using the Printer/Connection dialog box (Figure A.2). The dialog box can be opened using the Control Panel's "Printer" command from the Setup menu, or using the "Printer setup" or "Print" command from the PageMaker File menu and clicking on the "Setup" command button.

Your printer is now installed and ready to use with PageMaker. When you start PageMaker, you will be asked to designate your target printer. Chapter 2 gives you instructions on selecting a target printer.

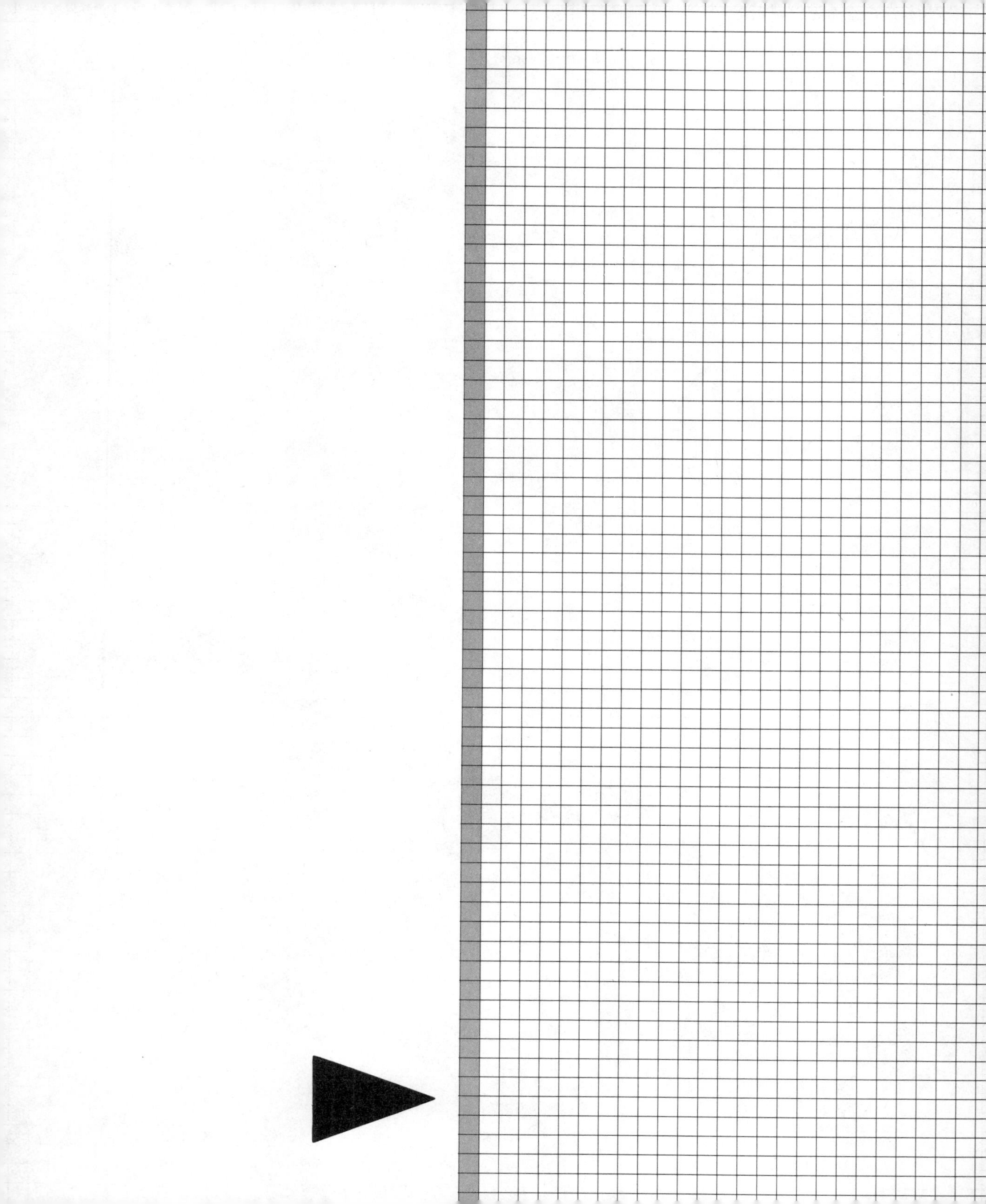

B KEYBOARD EQUIVALENTS TO MOUSE COMMANDS

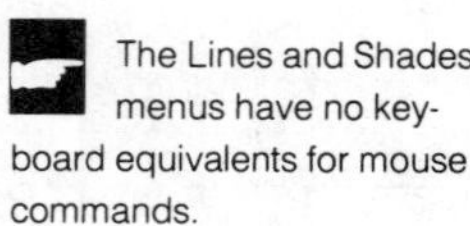
The Lines and Shades menus have no keyboard equivalents for mouse commands.

Many of the menu command options may be selected with keyboard commands instead of the mouse. The keyboard equivalents to mouse-initiated commands are listed in the pull-down menus next to the commands. Some of these commands are performed with the function keys (labeled F1, F2, F3, etc., on your keyboard). Depending on the keyboard you are using, the function keys are located on the left side or along the top of the keyboard.

Another group of commands is performed by using the Ctrl key with specific alphanumeric keys. In the pull-down menus, the Ctrl key is indicated with the caret (^) symbol. To specify a command using the Ctrl key, hold it down while you press the appropriate letter or number in the command.

There are a few commands that require you to hold down the Shift key while pressing another key. PageMaker indicates the Shift key in the pull-down menus with the abbreviation *Sh.* Some commands require you to hold down the Alt key as well. The following tables list the keyboard equivalents to mouse-initiated commands.

▶ FILE MENU KEYBOARD EQUIVALENTS

Command	**Keyboard alternative**
In PageMaker 3.0:	
New	^N
Open	^O
Save	^S
Place	^D
Print	^P
In PageMaker 1.0 and 1.0a:	
Save	^S
Place	^D
Print	^P

▶ EDIT MENU KEYBOARD EQUIVALENTS

Command	**Keyboard alternative**
In PageMaker 3.0:	
Undo	Alt Backspace
Cut	Sh Del

Copy	^ Ins
Paste	Sh Ins
Clear	Del
Select all	^A
Bring to front	^F
Send to back	^B

In PageMaker 1.0 and 1.0a:

Undo	Sh Esc
Cut	Del
Copy	F2
Paste	Ins
Clear	Sh Del
Select	^A
Bring to front	^F
Send to back	^B

► OPTIONS MENU KEYBOARD EQUIVALENTS

Command	**Keyboard alternative**
In PageMaker 3.0:	
Snap to rulers	^Y
Snap to guides	^U
Style palette	^E
Color palette	^K
In PageMaker 1.0 and 1.0a:	
Snap to guides	^M

► PAGE MENU KEYBOARD EQUIVALENTS

Command	**Keyboard alternative**
In all versions of PageMaker:	
Actual size	^1

75% size	^7
50% size	^5
Fit in window	^W
200% size	^2
Go to page	^G

► TYPE MENU KEYBOARD EQUIVALENTS

Command	**Keyboard alternative**
In PageMaker 3.0:	
Normal	F5
Bold	F6
Italic	F7
Underline	F8
Type Specs	^T
Paragraph	^M
Indent/tabs	^I
Align left	^L
Align center	^C
Align right	^R
Justify	^J
In PageMaker 1.0 and 1.0a:	
Normal	F5
Bold	F6
Italic	F7
Underline	F8
Type specs	^T
Indent/tabs	^I
Align left	^L
Align center	^C

Align right	^R
Justify	^J

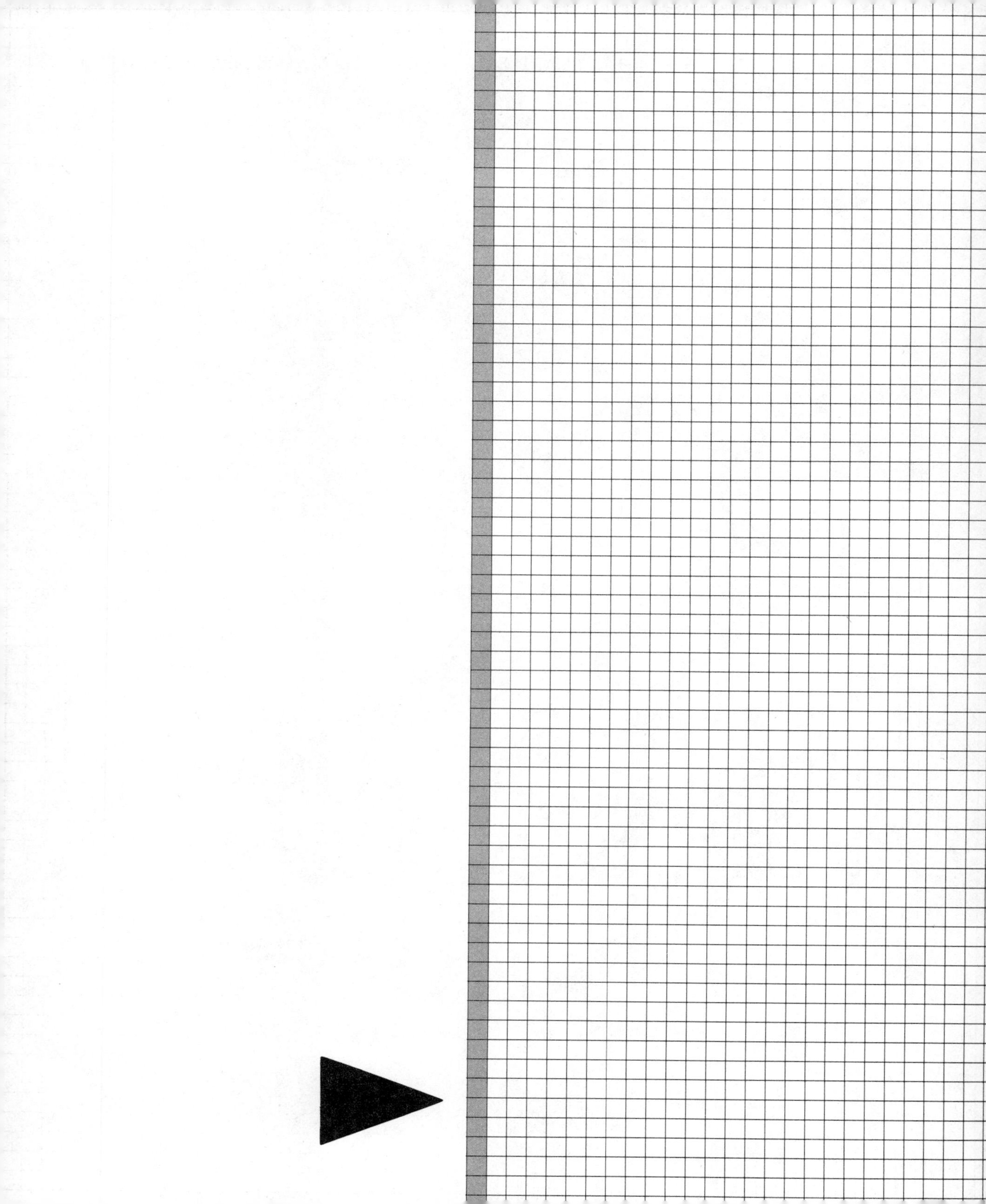

C PAGEMAKER DEFAULT SETTINGS

There are two types of default settings: *application defaults* and *publication defaults.* PageMaker automatically selects application defaults. They are active each time you begin working with PageMaker, and to change them you must make your selections from the desktop before you open a publication. Your changes will then apply to every new PageMaker publication.

Publication defaults are only active for the current publication. Each time you make a new selection with the pointer tool, you change the publication defaults. As you've already noticed, the selections you make while you are within a publication are only active for that publication; when you open a new publication all the application defaults are restored.

Both application and publication defaults can be changed by selecting from the list of options displayed under the PageMaker menus. Application defaults are changed from the desktop before opening a new or existing publication, and publication defaults are changed once the publication is begun. The following tables indicate the application defaults used by PageMaker in each menu before you make any changes.

▸ FILE MENU DEFAULTS

Setting	Default	Command
Page size	Letter	Page setup
Orientation	Tall	Page setup
Single or double-sided	Double-sided	Page setup
Starting page #	1	Page setup
# of pages	1	Page setup
Facing pages shown for a double-sided publication	Facing pages	Page setup
Margins	Inside: 1 inch Outside, Top, and Bottom: 0.75 inches	Page setup
Printer	Windows printer	Target printer (1.0 and 1.0a), Printer setup (3.0)

► EDIT MENU DEFAULTS

Setting	Default	Command
Unit of measure	Inches	Preferences
PageMaker 3.0 adds these defaults:		
Measurement system	Inches	Preferences
Vertical ruler	Inches	Preferences
Greek text below	6 pixels	Preferences
Stretch text above	24 pixels	Preferences
Vector text above	24 pixels	Preferences
Guides	Front	Preferences

► OPTIONS MENU DEFAULTS

Setting	Default	Command
Corner style of boxes	.25-inch radius	Rounded corners
Rulers	Off	Rulers
Zero point	Unlocked	Zero lock
Nonprinting guides	On	Guides
Snap to guides	On	Snap to guides
Number of columns	1	Column guides
Space between columns	0.167 inch	Column guides
Toolbox	On	Toolbox
Scroll bars	On	Scroll bars
Font name and size	Tms Rmn or similar font in 12 point or next available size on target printer	Type specs
PageMaker 3.0 adds these defaults:		
Autoflow	Off	Autoflow

Wrap option	None icon	Text wrap
Text flow	(No icon is selected)	Text wrap
Standoff in inches	(No entries in Left, Right, Top, Bottom)	Text wrap
Color	Black	Define colors
Styles	No style	Style palette
Colors	Black	Colors palette
Guides	Displayed	Guides
Lightness	50%	Image control
Contrast	50%	Image control
Screen	Dot	Image control
Screen angle	45 degrees	Image control
Screen frequency	53 lines per inch	Image control

► TYPE MENU DEFAULTS

Setting	**Default**	**Command**
Type style	Normal	Type specs
Leading	Auto	Type specs
Type position	Normal	Type specs
Capitalization	Normal	Type specs
Hyphenation	Auto	Paragraph
Pair kerning	Above 12.0 points	Paragraph
Left, right, and first line indents	0	Paragraph or Indents/Tabs
Paragraph spacing before or after	0	Paragraph
Paragraph alignment	Left	Paragraph
Tab alignment	Left	Indents/Tabs
Tab leader	None	Indents/Tabs
Tab stops	Every 0.5 inch	Indents/Tabs

Spacing between words	Minimum: 50% Desired: 100% Maximum: 200%	Spacing
Spacing between characters	Minimum: 0% Maximum: 25%	Spacing
Hyphenation zone	0.5 inch	Spacing
Reverse type	Off	Reverse type

PageMaker 3.0 adds these defaults:

Position	Normal	Type specs
Case	Normal	Type specs
Pair Kerning	Auto above 12 points	Paragraph
Spacing attributes	0	Paragraph
Word space	Minimum: 50% Desired: 100% Maximum: 200%	Spacing
Letter space	Minimum: –5% Desired: 0% Maximum: 25%	Spacing
Auto leading	120%	Spacing
Leading method	Proportional	Spacing
Font name and size	Tms Rmn or similar font in 12 point or next available size on target printer	Type specs

► LINES MENU DEFAULTS

Setting	**Default**	**Command**
Line style	1pt	Lines
Reverse line	Off	Reverse line

► SHADES MENU DEFAULTS

Setting	**Default**	**Command**
Shades	None	Shades

► PAGE MENU DEFAULTS

Setting	Default	Command
Page number	1	Go to page
Insert page(s)	1 after current page	Insert pages
Remove page(s) through	1, 1	Remove pages
Display master item	On	Display master items

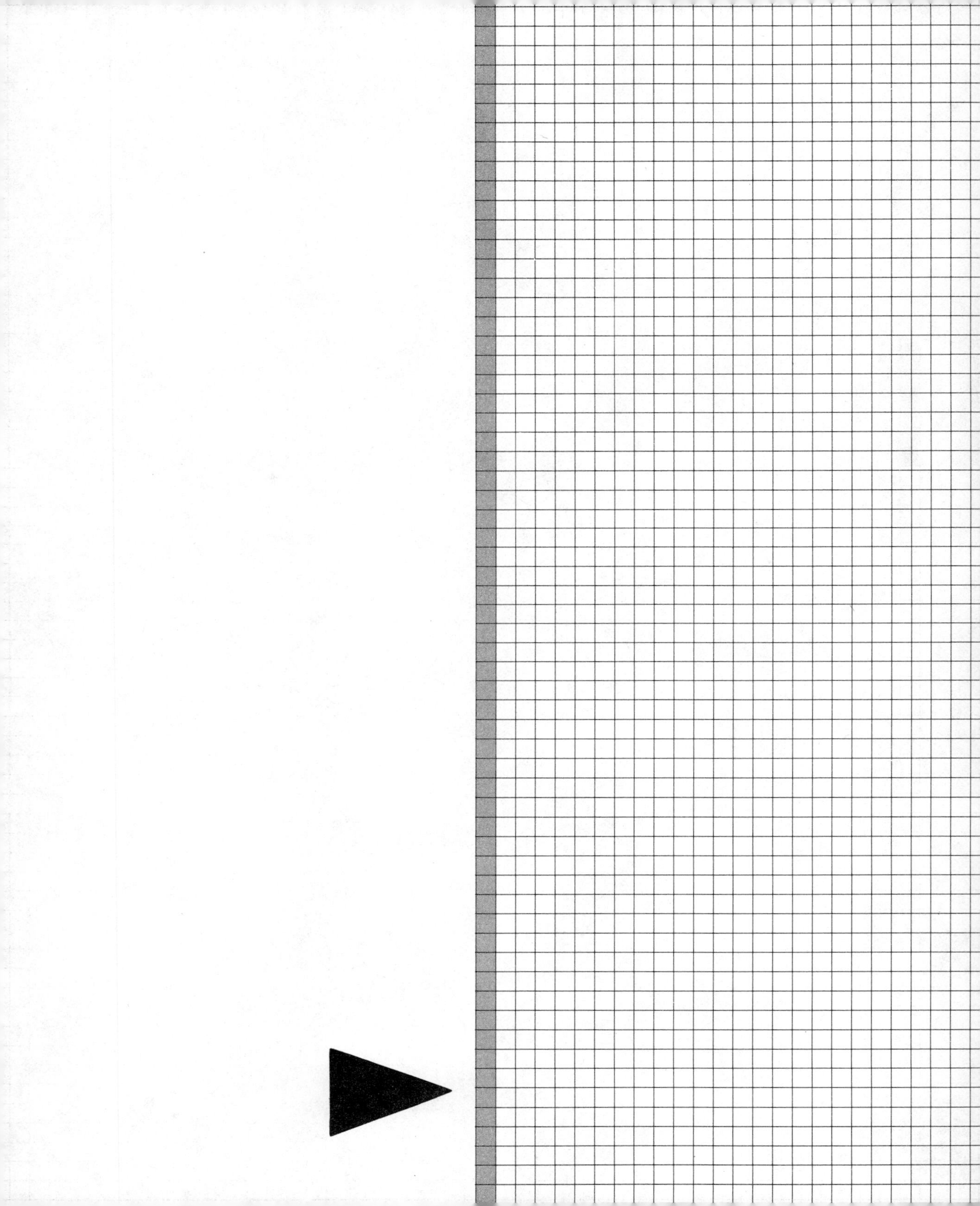

D GLOSSARY

Actual size A view that shows a page in the publication window at approximately the same size it will print. Because it is actual size, in most cases not all the page can be seen at once on the screen.

Alignment The way text is placed in a column, aligned to the left guide, right guide, centered, or justified between both column guides.

Autoflow Flowing text continuously into columns, page after page.

Baseline The imaginary line on which letters in a line of text rest.

Bit-mapped graphic A graphic created with a paint-type program and composed of a series of dots.

Boilerplate A standard design or format to be used over and over again.

Camera-ready High-quality, laser printed pages that can be photographed to produce printing plates.

Cancel The command button used to exit a dialog box without making selections.

Check box A small square inside a dialog box that contains a check mark if a function is turned on, and is empty if that function is turned off.

Cicero A unit of measure used to measure font size. It is the equivalent of 4.55 millimeters and is commonly used in Europe.

Clicking the mouse Pressing and releasing the mouse button quickly to perform a function.

Clipboard The holding place within Windows where PageMaker stores text or a graphic temporarily.

Close pub The File menu command used to close a publication.

Colors palette The colors you can select from when adding color to text or graphics.

Column guides Vertical, nonprinting dotted lines that mark the boundaries of the columns you create with PageMaker.

Corner style One of six types of corners that can be selected for a box drawn with PageMaker's rounded corners box tool.

Crop marks Intersecting lines printed at the corners of a page if the page size is smaller than the paper size. These marks show where the paper should be cut.

Cropping tool The tool in the PageMaker Toolbox for trimming or cropping parts of a graphic placed in PageMaker.

Crossbar The pointer shape displayed on the screen when you have selected one of the drawing tools from the Toolbox.

Cutout The area in a publication where two colors overlap. PageMaker deletes the background color in the overlapping area.

Default The option PageMaker selects unless you specify differently.

Desktop The blank gray screen PageMaker displays when you do not have a publication open.

Desktop publishing Using page processing software such as PageMaker to produce personal computer generated publications.

Diagonal line tool The tool in the Toolbox used to draw a line in any direction.

Dialog box A box that is displayed in the middle of the screen asking you to provide more information so PageMaker can perform the selected task. A dialog box can contain up to six elements: option buttons, a list box, command buttons such as OK or Cancel, scroll bars, text boxes, and check boxes.

Discretionary hyphen The hyphen that you can manually add to your publication to let PageMaker know where you want hyphenation to occur.

Directory A section of your hard disk with its own unique name in which a group of related files are stored.

Downloadable fonts The software fonts you can add to your printer.

Double-clicking Pressing and releasing the main mouse button two times quickly in order to perform a function.

Double-sided publication A publication that is printed on both sides of a page. The front side is odd-numbered and the back side is even-numbered.

Dummy A template publication containing the layout grid, boilerplate text, and graphics used for creating more than one publication with the same design.

Edit menu The menu that contains editing commands, including the Clipboard commands.

Em A unit of measure equal to the point size of the type being used.

En A unit of measure equal to one half the width of an em.

Encapsulated PostScript (EPS) The programming code used by some graphics applications to generate graphics.

Export The File menu command used to copy text in PageMaker back out to a word processing file.

Facing pages The two pages opposite each other in a double-sided publication. The page on the left side is even numbered, and the page on the right side is odd numbered.

Flowing text Placing text on the page from a loaded text icon.

Font The complete set of numbers, letters, and special characters in a particular typeface.

Formatting Applying paragraph and type specifications to your publication.

Grabber hand Moves the page in the publication window using the Alt key in combination with the pointer tool.

Graphic A shape drawn with one of PageMaker's drawing tools, or an illustration created using graphics software and placed in PageMaker.

Graphic boundary The dotted line boundary of an imported graphic that defines the text wrapping area.

Greeked text Garbled text that is displayed when the window view is small and text is unreadable.

Hairline The thinnest possible line, 0.25 point, drawn with the PageMaker line tool and generally used to define columns on a page.

Handles Used for manipulating text and graphics. Windowshade handles are the horizontal lines at the top and bottom of a text block. Corner rectangle handles surround both text and graphics. Graphics also have four side handles.

Highlighting text Defining a section of text with the text tool by dragging the mouse over it. This causes the text to appear in reverse video on the screen.

I-beam The shape of the pointer when you select the text tool.

Icon A graphic representation of a PageMaker tool or function.

Insertion point The point in the publication window where text will be inserted. It is indicated by the blinking text bar.

Inside margin The margin along the inside binding edge of a page: the right margin on a left-hand page, and the left margin on a right-hand page.

Kerning Adjusting the spacing between letters.

Layout A logical arrangement of text and graphics on a page.

Layout grid A collection of nonprinting guides used to help align text and graphics on a page.

Leading The amount of vertical space between the tops of the capital letters in two successive lines of text. Leading is measured in points.

Line style The design of a line selected from the Lines menu.

Main mouse button The mouse button used to carry out most of the commands used in PageMaker—usually the left-most button on the mouse.

Manual text flow Placing text column by column.

Margin guides The nonprinting dotted lines that mark the top, bottom, left, and right boundaries of a page.

Master items The elements placed on a master page that will appear on all pages of the publication unless specifically removed.

Master pages Pages used to define repeating items in a publication. They are accessed using the L or R page icons at the bottom of the publication window.

Menu bar The highlighted bar at the top of the publication window that contains the menu titles.

Option button The round selection area in a dialog box that you highlight to select an option displayed in the dialog box.

Outside margin The unbound margin of a publication: the left margin on a left-hand page and the right margin on a right-hand page.

Oversize publication A publication whose page size is larger than the paper size it will be printed on.

Page icon The numbered icons displayed at the bottom of the publication window used to display the pages of a publication.

Page orientation The page position, either tall or wide, defined in the Page Setup dialog box.

Palette A small window overlaying the publication window that is used for selecting colors or styles.

Pasteboard The area in the publication window that surrounds the pages of your publication. The pasteboard is a blank area for developing text and graphics, and for storing text and graphics until they are placed on the page.

Perpendicular line tool The line tool from the Toolbox used to create lines at 45-degree angles.

Pica A unit of measure that equals 1/6 of an inch. A pica is used to measure type size.

Pixel The name for each of the dots that compose an image on the screen.

Place The File menu command used to import text and graphics created outside of PageMaker.

Placeholder The place in a template reserved for inserting final text and graphics.

Point A unit of measure equal to 1/72 of an inch, or 1/12 of a pica. Used to measure type size.

Pointer The icon shaped like an arrow that is used to make selections.

PostScript A page description language used by the Apple LaserWriter and Linotype machines.

Publication window The window that is displayed in PageMaker when you start a new publication or open an existing one.

Registration mark The mark that helps you align the pages in a color overlay.

Reverse video The inverted background display of text or graphics. If the text or graphic is black, the background is white; if the text or graphic is white, the background is black.

Rounded-corner box tool The tool from the Toolbox used to create boxes with rounded corners. You may select the slope of the rounded corner using the Rounded Corners option from the Options menu.

Ruler guides Nonprinting horizontal and vertical lines that help align text and graphics on the page.

Scaling A Print menu option that lets you scale your publication smaller or larger than 100%.

Scanner An electronic device that scans a graphic on paper and inputs it into the computer.

Scroll bars Bars located on the right side and at the bottom of the publication window used for moving the page(s) of your publication in the window.

Snap to guides An Options menu selection that helps you place text accurately between the guides.

Style sheet A set of formatting commands, including type and paragraph specifications, tabs and indents, and color, that can be applied to blocks of text.

Style tag A marker used in your word processed file to apply PageMaker's styles to your word processed text.

System menu The Windows menu that is available within PageMaker as well as Windows.

Target printer The printer selection you make at the beginning of a publication to indicate the printer you will use for the final version of the publication.

Template A standard design or format to be used over and over again.

Text block The text between two text handles. One story can be divided into several threaded-together text blocks.

Text box A space within a dialog box in which you must type information.

Text icon An icon that resembles a page of text. It is loaded with text from your word processor for placement in a publication.

Text tool The editing tool located in the Toolbox.

Text wrap The Options menu command that lets you wrap text around graphics using the graphics boundary.

Threaded text blocks Separate text blocks that are connected or threaded together to form one story.

Thumbnail printout Up to 16 miniature copies of the pages of a publication printed on one page.

Tiling Printing a portion of a page. Used for an oversized publication.

Toolbox The box in the top right-hand corner of the publication window that contains the PageMaker graphics and text tools.

Windowshade handles The handles at the top and bottom of text blocks.

Zero point The intersection of the zeroes on the horizontal and vertical rulers in the publication window.

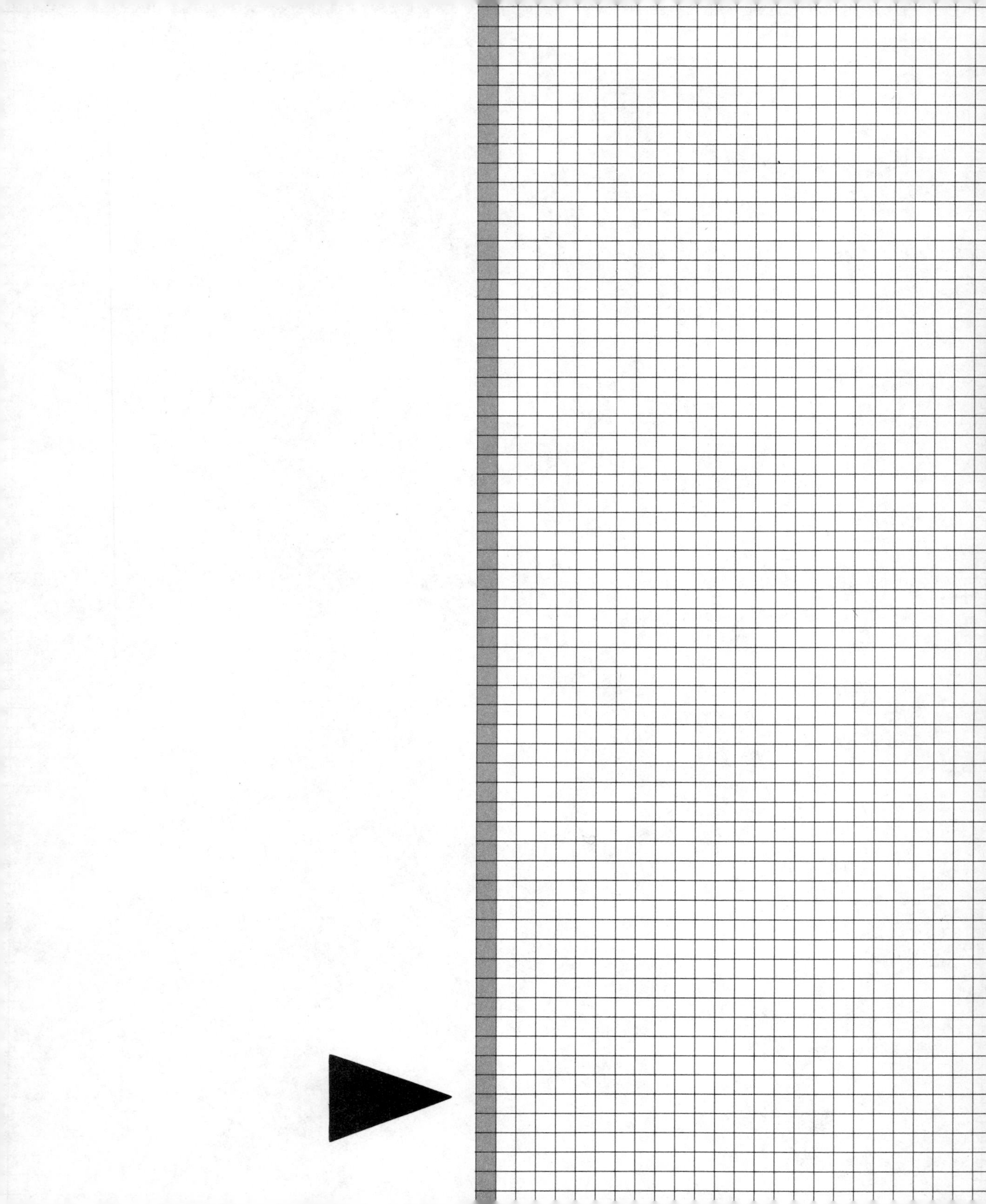

E FURTHER READING

Beach, Mark. *Editing Your Newsletter: A Guide to Writing, Design and Production.* Portland, Oregon: Coast to Coast Books, 1982.

Bevington, William; Sanders, Norman. *Graphic Designer's Production Handbook.* New York: Hastings House Publishers, Inc., 1982.

Bruno, Michael H., ed. *Pocket Pal, A Graphic Arts Production Handbook,* 13th ed. New York: International Paper Company, 1983.

Damerest, William A. *Clear Technical Reports.* New York: Harcourt Brace Jovanovich, 1972.

Davis, Fred; Barry, John; Wiesenberg, Michael. *Desktop Publishing.* Homewood, Illinois: Dow Jones-Irwin, 1986.

Donahue, Bud. *The Language of Layout.* Englewood Cliffs, New Jersey: Prentice-Hall, 1978.

Felici, James; Nace, Ted. "Typesetting Point by Point." *PC World,* July 1986, pp. 170-181.

Grout, Bill; Athanasopoulos, Irene; Kutlin, Rebecca. *Desktop Publishing From A to Z.* Berkeley, California: Osborne McGraw-Hill, 1986.

Hamilton, Edward A. *Graphic Design for the Computer Age.* New York: Van Nostrand Reinhold Co., 1970.

McClelland, Deke; Danuloff, Craig. *Desktop Publishing Type and Graphics.* Florida: Harcourt Brace Jovanovich, Inc., 1987.

Miles, John. *Design for Desktop Publishing.* San Francisco, California: Chronicle Books, 1987.

Parker, Roger C. *Looking Good in Print.* North Carolina: Ventana Press, Inc., 1988.

Rehe, Rolf F. *Typography: How to Make It Most Legible.* Carmel, Indiana: Design Research International, 1974.

Romano, Frank J. *The Typencyclopedia: A User's Guide to Better Typography.* New York: R. R. Bowker Co., 1984.

Rosenthal, Steve. "Composition and Layout Come to the Desktop." *Business Software,* November 1986, pp. 14–16, 18–23.

Seybold, John; Dreasler, Fritz. *Publishing from the Desktop.* Bantam Books, 1987.

Spiegelman, Marjorie. "Page Makeover: Make Your Price List Sell." *Publish,* September/October 1986, pp. 76–77.

Spiegelman, Marjorie. "Page Makeover." *Publish,* November/December 1986, pp. 84–85.

Spiegelman, Marjorie. "Page Makeover." *Publish,* January/February 1987, pp. 64–65.

White, Jan V. *Editing By Design: A Guide to Effective Word-and-Picture Communication for Editors and Designers.* New York: R. R. Bowker Co., 1982.

Will-Harris, Daniel. *Desktop Publishing with Style.* Indiana: And Books, 1987.

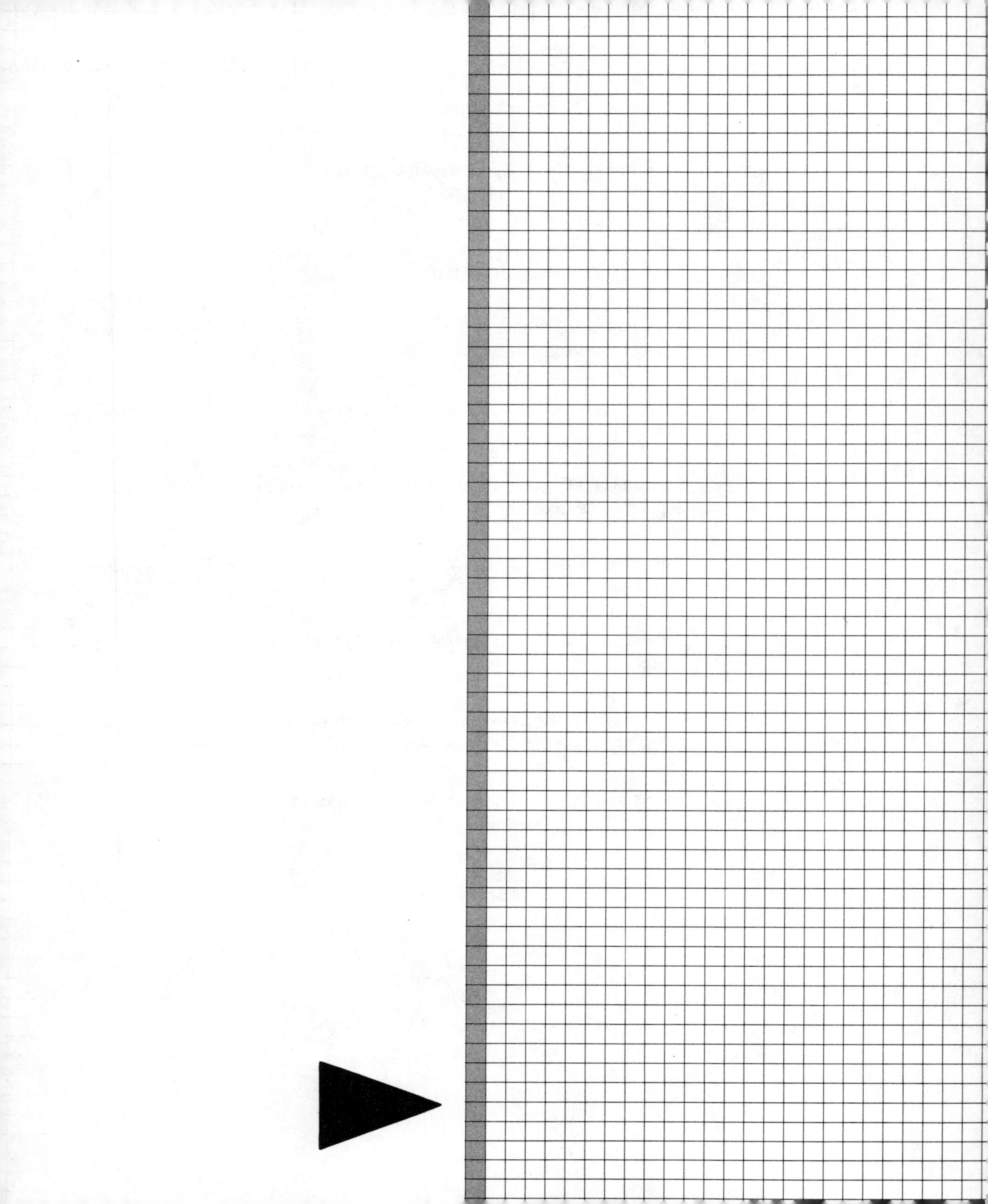

F PAGEMAKER-COMPATIBLE HARDWARE AND SOFTWARE

This appendix lists the following types of hardware and software that are compatible with PageMaker: word processors; DCA-formatted files; draw, paint, and clip-art programs; scanners and scanning software; printers; and typesetters.

▶ PAGEMAKER-COMPATIBLE WORD PROCESSORS

- HP AdvanceWrite
- HP Executive MemoMaker
- Microsoft Word
- MultiMate
- Lotus Manuscript
- Olivetti Olitext Plus
- Samna Word
- Windows Write
- WordPerfect
- WordStar 3.3, 4.0
- XyWrite III

▶ PAGEMAKER-COMPATIBLE DCA-FORMATTED FILES

- AdvanceWrite
- Office Writer
- Samna Word
- WordStar 2000
- Lotus Manuscript
- IBM DisplayWrite 3, 4
- Volkswriter 3

▶ PAGEMAKER-COMPATIBLE DRAW PROGRAMS

- Windows DRAW
- In-a-Vision
- Targa Board (TIPS; EPS)
- Pro 3-D
- AutoCAD (ADI format)
- Lotus 1-2-3 (PIC)
- Symphony (PIC)
- Instinct
- Diagraph Windows
- Freelance (CGM)

Harvard Graphics (CGM)
DB Graphics (CGM)
ChartMaster (NAPLPS)
Autumn (NAPLPS)
Chart (NAPLPS)
DiagramMaster (NAPLPS)
Picture It (NAPLPS)
Windows GDI Metafiles
HPGL Plotter Language
Tektronix Plot-10 files

▶ PAGEMAKER-COMPATIBLE PAINT PROGRAMS

Targa Board (TIFF)
HP Scanning Gallery
Windows GRAPH (TIFF)
PC Paint Plus
PC Paintbrush
PC Paintbrush for Windows
Mirage
Windows Paint
PC Paint
Publisher's Paintbrush
MacPaint
Dr. Halo DPE (TIFF)
Energraphics (TIFF)
PostScript Adobe Illustrator (EPS)

▶ PAGEMAKER-COMPATIBLE CLIP-ART PROGRAMS

DeskTop Art

PC Quik-Art

ClickArt

PicturePak

Micrografx Windows Clipart

HP Graphics Gallery Portfolios

▶ PAGEMAKER-COMPATIBLE SCANNERS AND SCANNING SOFTWARE

AST TurboScan
Vidar 4220, 6220
Canon IX-12
Scan-Do

Datacopy 730
JetReader
Dest PC Scan Plus
PC Scan 1000
HP ScanJet
IBM 3117, 3118
Microtek MS300A
Princeton Graphics LS-300
WIPS
PC Image
PublishPac
PC Paintbrush
Scanning Gallery
HALO DPE
ScanMate
Ricoh IS-30

► PCL PRINTERS SUPPORTED BY PAGEMAKER'S PCL DRIVER

Apricot Laser
Epson GQ-3500
HP LaserJet
HP LaserJet Plus
HP LaserJet 500 Plus
HP LaserJet Series II
HP LaserJet 2000
Kyocera F-1010 Laser
Quadram QuadLaser 1
NEC Silentwriter LC 860 Plus
Tandy LP1000
Tegra Genesis
Wang LDP8-DSK

► POSTSCRIPT PRINTERS SUPPORTED BY PAGEMAKER

Agfa P400PS
Apple LaserWriter
Apple LaserWriter Plus
AST PS-R4081
Dataproducts LZR 2665
Digital LN03R ScriptPrinter
Digital LPS Print Server 40
IBM Personal Pageprinter
Linotronic 100/300/500
NEC SilentWriter LC-890
QMS-PS 800, 800A, 800 Plus
TI OmniLaser
Varityper VT-600
Wang LCS15-DSK

► PAGEMAKER-COMPATIBLE TYPESETTERS

Linotronic 100 (up to 1270 dpi)

Linotronic 300 (up to 2540 dpi)

Compugraphic 8000, 8400, 8600, 9600, and Editwriter

Varityper 6700, 6710, 6720, 6750, Comp/Edit and Comp/Set using MicroSetter

► PAGEMAKER-COMPATIBLE DOT-MATRIX PRINTERS

Advanced Matrix Technology OfficePrinter

Epson FX-80, LQ 2500

Fujitsu DL2400

IBM Proprinter

NEC P5XL (color)

Okidata 92/93, 192/193

Texas Instruments 850, 855

Toshiba P1351

Wang PC-PM016

► OTHER PRINTERS SUPPORTED BY PAGEMAKER

AST Turbo Laser

Epson GQ 3500

HP PaintJet

HP DeskJet

IBM Pageprinter 3812

INDEX

D

E

F

G

H

I

N

O

P

Q

R

S

T

U

V

W 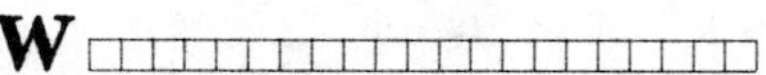

Z

Selections from The SYBEX Library

DESKTOP PUBLISHING

The ABC's of the New Print Shop
Vivian Dubrovin
340pp. Ref. 640-4
This beginner's guide stresses fun, practicality and original ideas. Hands-on tutorials show how to create greeting cards, invitations, signs, flyers, letterheads, banners, and calendars.

The ABC's of Ventura
Robert Cowart
Steve Cummings
390pp. Ref. 537-9
Created especially for new desktop publishers, this is an easy introduction to a complex program. Cowart provides details on using the mouse, the Ventura side bar, and page layout, with careful explanations of publishing terminology. The new Ventura menus are all carefully explained. For Version 2.

Mastering COREL DRAW!
Steve Rimmer
403pp. Ref. 685-5
This four-color tutorial and user's guide covers drawing and tracing, text and special effects, file interchange, and adding new fonts. With in-depth treatment of design principles. For version 1.1.

Mastering Ventura (Second Edition)
Matthew Holtz
613pp. Ref. 581-6
A complete, step-by-step guide to IBM PC desktop publishing with Xerox Ventura Publisher. Practical examples show how to use style sheets, format pages, cut and paste, enhance layouts, import material from other programs, and more. For Version 2.

Understanding PFS: First Publisher
Gerry Litton
310pp. Ref. 616-2
This complete guide takes users from the basics all the way through the most complex features available. Discusses working with text and graphics, columns, clip art, and add-on software enhancements. Many page layout suggestions are introduced. Includes Fast Track speed notes.

Understanding PostScript Programming (Second Edition)
David A. Holzgang
472pp. Ref. 566-2
In-depth treatment of PostScript for programmers and advanced users working on custom desktop publishing tasks. Hands-on development of programs for font creation, integrating graphics, printer implementations and more.

Ventura Instant Reference SYBEX Prompter Series
Matthew Holtz
320pp. Ref. 544-1, 4 3/4" × 8"
This compact volume offers easy access to the complex details of Ventura modes and options, commands, side-bars, file management, output device configuration, and control. Written for versions through Ventura 2, it also includes standard procedures for project and job control.

Ventura Power Tools

Rick Altman

318pp. Ref. 592-1

Renowned Ventura expert, Rick Altman, presents strategies and techniques for the most efficient use of Ventura Publisher 2. This includes a power disk with DOS utilities which is specially designed for optimizing Ventura use. Learn how to soup up Ventura, edit CHP files, avoid design tragedies, handle very large documents, and improve form.

Your HP LaserJet Handbook

Alan R. Neibauer

564pp. Ref. 618-9

Get the most from your printer with this step-by-step instruction book for using LaserJet text and graphics features such as cartridge and soft fonts, type selection, memory and processor enhancements, PCL programming, and PostScript solutions. This hands-on guide provides specific instructions for working with a variety of software.

DESKTOP PRESENTATION

Mastering Harvard Graphics

Glenn H. Larsen

318pp. Ref. 585-9

Here is a solid course in computer graphing and chart building with the popular software package. Readers can create the perfect presentation using text, pie, line, bar, map, and pert charts. Customizing and automating graphics is easy with these step-by-step instructions. For Version 2.1.

OPERATING SYSTEMS

The ABC's of DOS 4

Alan R. Miller

275pp. Ref. 583-2

This step-by-step introduction to using DOS 4 is written especially for beginners. Filled with simple examples, *The ABC's of DOS 4* covers the basics of hardware, software, disks, the system editor EDLIN, DOS commands, and more.

ABC's of MS-DOS (Second Edition)

Alan R. Miller

233pp. Ref. 493-3

This handy guide to MS-DOS is all many PC users need to manage their computer files, organize floppy and hard disks, use EDLIN, and keep their computers organized. Additional information is given about utilities like Sidekick, and there is a DOS command and program summary. The second edition is fully updated for Version 3.3.

DOS Assembly Language Programming

Alan R. Miller

365pp. 487-9

This book covers PC-DOS through 3.3, and gives clear explanations of how to assemble, link, and debug 8086, 8088, 80286, and 80386 programs. The example assembly language routines are valuable for students and programmers alike.

DOS Instant Reference SYBEX Prompter Series

Greg Harvey
Kay Yarborough Nelson

220pp. Ref. 477-1, 4 3/4" × 8"

A complete fingertip reference for fast, easy on-line help:command summaries, syntax, usage and error messages. Organized by function—system commands, file commands, disk management, directories, batch files, I/O, networking, programming, and more. Through Version 3.3.

DOS User's Desktop Companion SYBEX Ready Reference Series

Judd Robbins

969pp. Ref. 505-0

This comprehensive reference covers DOS commands, batch files, memory enhancements, printing, communications and more information on optimizing each user's DOS environment. Written with step-by-step instructions and plenty of examples, this volume covers all versions through 3.3.

Encyclopedia DOS

Judd Robbins

1030pp. Ref. 699-5

A comprehensive reference and user's guide to all versions of DOS through 4.0. Offers complete information on every DOS command, with all possible switches and parameters -- plus examples of effective usage. An invaluable tool.

Essential OS/2 (Second Edition)

Judd Robbins

445pp. Ref. 609-X

Written by an OS/2 expert, this is the guide to the powerful new resources of the OS/2 operating system standard edition 1.1 with presentation manager. Robbins introduces the standard edition, and details multitasking under OS/2, and the range of commands for installing, starting up, configuring, and running applications. For Version 1.1 Standard Edition.

Essential PC-DOS (Second Edition)

Myril Clement Shaw
Susan Soltis Shaw

332pp. Ref. 413-5

An authoritative guide to PC-DOS, including version 3.2. Designed to make experts out of beginners, it explores everything from disk management to batch file programming. Includes an 85-page command summary. Through Version 3.2.

Graphics Programming Under Windows

Brian Myers
Chris Doner

646pp. Ref. 448-8

Straightforward discussion, abundant examples, and a concise reference guide to graphics commands make this book a must for Windows programmers. Topics range from how Windows works to programming for business, animation, CAD, and desktop publishing. For Version 2.

Hard Disk Instant Reference SYBEX Prompter Series

Judd Robbins

256pp. Ref. 587-5, 4 3/4" × 8"

Compact yet comprehensive, this pocket-sized reference presents the essential information on DOS commands used in managing directories and files, and in optimizing disk configuration. Includes a survey of third-party utility capabilities. Through DOS 4.0.

The IBM PC-DOS Handbook (Third Edition)

Richard Allen King

359pp. Ref. 512-3

A guide to the inner workings of PC-DOS 3.2, for intermediate to advanced users and programmers of the IBM PC series. Topics include disk, screen and port control, batch files, networks, compatibility, and more. Through Version 3.3.

Inside DOS: A Programmer's Guide

Michael J. Young

490pp. Ref. 710-X

A collection of practical techniques (with source code listings) designed to help you take advantage of the rich resources intrinsic to MS-DOS machines. Designed for the experienced programmer with a basic understanding of C and 8086 assembly language, and DOS fundamentals.

Mastering DOS (Second Edition)

Judd Robbins

722pp. Ref. 555-7

"The most useful DOS book." This seven-part, in-depth tutorial addresses the needs of users at all levels. Topics range from running applications, to managing files and directories, configuring the system, batch file programming, and techniques for system developers. Through Version 4.

MS-DOS Advanced Programming

Michael J. Young

490pp. Ref. 578-6

Practical techniques for maximizing performance in MS-DOS software by making best use of system resources. Topics include functions, interrupts, devices, multitasking, memory residency and more, with examples in C and assembler. Through Version 3.3.

MS-DOS Handbook (Third Edition)

Richard Allen King

362pp. Ref. 492-5

This classic has been fully expanded and revised to include the latest features of MS-DOS Version 3.3. Two reference books in one, this title has separate sections for programmer and user. Multi-DOS partitons, 3 1/2-inch disk format, batch file call and return feature, and comprehensive coverage of MS-DOS commands are included. Through Version 3.3.

MS-DOS Power User's Guide, Volume I (Second Edition)

Jonathan Kamin

482pp. Ref. 473-9

A fully revised, expanded edition of our best-selling guide to high-performance DOS techniques and utilities—with details on Version 3.3. Configuration, I/O, directory structures, hard disks, RAM disks, batch file programming, the ANSI.SYS device driver, more. Through Version 3.3.

Programmers Guide to the OS/2 Presentation Manager

Michael J. Young

683pp. Ref. 569-7

This is the definitive tutorial guide to writing programs for the OS/2 Presentation Manager. Young starts with basic architecture, and explores every important feature including scroll bars, keyboard and mouse interface, menus and accelerators, dialogue boxes, clipboards, multitasking, and much more.

Programmer's Guide to Windows (Second Edition)

David Durant
Geta Carlson
Paul Yao

704pp. Ref. 496-8

The first edition of this programmer's guide was hailed as a classic. This new edition covers Windows 2 and Windows/386 in depth. Special emphasis is given to over fifty new routines to the Windows interface, and to preparation for OS/2 Presentation Manager compatibility.

Understanding DOS 3.3

Judd Robbins

678pp. Ref. 648-0

This best selling, in-depth tutorial addresses the needs of users at all levels with many examples and hands-on exercises. Robbins discusses the fundamentals of DOS, then covers manipulating files and directories, using the DOS editor, printing, communicating, and finishes with a full section on batch files.

Understanding Hard Disk Management on the PC

Jonathan Kamin

500pp. Ref. 561-1

This title is a key productivity tool for all hard disk users who want efficient, error-free file management and organization. Includes details on the best ways to conserve hard disk space when using several memory-guzzling programs. Through DOS 4.

Up & Running with Your Hard Disk

Klaus M Rubsam

140pp. Ref. 666-9

A far-sighted, compact introduction to hard disk installation and basic DOS use. Perfect for PC users who want the practical essentials in the shortest possible time. In 20 basic steps, learn to choose your hard disk, work with accessories, back up data, use DOS utilities to save time, and more.

Up & Running with Windows 286/386

Gabriele Wentges

132pp. Ref. 691-X

This handy 20-step overview gives PC users all the essentials of using Windows -- whether for evaluating the software, or getting a fast start. Each self-contained lesson takes just 15 minutes to one hour to complete.

COMMANDS AND FUNCTIONS ARRANGED BY MENU

Edit Menu

Command	Function
Cut	Removes selected text or a graphic from a publication and puts it in the Clipboard
Clear	Deletes selected text or a graphic from a publication
Paste	Places an item from the Clipboard into a publication
Copy	Places a copy of selected text into the Clipboard
Preferences	Indicates a measuring system
Undo	Reverses your most recent action
Select all	Selects an entire story or page when using the text tool
Bring to front	In overlapping text and graphics, brings the background item to the foreground
Send to back	In overlapping text and graphics, moves the foreground item to the background

File Menu

Command	Function
New	Starts a new publication
Save as	Saves your work as a publication or a template
Printer setup	Designates your target printer
Save	Saves changes to your publication or template
Open	Opens an existing publication or template
Exit	Closes a publication and returns you to the DOS prompt (or the MS-DOS Executive Window if you have a full version of windows)
Close	Closes the publication window and returns you to PageMaker's desktop
Place	Places files from other applications into PageMaker
Revert	Restores the last-saved version of a publication or template
Export	Saves the selected text as a formatted file for a word-processing application, or as a text-only file
Page setup	Sets most of the options you specified with the "New" command when starting the opened publication
Print	Prints your publication or template

Options Menu

Command	Function
Rulers	Displays the rulers
Zero lock	Locks down the zero point
Column guides	Creates column guides
Guides	Toggles between visible and hidden guides
Snap to guides	Makes the column, margin, and ruler guides snap text and graphics into place
Lock guides	Locks column and ruler guides in place
Autoflow	Flows an entire text file onto the pages of a publication
Text wrap	Controls how text flows and wraps around graphics
Define colors	Lets you create, name, and apply colors for text and graphics
Image control	Controls brightness and contrast, and changes the print screen for paint-type graphics and scanned images
Rounded corners	Creates rounded or square corners on rectangles and squares drawn in PageMaker
Toolbox	Displays the Toolbox
Scroll bars	Displays the scroll bars
Styles palette	Displays the Styles palette
Colors palette	Displays the Colors palette